Writing Democracy

Time and the World: Interdisciplinary Studies in Cultural Transformations

Series editor: Helge Jordheim, University of Oslo, Norway

Published in association with the interdisciplinary research program Cultural Transformations in the Age of Globalization (KULTRANS) at the University of Oslo.

Time is moving faster; the world is getting smaller. Behind these popular slogans are actual cultural processes, on global and local scales, that require investigation. *Time and the World* draws on research in a wide range of fields, such as cultural history, anthropology, sociology, literary studies, sociolinguistics and law and sets out to discuss different cultures as sites of transformation in a global context. The series offers interdisciplinary analyses of cultural aspects of globalization in various historical and geographical contexts, across time and space.

Volume 1
From Antiquities to Heritage: Transformations of Cultural Memory
Anne Eriksen

Volume 2
Writing Democracy: The Norwegian Constitution 1814–2014
Edited by Karen Gammelgaard and Eirik Holmøyvik

Upcoming Volumes
Conceptualizing the World
Edited by Helge Jordheim and Erling Sandmo

Understanding Transformations in the Context of Globalization
Edited by Vidar Grøtta, Rana Issa, Helge Jordheim and Audun Solli

Writing Democracy

The Norwegian Constitution 1814–2014

Edited by

Karen Gammelgaard and Eirik Holmøyvik

berghahn
NEW YORK · OXFORD
www.berghahnbooks.com

Published in 2015 by
Berghahn Books
www.berghahnbooks.com

© 2015 Karen Gammelgaard and Eirik Holmøyvik

Library of Congress Cataloging-in-Publication Data

Writing democracy: the Norwegian Constitution, 1814-2014 / edited by Karen
Gammelgaard and Eirik Holmøyvik.
    pages cm. -- (Time and the world: interdisciplinary studies in cultural
transformations series)
    Includes bibliographical references.
    ISBN 978-1-78238-504-2 (hardback: alk. paper) -- ISBN 978-1-78238-505-9 (ebook)
    1. Constitutional history--Norway. 2. Constitutional law--Norway--Interpretation and
construction. 3. Democracy--Norway. I. Gammelgaard, Karen, editor. II. Holmøyvik,
Eirik, editor.
    KKN2101.W75 2014
    342.48102'9--dc23

                                                                    2014019631

British Library Cataloguing in Publication Data

A catalogue record for this book is available from the British Library

ISBN 978-1-78238-504-2 (hardback)
ISBN 978-1-78238-505-9 (ebook)

▶● ●◀

Contents

▶● ●◀

Figures

▶• •◀

Acknowledgements

The present volume is the result of a collective scholarly project that authors have been engaged in from its launch in Easter 2010. Many institutions and people encouraged and supported work on the project.

First, we thank the Norwegian Research Council's Norwegian Constitution Bicentennial 2014 Research Initiative for providing us with a grant. Institutionally, our project emanates from activities in the fruitful academic environment created by the interfaculty research area KULTRANS at the University of Oslo, 2008–2013. We are grateful to Helge Jordheim, academic director of KULTRANS, for all economic, academic, and collegiate support, and to Beate Trandem, senior executive officer of KULTRANS, for her numerous and high-quality services. The grants provided by the Norwegian Research Council and KULTRANS allowed us to hire Anna Young as a project assistant. We credit her for meticulous work when we most needed it. Copy editor Frank Azevedo held a workshop for project authors that greatly helped us solve problems of communicating, in English in 2013, about a document written in Norway in 1814. Also, Frank went through the entire manuscript, inspiring us with many new questions along with valuable suggestions for solutions. Further, we express our gratitude to postdoctoral fellow Tone Brekke, who served in the project leadership and on the editorial team as long as her health allowed her to do so, and to colleagues at the University of Oslo—Professor Bjørn Erik Rasch, Associate Professor Kirsten Sivesind, and Professor Johan Tønnesson—who in various stages of the research project shared with us their enthusiasm for the Norwegian Constitution.

Many people contributed in many ways to the individual chapters. The people are too numerous and the variety of help and advice is too complex to list here; however, unmentioned does not mean unrecognized. Finally, we thank Berghahn Books for tackling a volume of this kind, the editorial board of the series whose positive response encouraged our work, and last but not least the anonymous reviewers whose excellent recommendations we have been happy to follow.

The editors,
Oslo and Bergen, 22 November 2013

►● ●◄

Note on Interdisciplinarity and Stylistic Conventions

This volume brings together experts from several disciplines to work jointly on researching the Norwegian Constitution as a text: legal studies, history, linguistics, sociology, history of concepts, and literary studies. The Constitution matters to researchers in different ways and with different significance, and when examining the Constitution, researchers have differing interests and methodologies. Methods differ accordingly, but all authors focus on framers' or other participants' textual practices. The Constitution's textuality serves as the meeting point for all involved authors.

This shared focus of research interest, however, is not the only way in which authors engage in textual practices. The writing of the chapters in this volume adds yet another act of textual practice to those countless others sparked off by the 1814 Norwegian Constitution. In this volume, authors put into text their research on the Norwegian Constitution. Because they are part of a joint research project, all chapters have been presented in early versions to all project participants. All have received valuable criticism from participants representing other disciplines.

All authors face the challenge of writing for an interdisciplinary readership. Therefore, they have attempted not to use the terminology and jargon of their respective disciplines. Nonetheless, specialized terminology cannot always be avoided. For example, when authors with a background in legal studies refer to "positive law," this term means law that is valid. Similarly, when linguists speak of "pragmatics," they refer to a very specific body of literature dealing with people's ability to do something with words and texts, as indicated above. We hope that such disciplinary jargon is largely avoided in the present volume, although we are aware that the absence of disciplinary terms may lead to a lack of precision.

In the process of putting their research into text, this volume's authors have followed a set of shared stylistic conventions.

The text (in the sense of artifact) that most authors use as their point of departure for analysis is the printed edition of the 17 May 1814 Norwegian

Constitution (Kongeriget Norges Grundlov 1814). This edition is reprinted in Appendix A. The original text exists also as a handwritten document; its scanned version can be found at Stortinget's website (*Dokumentet Grunnlova av 17. mai 1814*). The 17 May 1814 Constitution's wording can also be read as a digital document, published on the Internet by Stortinget (*Grunnloven fra 1814*). Moreover, some draft versions are accessible on the Internet, including the influential draft by Eidsvold deputies Johan Gunder Adler and Christian Magnus Falsen (Adler and Falsen 1814).

To quote the 1814 Norwegian Constitution in English, authors as a rule quote the English-language translation "pursuant to order of Government" (The Constitution of the Kingdom of Norway 1814).[1] This translation is reprinted as Appendix B.[2] The use of this translation entails some problems because the translation is somewhat inconsistent and clumsy. For example, a contemporary copy editor may well find that the following formulation needs work: "Nobody must be punished for any writing unless he has either willingly and evidently shown himself disobediently to the law" (Article 100).

Moreover, the translation of some articles is imprecise, bordering on changing the original's meaning. A case in point concerns the important Article 100. The original states, "Pressefrihet bør finde Sted" (literally, "liberty of the press shall take place"). However, the 1814 English-language translation states, "An intire [sic] liberty of the press shall take place." Probably, the anonymous translators wished to explain to the English-speaking public the character of the newly introduced liberty by adding "intire." In any event, readers may find quotations from the 1814 English-language translation of the Norwegian Constitution somewhat strange.

However, to emphasize that all documents (including official translations) are produced in specific historical situations, we have chosen to quote the 1814 documents in their historical form. Therefore, we keep forms such as "every one" (in two words) and "intire" for "entire."

In some cases, the use of specific terms in the authorized 1814 English-language translation has guided our diction. For example, we refer to the men at Eidsvold as "deputies," not as, for example, "delegates." "Deputy" was the word that the anonymous translators of the 1814 Constitution reached for when they had to transform into the English language the new experience of 1814, namely, that representatives of the people could assemble and put into text their ideas of government and the protection of human rights. On other occasions, however, our diction has been motivated mostly by our wish for clarity for international readers; therefore, we use recognizable terms, even when they conflict with the 1814 English-language translation. A case in point concerns the translation of Storthinget. In the 1814 English-language translation, Storthinget was translated as "National Assembly." However, we most often translate Storthinget as "the Norwegian parliament."

Regarding English-language translations of other constitutions and documents, each author is responsible for the translations of the passages that he or she quotes. In most cases, translations are by the authors. We have chosen this solution because not all constitutions and other material quoted in the volume exist in authorized translations; because from a legal perspective, translations of nineteenth-century constitutions are highly problematic; and because chapter authors may wish to emphasize different aspects of the quoted parts of the constitutions, aspects that might not be clearly communicated were all authors to quote one authorized translation.

All historical names are given in their contemporaneously most used orthographic form. Hence, today's place names Eidsvoll, Oslo, and Trondheim appear as Eidsvold, Christiania, and Trondhjem, respectively. Around 1814, however, Norwegian orthographic praxis was far from stable. Many words had several different written forms. For example, the name of the northern city of Trondhjem also appeared as Throndhiem, Tronhiem, and Throndhjem. Note that Eidsvold was written thus in contemporary Danish-Norwegian, but that the English-language translation "pursuant to order of Government" of 1814 applies the spelling "Eidswold" (with a "w"). Other names were written inconsistently, too. For example, the spelling of the loanword for "constitution" appeared as both Konstitution and Constitution. Also, regarding relevant institutions, spelling in this volume adheres to that of contemporaneous documents, for example, Rigsforsamling (National Assembly), not Riksforsamling, the latter spelling preferred since 1918. In 1814, all nouns in Danish-Norwegian were written with initial capitals, for example *Grundlov, Konge* (constitution, king). This praxis began to change slowly, beginning in 1877. For example, until 1899, "Stortingets forhandlinger" (Stortinget's proceedings) was written with initial capitals in both nouns.

An exception to the rule of applying contemporaneous orthography concerns the name of the Norwegian parliament, Stortinget. Although until 2014 the Constitution's text displayed the spelling "Storthinget" (with an "h"), from about 1900, the widespread convention in all other Norwegian documents has been to use the spelling "Stortinget" (without an "h"). We follow this convention, so that when referring to the Norwegian parliament after about 1900, we write "Stortinget." On some occasions, the indefinite grammatical form of the name appears: "Storting." Readers should understand both to mean simply "parliament" when reading them in English-language text in this volume.

Titles of books and other documents are given in the original language (in italics), followed by translation when necessary. If the document exists as a published English-language translation, the title of this translation is used and italicized. When giving Norwegian book and document titles, we adhere to the Norwegian praxis of using a hyphen, not an en dash, in number spans, for example, *Dokument 12:25 (2011–2012)*. Quotes from other languages (for example, French and German) follow the orthographic forms used in the original sources. Sources and references are listed in the general bibliography inserted at the end of the volume.

NOTES

1. The chapter by Gammelgaard quotes an 1895 English-language translation of the 4 November 1814 edition translated by US senator Knute Nelson, and the chapter by Visconti quotes a 2013 English-language translation published on Stortinget's website.
2. Whereas the 1814 English-language translation "pursuant to order of Government" should most likely be seen as an attempt to inform an important international player of developments in Norway, the 1814 Norwegian Constitution also attracted interest in independent political and intellectual circles in London. Such interest is evidenced by other contemporaneous translations, such as that by Jens Wolff (1814).

▸• Introduction •◂

The Norwegian Constitution as a Text

Karen Gammelgaard and Eirik Holmøyvik

Celebrating Democracy's Textual Practices

In 2014, the Norwegian Constitution has existed for two hundred years. Adopted on 17 May 1814, it is the oldest functioning constitution in Europe. Only the US Constitution (adopted in 1787) is older. The beginnings of the Norwegian Constitution, as well as its longevity, have been accompanied by dramatic events, including the breakup of the long-lasting union with Denmark in early 1814, war with Sweden (summer 1814), union with Sweden (1814–1905), German occupation (1940–1945), and two referenda on Norway's place in European cooperation structures (1972 and 1994). All these events have been topics of comprehensive research and will indisputably continue to be so.

This volume's authors, however, take a different approach. Rather than focusing on events, they focus on practices connected with putting the Constitution into text, with setting down in a document the rules of government and human rights, and with interpreting that document. These practices may lack palpable outward dramatics because they most often take place in forums—conference rooms, meeting rooms, studies—where the drama of conflicting interests occurs not as physically tangible fights but in represented shape only: as words, sentences, and paragraphs. The lack of outward drama is also caused by the fact that textual practices often concern political decisions on a micro level (Chilton 2004: 4). Such practices have the character of everyday, often meticulous, work. Nonetheless, these easily overlooked practices, and not least the sum of many such practices, may have consequences as significant as actions unfolding on real battlefields. In many ways, these textual practices lie at the heart of a well-functioning democracy. It is the shared recognition of textual practices' significance that sparked this volume's authors to scrutinize practices that relate to the Norwegian Constitution as a text.

Consequently, this volume's authors investigate textual practices that preceded and accompanied the Norwegian Constitution's framing in spring 1814, be such practices investigated as instances of contemporaneous textual culture, as the embedding of the Constitution's text in other documents, as concerning the changing meaning of concepts, or as concerning the relation between real time and time construction in the Constitution's text. Recognizing the seminal importance of 1814 textual practices for Norwegian democracy, other authors take a geographical avenue—investigating how the Norwegian Constitution's textual practices interweave with transnational and international textual practices—or take a historical avenue to investigate how the Norwegian Constitution has been interpreted and amended in its 200-year existence. Fundamental to all investigations is the shared understanding that ever since 1814, the Constitution has been central to Norwegian democracy.

Although the authors research the Constitution as a text, all emphasize that textual practices imply and depend upon realities outside the text: people engage in many actions that do not involve texts (or that involve texts only peripherally). Yet, people also write texts, they negotiate how texts should be written, and they debate how texts should be disseminated, interpreted, enacted, and changed. A focus on the Constitution's text therefore helps us scrutinize both its complex prehistory and its history of changes and interpretations.

We have entitled the volume *Writing Democracy: The Norwegian Constitution 1814–2014*, and we will use this introduction to initially define the title's first two words.

Writing

We understand "writing" broadly, as all activities connected with putting something into text, with setting something down in a written document. Therefore, focusing on such activities, authors of this volume investigate those processes where participants negotiate the meaning of words and concepts, draw on available grammatical rules and stylistic conventions, use channels of dissemination, and engage in interpretation. Many other activities enabled the framing of the Norwegian Constitution in 1814 and its continuous application. Yet this volume focuses on practices connected with putting something into text.

The textual character of the Constitution is generally overlooked. One cause of this oversight is perhaps the Constitution's status as a national myth: the Norwegian public seems less interested in the text, which is understood as a given and stable entity, and more interested in how the Constitution relates to phenomena outside the text. People tend to see the effects of the Constitution more clearly than they see the Constitution itself. Thereby, the Constitution conforms to a general paradox: social life is permeated by texts at every level, yet precisely because of this omnipresence, the texts per se are overlooked.

The Norwegian Constitution was framed in spring 1814 by one hundred and twelve deputies gathered at what was then termed *Rigsforsamlingen* (literally, "the realm's assembly"). Today, such a gathering would be referred to as a constitutional assembly. The deputies' main task was to put down on paper—in words, sentences, and paragraphs—ideas of the foundations of government and the protection of human rights in Norway. A written document emerged from this activity. To emphasize the legitimacy of their putting ideas on paper, deputies took another textual step: they added their signatures to the document. By this daring gesture—which demonstrated that government is created by and subject to the wants of the people—they changed ideas of government and human rights into the legal foundation for the Norwegian state.

The deputies first wrote the Constitution in longhand. The document that resulted from this setting down of principles for Norway's system of government and the protection of human rights was intended to function as an object that all inhabitants of Norway could access (see Warner et al. in this volume). To achieve this aim, dissemination was required. Already on 17 May, deputies decided that their jointly produced and adopted document should be published in print. On 30 May, the committee appointed for carrying out this task announced that the Constitution was published and was on sale in all post offices in Norway. Many copies of the first two printings, in Danish, the written language in Norway at the time, were sold. A third Danish edition, a French-language edition, and an English-language edition were released somewhat later and in very limited numbers (Nielsen 1997: 75–76).

By setting down on paper the principles for Norway's government and the protection of human rights, the 1814 deputies followed the example set by American revolutionaries in 1776, including textual deeds such as the Declaration of Independence by the first thirteen states of the United States of America and the Constitution of Virginia. Spurred on by the French Revolution in 1789, constitution makers in the following decades in Europe and in the Americas engaged in similar activities. The international movement of Enlightenment philosophy served as a shared intellectual background. To call attention to how in this period, the heyday of constitutionalism, traditional concepts of "constitution" succumbed to new and radically different concepts, the constitutions that emerged out of these new impulses are often called "modern constitutions," "revolutionary constitutions," or "Enlightenment constitutions." In the present volume, authors use all three terms, depending on their perspective.

In addition to the international impetus of constitutionalism, which traveled across boundaries and time most often in the form of texts—pamphlets, books, newspapers—the Norwegian framers were influenced by the traditions of government in the state that they had belonged to until the beginning of 1814, namely, the authoritarian twin kingdoms of Denmark-Norway.

Influences from this tradition came from legal and administrative concepts used in the twin kingdoms' governance, from ideas and experiences of the emerging institution of a public sphere, and from the Danish-Norwegian systems of language, genres, and dissemination.

The act of putting something into text presupposes readers able to read the planned text. In early nineteenth-century Norway, literacy was fundamental to the Constitution's success. Literacy in Norway gained momentum after the 1739 rescript that introduced the principle of compulsory school attendance for rural children. The rescript prescribed two elementary disciplines: reading and Christian studies. In towns, school attendance was not compulsory until 1848, and some literacy statistics show higher illiteracy rates in towns than in the countryside (Byberg 2008: 4). However, the amount of printed matter published and disseminated in the four decades before 1814 indicates widespread literacy (Fet 1995). Because literacy was not confined to the Norwegian elite, the Constitution could be read and discussed by large groups of inhabitants, not only by the privileged few, as far as its material text could be disseminated.

The language used in written communication in Norway circa 1814 was Danish. Therefore, when in 1814 at the Constitutional Assembly deputies framed the document that they entitled *Kongeriget Norges Grundlov* (The Constitution of the Norwegian Kingdom), they wrote in Danish. Even though differences existed between spoken Norwegian and spoken Danish (Vikør and Torp 2000: 118), it was not until about 1850 that the campaign for a distinct Norwegian language began (Hyvik 2010). Until then, in general, people in Norway did not regard Danish as foreign. That role was played by the typologically more different languages of Latin, German, and French. In the words of literacy historian Jostein Fet (2003: 362; quoted in Hyvik 2010: 116): "Writers had no choice. Danish was the only written language they knew. All who had political, legal, and economic power in society used Danish."[1]

Text practices connected with the Constitution did not cease by the very act of framing the Constitution's text in the spring of 1814. Already in November 1814, the Constitution's text was amended to reflect the union with Sweden. And since 1814, the Constitution's text has been amended, translated, reprinted, and interpreted in an incalculable number of acts: democratic activities include interpretation of the Constitution's text and very often the writing of new texts. Consequently, today the Constitution is entangled in a comprehensive net of texts, domestic and international, old and new. To mention just those textual acts that are probably most easy to count, namely, constitutional amendment proposals, 559 proposals were made between 1905 and 1996. Far from all proposals have been adopted; nevertheless, between 1814 and 2001, on average more than one amendment has been adopted yearly (Rasch 2011). We may only guess how many times the Constitution has been the focus of textual practice in the sense of reading and interpreting. Also, those interpretative practices that result in new texts—laws, court decisions, textbooks on constitutional law, and many other very different texts, such as young students' speeches for local communities throughout Norway on Constitution Day, 17 May—we may only roughly estimate: their number runs to hundreds of thousands. The transformation of the Constitution's text—understood as a physical entity on paper—into digital form accessible on the Internet adds to the daunting task of identifying how textual practices coshape Norwegian democracy. This situation also explains why this volume's authors may investigate only some aspects of the Norwegian Constitution's textuality.

To introduce a way of dealing theoretically with the relation between text and interpretation, let us begin by emphasizing that any text lives also in its interpretations. In many ways, readers are as active as authors are in creating a given text's meaning. By approaching the Norwegian Constitution analytically through such notions of textuality, the Constitution may exist in three modes for readers: as an artifact, as an individual interpretation, and as a social object (Gammelgaard 2003).

As an artifact, the Constitution has a material existence as a vehicle carrying linguistic and other signs. Thus, the Constitution appears as different things when handwritten on paper, printed as a booklet, and accessible in digital form on the Internet. It also appears as different things when translated into different languages and when written in the varying historical shapes of single languages. Further, the Constitution appears as yet another material object whenever amendments are made. Finally, each different graphic design makes the Constitution appear to be a new artifact.

Through individual interpretations, the Constitution exists whenever anybody reads it and forms his or her idea of its meaning. Such individual interpretations form a basic precondition for citizens' understandings of democratic participation provided by the Constitution. As researchers, we may access such individual interpretations when people reveal them in the form of new texts, spanning such diverse pieces as rulings by Supreme Court judges, amendments by parliamentarians, instructions by civil servants, and speeches on Constitution Day.

As a social object, the Constitution exists as an entity lodged in the collective national consciousness. Most often, when Norwegians express statements such as "The Constitution says" or "This violates the Constitution," they refer to the Constitution as social object. They refer to the general, socially shared idea of the Constitution's meaning, rather than to any of its many material varieties. They refer to general ideas about democracy rather than to the letter of the Constitution. Constitutions are particular in that entire institutions are erected to interpret them, such as the study of constitutional law, courts of impeachment, and procedures of constitutional amendments. All of these institutions have played influential parts in establishing the contemporaneous, socially shared understanding of the Norwegian Constitution.

The three modes of existence change at different paces. The Constitution as artifact changes hand in hand with every new vehicle and amendment. Also, individual interpretations change quickly: new interpretations appear with every individual reading. On the other hand, the Constitution as social object changes gradually according to the changes of new "Constitution artifacts" and according to continuous individual interpretations. The relative stability of the Constitution as social object is the reason that in 2014, Norwegians celebrate the Constitution's bicentennial.

So, there is a certain ambiguity in a text as old as the Norwegian Constitution. This ambiguity may be demonstrated perhaps most easily on the level of individual words, the Constitution's diction. In one sense, its words are temporal anchors that bind the Constitution to a given historical moment: the Constitutional Assembly in 1814 or the time of later amendments. Yet, simultaneously, its words often point to generic concepts and institutions in existence at any given time. Over time, concepts' and institutions' contents may change, so that in a sense the Constitution is changed too even though the text's diction remains the same. Take the word "king," for example. In a monarchical constitution such as the Norwegian Constitution, "king" is one of the most frequent words. Yet the Norwegian king holds a very different constitutional position today compared to his position in the nineteenth century, even though corresponding changes in the Constitution's text have been minimal. During its two hundred years of life, the Constitution has seen numerous amendments and interpretations that have transformed it into what it is today (see Sand, Madzharova Bruteig, and Kalleberg in this volume). In the course of all these amendments and interpretive changes, even the meaning of the very word "constitution" has changed (see Holmøyvik in this volume).

Some aspects of the Constitution's textuality relate to influences from foreign constitutions and international treaties—and to Norway's influencing foreign constitutions. International in its historical origin, the Constitution interconnects transnationally with foreign constitutions, international legal documents, political pamphlets, literary texts, and other texts transmitting ideas of politics, rights, government, and social formations. Consequently, the Constitution is entwined in layers and networks of other texts that cut across and challenge our modern notions of genres and disciplines. In investigating the characteristics of the Norwegian Constitution, this volume's authors include and compare it with many other constitutions, such as the US Constitution (1787); the French constitutions of the 1790s; the Batavian Republic's constitution (1798); the constitutions of Poland (1791), the Helvetic Republic

(1798), and Spain (1812); constitutions of the Habsburg Empire, 1848–1849; and the Italian Constitution (1948).

Framed in different historical situations, set down in different languages, and solving questions of government and protection of human rights in many different countries, all modern constitutions nevertheless share one very palpable feature: they create a new state of affairs. In so doing, constitutions eliminate the boundaries between text-specific matters (orthography, diction, segmentation) and the external reality. This specific feature, to exist as a text and simultaneously influence the world outside the text, is closely linked with the category of linguistic performativity, that is, human beings' ability to do things with words (Austin 1962). However, as emphasized by the Italian linguist Jacqueline Visconti (2009b, and in this volume), constitutions do things with words in a very specific way: they *create* something with words. A country's system of government and its protection of human rights are created by the framers' very act of putting down the principles of this system and this protection as a text and by the framers' accompanying act of solemnly announcing that this text is to function as the country's constitution.

Many authors in this volume address this specific pragmatic quality of the Norwegian Constitution to establish, initiate, found, create, and set up Norway's government and its protection of human rights. Identifying this quality, authors make use of very different theoretical apparatuses. In their coauthored chapter, William B. Warner, Eirik Holmøyvik, and Mona Ringvej discuss how the constitutive act in 1814 interwove with supplementary textual acts in a carefully orchestrated whole. The uniqueness of the act is highlighted: what the Norwegian framers did in 1814—their bold move from absolutism to democracy—cannot be recreated. They acted in a historically exceptional moment. Ulrich Schmid investigates how the Norwegian Constitution functioned as a rhetorical phenomenon of its time. He detects phrasings of constitutions' performative quality in Hegel's understanding of "poetry" and relates Hegel's understanding to Austin's work. The linguistic line of inquiry is resumed by Jacqueline Visconti and Karen Gammelgaard, who perform detailed contrastive analyses of constitutional texts. Helge Jordheim and Dag Michalsen add temporal dimensions. Michalsen stresses that modern constitutions are oriented toward the future: they establish what is to be. Premodern constitutions merely summed up rules and principles already in use. Jordheim argues that the present tense indicative verb forms so typical of constitutions may also be considered an expression of the built-in orientation of constitutional texts toward eternity.

The intriguing quality of constitutions, the quality of *constituting* something in the world, also distinguishes constitutions from many other kinds of texts that have been important in the long history of developing democracy and human rights. For example, their specific pragmatic quality distinguishes constitutions from declarations of human rights, whose qualities as speech acts may be described as *confirming* (rather than constituting) rights that already exist and are unquestionable (Hunt 2007: 115–116).

So far, research on the Norwegian Constitution has lacked the textual perspective. Significantly, the few academic works dealing with the Constitution from a textual perspective are by librarians: the comprehensive bibliography, by Ragnar Anker Nielsen (1997), of all kinds of texts published in Norway in 1814; the database "Norge i 1814 - bibliografi" (Norway in 1814: Bibliography) located at the National Library in Oslo; and the investigation by Ruth Hemstad (2013) into Swedish 1814 propaganda in Norway. Because of the lack of text-oriented research on the Norwegian Constitution, this volume's authors have sought inspiration in analyses of other constitutions and declarations. One source of inspiration is analyses in the tradition of stylistics, for example, Stephen E. Lucas's analysis (1990) of the US Declaration of Independence. Another source of inspiration is works by historians who are fascinated by the historicity of words, concepts, and texts. One such strand of historiography is represented by the so-called *Begriffsgeschichte* (history of concepts), as elaborated by German philosopher of the history of concepts Reinhard Koselleck and, regarding the very concept of constitution, as elaborated by Dieter Grimm and Heinz Mohnhaupt (1995). Another central inspirational work is that of American historian Lynn Hunt (2007), who traced the impact of fictional works on people in the eighteenth century. She argues that impulses from these texts led many readers to understand that their fellow men (including women and slaves) shared feelings and the capacity to suffer physical and psychological pain.

Democracy

Democracy may be understood simply as majority rule. Constitutions provide substantive and procedural limits to majority rule (Elster 1998: 2). Today, democracy is generally understood as involving some kind of constitutional restraints, unlike in the eighteenth century, when democracy was understood in the Aristotelian sense as unrestrained direct democracy (Aristotle 1996: 71–72). The modern, most often written, constitutions have thus become closely connected to modern conceptions of democracy. The theoretician of deliberative democracy John S. Dryzek emphasizes that while the concept of democracy and its constituting components are continually disputed, undisputed components are those of legitimacy and legality. Legitimacy includes acceptance, the moral rightness, freedom, transparency, and competence in the process of acceptance. "When it comes to political structures and public policies in particular, it is also common to add a requirement of legality: to be legitimate, a decision must be legal or constitutional" (Dryzek and Niemeyer 2010: 21).

Like most contemporary constitutions, the 1814 Norwegian Constitution did not contain the word *demokrati* (democracy). Not until 2012 did the word "democracy" gain its current prominent position in the Constitution. Following the abolishment of the state religion that year, Article 2 was amended to state the basic values enshrined in the Constitution: "Værdigrundlaget forbliver vor kristne og humanistiske Arv. Denne Grundlov skal sikre Demokratiet, Retsstaten og Menneskerettighederne." In the Norwegian parliament Stortinget's English translation, Article 2 reads: "Our values will remain our Christian and humanistic heritage. This Constitution shall ensure democracy, a state based on the rule of law and human rights."

Perhaps not coincidentally, the first mention of democracy in the Constitution came in Article 100, on the freedom of expression. The 2004 constitutional amendment of this article listed "the grounds of freedom of expression," among them "the promotion of democracy" (see Kalleberg in this volume).

Despite these late introductions of the very word "democracy," during the last two centuries, Norwegians have considered the adoption of the Constitution on 17 May 1814 as the decisive point in the development of Norwegian democracy. For the framers in 1814, however, it made no sense to call the form of government democratic. They understood democracy in the Aristotelian sense as direct democracy, and not in the modern sense as representative democracy subject to constitutional restraints. Instead, Article 1 said, and still says, that "the form of government is a limited and hereditary monarchy." The key word here is "limited." As explained by Christian Magnus Falsen (1782–1830), a preeminent member of the 1814 Constitutional Assembly, the Constitution established "a monarchy limited by democracy" ("et Monarkie indskænket ved Demokratie") (Falsen 1817: 6). Falsen and his contemporaries viewed the Constitution as democratic because it limited monarchy by making the people an integral and decisive part of the political system. The Constitution granted 45 percent of all men above the age of twenty-five the right to elect representatives to the legislative assembly, Storthinget, the Norwegian parliament (Kuhnle 1972: 388). Through representatives in Storthinget, legislation—the principal instrument for societal reform and development—was in the hands of the people through majority rule.

"The people" are the core of any democracy, and democracy's substance and scope rest upon how "the people" are defined. Just as the noun *demokrati* (democracy), the noun *folket* (the people) has a different constitutional meaning in today's Norway than it did in 1814. The 1814 Constitution, like other contemporary constitutions, distinguished between what the French 1791 constitution famously called "active" and "passive" citizens (Sieyès [1789] 1994: 199). The distinction referred to those with and without the right to vote and to be elected the people's representatives in political institutions. So when Article 49 in the 1814 Norwegian Constitution stated, "The people exercises the legislative power at the National Assembly,"[2] this "people" was defined in Article 50 as male property owners above the age of twenty-five. Universal suffrage in Norway was not introduced until ninety-nine years later, in 1913, by constitutional amendment. By this amendment, the Constitution's concept of "the people" in Article 49 changed its meaning, too, because "the people" now referred to all Norwegian citizens, male and female, above the age of eighteen.

Today, we may object that a constitution that refused the vote to women and the poor was hardly consistent with modern concepts of democracy. But if we consider that the 1814 Constitution replaced an absolute monarchy where no parliament existed and no citizens had the right to vote or to participate in politics, then the 1814 Constitution was truly the first step toward democracy in Norway. Among other things, this shared idea is reinforced in popular celebrations throughout Norway each year on Constitution Day, 17 May. Today's Norwegian democracy has evolved within the institutional structures and normative framework established by the 1814 Constitution. As of today, Norway ranks, indisputably, among the most democratic countries in the world, as evidenced, for example, by recurrent top scores in international democracy rankings of indexes (Norway ranks number one both in the *Democracy Index 2012* [2012] and in the *Democracy Ranking 2013* [Campbell et al. 2013]).

Historical Context

All chapters in this volume relate directly or indirectly to the Norwegian Constitution as a text. However, constitutions are rarely if ever disconnected from political and historical contexts. The 1814 Norwegian Constitution is no exception. Events in 1814 are intimately connected to the Constitution; likewise, later events are connected to the Constitution's contemporaneous legal and cultural positions.

In the broad European context, the Napoleonic Wars and France's defeat to the Allied powers, among them Sweden, form an international link and backdrop to the Norwegian Constitution. From 1380 to 1814, Norway was a part of the twin kingdoms of Denmark-Norway, an absolute monarchy since 1660.[3] In the Napoleonic Wars, Denmark-Norway sided with Napoleon to the end, and lost. For the Danish king, it meant the loss of Norway, because the peace settlement with Sweden in the Treaty of Kiel (signed on 14 January 1814) required him to renounce his claim to the Norwegian throne and required Norway to enter into a union with Sweden under the Swedish king.[4] For Norwegians, however, the breakup of the ancient union with Denmark and its political system and institutions was the fateful moment—the kairos—that made possible full independence for the first time since the Middle Ages.

In Norway, news of the Treaty of Kiel sparked resistance instead of submission to Swedish claims. As a natural corollary, cries for independence brought cries for a constitution. The figurehead of Norwegian resistance was the Danish prince Christian Frederik (1786–1848), the heir presumptive of Denmark-Norway (his cousin, King Frederik VI, had no male heirs). In 1813 he had been sent as vice-regent to Norway to promote the Norwegians' loyalty to the royal house. However, after learning about the Treaty of Kiel, and upon realizing that he could not claim the Norwegian throne by right of inheritance, he established a provisional government and organized the election of a constitutional assembly (see Warner et al. in this volume).

In the months leading up to the Constitutional Assembly, the new constitution was on everyone's minds. Private draft constitutions and suggestions were written and sent, or brought along, by deputies to the Constitutional Assembly, some twenty-seven of which are known today (Holmøyvik 2012: 290–307). An enterprising newspaper editor even launched a constitution-writing contest with a money prize for the three best drafts (Bergsgård 1943: 264).

On 10 April 1814, 112 elected deputies from most parts of Norway assembled in a manor house at Eidsvold, a small town about fifty kilometers north of today's capital, Oslo, then called Christiania.[5] The deputies were quite young; the average age was forty-two years, and many leading deputies were still in their thirties. Considered by social class, more than half of the deputies (fifty-seven) were senior government officials (judges, magistrates, priests, or military officers) and thus represented Norway's political and intellectual elite. Yet the country's farming majority was still substantially represented, with about one-third of the deputies (thirty-seven). The remainder eighteen representatives were merchants, manufacturers or large landowners. These men were the Constitution's framers.

Known as *Eidsvoldsmænd* (Eidsvold men), they have ever since enjoyed an almost mythical position in Norwegian national consciousness (panegyric works include, for example, one by Heggtveit [1888]). In this volume, authors refer to them as "deputies," a neutral term as to gender. However, it should be noted that in many passages, when authors apply what may seem to be gendered diction, this diction reflects the times and the situation, when only men were allowed to vote and participate.

At the Constitutional Assembly in the spring of 1814, most deputies participated little in the discussions. The actual framing was done by a smaller group of deputies, who debated and decided the principles and details in the Constitution. The fifteen members of the Constitutional Committee, elected by the Constitutional Assembly to draft the Constitution, had the greatest influence on the final text. Among them were some of the most knowledgeable and capable deputies at the Constitutional Assembly, but socially they all represented the small national elite of senior government officials and wealthy landowners. These fifteen men were the true framers of the Constitution, because the Constitutional Assembly eventually made few major changes to the Constitutional Committee's draft (Bergsgård 1943: 293). Moreover, the plenary discussions at the Constitutional Assembly lasted only eight days, and the latter half of the 110 articles in the Constitution were debated and decided in only two days. If we include the Constitutional Committee's work, the Constitution was drafted, discussed, and decided in only sixteen days (Holmøyvik 2012: 409). That is a short time to reflect upon and develop an entirely new system of government, with its institutions, procedures, and distribution of competences. Yet it is often the case that constitution-making processes take place in less than ideal conditions for reaching agreement upon fundamental issues like the basic principles of government (Elster 1995: 394). For the Constitutional Assembly, urgency was dictated by Norway's precarious political situation in the spring of 1814. In the short term, the Constitution was primarily a Norwegian declaration of independence against the Swedish king's claim to Norway according to the Treaty of Kiel (see Warner et al. in this volume).

These pressures of time imply that the subject of this volume is a document that was framed in only sixteen days; it nevertheless succeeded in establishing a new state that has lasted two hundred years. This imbalance between framing time and longevity may seem paradoxical. Nonetheless, the Norwegian Constitution exemplifies that textual practices may have not only significant consequences, but also long-lasting ones.

At the time of its adoption, however, few could imagine that the Constitution would last so long. The elite of Sweden, surely, did not imagine the strength of the Norwegian Constitution. The real ruler of Sweden was Crown Prince Carl Johan, who in 1810 had been adopted by King Karl XIII. Née Jean Baptiste Bernadotte (1763–1844), Carl Johan had served as a prominent general in Napoleon's army. He was intent on conquering Norway to compensate for Sweden's loss of Finland to Russia in 1809 and thus regain Sweden's status among the European powers. At Eidsvold, the deputies were well aware of the Treaty of Kiel and Carl Johan's ambition. In light of this harsh political reality, the fate of the constitutional project must have seemed uncertain. After fruitless negotiations, Sweden invaded Norway in the summer of 1814. The war was a short one and ended with the Convention of Moss (signed on 14 August 1814). There, the newly elected Norwegian king, Christian Frederik, agreed to lay down his crown, having reigned for only three months.[6] In his place, the king of Sweden ascended the throne, and through him, Norway entered into a union with Sweden.

The union with Sweden, however, did not mean the loss of Norwegian independence. Instead, the Swedish king promised in the Convention of Moss to accept the Constitution adopted at Eidsvold, subject only to changes necessary to accommodate a shared monarchy with Sweden. As king of Norway from 1818 to 1844, Carl Johan would later attempt to reform the Constitution and to increase the king's power in relation to Storthinget (see Warner et al. in this volume). In 1814, however, he accepted the Norwegian Constitution, despite its being far more radical than the Swedish Constitution of 1809. Carl Johan's promise helped quell resistance to the union, as well as securing his and King Karl XIII's claim to the Norwegian throne according to the Treaty of Kiel. The timing was critical because the Great Powers[7] of Europe were preparing for the Congress of Vienna in September 1814, where they would settle the many claims and land disputes arising after the Napoleonic Wars.

A revised Constitution was adopted by Storthinget, sitting in an extraordinary session on 4 November 1814. The constitutional revision marks the end of Norway's struggles in 1814. In less than a year, Norway passed from an absolute monarchy, in a union with Denmark, to a constitutional monarchy, in a union with Sweden, while retaining arguably the most democratic constitution in Europe at the time (see Gammelgaard in this volume).

Two constitutional texts are textual evidence of the dramatic events in 1814: the 17 May Constitution and the revised 4 November Constitution. The 4 November Constitution had 112 articles compared to the 110 articles of the 17 May Constitution. Most amendments in the 4 November Constitution sought to accommodate Norway's having a king (and head of the executive power) in common with Sweden, but other amendments sought to protect Norwegian institutions, such as the Council of State and the military, from Swedish influence. The constitutional revisions, however, made no changes in the vast majority of the articles or in the political system. Therefore, the 4 November Constitution has always been considered a revision of the 17 May Constitution, rather than a new constitution. For the same reason, today's Constitution's text, despite all its later amendments, is dated 17 May 1814 as well.

During the two hundred years since its adoption, the Constitution has undergone significant changes both in text and in law. In the nineteenth century, the interpretation of the Constitution was a continuous source of conflict between the legislative and executive branches. With a king residing in Sweden's capital, Stockholm, instead of in Norway's capital, Christiania, questions of separation of powers between the executive and legislative branches quickly became questions of protecting Norwegian sovereignty from Swedish influence.

The most significant constitutional change in this period did not come about as a result of a formal constitutional reform, but evolved through practice, interpretation, and piecemeal constitutional amendments. This change was the move to a parliamentary system, starting at the end of the nineteenth century. The parliamentary system was a radical break from the separation of powers system in the 1814 Constitution, because it made the executive branch subordinate to the legislative branch. In the 1814 Constitution, the king appointed and dismissed the governments, and the governments acted independently of Storthinget. After decades of discussion, which culminated in the impeachment and conviction of the government in 1884, the Constitution was amended that year to allow government ministers to appear in Storthinget (see Sand in this volume).[8] This amendment radically altered the separation between the executive and legislative branches. In the following decades, practice established that the king could not appoint a government that lacked majority support in Storthinget. Simultaneously, the king's personal power withered and the government became the dominant institution in the executive branch. A constitutional amendment of Article 31 in 1911 formally put an end to the king's exclusive and personal exercise of the executive power by making all executive decisions subject to approval in the Council of State. Yet only in 2007 was the parliamentary system explicitly introduced into the Constitution's text.

Characteristically, the more comprehensive constitutional reforms in Norway have been limited to specific issues arising from specific needs. In 1903, the Constitution's language form was revised to be in accordance with linguistic developments in Norwegian administrative language. The breakup of the union with Sweden in 1905 reversed many of the constitutional amendments introduced in 1814 in the 4 November Constitution. In the decades following the end of World War II, the emergence of international organizations such as the United Nations (UN), the North Atlantic Treaty Organization (NATO), and in particular the European Union (EU) spurred Stortinget into adopting a specific procedure in Article 93 to allow the transfer of sovereignty to international organizations. Recent reforms include the 2004 revision of Article 100 on the freedom of expression, a revision of the Court of Impeachment, and the move from a bicameral parliamentary system to a unicameral system in 2007. In 2012, the principle of the separation of church and state required several constitutional amendments and removed one of the key features of the 1814 Constitution, namely, the close connection between church and state. In May 2014, another reform of the Constitution's language form was adopted (see Madzharova Bruteig in this volume), as well as a comprehensive reform of the Constitution's human rights protection.

All in all, then, today's Constitution differs both textually and substantively from the document first adopted on 17 May 1814. In addition to formal amendments, the Constitution has also been subject to extensive interpretation over the years (Holmøyvik 2013). In some cases, interpretation has replaced formal amendment in the sense that the same constitutional text has taken on a new legal meaning. In the absence of a complete constitutional reform, interpretation has been crucial for the 1814 Constitution's text to remain relevant and up-to-date.

Chapter Survey

The present volume has four sections, each containing three chapters. Chapters in the first section embark on analyzing the Constitution as a text. In the first chapter, William B. Warner, Eirik Holmøyvik, and Mona Ringvej focus on events in Norway in 1814 as seen through the Constitution and the documents that functioned as what the three authors term its "envelopes." This approach allows for discussions of contemporaneous perceptions of democracy. In particular, the authors emphasize how processes leading to the framing of the Constitution, such as preparatory and accompanying negotiations, and even its very framing were vital for the Constitution's adoption, longevity, and legacy. In the second chapter, Eirik Holmøyvik investigates the development of the very concept "constitution" and its manifestations in terms used by legal scholars and Eidsvold deputies around 1814. In the Danish language and legal terminology, the US and French constitutions of the late eighteenth century activated a new understanding of the "constitution" concept. Holmøyvik shows how this new understanding of "constitution" shaped the Eidsvold deputies' vision of the 1814 Norwegian Constitution. In the last chapter in this section, Dag Michalsen adopts an analytical view of constitutions' textuality. He identifies different connections between constitutions and texts, connections that go beyond today's widespread identification between government and the protection of human rights on the one hand and an exhaustive formal written document on the other. By using historical as well as contemporary examples, Michalsen challenges our conception of what a constitution is in terms of its textual basis.

Chapters in the second section focus on the Norwegian Constitution in transnational conversations. Ulrich Schmid discusses the poetics of the international constitutionalism movement. In addition to the well-known US and French constitutions, he includes in his discussion the Spanish Constitution of 1812, the Polish Constitution of 1791, and several Swiss constitutions. In the fifth chapter, Karen Gammelgaard compares the 4 November 1814 Norwegian Constitution with constitutions in the Habsburg Empire in 1848 and 1849 to determine the characteristics of what she terms "the transnational constitution genre." Her genre identification is resumed in the sixth chapter, by Jacqueline Visconti, who compares the discursive patterns of the current Norwegian Constitution (of 2012) with those of the Italian Constitution of 1948. She identifies a set of patterns shared by both constitutions and thus confirms Gammelgaard's thesis of the existence of a transnational constitution genre.

In the third section, the chapters concentrate on historical transformation. Helge Jordheim discusses the various concepts of time involved in writing the 17 May 1814 Constitution. He detects a tension between the present tense of verbs used in the Constitution and the "fateful moment," that is, the dramatic historical events surrounding the deputies' work with the document. In addition, Jordheim identifies a tension between what he terms "monarchical time" and "republican time," both inscribed in the Constitution's text. In the eighth chapter, Inger-Johanne Sand studies the transformation of political and legal codes in the Norwegian Constitution. Analyzing three cases—parliamentarism, human rights, and international cooperation—she emphasizes the difference between the Constitution's text and how this text has been interpreted over the last two hundred years. Yordanka Madzharova Bruteig focuses on the Constitution's language form. A central component in its textuality, namely, its antiquated language form (which resembled Danish more than modern Norwegian), was a topic for Stortinget's members in recent years. Stortinget adopted linguistically renovated editions of the Constitution before its bicentennial in 2014, and Madzharova Bruteig investigates how procedural, political, and institutional factors have influenced discourse on this topic.

Chapters in the final section scrutinize the Norwegian Constitution's Article 100, the article on freedom of expression. The particular focus on this article coincides with the volume's general focus on text. Article 100 guarantees that texts can be disseminated to the public without the author fearing persecution by state authorities for his or her opinions. Therefore, Article 100 may be regarded as a *metatext:* a text about texts. It establishes the foundations for deliberative democracy in Norway. Indeed, many historians argue that among all the articles in the 1814 Norwegian Constitution, only Article 100 was truly democratic. In his chapter, Kjell Lars Berge investigates a crucial precondition for the creation of Article 100, namely, the period 1770–1799, when Denmark-Norway enjoyed exceptional freedom of expression. This freedom is often explained by the dealings of Johann Friedrich Struensee, a German doctor and Enlightenment zealot who gained influence over the mentally ill king of Denmark-Norway, Christian VII. However, Berge adopts a perspective that instead directs attention to structural issues connected with the emerging institution of public opinion. In the eleventh chapter, Mona Ringvej analyzes conceptions of freedom of expression among the deputies at Eidsvold. She demonstrates how (apparent) unity was emphasized rather than dissent, and compares ideas of freedom of expression with general ideas of democracy. Article 100 was kept unchanged from 1814 until 2004. That year Stortinget adopted a revised Article 100 in order to bring the Constitution's protection of the freedom of expression, hailed as a cornerstone of democracy, up-to-date with the demands of a modern society (*Innst. S. nr. 270 [2003–2004]*). Ragnvald Kalleberg traces how this revision was heavily influenced by scholarly texts. Among other things, his analysis of the 2004 revision of Article 100 may serve to illustrate how, in the Norwegian tradition, the amendment procedure takes place. Kalleberg concludes his chapter, and the volume, by discussing how the revised Article 100 meets current challenges in the unfinished historical project of democracy.

NOTES

1. English-language translations are by the authors.
2. We quote from the 1814 English-language translation "pursuant to order of Government" (*The Constitution of the Kingdom of Norway* 1814).
3. The Danish historian Ole Feldbæk notes, however, that at no point was the Danish-Norwegian absolutism identical to the king's personal rule (Feldbæk 1982: 74–83). In particular, from the middle of the eighteenth century, the Danish-Norwegian monarchs were weak and therefore left it to the Council of State and the state administration to rule on their behalf.
4. While the breakup of the union with Denmark is a significant event in Norwegian history, culture, and self-understanding, in Denmark, the loss of Norway in 1814 has been reflected on relatively little. However, the breakup of the twin kingdom's more than 400-year coexistence had far-reaching implications for how national identities have since been constructed in both Denmark and Norway (Glenthøj 2012).
5. Because of the great distance and slow postal communication, the northernmost parts of Norway received news of the Constitutional Assembly too late to organize elections and send deputies. From 1877, Christiania was also spelled "Kristiania" (with an initial "K").
6. In October 1814, Christian Frederik left for Denmark, where he eventually ascended the throne in 1839 and reigned as an absolute monarch until his death in 1848. In Denmark, absolutism was finally abolished with the constitution of 1849, which introduced the separation of powers and an elected parliament. The Norwegian 1814 Constitution was one of several sources of inspiration for the Danish framers.
7. Following the Congress of Vienna in 1814–1815, Austria (the Habsburg Empire), Russia, Prussia, the United Kingdom, and later France became known as the Great Powers of Europe. The title signified these powers' superior status compared to that of the other European states.
8. The principal question in the impeachment case was whether the king had to consent to constitutional amendments. This was a highly contested issue at the time. Article 112 in the Constitution said nothing about royal involvement in constitutional amendment, but the text was interpreted in the light of its context, of the separation of powers doctrine, and of established practice for constitutional amendment. Ultimately, the Court of Impeachment ruled that royal consent was not required for constitutional amendment. The government was then convicted for acting contrary to the Constitution by contributing to the king's decision to veto the constitutional amendment that would allow government ministers to appear in Storthinget.

►• Part I •◄

EMBARKING ON THE MATTER

The Thing That Invented Norway

William B. Warner, Eirik Holmøyvik, and Mona Ringvej

A Bridge of Things

If one wished to place the emergence of Norway as a modern, independent nation, one could not do better than to repair to Eidsvold on 17 to 19 May 1814 and take in the scene where a consensus was achieved through reciprocal exchange between 112 deputies and Prince Regent Christian Frederik. On 17 May, the deputies had declared their newly signed Constitution "to be the fundamental law of the Kingdom of Norway, which all and every one shall obey"; elected the prince regent as the new king of Norway; and rejoiced in the "hope" that he would "accept of a crown, voluntarily offered You by a free people."[1] However "freely" given, this crown came with 110 carefully specified conditions, the articles of the Constitution of the Kingdom of Norway. Two days later, on 19 May, the prince regent's response carefully balanced his acceptance of the crown with a vow to uphold the Constitution:

> I accept the crown of Norway as the gift of a constant and sincere people, as a pledge of its attachment to me and my royal family.
> *I promise and swear to reign the Kingdom of Norway according to its Constitution and Laws; so help me God and his holy word.*
> Eidswold, the 19th May 1814
> Christian Frederik. (*The Constitution of the Kingdom of Norway* 1814: 40)

By coupling his acceptance of the "gift" of the crown with a vow, marked with italic emphasis in the text and as a sacred pledge (*"so help me God and his holy word"*), the new king had accepted the relatively recent notion that though he was a king, his authority was derived from a written constitution. It is worth remarking the strangeness of this moment. It is not just that the prince regent had internalized the Enlightenment critique of absolutism, where, to quote Anglo-American revolutionary Thomas Paine in his pamphlet *Common Sense* from 1776, "The Law Is King" (Paine [1776] 2004: 75).

It is as if the Constitution of Norway were a thing with an uncanny incorporating power. After accepting this potent new gift—a crown wrapped in a constitution—Christian Frederik finds himself inside of, and subordinate to, the Constitution, "which all and every one shall obey."

How did the Eidsvold delegates and the prince regent use constitution writing as a way to invent Norway as "a free, independent and indivisible Realm" (Article 1)? How was their constitution indebted to but also distinct from Enlightenment constitutions framed in other nations?[2] And finally, how, after the king of Sweden arrived at the frontiers of Norway in the fall of 1814 to demand Norway as properly his by the articles of the Treaty of Kiel, did this Constitution become the vital thing that guaranteed Norwegian political autonomy during the nineteenth century, even while Norway submitted to a formal union with Sweden? It all depended upon drafting and implementing a new constitution. Thus, this constitution turned out to be a mighty thing. From the vantage point of the technology-consumed twenty-first century, we might say that it was the Enlightenment's most powerful technology for bringing about the sort of radical change that was called for in the spring of 1814.

We can grasp how constitutions can drive change by developing a new understanding of the centrality of "things." It is not difficult to tell the story of the constitutional invention of Norway by engaging different early meanings of the word "thing," as found in Danish and English dictionaries. The English word "thing" has strong etymological links with the Old Danish *thing* and contemporary Norwegian *ting* and their equivalents in the host of those northern European languages used around the North Sea. The most comprehensive dictionary of the Danish language between 1700 and 1950 offers this etymological account of the two entries, identified by Roman numerals, *Ting* (case) and *Ting* (assembly): "*I. Ting* … old Danish *t(h)ing*, elder Danish *thing*, old Norse þing, English *thing* (Old English þing), German *ding* … actually the same word as *II. Ting* with semantic development: assembly at the *Ting*—case being discussed there—state of affairs, case in general—object."[3] When news of the Treaty of Kiel arrived in Norway, the treaty and its appalling implications for Norway became the "thing" on everyone's mind: "A matter with which one is concerned (in action, speech, or thought)."[4] In order to gather the power to oppose the Treaty of Kiel, the prince regent convened a meeting with a group of distinguished and influential Norwegians, a famous meeting called the *Notabelmøtet* (meeting of notables). These notables convinced the prince to gather a representative assembly, one inspired by the revolutionary constitutionalism of the past century, but also by the Norse tradition that extended back to the Middle Ages, of holding a *thing* (*ting*), "A meeting, an assembly; esp. a deliberative or judicial assembly." The meeting at Eidsvold was the first gathering of representatives from all of Norway.[5] Their charge was to write a "constitution," another kind of "thing": "that which is stated or expressed in speech, writing, etc.; a saying, an utterance, an expression, a statement." To put it more colloquially, a constitution would enable the people of Norway to "say their thing." Once written, the Constitution emerged as another kind of "thing," "that which is done or to be done; a deed, an act, a transaction," for example, the exchange that we have described above between the deputies and the king so as to activate their new "thing," the Constitution of Norway. Now the Constitution becomes a more concrete thing, "an entity of any kind": a material document written upon parchment, a text published as a pamphlet for dissemination across Norway, and, over the course of the nineteenth and twentieth centuries, as the "thing" to celebrate as a symbol of Norway's stubborn autonomy. A matter of concern, a deliberative assembly, a statement, a transaction, a text, a document, and a symbol: these things are constituents of Norway's constitution of itself as an independent nation. We imagine our skeptical reader asking: why use a word and concept so vague and indefinite as "thing" to describe the political action of Norwegians in the spring of 1814? To which we reply: it is precisely the vague and indefinite character of things that allows them to serve their mediating function as a bridge toward an as yet indefinite future.

Gathering the Deputies at Eidsvold

News of the Treaty of Kiel precipitated a political crisis in Norway, a time of anxiety and uncertainty, what the deputies would describe in their address to the prince regent as "a time of danger and misery" (*Riksforsamlingens forhandlinger* 1914–1918: 1:13). In such a crisis, the events that cascade into the present seem fraught with the future. If Norwegians did not find a way to act, and act with decision, others, such as Crown Prince Carl Johan of Sweden, would surely decide Norway's future for them. When Christian Frederik received the news of the Treaty of Kiel, he reacted with resentment. Being an heir to the Danish-Norwegian throne himself and functioning at the time as governor of Norway, his loyalties were primarily absolutist and dynastic. Historians have repeatedly debated the motives of Christian Frederik in the months to come, but it seems obvious that certain elements of his actions sprang from a sincere sense of affinity with the Norwegians, a feeling that was entangled with the dynastic outlook of the absolutist monarchies: he saw himself as the savior of Norway (Raabe 1914). As cousin of the Danish king who had betrayed the Norwegians by giving Norway to Sweden, he took it as his duty to save the Norwegians for the royal family, perhaps even to see the two countries united again. At the same time, it was essential to save Norway from the archenemy, namely, the Swedes, headed by Crown Prince Carl Johan.

Christian Frederik wanted to fight for Norway's autonomy. He was probably the only one who could take it upon himself to do so, since he was both governor and an heir to the throne of the kingdom that had just given the country away. But how to oppose a peace treaty supported by all the important dynasties of Europe? To them, Norway lawfully belonged to Sweden. Christian Frederik was about to embark upon a struggle for freedom for a nation that had not been an autonomous state or administrative unit for more than four hundred years. It was a nation with hardly any man-made resources: infrastructure, military forces, or economic power. It had no administrative strongholds, nothing but this one person, a prince, with some executive power and a great deal of motivation. But what were his potential resources for this struggle? Only a people and a declaration, a written constitution backed by the sovereign will of the people. In order to mobilize this latent power, he had to gather the representatives of this people so that they could condense this power in some thing, the text of a written constitution.

However, Christian Frederik did not immediately grasp this strategy. He first sought to gather support for his project of declaring Norway a sovereign state in opposition to the treaty, and he thought he could do so as heir to the throne. After the political crisis had calmed down, he planned to offer the people of Norway a new constitution, one that he and a council of higher deputies would design. But plans soon changed. In the following months, powerful political currents carried all the agents toward certain new principles. Christian Frederik could not claim the throne of Norway based upon his dynastic position. In the wake of the Enlightenment revolutions that had spread across Europe, this new nation had to be built upon the one principle that could secure its legitimacy: the people's sovereignty. Though Christian Frederik would be welcome to the throne of Norway, it would not be his by inheritance, but rather would be offered him by the people of Norway. Simultaneously, throughout the towns and countryside, discussions became focused on the need for a new constitution. And the constitution would have to come before the king.

These early months of 1814 present an epoch of remarkable political tumult taking the form of town gossip, of discussions in dinner parties and clerical meetings, of local newspaper reading, and of intense activism from the pastors each Sunday in church. The actors circulated among these different meeting places, occasionally giving center stage to the messages in the press as well. It was an intensely concentrated clamor, with discoursing and listening, and analyzing of the political situation from day to day. On their own initiative, and already in January, some Norwegians began drafting constitutions. Later on, the papers would invite readers to do so as well. The consensus for a constitution was so broad that it is in fact difficult to see where the idea of constitutional government first showed up, or how it won the day. But through letters, gossip, discussions, toasts at dinner parties, and exchanges in the streets, it did. Within the sources from these months, there are expressions of bewilderment at the situation, over what is really going on (Riis 1864). But at the center of it all, we find single-minded focus upon the great question: how could a new constitution be designed with the greatest possible legitimacy within the shortest possible time? A gathering of deputies was the logical answer to the question. Such a gathering would secure internal support from the people of Norway, an absolute precondition for any hope of success in their struggle against the international Treaty of Kiel. And it would have to happen quickly.

The new strategy emerged by 19 February, when Christian Frederik and his group of prominent friends, the notables, gathered at Eidsvold. The consensus that popular sovereignty would be the only legitimate ground for his project speeded the call for the election of a representative assembly. This first meeting at Eidsvold was, as everything else in this process, an informal meeting of friends and helpers, designed to enable the prince to understand the mental climate of the Norwegians. At the meeting, Christian Frederik received a unanimous message: he could not claim Norway through his position as heir to the Danish throne. Another factor contributed to the prince's willingness to accept this judgment. The Swedes approached the Norwegians after the Treaty of Kiel as friends and offered Norway a free, liberal constitution as a relief from the absolutist tradition of the Danes.

In spite of an initial reluctance, Christian Frederik now embraced change with great enthusiasm, and three days later he had written all the necessary documents in order to initiate an electoral process. Letters were written to, among others, the pastors, who would have the task of organizing primary elections in church as soon as the next week, if they could. They were to make the parish swear an oath to uphold the nation's autonomy, and thereafter all men above the age of twenty-five could elect candidates, who would then meet with candidates from the whole *Amt* (county) and elect two deputies among themselves to attend the assembly at Eidsvold, which was to convene on 10 April (Jæger 1916).

There was no time for delay of any sort. This forced all the organizers to improvise wherever they found Christian Frederik's instructions vague or difficult to follow. There were two noteworthy features of this process. The first feature helped to ensure that the gathering at Eidsvold would be representative. The prince decided that, among autonomous males who earned their own living, all social strata should be represented. He designated the number of delegates to be elected from each social stratum or estate, and, surprisingly, he wanted peasants and military representatives in addition to the burghers and civil servants. This approach secured the broad popular legitimacy of the project, which probably contributed to the durable result. All in all, these procedures helped bind the prince and the people together, across the estates and across the geographical diversity of the country.

A second aspect of the gathering of deputies increased the likelihood that they would achieve a consensus good enough to act as one body. The deputies were not representatives of any party, and they were not provided with any instructions from their electing bodies. Instead, they were elected solely as representatives of their local community. By serving as individuals, the 112 who met at Eidsvold could be moved by the discussions to change their minds, and each deputy could contribute freely in shaping the constitution. This political autonomy helps explain the quiet and orderly character of the oppositional activity at Eidsvold. There was little tumultuous agitation or thorough debate concerning clearly defined alternative positions. Quite the opposite: the discussions were so insistently driven in a certain direction that some critics privately complained that the atmosphere constrained debate.

The deputies met at Eidsvold on 10 April, went to church as their first duty, and then proceeded to deliver a new constitution within five weeks. This astonishing speed was the result of a broadly shared set of principles, including popular sovereignty, limited monarchy, and Norwegian autonomy. As the deputies deliberated, fewer and fewer dared to question the project of an autonomous state versus a union with Sweden. This narrowing of options contributed to the productiveness of the gathering but resulted in a kind of consensual censorship. As the very first national *Thing* (*ting*), this body was not encumbered by rules that could slow down deliberation. Not even those rules invented during the process were strictly followed (Jæger 1916). Instead, the deliberations were driven by the imperative to establish a binding "fundamental law," so that deputies could publicly establish Norway's legitimate autonomy as soon as possible. Further, this autonomy could be most effectively achieved through a constitution that included an energetic executive power, which could be immediately embodied in Christian Frederik.

The Constitutional *Thing* as an Enlightenment System

How did it happen that the people of the seventeenth and eighteenth centuries began to use something as insubstantial as words to ground the agencies and institutions of government? The development of the Enlightenment-era constitutions should be understood as an extension into politics of the era's most prestigious new genre for explaining the world, the system (Siskin 2010). Throughout the Enlightenment, knowledge advanced by casting its explanations into the form of a "system." This was the word used by Isaac Newton in his *Principia Mathematica* (1687), and the third volume was even entitled *De mundi systemate* (On the System of the World). The most advanced thinkers of the Enlightenment were fascinated with the explanatory power of Newton's development of the genre he called "system." Newton had shown that certain laws could explain how the parts of a system—like the planets, the moons, and the sun that composed a single solar system—were held in place by a balance of gravitational forces. Newton's account of gravity used mathematical proofs and diagrams to develop an abstract model that disclosed something true about reality. Newton's breakthrough was as much formal as explanatory. His systematic account demonstrated the power of the genre of the "system" to reconcile dynamic change with regularity, periodicity with a complex and contingent reality. Those who drafted systems in the wake of Newton's system sought to accomplish something equally truthful and effective for other branches of knowledge. Carl Linnaeus sought to classify all the plants in the world as part of one *Systema Naturae* (1735), and Denis Diderot organized the *Encyclopédie* (1751–1772) so its thousands of articles were branches of a single "tree of knowledge." John Locke developed a systematic history of politics (from the state of nature to modern political systems) in *The Two Treatises on Government* (1689), and Montesquieu attempted a still more systematic account of government in *De l'esprit des lois* (The Spirit of Laws) in 1748. The new constitutions of the Enlightenment differ from medieval legal systems by being systematic in this special generic sense developed during the Enlightenment; that is, they are descriptive as well as prescriptive, and they are designed to discover in, and confer upon, a nation's polis the same elegant order and complex balance that the Enlightenment natural philosophy had discovered in nature (see Holmøyvik in this volume.)

The drafters of the Norwegian Constitution adopted the same general structure as other Enlightenment systems: (a) the systems were made of parts that constituted a whole; (b) the system could "talk with itself" (for example, among its parts, through cross-references); and (c) the systems should be self-contained and complete. The Norwegian Constitution of 1814 consisted of 110 articles, which were organized into five main parts:

A. Of the form of Government and the Religion   Articles 1–2

B. Of the Executive Power, the King and the Royal Family   Articles 3–48

C. Of Burghership and the Legislative Power   Articles 49–86

D. Of the Judicial Power   Articles 87–92

E. General Rules   Articles 93–110

This arrangement of articles is the outcome of the drafters' combining a pragmatic understanding of politics with certain fundamental axiomatic principles of Enlightenment political theory (like the "separation of powers," a term that appears in three of the five parts of the constitution) in order to build a model for a government. Constitution framing is at once conservative (it builds upon what has been), constructive (it shapes a model), and speculative (it figures a new, not yet existing scheme of government) (see Michalsen in this volume).

After the Enlightenment, systems were decried by the Romantics as cages that enslave the imagination, or, after the rise of bureaucratic systems in the twentieth century, as sinister instruments of control. But Enlightenment systems were based upon a skeptical experimental epistemology whereby systems modeled the world, were tested, and then were open to modification. Thus, to sustain their efficacy over time, the Enlightenment constitutions were provided with amendment procedures so alterations could be made, with the proviso, in the case of the Norwegian Constitution, that those who draft amendments "do not alter the spirit of this Constitution" (Article 110). In other words, the Constitution was not a system imposed upon reality, but one that was in a highly mediated "dialogue" with it.

The framers at Eidsvold accommodated the complexity of their political situation by practicing the art of mixing. The deputies and prince regent created a form of government that preserved by mixing a few of the best old features of monarchy (the king as the representative of the nation; the continuities of a hereditary monarchy) with the best new features of the Enlightenment republics (popular sovereignty as expressed through their representatives, a separation of powers, recognition of human rights). We can see this mixing in the compromise of Article 1: "Its form of government is a limited and hereditary monarchy." The article reconciles Enlightenment political science—the very idea that governments have "a form," that the monarch's power must be "limited"—with the continued existence of a monarchy that would be "hereditary." Such an outcome is a compromise between, on the one hand, Norway's experience of Danish absolutism and, on the other, her memory of the autonomy the framers associated with medieval kings of Norway. This selective use of Norwegian history as well as the crucial facilitating role of the prince regent at Eidsvold helped to account for the main way the Norwegian Constitution diverges from other Enlightenment constitutions. In them, the powers of the legislature are described before the powers of the executive are. This ordering gives formal expression to the primacy of the legislature as the embodiment of the people's sovereignty. But in Norway, the order was reversed, such that the powers of the executive and the king were described first. In addition, nearly half of the articles are devoted to describing the monarchy. Putting the king first reflects the historical process that led to Eidsvold, where the king was the prime mover in gathering deputies, in defining the task, and in collaborating in framing a new constitution. Finally, the executive is honored with first place because, as we shall see, it was through his swift assent that the Constitution could be brought into effect. Not for reasons of political theory, but rather for the most pragmatic reasons, putting the king first made good sense.

Putting Norway's king first did not just involve political expediency. It also is a clue that Norway was borrowing from the limited constitutional monarchy that England had opened in 1688–1689, when Parliament removed the anointed monarch, James II. James II had sought to rule England as an absolutist sovereign in the style of France's Louis XIV. Parliament's alternative was a new form of mixed government, by which a new king and queen (William and Mary) were offered the throne of England in exchange for their signing Parliament's An Act Declaring the Rights and Liberties of the Subject and Settling the Succession of the Crown (1689), known ever since as the Bill of Rights. Because of the way that document itemized the powers of the Parliament (to tax, to control succession, to raise an army, etc.), it is the first experiment with what would come to be called "limited monarchy." The key point for our understanding of the Norwegian Constitution is that although it is grounded in the Enlightenment constitutions (as to the assertion of popular sovereignty, representative government, and individual rights and liberties), its content—a limited monarchy—also borrowed from the older model of Britain in 1688, where the Bill of Rights and the Magna Carta were enshrined in eighteenth-century political theory as constituents of England's mixed "constitution" (see Holmøyvik in this volume; Schmidgen 2012). During the Enlightenment, British politician Edmund Burke, in his polemics against the French Revolution, would use eighteenth-century political theory to defend the English constitution against French innovations. By Burke's account, England's successive modifications of law and practice, over the course of centuries, produced a wise mixture: the monarch remains as the unifying embodiment of the nation, while Parliament represents, respectively, the nobility (the Lords) and the people (the Commons). A Burkean revaluation of this native political tradition seems to have been at work in the somewhat Romantic choice of a name for the legislative branch of the Norwegian government. The framers did not choose the name that had been consistently applied to describe their own body—Rigsforsamlingen (National Assembly)—but instead returned to the old Norse usage of the *ting* by adopting the name Storthinget (later Stortinget).

The Actions that Framed the Delivery of the Constitution to the People

A constitution is not the act of a government, but of a people constituting a government.
—Thomas Paine, *Rights of Man*

The gathering at Eidsvold unfolded in uncertainty. Such a time of crisis— where paths to different futures open—might be a moment where the course of history could, if faced with decision and resolve, be given an auspicious new direction. However, for skeptics inside and outside of Norway, this so-called constitution might appear as little more than the contrivance of 112 disaffected Norwegians, conspiring at a country estate with one renegade Danish prince. How could the deputies and prince make this constitution appear as the outcome of a grander process, one invoked by Thomas Paine's resonant phrase as "a people constituting a government"? They did so by wrapping the new constitution in four discrete actions, each articulated in a separate document so these actions could serve as an envelope to deliver the constitution to the people. We might say, in modern computer jargon, that these actions put the constitution "online":

1. Declaration: a one-sentence declaration with 112 signatures, each confirmed with a stamp.
2. Election: the deputies' address to the prince offers him the crown. (Enclosure: the Constitution with 110 articles.)
3. Ratification: the king's answer accepts the crown and vows to uphold the Constitution.
4. Publication: a committee of three deputies attests that the published Constitution is correct.

This sequential list of documents, which we will discuss in more detail below, allows us to trace the constituents of this decisive exchange between the deliberative body of deputies (the "thing" [*ting*]) and the prince who would be king. The Constitution is linked to the people by making it an enclosure in a carefully choreographed correspondence between the people's deputies, acting as *declarers, signers,* and *electors,* and the prince, who *countersigns* the Constitution to which he *vows* allegiance and, simultaneously, *proclaims* the document to be the law of the land. Although the Norwegian Constitution is written, like all other constitutions, in an indicative "timeless" present tense (see Jordheim in this volume), it emerges out of a political crisis with an active temporality, reminding anyone who might have forgotten that the Constitution was both a political and a legal document.

These four actions, each of which is given a publishable textual form, allow those who were not at Eidsvold to grasp the process of constituting the Kingdom of Norway. These constituents have commonalities with, as well as differences from, Enlightenment antecedents in the United States (1789), France (1791), and Spain (1812).

First action: A one-sentence declaration by the deputies is the first step in giving the constitution the force of law: "We the signed, Deputies of the Kingdom of Norway, hereby declare [*erklære*] this Constitution [*Constitution*], sanctioned by the National Assembly [*Rigsforsamlingen*], to be the fundamental law [*Grundlov*] of the Kingdom of Norway, which all and every one shall obey." What could justify such an audacious declaration? This declaration has several of the distinct features of the declarations that preceded it. First, in English law, a "declaration" provides an explanation for the willed violation of the law, here Swedish rule over Norway. Relevant comparisons would be the English Parliament's declaration of 1689 (the Bill of Rights) or the US Declaration of Independence, justifying renunciation of British sovereignty over the thirteen signing states. Second, precisely because these men did something that was *not* grounded in any already existing authority, this Norwegian declaration and constitution both have a circular self-authorizing character: each claims authority through an enunciation that then provides a retroactive justification for itself. In other words, the performance produces the authority that underwrites the performance (see Derrida 1986; M. Warner 1990: 102–104; Schmid; Gammelgaard; Visconti in this volume.) To make themselves publically accountable for this declaration, each of the 112 deputies signed the declaration that followed the text of the Constitution, and then affixed his personal seal next to his signature. Finally, this declaration gives retroactive coherence to a "we" that acts together with these words. On the one hand, this "we" is specific and public (the list of signatures made it so). But on the other hand, this "we" also had an expanding and incorporating character, because the particular voices of 112 deputies are merged into one declaration, and through an explicit assertion of the representative function of this body, these 112 aspire to speak, in one authorial voice, for the whole nation (see also Schmid in this volume).

The declaration that is appended to the Constitution allows us to see the way in which the Constitution itself served as a kind of declaration of independence. Thus, by 17 May 1814, the Constitution was more than the tangible outcome of the course for independence set by Christian Frederik and his allies some months earlier. The very first words of Article 1 assert as a legal fact, in nakedly performative language, that "[t]he Kingdom of Norway is a free, independent and indivisible Realm." These words were the kernel of the constitution project: the wording, "a free, independent and indivisible Realm," appeared as the first of ten basic principles for the Constitution defined in its early stages by the Constitutional Assembly. On this single point, the otherwise divided assembly at Eidsvold acted unanimously (*Storthings-Efterretninger 1814–1833* 1874: 1, 9–10). Of course, independence was far from a fact. Although the project was incomplete, the prospects for independence were in fact quite grim. But the bold performative language of Article 1, like that of the signed declaration, displays a sublime indifference to those, like Carl Johan, who would be incited to action by claims to Norwegian independence.

Second action: The deputies write an address to the prince regent that braids together three steps, an address that the deputies hope the prince will countersign. First, their Constitution has followed Enlightenment separation of power theory by distributing "sovereign power, in such a manner, that legislation is deposited into the hands of the people, and the executive power into the hands of the King"; second, they have had the "dear and sacred duty … to elect a King," and they announce their choice in words that express intense personal affection for the prince regent: "Confidence, gratitude and love equally forced us to fix our regards on Your Royal Highness." Their address ends by expressing the "hope" that both Constitution and crown will be found "worthy of Your approbation." Constitution and king, king and Constitution, one cannot have one, the logic of this address by the deputies makes clear, without the other. Given the prince regent's indispensable support during the previous months for the gathering at Eidsvold, the address to the prince regent may seem to be a mere formality, a piece of self-conscious political theater. But we would maintain that neither the deputies nor the king are just acting (i.e., performing); they are *acting*.

Third action: In the first pages of this chapter, we quoted the words with which the king countersigns the Constitution, accepts the crown that has been offered him, and vows to subordinate himself to the Constitution. The tone and content of the words with which Christian Frederik accepts the throne imbue this action with an equable wisdom. First, he approves the deputies' choice of the "form of government": "a limited and hereditary monarchy" (Article 1). In his words, this choice will "guard the Constitution equally against the marks of despotism as against the abuses of a popular government." While these words express the common sense of his era, Christian Frederik couples this idea with words that makes the deputies' choice of a monarchy rather than a republic seem like a comfortable inevitability: "This old Kingdom calls for a King." He adds a fraternal and patriarchal sentiment that resonated more with a Burkean sense of the authority of custom than with the innovation advanced by the American founder Thomas Jefferson or by the French politician Maximilien de Robespierre: the king "should be the first friend and father to his people." Finally, he develops the metaphor for this exchange that we have noted above: "I accept the crown of Norway as the gift of a constant and sincere people." The metaphor of crown as gift might give some pause. After all, had not the prince regent been scheming all spring, first with the notables and then the deputies, to constitute an independent kingdom that would welcome Christian Frederik as its king? Nonetheless, the conceit of the crown as gift is a happy one. By reaffirming what the deputies had said near the end of their address—that the crown was "voluntarily offered" by "a free people"—the prince regent's gracious acceptance of the crown gives this inaugural exchange a positive moral valence. A people have freely offered the crown, as defined by the Constitution, and the fortunate and faithful monarch freely accepts their gift. In return, he vows to uphold the Constitution that comes with the crown. A circle had been squared: two terms that many Enlightenment revolutions had made appear incompatible—"monarchy" and "the sovereignty of the people"—had been reconciled by the exchange that delivered the Constitution to the people of Norway.

The prince regent magnifies the performative power of his message by the way he delivers his answer to the deputies. The public record makes it clear that the deputies of Eidsvold *write* an address to the prince regent inviting him to become the king of Norway. But his answer was delivered *orally*, "in the National Assembly." Although the prince regent had been present in Eidsvold for most of the five weeks of deliberation, and he had even invited different deputies to eat with him on successive evenings, the prince regent was by design not part of the deliberations. But, two days after the deputies' address of 17 May 1814, the prince regent appeared before the assembled deputies in person. With his words, he does much more than accept the crown. First, he addresses the deputies with an epithet that the drafting of a constitution has given new resonance: "Norwegians!" Then, he announces the closure of the constitutional process: "The high calling, to which you are elected by the trust of your fellow-citizens, is finished. The Constitution of Norway is founded; the Norwegian people has maintained its rights through you, its selected Deputies; it has maintained them for futurity." Here is a breathtaking display of the performative power of kingship. With these words, spoken before the deputies, he proclaims that the founding of Norway is coextensive with the completion of the Constitution. There will be no need to return the document to the people for their approval, as was the case, for example, with the US Constitution. Through the carefully structured exchange between prince and deputies, Norway has been "founded." He had been addressed as prince regent, but he replied as the king of Norway. Through his words, spoken before the deputies at Eidsvold and (by implication) before the people of Norway, the Constitution has become an operational instrument with the force of law.

Fourth action: The early Norse *ting*s often took place in open fields, under huge trees, or near prominent rock formations so that judicial or administrative deliberations were open to the people (Dölemeyer 2005). The deputies of Eidsvold, who had been deliberating inside and in private for five weeks, were finally ready to make things public. Three deputies were authorized to sign a short but vitally important document: "[We] do hereby attest, that this fundamental law of the Kingdom of Norway and the documents annexed to it, are, word for word, conformable to the chief records of the National Assembly." These words attest that the official printed versions of the Constitution, published in Danish, as well as in French and English, by Jacob Lehmann in Christiania on 31 May 1814, correspond to the manuscript records of the Constitutional Assembly (Nilsen 1997: 74–75).

We have noted above that the constitutional process was inscribed from its inception in a communication circuit between prince and notables, prince and people, the people's deputies and the people. This communication reached its climax in the publication of the Constitution. Now, finally, the prince and deputies would learn if their work appeared to the people of Norway to be what they claimed it was: legitimate, right, and worthy of general support. This precarious moment helps to explain the particularly careful shape given the four framing documents we have been interpreting. We can bring this idea to the fore by posing a question based on a counter-contingent scenario. Since the prince regent had been at Eidsvold for most of the five weeks of the deliberation, since deputies and the prince had been in daily communication with one another, why, once the constitutional draft was finished, did the prince regent not simply walk into the deputies' meeting room, vow allegiance to the Constitution, and accept the offered crown? The event would have been lively and momentous, and its spontaneous freedom would have reflected the warm trust that each evinced for the other. So why did each act of deputies and prince get broken down, in a labored manner, into a declaration, an address, an answer, and the order to publish, with each act recorded in a separate text? To pose this question helps us to see how the rhetoric of the Constitution—its need to persuade readers of the Constitution throughout Norway to support it—enters every aspect of the proceedings at Eidsvold. Once the Constitution had been completed, the deputies and the prince regent communicated with each other with exacting premeditation and formality so that what was done at Eidsvold could be shared, scrutinized, and interpreted by the people of Norway. In short, there was a dramatic "fourth wall" at Eidsvold and all who acted there knew that what was done was part of a performance, and further, that the success of that performance would help determine the fate of the Constitution.

The format of the official published Constitution supports the persuasive rhetoric of the new Constitution. The format carefully calibrates the relationship between the primary text—the Constitution—and what we have called the "envelope"—the four supporting documents. Following a title page of great simplicity—*Kongeriget Norges Grundlov / Christiania 1814. Trykt hos Jacob Lehmann* (The Fundamental Law of the Kingdom of Norway / Christiania 1814. Printed by Jacob Lehmann)—the primary document, the Constitution, is given no introduction, preamble, or justification. In other words, there is nothing to remind readers of the turbulent political crisis out of which it emerged. Rising above all that, the Constitution makes statements in the present tense and indicative mood, of what *is*: "Article 1: The Kingdom of Norway is a free, independent and indivisible realm." But the four "documents annexed to" the Constitution, which describe the *way* the Constitution was declared, countersigned by a prince, and put into effect, can be relegated to the back of the book, placed behind the Constitution, in an appendix. Because these documents document how the Constitution acquired its authority, they are still essential supports to the Constitution, but they do not invest the future in the same way that the Constitution aspires to do.

The exacting attention to procedure at Eidsvold suggests a cardinal feature of the emergence of a democratic political culture. For those seeking to found a new political system, *how* things are done becomes the kernel for what can be achieved. Thus, the communication protocols used before, during, and after the constitution making helped to define the values that would inform the new political system. A "protocol" was originally a small document that was placed before (*proto*) another document, specifying the terms of an agreement regarding how the following document should be read, as in the phrase "the protocols of a treaty." Protocols have long channeled diplomatic communication, but they have also been extended to prescribe modes of address in epistolary correspondence, to prescribe the correct method for repeating scientific experiments, and to prescribe the software code that allows computers to communicate with one another on the Internet (IP/TCP = Internet protocol/ transfer control protocol). More generally, protocols can be thought of as "enabling constraints," because they enable communication by shaping it in various ways. There are at least five protocols that shaped the constitution framing at Eidsvold; each helped sustain and give coherence to the process of instituting an independent Norwegian state (W. Warner 2013). To be a document that persuades the people of Norway to accept the document as their constitution, the constitution must observe the protocol of a *general and systematic address to the people*. Implicit in all four of the appended documents is the workings of what might be called the *public access protocol*: not only is the published Constitution distributed through post offices throughout the country almost immediately after it is drafted. The deliberations at Eidsvold, from the election of deputies to the writing of four supporting documents, also allow private deliberations to culminate in a publication that makes the drafting of the Constitution into something done for and before the public. Several features of the process at Eidsvold foregrounded what might be called the *legal procedure protocol*. The process had been initiated by the prince regent, who had been appointed by the previous, absolutist government of Denmark. The Constitutional Assembly enhanced its legal authority by being a "National Assembly" that represented the different localities of the Norwegian nation. That Constitutional Assembly enhanced its effective power by observing the *corporate action protocol*: what was done was done as one body. Thus, as we have noted above, although there was a minority of deputies who favored union with Sweden, all 112 deputies unanimously endorsed the completed document. The printed version of the Constitution included these names in the appendix, and, as we have seen, the supporting documents stage a spectacle of the unity and enthusiastic attachment between loving deputies and a grateful king. The loyalty pledged by deputies to the king and by the king to the new Constitution also evidences their observance of what might be called the *virtuous independence protocol*, as if they were saying, "By what we do and how we do it, we exhibit our disinterested concern for the welfare of the people, as well as our virtue, or manly courage" (virtue, derived from the Latin *vir,* meaning "man").

After Eidsvold, the Constitution Takes Root

In Norway, the Constitution has become intimately connected to an idea of the beginning of an independent nation, of a modern form of government, of a Norwegian identity, and so on. Legally speaking, any constitution is by definition the beginning of government institutions, relations with other states, and basic relations between state and individual. Yet this beginning itself cannot explain the longevity of the Constitution and its extraordinary symbolic power in Norway. Many constitutions were written in the decades before and after the Norwegian Constitution came into being, but for various reasons, few lasted very long. However, in the months and years immediately after Eidsvold, events conspired to give the Norwegian Constitution great symbolic importance and staying power. First, after the framing of the Constitution in the spring of 1814, there was a struggle in the fall of 1814 to preserve the Constitution as part of the union with Sweden. Second, there was a defense of the Constitution against an attempt at Swedish royal "reform" in the early 1820s. In both stages, the Constitution played the role of the principal bulwark of Norwegian sovereignty and independence. The result was an entrenchment of the Constitution in Norwegian identity and culture.

Stage one: Keeping the Constitution in a union with Sweden. The claim for independence in Article 1 was directed not only at the more than 400-year-long union with Denmark, but also against the ambitions of Sweden in particular. Given the Swedish military superiority, the Constitution became the principal weapon for the protection of Norwegian independence and sovereignty. After a short war in the summer of 1814, Norway was forced into a union with Sweden. When a union became a political fact, the Norwegians gave up their newly elected king, Christian Frederik, but fought hard to keep the Constitution. Besides its symbolic importance, the Constitution would sustain institutional autonomy. Remarkably, the future king Carl Johan accepted the Norwegian demand to keep the Constitution and to rule Norway according to it. By doing so, he became a king with two thrones who ruled through two constitutions, one Swedish and one Norwegian. It is safe to say that Carl Johan's concessions to the Norwegian demands helped sustain the claim made in Article 1 that Norway was "free" and "independent," and its "form of government" was a "limited" monarchy.

Even if Norway remained independent de jure, a union with Sweden nevertheless raised concerns. In the eyes of the Norwegians, the new king, who was invested with the new constitution's executive powers, was Swedish.

From this viewpoint, the king's constitutional prerogatives were likely entry points for Swedish influence and possible interference in Norwegian affairs. The union had obliged Norway to amend the Constitution in order to enable the executive power to be located in Stockholm instead of Christiania. However, in carrying out this amendment, Storthinget used their amending power to strengthen Norwegian sovereignty. Sitting in an extraordinary session, Storthinget framed amendments that shifted power from the king to Storthinget (Bergsgård 1945: 250–267; Seip 2002: 46).

In the revised Constitution of 4 November 1814, a separate Norwegian cabinet was established in Stockholm along with procedures to ensure that Norwegian matters were addressed with the advice of the king's Norwegian ministers. Further, the revised Constitution placed new restrictions on the king's originally unfettered prerogatives of war and peace by prohibiting him from garrisoning Swedish troops in Norway and from mixing the troops of the two nations. It also required that the use of Norwegian troops in aggressive war be subject to approval by Storthinget. At Eidsvold, the same prohibition had been proposed, but was then firmly rejected (Holmøyvik 2012: 465–466). But now, in the hands of a *Swedish* king, the use of Norwegian troops in a war of aggression abroad suddenly appeared as a realistic and harmful prospect. Finally, and of great symbolic significance, the important wording "free" and "independent" in Article 1 was left untouched save for the addition of "united with Sweden under one King." These amendments to the Constitution, enabling it to survive the tumultuous transition from Eidsvold into a union with Sweden, further entrenched its position as the bastion of Norwegian independence. The following decade would extend this trend.

Stage two: Resisting constitutional reform. Throughout the nineteenth century, Norwegians evinced an enormous reluctance to make any changes to the Constitution that would give more powers to the executive, for this would only increase Swedish influence over Norwegian affairs. The Constitution became untouchable on any matter involving the separation of powers. The episode that elevated this notion into an ideology was Carl Johan's forceful effort in 1821 to carry through a constitutional reform. Incited by the revival of the European monarchies following the defeat of Napoleon, the king argued that there was an imbalance of powers between the two branches of government, and that his reform would restore that balance (*Kongeriget Norges fjerde ordentlige Storthings Forhandlinger i Aaret 1824*: 40–41). In reality, his reform aimed to render Storthinget impotent and to bring it under the control of the king. Yet the king nevertheless asked Storthinget to amend the Constitution to give himself an absolute veto on legislation instead of the existing veto in Article 79 that could be overruled by having three consecutive sessions of Storthinget pass the same law. Further, the king wanted the right to dissolve Storthinget at any time, the right to decide which matters to discuss in Storthinget, the right to appoint its presidents, and so on. The royal proposals spurred a heated debate in newspapers and pamphlets. Not surprisingly, but showing a great deal of courage in the face of a fraught political crisis, Storthinget firmly rejected all of the king's proposals in 1824. King Carl Johan's blatant attack on Norwegian autonomy made Norwegians close ranks and rally around the Constitution. The tradition of publicly celebrating the Constitution on 17 May stems from the 1820s. On the matter of an absolute veto on legislation, Carl Johan asked for a constitutional amendment in every session of Storthinget until 1839. His request was always rejected. Through this struggle, because the Constitution served as a bulwark assuming Norwegian independence, the letter of the Constitution had become sacrosanct for all Norwegians (Seip 2002: 76; Steen 1954: 319).

However, there is an irony inherent in Norway's nineteenth-century exaltation of the Constitution of 17 May 1814. After the union with Sweden was dissolved in 1905, the people of Norway could finally enjoy the constitutional gift Christian Frederik had accepted in 1814. However, when this gift was unwrapped, it was a different thing than the one offered at Eidsvold in 1814. The form, structure, and words in the Constitution were largely the same, but the interpretation of its contents had changed. Though the king never attempted another comprehensive constitutional reform after the defeat in 1824, the struggle between the executive and legislative branches of government persisted. Instead of using the amendment process, the king attempted to strengthen his position through the means of constitutional interpretation, but to no lasting effect. The conflict reached its climax in 1884, when the entire cabinet was convicted by the Court of Impeachment in a monumental show of force by Storthinget. This episode marked the end of the original system of separation of powers in the Constitution, and the birth of the parliamentary system, where the executive branch became formally accountable to Storthinget. Moreover, the cabinet replaced the king himself as the actual executive power. After 1905, the king had the executive power in name alone (Mestad 2005: 403–408). Yet for a long time, this dramatic and fundamental change in the separation of powers left no trace in the text of the Constitution. Only in 2007, more than one hundred years after it became legal fact, was the Constitution formally amended to include the basic legal rules guiding the parliamentary system (see Sand in this volume).

The Ambivalent Legacy

There are good reasons to feel the weight of the Constitution of 17 May 1814, even as we celebrate it in 2014. Why do we return to 1814? First, the moment of the founding of the modern Norwegian nation, as distinct from the founding of its "brother" countries, Denmark and Sweden, promises to disclose the

"authentic element" of Norwegian freedom (see Arendt [1963: 456] on the Roman historians' periodic return to the founding of Rome). What happened at
Eidsvold seems to be a moment when, through a happy convergence of cir-
cumstance and action, events took on the miraculous character of a beginning.
It also seems to be a moment of a new birth of freedom. In her essay "What
Is Freedom?," the philosopher Hannah Arendt has described the difficulties
that beset anyone trying to define freedom (2000: 438–461). But her writing
suggests one way to think about the freedom won by the gathering at Eidsvold.
With a strong debt to ancient republican thought, Arendt defines freedom as
coextensive with an action that assumes the form of words and deeds that
are undertaken before the public and are animated by a shared principle. In
1814, freedom was experienced through the actions by which a principle was
realized: the independent sovereignty of Norway. When men have succeeded
in acting—for example, by winning their independence by framing a constitution—they later feel a certain pathos about that time of crisis, talk, doubt, and
action, for nothing in their later lives has had the sublime importance of those
deeds (Arendt 1963: 34).

Once founding action is distilled into the words of a constitution, it can become a mainstay of political continuity. Since 1814, monarchs have come and
gone, the town of Christiania has grown into the metropolis of Oslo, but the
Constitution abides. Whether one loves it or hates it, the Constitution turns
out to be the thing at the center of the whole thing called Norway. The Constitution becomes a *legacy* that one feels obliged to remember, protect, and
transmit. This gifted thing from the past may begin to feel like a debt. Why?
In part, this sense of debt results from our very different, belated relationship to the Constitution. For modern Norwegians it cannot be what it was for
the founders: a vague dream, a plan, something to weave out of their words,
thoughts, deliberations and then publish to the world. Instead, modern Norwegians, by living inside the institutional frame of the Constitution that the
founders stood outside of, can have no access to the founders' heady freedom
in making it. They may resent being stuck with the task of lugging this heavy
thing from the past into the future. Because the gift is never entirely severed
from the giver (Mauss 1954), Norwegians of today could even begin to resent
the gift givers in Eidsvold. To have access to their freedom (in Arendt's sense),
today's Norwegians must act again, but this act must take the more mediated
shape of "translation," in the many senses of that word.

In considering how to translate the Constitution so that it continues to be
central to Norway, Norwegians are confronted with a vexing choice. Should
they continue the relatively conservative approach to constitutional change,
one that served Norway so well in the nineteenth century, when resistance
to changing the Constitution enabled it to serve as a bulwark of Norway's independence? In Norway, the historical reluctance to amend the Constitution

is often referred to as "constitutional conservatism" (*grunnlovskonservatisme*) (Andenæs and Fliflet 2006: 55; Helset and Stordrange 1998: 67–68). In fact, the Norwegian Constitution encodes this reticence about change in its own language. The last sentence of Article 110, the last article of the Constitution, offers a harsh admonition with regard to amending the Constitution: "Yet such an alteration must never be inconsistent with the principles of this fundamentel [*sic*] law, but only concern modifications in particular cases, which do not alter the spirit of this Constitution, to which alteration the consent of two thirds of the National Assembly is required." This sentence transmits the founders' arduous caution to later generations, and that caution might be translated into this American colloquialism: "Don't mess up a good thing." Using an implicitly Romantic metaphor cluster, the language from Article 110 suggests that the Constitution is a unified and living thing, whose "principles of this fundamentel [*sic*] law" (*Grundlovs Principer*) are animated by a precious vitality, the Constitution's "spirit" (*Constitutions Aand*). Care must be taken—the framers warn—that "alterations" made to the Constitution by Storthinget not kill its "spirit." Article 110's warning against killing the spirit of the Norwegian Constitution suggests that amendments—small additions that preserve the completeness of the whole—could become what French philosopher Jacques Derrida later referred to as "dangerous supplements," because they could always supplant what they pretend to supplement (Derrida 1967).[6]

But refusing to amend the Norwegian Constitution courts the danger that it will become an antiquated old thing, a respected monument, but irrelevant to the conduct of government or national political life. In order to stay central to the nation, every constitution must be open to change. And in fact, during the Constitution's two hundred years of history, and despite the formal rules that make amending it a protracted and arduous process, and despite its being written in an antiquated form of Danish, Norway's Constitution has successfully been updated (see Sand; Madzharova Bruteig; Kalleberg in this volume; Smith 2012: 102–104). Besides removing offensive articles (against Jews and Jesuits), Stortinget has, over the years, included special cultural rights for the Sami peoples, granted women the vote, extended powers to international agencies, charged the authorities of the state with creating conditions "enabling every person capable of work to earn a living by his work," and, finally, made it a right of Norwegians that their "natural resources ... will be safeguarded for future generations."[7] In recent years, Stortinget has also revised the Constitution to reflect changes in the political system. In 2007, key elements of the parliamentary system were written into the Constitution, the bicameral system was abolished, and the Court of Impeachment was modernized. Finally, the separation of church and state led to the amendment, in 2012, of several articles in the Constitution, including a completely revised Article 2, which for the first time defines the basic values to be guaranteed by the Constitution:

democracy, the rule of law, and human rights. However, a liberal practice of amendment courts a new danger. If, for example, Stortinget continues to update what is meant by "freedom of expression" in the crucial Article 100, it risks introducing period-specific detail that might result in restricting the very freedom it intends to protect. Thus, the original version of Article 100 was relatively terse (see Berge; Ringvej in this volume), but in the 2004 revision, Article 100 now provides "grounds for freedom of expression," which include "seeking truth," "promotion of democracy," and "the individual's freedom to form opinions." By opening themselves up to the German philosopher Jürgen Habermas's enlightened ideals for democratic communication (see Kalleberg in this volume), has Stortinget placed a date stamp upon Article 100? Once one has read the many prescriptions and exclusions found in Stortinget's revised Article 100, as amended in 2004, one might well ask, who now has the primary agency in defining freedom of expression, the citizens of Norway or Stortinget? The revised Article 100 may compromise freedom of expression by providing too much detail and by specifying the normative "grounds" for freedom of expression. It is not difficult to imagine the day when a drama troop, an edgy comedian, a fringe religious group, or anyone promoting strange ideas might find that they have violated Article 100, because they have failed to live up to the high-minded ideals for freedom of expression in the public sphere. If a constitutional overspecification of basic rights leads to their narrowing, the citizens of Norway may long to return to the vague but open abstractions of the good old Constitution framed and adopted at Eidsvold.

In this chapter, we have explored the Constitution of Norway as process and thing, history, and genre. We hope that this chapter serves as an antidote to the familiar tendency to anthropomorphize and humanize the Constitution, for example, by imagining it as the "voice of the people." To engage in that kind of Romantic vitalism obscures the power of a constitution, once it has been completed, adopted, and put into force, to become a semiautonomous object, a potent thing to be admired, interpreted, litigated, venerated, or even deplored. It certain ways it serves in the place of the body of the king within an absolutist monarchy as the one thing that can hold the nation together. It too shimmers as a symbolic embodiment of the nation. Here it is useful to invoke an influential formulation of the French political theorist Claude Lefort. In democracy, the locus of power is no longer the body of the king, or any group of persons, but *"an empty place"* inaugurating "a history in which people experience a fundamental indeterminacy as to the basis of power, law and knowledge" (Lefort 1988: 17–19; italics in original). In or near that empty place sits the Constitution, becoming the common reference point for those marshaling political complaints, questions, and statements. Remembering Eidsvold two hundred years later, tracing, for example, the recent history of Article 100, we have found that the Constitution of 1814 did not bring closure or consensus to Norway's politics. Instead, the intricate history of the Constitution reminds us that democracy rests less upon settled institutions than upon a practice of politics that must be always ready to begin again.

NOTES

1. All English-language quotations from the Constitution and its supporting texts come from the official English-language translation published by Jacob Lehmann in Christiania in the spring of 1814 unless otherwise noted (*The Constitution of the Kingdom of Norway* 1814).

2. The comparative nature of this volume allows us to explore the reasons for the distinctive features of Norway's Constitution as noted by scholars: longevity (except for the US Constitution, which preceded it by twenty-five years, it is the oldest constitution still in force in the world); celerity (it was written, debated, and accepted in five weeks); monarchical; and remarkably consensual (all 112 delegates signed the final Constitution). Finally, it is difficult to think of another nation where the Constitution Day celebrations are as robust and sustained as in Norway.

3. *Ordbog over det danske Sprog*, s.v. "I. Ting." Translation by Karen Gammelgaard. All abbreviations in the original are spelled out in the translation.

4. This definition of "thing" and those that follow of "thing" and "constitution" in this paragraph are from the *Oxford English Dictionary*, Third Edition, 2008.

5. Our discussion of the way the Norwegian Constitution embeds its own preamble and declaration of independence is offered as an alternative to (a) those scholars who have noted the absence of an explicit preamble in the Norwegian Constitution that names the speakers and describes the occasion of the constitution (for example, the preamble of the US Constitution); and (b) those scholars who have noted the absence within the Norwegian constitutional process of the declarations of rights and independence that served as first steps toward constitution writing in both the American and French revolutions.

6. Such a concern looms large in the current debate about modernizing the Danish language within which it was written. Could an authorized, modern Norwegian translation kill the "spirit" it is supposed to translate?

7. Quoted from the official English-language translation of the current Norwegian Constitution.

⊢• 2 •⊣

The Changing Meaning of "Constitution" in Norwegian Constitutional History

Eirik Holmøyvik

Concepts and Change

The meaning of concepts is not constant.[1] A concept can have different meanings at different times and places in history. Yet the word that expresses it need not change. This flexibility is possible because concepts are linguistic carriers of a rich social-political context of meaning and experience (Koselleck 2004: 85). According to German historian Reinhart Koselleck and his theory of *Begriffsgeschichte*, concepts may take on a new meaning when new experiences alter society's expectations of a possible future presupposed by previous experience (Koselleck 2004: 262).[2] Koselleck implies that neither concepts nor the ideas they refer to are historical constants (see Koselleck 2004: 81–89). In short, the changing meaning and use of concepts reflect changes in the social, political, or, as in this case, legal phenomenon to which the concept refers. The study of concepts can thus be useful in historical studies to trace substantive developments over time. Sometimes, concepts can be agents of change.

"Constitution" is such a concept.[3] In politics and law, and more specifically in constitutional law, "constitution" has been a key concept since the late eighteenth century. Despite the term having been a part of the legal and political vernacular far longer, our modern understanding of it dates from this period. Historically, then, "constitution" is a variable concept, and it acquired a new meaning and significance in this period. This change is, of course, largely due to the wave of written constitutions in the wake of the American and French revolutions in 1776 and 1789, respectively. Yet the written constitution as such was not a novelty then, even though these constitutions did introduce a new form, new institutions, and new terminology. For "constitution" as a concept, the real significance of the written constitutions of the late eighteenth century was their contents. These constitutions represented a new conception of the state and its relations to the individual by establishing government on rational principles such as separation of powers, the sovereignty of the people, and human rights.[4] Consequently, "constitution" became a normative concept in the sense that specific material requirements had to be met in order for a legal document to qualify as such a constitution.

In this chapter, we shall see how such a change in the use and meaning of the term "constitution" took place in the Norwegian legal and political vernacular at the turn of the eighteenth century. In Norway, this process was completed with the adoption of the Constitution of 1814. Here, the changing usage and meaning of the term "constitution" signified a break with the past due to the fact that when the framers of the Norwegian Constitution used this concept in 1814, they had in mind a specific type of legal instrument and, more importantly, a specific vision of government.

International and Historical Context

Constitution and Leges Fundamentales

In seventeenth-century Europe, before the wave of written constitutions in the late eighteenth century, the common term for the legal norms concerning a state's government was *leges fundamentales* (fundamental laws) and its various national translations (Grimm and Mohnhaupt 1995: 63). The legal basis for such fundamental laws was often a contract between the prince and the estates. Contrary to other laws, fundamental laws were superior to the prince's will and thus legally binding for him. Important matters often settled in fundamental laws were jurisdiction, succession, and privileges.

A number of fundamental laws were written. In his *Commentaries on the Laws of England* from 1765, the famous British jurist William Blackstone named the Magna Carta of 1215, the Bill of Rights of 1689, and the Act of Settlement of 1701 as fundamental laws for England (1765–1769: 1:123). In Sweden, the form of government (*Regeringsformen*) of 1719 styled itself in the preamble as a fundamental law for the realm (*fundamental lag*). And most relevant for our topic, in Denmark-Norway the *Lex regia* of 1665 (*Kongeloven*) defined itself in the preamble as a fundamental law (*fundamental Low*).

Until the end of the eighteenth century, the concept "constitution" was used in European legal terminology in more than one context. In one common usage, it referred simply to ordinary statutes. In the political context, however, it was used in a broad and empirical sense referring to the state's general condition and composition (Grimm and Mohnhaupt 1995: 100; Stourzh 1988:

40–42; Baker 1990: 254). In this context, a state's constitution was an analogy from medical terminology and the human body's constitution. "Constitution" was a descriptive concept referring to the actual political and social condition and composition of the state as a political body.[5]

As we can see, this meaning of "constitution" is quite far from its later meaning, which is that of a specific legal concept referring to the superior legal norms defining the government, its branches, and its relation to the citizens. The closest equivalent to the modern meaning of "constitution" was, rather, the concept of "fundamental laws." During the eighteenth century, however, the meaning and use of the concept "constitution" changed and merged with that of "fundamental laws" in that both referred to specific superior legal norms concerning the government. This development was, of course, not uniform across Europe. The following is just a brief outline to define the context for the development of the concept in Norwegian constitutional history.

In England, the two concepts merged during the Glorious Revolution (Stourzh 1988: 43; Grimm and Mohnhaupt 1995: 44–48, 102–103). In the often cited resolution by Parliament in 1688 declaring the abdication of James II, Parliament declared "that king James the second, having endeavoured to subvert the constitution of the kingdom, by breaking the original contract between king and people; … having violated fundamental laws; and having withdrawn himself out of the Kingdom; has abdicated the Government; and that the Throne is thereby vacant" (quoted in Blackstone 1765–1769: 1:204). From this declaration, it is clear that "constitution" is a term of legal value referring to the organization of government and linked to the fundamental laws. This reference is something more precise and distinctly legal than a reference to the state's general condition and composition. Yet, in eighteenth-century English political and legal vernacular, "constitution" was still a historical-empirical concept referring to fundamental principles of government based upon piecemeal institutional practices, laws, customs, and traditions rather than referring to an act defining the government and its formal structure. Such was the definition offered by the English politician Henry St John Bolingbroke in 1733–1734:

> By constitution we mean, whenever we speak with propriety and exactness, that assemblage of laws, institutions and customs, derived from certain fixed principles of reason, directed to certain fixed objects of publick good, that compose the general system, according to which the community hath agreed to be governed. (Bolingbroke [1733–1734] 1809: 157)

A similar notion of "constitution" is found in one of the most famous eighteenth-century books on law and government, Charles de Montesquieu's *De l'esprit des lois* (The Spirit of Laws) from 1748. For Montesquieu, "constitution" was an ambiguous concept, used both in the broad sense as referring to a state's general condition and composition, to which he argued laws had to be adapted, and in a political context as referring to a specific organization of a state (Grimm and Mohnhaupt 1995: 42–43).[6] It was in the latter political sense that he spoke of the English "constitution" in the famous book 11, chapter 6 of *De l'esprit des lois*. Here, "constitution" was not a specific act constituting government, but a historical-empirical concept referring to "the fundamental order of a state, the mode of political existence of a nation or people, the essential disposition of the elements or powers composing a form of government" (Baker 1990: 255). When Montesquieu spoke of the English constitution, he did not refer to specific legal norms, but rather to the actual political and social organization of the English government and its principles.

The Changing Meaning of "Constitution" in the Late Eighteenth Century

In the second half of the eighteenth century, the meaning of the concept "constitution" gradually changed from having a descriptive function to having a specific legal function as the normative foundation of the state and its political organization. Behind this shift in meaning lay two novel ideas articulated for the first time by Swiss jurist Emmerich de Vattel in his widely read *Droit des gens* (The Law of Nations) from 1758. He defined "la *Constitution de l'Etat*" as the "règlement fondamental qui determine la maniére dont l'Autorité Publique doit être exercée" (the fundamental regulation that determines the manner in which the public authority is to be executed) (Vattel 1758: 31; italics in original). At the core of this definition was the idea that the "constitution" was the normative foundation and not the result of a state's political organization. At the height of the Enlightenment, this idea was inseparably linked to the principle of popular sovereignty. In other words, the "constitution" was to be an act of the people as a whole establishing the government. As such, it was a materialization of the social contract and man's transition from the natural state to society. The second notion inherent in Vattel's definition was that the "constitution" was a legal norm superior to the government and its laws, resolutions, and acts. To Vattel this superiority was only a logical consequence of his definition, because "c'est de la Constitution que ces Législateurs tiennent leur pouvoir; comment pourroient-ils la changer, sans détruire le fondement de leur Autorité?" (it is from the constitution that those legislators derive their power; how then can they change it without destroying the foundation of their own authority?) (1758: 37). Thus, the function of a constitution was to define the public powers in the society and, importantly, their competences and limits.

Later writers picked up Vattel's definition of "constitution" and it eventually became common in the late eighteenth century.[7] With the first American state constitutions in 1776, the term "constitution" was linked to written legal documents, given by sovereign peoples, that contained legal norms superior to the powers of state and imposed limitations on the government by defining individual rights (Grimm and Mohnhaupt 1995: 104–105). From now on, a "constitution" was no longer a description of the actual organization of the state and its institutions, but rather its very constitutive and normative foundation.

The distinction between these two conceptions of "constitution" had an ideological and political significance that contemporaries were acutely aware of. Because it was rooted in practice and custom, the older understanding of "constitution" meant the preservation of the established social and political order. The new understanding of the word, on the other hand, heralded a regeneration of the state based upon predetermined rational political principles. In his famous 1791 criticism of the French Revolution and its rational constitutionalism, English politician Edmund Burke articulated this distinction by saying that the English "constitution" was not based upon a prior right, but on an "*entailed inheritance* derived to us from our forefathers" (Burke [1791] 1999: 121; italics added). On the modern, and for him particularly French, understanding of "constitution," Burke said, "The very idea of the fabrication of a new government is enough to fill us with disgust and horror" ([1791] 1999: 119). Equally famous is the Anglo-American revolutionary Thomas Paine's response to Burke in his *Rights of Man* from 1791, saying that "a constitution is a thing *antecedent* to a government, and a government is only the creature of a constitution" (Paine [1791] 1894: 310; italics added). The implication in Paine's argument is that the unwritten English "constitution" based upon traditions and customs did not in fact qualify as a constitution at all. Paine thus made a distinction between what we may call *empirical* and *rational* constitutions.[8] The former rested upon traditions and customs, while the latter pretended to rest upon rational political principles disconnected from the existing social and political fabric of the state.[9] In France, the lawyer and a leading member of the Constituent Assembly of 1789 Jean-Joseph Mounier made a similar argument in his *Nouvelles observations sur les états-généraux de France* (New Observations on the Estates General of France). He concluded that France did not have a constitution at all (Mounier 1789: 182). According to Mounier, the unwritten French fundamental laws based upon ancient customs did not qualify as a constitution. A constitution, he said, defined the government's jurisdiction and limited its power—two features missing in the old constitutional order under absolutism. What Mounier had in mind was, of course, the modern written constitution as defined by Vattel, and writing one became a key task for the French revolutionaries of 1789.

Constitution as a Normative Concept

The French revolutionaries of 1789 followed their American predecessors of 1776 and defined the state's new and written legal foundation as a "constitution." In so doing, they linked the understanding of the concept to the expectations regarding which principles the new state was to be founded upon. As Mounier had concluded, a constitution was not just any collection of legal rules for organizing the state. It also had a normative function. Many of the constitutions of that period were preceded by rights declarations containing the rational political principles that, in the words of the 1776 Virginia Declaration of Rights, were to be "the basis and foundation of government." The declarations asserted the sovereignty of the people, which the constitutions transformed into systems of elections and representation. The constitutions transformed another key principle, the equality of rights, into the abolition of nobility and equality before the law. Finally, the principle of separation of powers caused constitutions to organize the government in separate and independent legislative, executive, and judicial branches. In fact, all constitutions in the late eighteenth century were at least formally organized according to this formula. Ever since Montesquieu, the separation of powers was widely regarded as a prerequisite for liberty. As such, it was one of those political principles of the age that were inextricably linked to the concept "constitution." The famous Article 16 of the French *Déclaration des droits de l'Homme et du Citoyen* of 1789 simply stated this as a fact: "Toute société dans laquelle la garantie des droits n'est pas assuré, ni la sèparation des pouvoirs déterminée, n'a point de constitution" (Any society in which the guarantee of rights is not secured or the separation of powers not determined has no constitution at all).[10] According to the French framers, of whom Mounier was one, there simply could not be a constitution without the separation of powers.[11] We see, then, that the separation of powers as well as other key components in the new written constitutions of the late eighteenth century had become fundamental expectations of a constitution. In this sense, "constitution" had become a normative concept.

Danish-Norwegian Law before 1814

Now we shift our attention to eighteenth-century Danish-Norwegian constitutional law. Between 1661 and 1814, Denmark and Norway formed an absolutist unitary state. Danish was the common written language (see Berge; Madzharova Bruteig in this volume). The Norwegian Constitution of 1814 was a result of a forced breakup of the union by the victors of the Napoleonic Wars, in which Denmark-Norway was among the losers. What I say about the development of legal terminology before 1814 thus applies to both Denmark and Norway.

Grundlov *in Legal Terminology under Absolutism*

Unlike most European states before the wave of written constitutions in the late eighteenth century, Denmark-Norway had had a written constitution since 1665—the *Lex regia*. This constitution was unique among its contemporaries in being the sole example of a written constitution for an absolutist state. In its preamble it referred to itself as a fundamental law (*fundamental Low*), and in Article 3 it referred to itself as the true *Grund og Grundvolds-Low* (basic law) of the realm. The *Lex regia* was thus a "fundamental law" and a *Grundlov*, which in this context were synonymous terms. *Grundlov* literally means "basic law," and is a Danish term equivalent to the German term *Grundgesetz*. At that time, we find the same link between *Grundgesetz* and "fundamental law" in German legal terminology (Grimm and Mohnhaupt 1995: 101).[12]

Following the *Lex regia*, later legal literature—predominantly natural law doctrine at the time—consistently referred to the positive legal norms concerning the government as *Grundlov*.[13] In the first Danish-language natural law treatise, famous writer and historian Ludvig Holberg's *Introduction til Naturens- og Folke-Rettens Kundskab* (Introduction to the Science of Natural Law and the Law of Nations) from 1716, the term *Grundlov* (plural *Grundlove*) was used to describe the legal norms that defined and limited the prince's power in a monarchy (Holberg 1716: 2:72).[14] For Holberg and other eighteenth-century authors, a *Grundlov* contained the legal norms that defined the government and its relation to the people. The legal basis for a *Grundlov*—as for fundamental laws elsewhere in Europe—was the at the time common idea of a contract between the prince and the people. One author, Andreas Schytte, professor of public law and politics, called the *Grundlov* a pact between prince and people, and a legal rule for both (1773–1776: 5:456–457).

Constitution *and* Forfatning *as Descriptive and Political Terms*

So far we have seen that in eighteenth-century Danish-Norwegian legal terminology, *Grundlov*, as synonymous with "fundamental law," was the term referring to the legal norms that defined the government and its limits. The term *Constitution*, on the other hand, had a different meaning in the Danish-Norwegian legal vocabulary at the time. As elsewhere in Europe, it could indeed have a political meaning by referring to the state's general condition and composition, in which positive constitutional law, or *Grundlov*, was just one of several components.

When referring to the broader notion of the state's general condition and composition, eighteenth-century Danish-Norwegian authors also used the term *Forfatning*.[15] Literally, *Forfatning* means "condition." As such, it is closely linked to "constitution" in its original medical meaning as an analogy for the body's constitution. Sometimes we also find it coupled with the term "state," as in *Statsforfatning*, literally meaning "the state's constitution."[16] Here, too, the Danish-Norwegian terminology mirrored contemporary German terminology, where *Verfassung* and *Statsvervassung* were used to convey the same meaning (Grimm and Mohnhaupt 1995: 71–75).

Thus, we see how eighteenth-century Danish-Norwegian legal terminology distinguished between *Grundlov*, on the one hand, and terms like *Constitution*, *Forfatning*, and *Statsforfatning*, on the other. The distinction between these terms might not always have been clear in common usage, though one thing was clear: only *Grundlov* was a proper legal term referring to positive constitutional law. I will demonstrate this distinction with some examples.

In law professor Lauritz Nørregaard's natural law treatise from 1784 (the first edition was published in 1776), *Natur- og Folke-Rettens første Grunde* (The Basic Principles of Natural Law and the Law of Nations), the distinction between *Grundlov*, as a specific legal term, and *Forfatning*, as a broader political term, is made evident. Probably addressing different usages of the term *Grundlov*, Nørregaard stated that one could use this term in both a broad and a narrow sense. In its broader sense, he said, *Grundlov* defined the true *Forfatning* of the state and the relation between the prince and his subjects (Nørregaard 1784: 318). With *Grundlov* in this broader sense and expressly linked to *Forfatning*, Nørregaard did not mean specific legal norms, but rather the idea of an original social contract that established the state and decided its form of government as either a monarchy, an aristocracy, a democracy, or a mixture of these. At that time, it was common to describe the state's basic political organization according to these four forms of government, but this classification did not have any legal meaning or status. When speaking of *Grundlov* in its narrow legal sense, on the other hand, Nørregaard implied that the term referred to specific legal norms, for example, to the rules of succession in a monarchy. *Grundlov* in the narrow sense was for Nørregaard "a law which limits the prince's power by prescribing the rules for how government is to be exercised" (1784: 321; my translation). As we can see, this understanding of *Grundlov* resembles the modern concept of "constitution." Here, we also see the distinction between *Grundlov* as a legal term and *Forfatning* as a descriptive nonlegal term. *Grundlov* might also be used in a broader and nonlegal sense as synonymous with *Forfatning*, but of these two terms, only *Grundlov* in its true and narrow sense was a legal term referring to positive constitutional law.

The same distinction between *Grundlov* in its broad and narrow senses was made by law professor Johan Frederik Wilhelm Schlegel in his natural law treatise from 1798, *Naturrettens eller den almindelige Retslæres Grundsætninger* (The Principles of Natural Law or General Jurisprudence). As Nørregaard used the term *Forfatning*, Schlegel used the term *Constitution* for the original social contract that decided the form of government, while *Grundlov* referred to positive law limiting the prince's power (Schlegel 1798: 2:93).[17] Thus, we see that in the Danish legal vocabulary at that time, *Constitution* did not yet refer to specific legal norms, but rather to the state's broader social and political composition, such as its form of government. Indeed, this was the common understanding of the term *Constitution* in late eighteenth-century Dernmark-Norway.[18] Another example is historian Tyge Rothe's 1781–1782 treatise on the ancient Nordic state. Here, Rothe discussed the idea of an ancient Nordic *Constitution* as a mixture of democracy and monarchy (1781–1782: 1:125). By the term *Constitution*, Rothe was clearly referring to the form of government and its implications for the state's social and political composition.

The Normative Effect of Constitution and Forfatning

Despite not having a specific legal content, like *Grundlov*, the terms *Forfatning* and *Constitution* were not entirely without a normative effect. Rather than having the effect of positive law, these terms could be used in a legal argument as expressing *jus publicum universale,* that is, general principles of public law based on natural law (see Stolleis 1988: 291–297). Andreas Schytte held that such principles, too, were valid sources of law (1773–1776: 5:454–455). In particular, he said, knowledge of a state's general condition and composition—its *Constitution* or *Forfatning*—was of value in interpreting positive constitutional law—the *Grundlov*, that is. In Danish-Norwegian constitutional law, we find the most notable example of such use of *Constitution* and *Forfatning* as normative terms in the legal opinions of Henrik Stampe, the crown's senior judicial adviser between 1753 and 1784.[19] One of his functions was to give reasoned legal opinions on state matters. In a series of legal opinions in the 1750s and 1760s, he repeatedly argued that the *Constitution* and *Forfatning* of Denmark-Norway prevented the executive branch of government from interfering in judicial affairs.[20] Stampe resorted to these terms in trying to keep separate the executive and judicial functions. His argument had to follow from general principles in the *Constitution* and *Forfatning* rather than from positive constitutional law, because the *Grundlov*—the *Lex regia*—unequivocally placed all power in the king's hands. Thus, strictly legally speaking, the king did exercise both functions. For Stampe, however, this strict legal interpretation did not mean that the actual exercise of royal power by subordinate institutions was unrestrained, and not subject to certain principles flowing from the state's *Constitution*. What Stampe had in mind here was Montesquieu's principles for a monarchical government in *De l'esprit des lois*. According to Montesquieu,

to ensure objective decisions by independent courts of law, the prince's ministers should not exercise judicial powers ([1748] 1961: 1:86–87). Because Denmark-Norway, too, was a monarchy, Stampe believed that this principle was
also part of the Danish-Norwegian *Constitution*. Consequently, government
had to be organized and power exercised in accordance with the true principles for a monarchy, in other words, in accordance with its "constitution."

Signs of Conceptual Change around 1800

So far, we have seen that in eighteenth-century Danish-Norwegian legal terminology, *Forfatning* and *Constitution* were synonymous terms distinct from
Grundlov and referring to the form of government or, more broadly, to the
state's political condition and composition. I might add that we are also speaking of terminology in the 1780s and 1790s—a time when the term "constitution" had obtained its modern and specific legal meaning in America and
France.[21] Yet at the turn of the century, we do see some signs of conceptual
change, most probably because of the effect of new written constitutions in
America and particularly in France.[22]

In Schlegel's natural law treatise from 1798, we can indeed sense a certain tension between the old and the new understanding of "constitution."
Following traditional natural law doctrine, Schlegel's treatise contained a
discussion of the various government forms: monarchy, aristocracy, democracy, and mixed governments. Yet when discussing popular assemblies in
democratic governments, Schlegel wrote that "certain constitutions" (*vise
Constitutioner*) required a two-thirds majority to pass a resolution (1798:
2:161). In the same chapter, he wrote that "the constitution" (*Constitutionen*)
should decide the requirements for elected representatives (Schlegel 1798:
2:157). From the context, and in using the definite form and referring to specific legal rules, Schlegel clearly had in mind the new written constitutions
at that time. He specifically mentioned and discussed the US Constitution of
1787 and the French Constitution of 1795. Interestingly, Schlegel filled the
ancient concept of the democratic form of government with new content
from the then new written constitutions, and consequently, his understanding of "constitution" also changed within this context. In later chapters on
aristocratic and monarchical governments, however, he returned to the old
and broader understanding of "constitution" as referring to the form of government (Schlegel 1798: 2:167, 172). We thus see that the new understanding of "constitution" had made its first impression in turn-of-the century
Danish-Norwegian legal terminology, but that understanding was highly de-
pendent on context. When Schlegel referred to the new written constitutions
in France and other countries, he used the concept "constitution" in its new
meaning.[23] When writing within the traditional categories of the natural law

genre, however, he maintained the old distinction between *Constitution* and *Grundlov*.

The Norwegian Constitution of 1814

Conceptual Change in the Constitution

Keeping in mind the traditional distinction between *Constitution* and *Grundlov* in eighteenth-century legal terminology, we now consider the Norwegian Constitution of 1814. What becomes obvious when looking at the constitutional text, its drafts, and the sources from the Constitutional Assembly in 1814 is that the two terms have become synonymous in the sense that both refer to the new written constitution. This new synonymy implies a shift in the meaning of both concepts. *Constitution* is no longer a nonlegal term referring to the state's political condition and composition or to its form of government. Rather, *Constitution* has taken on its modern and legal meaning, referring to a specific set of legal rules that define and limit the government. So, too, for the term *Grundlov*. Both in form and in content, the 1814 Constitution was largely modeled on contemporary US and French constitutions. This aspect gave it a distinctly different legal character than the former *Grundlov*—the absolutist *Lex regia*—had. Nor was the new constitution in accordance with older notions of "fundamental laws" as being contracts between prince and people. The 1814 Constitution was, in accordance with Vattel's definition, considered an act of a sovereign people by an elected constitutional assembly (Holmøyvik 2012: 417–419).

If we consider the sources from the Constitutional Assembly, we find that the term most commonly used for the 1814 Constitution is not *Grundlov*, but rather *Constitution*. The assembly's official protocol consistently uses this term, and the group of representatives commissioned to write the official draft was officially called Constitutions Comiteen (the Constitutional Committee). The committee referred to its draft as both *Grundlov* and *Constitution*, but the text of the draft used only *Constitution*. Of the seventeen private drafts written in preparation for the Constitutional Assembly, eight used *Constitution* exclusively, six used both *Constitution* and *Grundlov*, and three used *Grundlov* only.[24] In the final text of the Constitution, the term *Constitution* is the predominant one. It is used in the title and in thirteen articles, while *Grundlov* is used in only two articles. Yet clearly both terms refer to this document and they are clearly synonymous. Article 110, on constitutional amendment, for example, refers to "this *Constitution*" and "this *Grundlov*" in the same sentence: "Naar Rigsforsamlingen har antaget denne Constitution, vorder den Rigets Grundlov" (This Constitution, when sanctioned by the National Assembly, becomes the fundamental law of the Kingdom).[25] Clearly, the framers thought these terms had the same meaning.

Considering its pre-1814 usage, we see that the term *Constitution* has taken on a new and specifically legal meaning as referring to a written document containing the legal norms defining the government, its institutions, and its limits. In other words, the concept "constitution" defined by Vattel in 1758 and adopted by the US and French written constitutions had entered and changed the Norwegian legal vocabulary.

The Effect on Other Terms

With the adoption of the 1814 Constitution, we also see that the new meaning of *Constitution* also effected a change in the meaning of terms like *Forfatning, Statsforfatning,* and *Regieringsform.* Before the 1814 Constitution these terms had been used as synonyms for *Constitution* in its older meaning, but now they too were transformed by the new meaning of *Constitution.* Thus, at the Constitutional Assembly as well as in later Norwegian legal terminology, we find all of these terms referring to the 1814 Constitution.[26] One example of this conceptual plurality is the title of the first Norwegian textbook on constitutional law following the 1814 Constitution, written by the later prime minister Frederik Stang in 1833. It was titled *Systematisk Fremstilling af Kongeriget Norges constitutionelle eller grundlovbestemte Ret* (A Systematic Treatise of the Kingdom of Norway's Constitutional Law or Law Determined in the *Grundlov*). As we can see, the title gives equal status and meaning to *Constitution* and *Grundlov.*

In modern Norwegian legal terminology, the terms *konstitusjon, grunnlov, statsforfatning,* and *forfatning* can all refer to the Norwegian Constitution as a specific legal document and as a legal-political institution, although their scope may differ depending on the context. *Grunnlov* normally refers only to the written Constitution. The other terms, depending on the context, may also refer to unwritten constitutional norms and to lower-ranking legal norms concerning the government. Today, constitutional law as a legal discipline is often referred to as *statsforfatningsrett,* and Norwegian textbooks on constitutional law have traditionally had titles like *Norges nuværende statsforfatning* (Aschehoug 1891–1893), *Lærebok i den norske statsforfatningsret* (Morgenstierne 1926–1927), *Norges statsforfatning* (Castberg 1964), *Norsk statsforfatningsrett* (Helset and Stordrange 1998), and *Statsforfatningen i Norge* (Andenæs and Fliflet 2006). A 2009 textbook on Norwegian constitutional law, however, is titled *Konstitusjonelt demokrati* (Constitutional Democracy). Using the term *konstitusjon* instead of *statsforfatning* in the title, and consistently using *konstitusjon* instead of *grunnlov* for the written Constitution itself, is a clear break with traditional terminology. This break may actually signify a shift in the view on constitutional law. In the introduction, author Eivind Smith makes clear that his textbook does indeed differ from previous Norwegian textbooks on constitutional law (Smith 2012: 7). Significantly, his book breaks with tradition both in terms of structure and to some extent in content.

Causes for the Conceptual Change

The primary cause of the merger of all these terms into the modern concept "constitution" was the prospect, following the break with Denmark and absolutism, of a new and modern constitution for an independent Norwegian state. Such a full-scale conceptual change was impossible before 1814 despite knowledge of the modern concept "constitution" through constitutional literature and written constitutions. As evidenced by Schlegel, these were new experiences that could not replace the old until there existed the prospect of a new constitution without the old government's institutional and intellectual framework. Using Koselleck's above-mentioned dichotomy between experience and expectation, we might say that it was the prospect of a new and fundamentally different constitution that finally shifted Norwegians' expectations toward the modern concept "constitution." The very idea of a new Norwegian Constitution in 1814 was necessarily linked to the new constitutions in America and in France, all of which were titled as such. The Norwegian Constitution of 1814 was intended to be a constitution in this sense. Unsurprisingly, therefore, the older terminology was transformed by the new meaning of "constitution."

The Normative Dimension of the New Concept of "Constitution"

The new meaning of the concept "constitution" was not limited to the written form. For the Norwegian framers intending to write a constitution following the American and French models, the concept also carried with it an expectation of a specific content in accordance with these constitutions and their basic principles. This normative dimension of the concept is evident in the definition of "constitution" in the two most elaborate and influential of the private drafts written for the Constitutional Assembly.

The first of these drafts was written by Nicolai Wergeland, who also served on the important Constitutional Committee. According to his definition of *Constitution,* its object was "by deciding the separation of powers and the other aspects of society, to guarantee the object of the state, the enjoyment of the human and citizen rights and the promotion of everyone's happiness" (*Riksforsamlingens forhandlinger* 1914–1918: 3:261; my translation). In Wergeland's definition, we see that a "constitution" requires government to be organized according to the principle of separation of powers. Further, his definition presupposes the existence of human rights. Though more elaborately worded, his definition is essentially the same as in the above-cited Article 16 of the *Déclaration des droits de l'Homme et du Citoyen* from 1789, which clearly served as his model.[27]

We find a similar definition in the preamble to the draft of Johan Gunder Adler and Christian Magnus Falsen. The latter played a leading role at the Constitutional Assembly as leader of the predominant political faction there and as president of the Constitutional Committee. Because of this role and his and Adler's draft, Falsen is often called the father of the Norwegian Constitution. Adler and Falsen's draft was by far the most influential of the private drafts, and it was the principal source for the 1814 Constitution. In the preamble, the authors stated that:

> [the] *Constitution* of the state contains such provisions, which founded upon the steadfast foundation of natural rights determine the rules for the people's participation in the government, the relations between the legislative power and the executive power, management of public administration, the administration of justice, the organization of the national defense, the use of public funds and the promotion of knowledge. (*Riksforsamlingens forhandlinger* 1914–1918: 3:7–8; my translation)

Here, too, we see the separation of powers mentioned as an essential part of a "constitution," as well as popular participation in government and quite a few other issues that the authors considered necessary to regulate in a "constitution." Most of these were features of the foreign constitutions that had inspired the authors. The former two principles—the separation of powers and popular participation in the government—were indeed fundamental to the entire constitutional movement in the late eighteenth century and thus were essentially integrated into the contemporary understanding of the concept "constitution."

"Constitution" as a Vision of Government

What I am implying above is that some political principles, components, and institutional arrangements forming the basis of the first American and French constitutions had by 1814 become integrated into the very concept of "constitution" itself. The separation of powers is the prime example, being (at least formally) the core of most constitutions ever since. For the Norwegian framers, like the French, American, and other framers before them, a constitution without the separation of powers was unthinkable. The same holds true for the idea of human rights, the equality of rights, and popular participation in the government by means of voting rights and representation. Today these are fundamentals in every constitution, as they were for the Norwegian framers in 1814.

We might say, therefore, that the term "constitution" did subject the Norwegian framers in 1814 to what Reinhart Koselleck has called *Systemzwang* (systemic coercion) (1983: 18). By using the term "constitution," they accepted a specific type of constitution—the rational constitution based upon a certain set of rational political principles.[28] The precise contents of these principles might not have been clear at that time. Nor have they been permanently attached to the concept "constitution" ever since—the sovereignty of the people, for example, vanished for a time with the constitutions of the monarchical restoration in Europe in the decades following 1814 (see Gammelgaard in this volume). Yet at least at the time of the Norwegian Constitution in 1814, some principles were essential to the very concept "constitution." Thus, for the Norwegian framers, "constitution" was not only a legal term. It was also a vision of government.

NOTES

1. This chapter is based upon my study of the concept "constitution" (Holmøyvik 2012). I have translated into English all quotes from Danish, Norwegian, and French sources.
2. On Koselleck's theory of *Begriffsgeschichte* and the metahistorical categories *Erfahrungsraum* and *Erwartungshorizont,* see Koselleck (2004). Specifically on the concept of "constitution," see Koselleck (1983).
3. There is a substantive literature on the historical development of the concept "constitution." A principal study is Grimm and Mohnhaupt (1995). For the specific development in the French language, see Beaud (2009). For the specific development in the English language, see Stourzh (1988).
4. On the core components in modern constitutionalism, see Dippel (2005).
5. In the English language, a direct analogy from the human body is the concept "body politic" (Stourzh 1975: 106).
6. When Montesquieu used "constitution" in the political context referring to the government, he normally specified this as "constitution de l'Etat," "constitution du gouvernement," and so on; see Beaud (2009: 10–11).
7. On the reception of Vattel's definition in France, see Baker (1990: 256) and Beaud (2009: 9, 22–23).
8. I have borrowed this terminology from the Swedish historian Frederik Lagerroth (1973: 63).
9. The classic text on the distinction between these two historical types of constitutions is McIlwain (1940: 5). See also Caenegem (2009: 448–455).
10. In America, the necessity of separation of powers was stated in the declarations of rights for the constitutions of Virginia, North Carolina, and Maryland of 1776, Massachusetts of 1780, and New Hampshire of 1784.
11. The more or less general agreement upon the separation of powers obscures the important fact that there was hardly any agreement upon what the separation of powers actually entailed in practice; see Troper (1980: 157–60) and Casper (1997: 22).

12. The same is true for eighteenth-century Swedish terminology, where the term *grundlag* was a Swedish equivalent to "fundamental law" (Herlitz 1967: 148). The forms of government in 1719 and 1720 defined themselves as *fundamental lag*, while the form of government referred to itself both as a *grundlag* and as a *fundamentallag*.

13. So, too, in positive Danish constitutional law, where Andreas Höjer in a treatise from 1737–1738 defined the *Lex regia* as a *Grund-lov* (A. Höjer [1737–1738] 1783: 3).

14. See also Jens Schielderup Sneedorff's *Om den borgerlige Regiering* from 1757 (J.S. Sneedorff [1757] 1776: 92–103) and the 1760 Danish translation of Jean-Jacques Burlamaqui's *Principes du droit politique* (Burlamaqui 1760: 55ff.).

15. An example is Andreas Schytte's *Danmarks og Norges naturlige og politiske Forfatning* from 1777, which translates as "Denmark and Norway's Natural and Political Condition." Here, Schytte discussed the composition of the Danish-Norwegian state in multiple perspectives, politically, socially, culturally, and geographically.

16. An example is Andreas Höjer's above-mentioned constitutional law treatise and his discussion of the *Stats-Forfatningen* for the Duchy of Slesvig (A. Höjer [1737–1738] 1783: 36–49).

17. For Schlegel, *Constitution* was synonymous with form of government, which he called *Statsformen* or *forma imperii* (Schlegel 1798: 2:84). This terminology reveals Immanuel Kant and *Zum ewigen Frieden* as Schlegel's source.

18. We find another example of this understanding of *Constitution* in historian Frederik Sneedorff's published lectures on statistics from 1789 to 1790. According to Sneedorff, the *Grundlov* decided the *Constitution* of the realm as well as the duties of the prince and the people (F. Sneedorff 1795: 28). Here, too, *Constitution* simply referred to the form of government, which was one of many issues legally established in a *Grundlov*.

19. See Tamm (1997: 172–183) for the normative effect of this understanding of *Constitution* in the legislation of the 1790s.

20. For Stampe, the terms *Forfatning, Constitution, Statsforfatning,* and *Regieringsform* were synonymous, and he used them both alone and in combination, as in "vor Forfatning" (Stampe 1793–1807: 5:416; Stampe 1793–1807: 3:4–5), "vores Constitution og Forfatning" (Stampe 1793–1807: 3:611), "vaar Statsforfatning" (Stampe 1793–1807: 2:571), and "vores Regieringsform og Constitution" (Stampe 1793–1807: 3:448).

21. This was also the case in late eighteenth-century Germany; see Grimm and Mohnhaupt (1995: 107–108).

22. On the impact of the French Revolution and its ideas on Danish-Norwegian constitutional law and legislation in the 1790s, see Tamm (1997: 173ff.).

23. Another example of this is a pamphlet written by Enevold Falsen from 1802, where he wrote that the French revolutionaries had given themselves a *Constitution* (see E. Falsen [1802] 1821: 155).

24. For examples, see Holmøyvik (2012: 94–97).

25. Interestingly, in the official English-language translation of the Norwegian Constitution printed shortly after its adoption in 1814 and quoted here, the term *Grundlov* in Article 110 was translated as "fundamental law."

26. In modern Norwegian legal terminology, though, *regieringsform* is normally understood literally as "form of government," which is also its sole use in the text of the

Constitution. See Article 1, which says the form of government (*Regjeringsform*) is a limited and hereditary monarchy.

27. On the heavy influence from French constitutional law in Wergeland's draft, see Holmøyvik (2008: 184–188).

28. In his study of the Spanish constitution of 1812, Heinz Mohnhaupt concludes that the choice of the Spanish framers to use the term "constitution" was a conscious move away from the ancien régime (Mohnhaupt 2006: 90).

▶• 3 •◀

The Many Textual Identities of Constitutions

Dag Michalsen

Introduction

Since modern constitutionalism's beginnings in the last three decades of the eighteenth century, an increasing number of people worldwide have shared the idea that a written document represents a basic component in a constitution.[1] In general, we may say that today, the "constitution" concept is widely connected with texts. However, a constitution may connect with texts not only as a connection between a constitution and a written document. In this chapter, I discuss five possible connections between constitutions and texts. This discussion will focus on the Norwegian Constitution of 1814 and its connections with texts up until today.

This chapter has five sections, each of which focuses on a different one of five possible connection models between constitutions and texts. I start with the model of the Norwegian Constitution. This model may be referred to as the model of the modern constitution (see also Holmøyvik in this volume). In addition to shared ideas of popular sovereignty, separation of powers, popular participation in government, and human rights, this model stresses the identity between the adopted written constitutional document and constitutional law. Hence, the written document is regarded as the exhaustive core of constitutional law. The modern constitutional movement began in 1776 with the Constitution of Virginia and the US Declaration of Independence. In Europe, the movement ended in 1814–1815 with the European Restoration (Michalsen 2008: 11). The Norwegian Constitution was typical for its time and in this respect was just one of many constitutions that were framed in this period, such as—to mention just a few famous ones— the US Constitution of 1787, the French Constitution of 1791, the Polish Constitution of 1791, and the Spanish Constitution of 1812. The Norwegian

Constitution can be understood as exemplifying these first modern constitutions. Therefore, it may serve as the starting point for examining the heterogenic and problematic connection between constitutions and texts in general. I refer to the model of the Norwegian Constitution—the modern constitution—as representing monotextuality.

Other models of the connection between constitutions and texts exist, too. Most important is the British model, which is characterized by the coexistence of many written core documents. I refer to this model as representing multitextuality. This quality makes it difficult to define what represents the limits of the constitution's texts.

A third, even more problematic, model is the constitutional model of the Enlightenment philosophy, which presupposes that a constitution ultimately is a product of reason. According to this Enlightenment understanding, written documents should ideally serve as a transparent medium for rationality. Within this model, a constitution should be defined only by the insight of reason. This understanding means that an ideal Enlightenment constitution does not exist as a material, written document at all. Like every modern constitution, the Norwegian Constitution was influenced by this Enlightenment model. Owing to this philosophical influence, a tension between the textual and nontextual manifestation of reason came to characterize the making of the Norwegian Constitution. In this chapter, this tension will be addressed in the section on nontextuality.

A fourth model deals with the connection between constitutions and the texts derived from or enabled by constitutions. From the moment a constitution is adopted and put into force, a variety of texts are produced by the institutions that apply it. The most obvious examples of this institutional textual production are the secondary legal texts derived from a constitution, such as new rules regulating the constitutional powers of the legislative and executive branches of government. Besides these institutional texts, other categories also emerge. One important category is produced in the (academic) commentaries and interpretations of both the constitutional text itself and the secondary legal texts produced by the legal science. In addition, the practices enabled by and surrounding a constitution produce a number of other texts: political, ideological, and literary texts that interweave with the legal ones. In the Norwegian constitutional tradition, this specific connection between the Constitution and other texts is well-known; I will discuss some aspects of this fourth model, which I characterize as representing intertextuality.

Finally, constitutions as old as Norway's often come to serve as a symbol for a state, for a nation, or for an ideology. In this process, constitutions may transcend qualities connected with written documents and may attain visual, even auditory, dimensions. These aspects of a possible fifth model will be addressed in the conclusion.

Monotextuality: The Modern Constitution

One of the central qualities of the modern constitutions of the late eighteenth century was their specific and innovative textuality.[2] In contrast to constitutions of the era before modern constitutionalism, when the constitution concept did not require one written document or any specific documents at all, the modern constitution concept presupposed one legally formalized constitutional written document. The textuality of modern constitutionalism was evident in a number of ways. Most importantly, the constitutional document was adopted formally by a specific assembly. Therefore, the document's legality and textuality were closely connected. To change this type of constitution, the competent state organ must rewrite the original constitutional document, or portions of it, in the form of an amendment as dictated by the very same constitutional document. Because this understanding of the constitution concept presupposed that the constitutional document was exhaustive, the state organs could derive their legally binding authority only from this single document. They could not derive legally binding authority from any pretextual practices or authorities outside the written constitutional document. Owing to this circular dynamic, any additional legal document that regulated only parts of a constitutional order was not regarded as a constitutional document at all.

The modern constitution was constituted by two elements: the legal structure and working of a political organization (a state) and the relationship between this state and its citizens, often in the form of human rights. Because all modern constitutions adhered to this model, yet in different ways, each modern constitution contained dimensions of both universalism and particularism (Armitage 2007: 63ff.; see also Gammelgaard; Visconti; Schmid in this volume). Because of its universalism, each modern constitutional document was connected with literally hundreds of similar constitutional texts across states. These constitutional texts had the same character and they were all linked to the general constitution concept. Starting in 1776, with the first American revolutionary constitutions, modern constitutional writing evolved as a global practice, although with great political and ideological varieties: from the truly liberal democratic constitutions to the many authoritarian ones.

Into this formalized and politicized constitutional textual tradition a new relationship with time was introduced. From 1776, the modern constitution was fundamentally understood as a normative and *prescriptive* concept (Grimm and Mohnhaupt 1995: 101–112; Holmøyvik in this volume). Constitutions did not, as before, describe only a particular actual social state. In addition, they now normatively prescribed a political vision and, consequently, the type of social and cultural transformations that would be brought about by the state created by the constitution. A constitution should govern the state and structure its legal character. Therefore, the Norwegian Constitution of 1814 did not establish only Norwegian statehood and the state's system of governance; it also laid the foundation for Norway's legal, political, and cultural identity as well.

At last, the modern constitution concept presupposed that the act of writing down the constitution involved the performative idea that the act itself brought about new sociopolitical realities (see Warner et al.; Visconti in this volume). The extraordinary number of constitutions drafted and adopted in the decades around 1800 speak of this confidence in the effects of legal acts. For example, for the period from 1790 to 1814, the database "Constitutions of the World from the late 18th Century to the Middle of the 19th Century Online" lists more than a hundred adopted and drafted constitutions and constitutional documents.[3] Legal confidence and legislative optimism of this period were not only visible in constitutional practice, but were equally visible in the practice of civil law codifications like the French *Code civil* from 1804.

Multitextuality: The Premodern Constitution

The rise of modern constitutionalism changed constitutional practice in fundamental ways. The ideas of the connection between constitutions and texts, however, did not change overnight; indeed, the modern monotextual model is debated even today. Around 1800, regarding constitutional orders, three types of states existed: (1) states adhering to the modern constitutional model, (2) constitutional states in the sense of having a certain constitutionalism in the business of government but lacking a modern constitution (Caenegem 1995: 98–150), and (3) absolute states lacking any constitutional arrangement, such as Russia. Within these three categories, great differences existed. Here, I focus on the connection between constitutions and texts in the second category: constitutional states not founded on a modern constitution.

The paradigmatic example of this second category is the British constitution (Lyon 2003). Before 1700, the English political vocabulary used the word "constitution" variously, for example, to convey meanings such as "the action of constituting, making, establishing"; "appointment"; "ordinance, settled arrangement, institution"; and "nature, character, or condition of mind."[4] However, "constitution" slowly came to mean one legal-political order. This change is documented in a number of parliamentary acts. One early example of this change is the following quotation from a famous resolution by Parliament in 1688: "that King James II, having endeavored to subvert the constitution of the kingdom, by breaking the original contract between king and people … having violated the fundamental laws", and was consequently considered to have abdicated the government (quoted in Grimm and Mohnhaupt 1995: 47). Here, "constitution" is explicitly coupled with plural texts, "the fundamental laws." After 1700, the British constitution was understood as having a rather vague yet more varied textual basis, both because there were now numerous documents that were seen as the textual basis for the "living constitution" and because, unlike in modern constitutions, Parliament, with a simple majority, had the authority to change these documents through new legal acts. In his research on British constitutional documents from the period around 1800, the constitutional historian Harry T. Dickinson (2005) enumerates fifteen acts, not counting the numerous ones from before 1776 (such as the Bill of Rights of 1689).[5] Dickinson points to the heterogenic and varied textual status of the British constitution: "[W]hat cannot be done in Britain in this period—unlike in a growing number of advanced countries elsewhere in the world at this time—is to produce the full and agreed text of the British constitution" (Dickinson 2005: 11). Perhaps, therefore, it is not surprising that the British constitution ceased to be a formal model for political reform in Europe after the breakthrough of the modern constitutionalism that so specifically required one exhaustive core written document, *the* constitutional text. However, the mere existence of an alternative makes it clear that to create a constitution, legislators need not necessarily follow the single model of the monotextual modern constitutions.

Models similar to the British one existed on the Continent in the prerevolutionary era. The seventeenth and eighteenth century saw the production of a number of legal and constitutional documents referred to as *leges fundamentales* (Grimm and Mohnhaupt 1995: 62–66). These documents were often agreements between monarchs and estates concerning taxation, rules of succession, elections of kings, and other issues that might be viewed as fundamental for governing the realm. The purpose was to establish procedures for the estates' acceptance of the king's decisions. But even if these arrangements to some extent aimed at limiting kingship's power, we should not regard these documents as having any distinct legal force. They were certainly not comparable with the modern constitutions. The way of constitutionally viewing the variety of legal texts as equally relevant becomes evident in the following quotation from a French journal in 1780, one that enumerated several types of laws that amounted to French constitutional laws:

> Les loix Fondamentales, ou écrites, ou attestées par une tradition constante, ont pour objet, la succession au Trône, les droits du Roi, la constitution de l'Etat, l'essence des Tribunaux, la forme de la Législation, la liberté, la sûreté et le bonheur des Peuples. (*Journal encyclopédique ou universel* 1780: 169)

> (The fundamental laws, or written laws, or laws certified by a continuous tradition, have as their object the succession to the throne, the king's rights, the state's constitution, the fundamentals of the judiciary, the form of legislation, the liberty, safety and happiness of the people.)[6]

Nontextuality: The Constitution as Reason's Insight

The modern constitution concept emerged out of the idea of the social contract. In the eighteenth century, the idea of the social contract was—although with many political varieties—that sovereignty should be legitimized and based on a contract between the sovereign and his subjects. The social contract regulated both parties' rights and duties. This social contract was regarded as the ideological basis for each particular constitution. However, this original social contract did not exist in any written form. It existed only in derived forms, namely, the written constitutions. Leading philosophers of the social contract, such as Jean-Jacques Rousseau and Immanuel Kant, do not refer to any actual written documents in which the original social contract might have been articulated. In *Du contrat social* (On the Social Contract) of 1762, Rousseau maintains that the people permanently have the right to change the particular social contract that governs their state. Thus, with Rousseau, the original (unwritten) social contract is transformed into a particular constitution, becoming a particular interpretation of that unwritten social contract (Rousseau [1762] 1978: 2: XII). Kant views this issue somewhat differently (see Kant 1797). Because, for Kant, the logic of reason constitutes the state of law and emerges out of the state of nature, he argues that written documents are unnecessary to define the content of the constitution. In the realm of philosophical reason, he holds, no foundational texts exist. Therefore, for Kant, only human nature can serve as the fountain for defining the ideal constitution.

Kant's model of constitutionalism was very important in constitutional debates around 1800, that is, in the period of modern constitutionalism, and he therefore influenced Norwegian constitutional politics in 1814 (Michalsen 2008). In his philosophical writings, Kant defines reason as the authority of natural law. The idea is that essentially reason demands that a certain type of constitution be implemented in society, a constitution defined through the people's sovereignty and the separation of powers; in short, what Kant calls a "republican constitution." This republican constitution was intended to secure the principle of freedom. To implement this constitution meant to introduce a specific relationship between statehood, citizens, and legislation explained by the purpose it serves. I refer to this specific relationship as "constitutionalization." This constitutionalization dictates the realization of the material principles of constitutionalism in society. Therefore, Kant claims, it is reason that originally defines the aims of a concrete state's constitution and the specific ways in which its legislation should be implemented. These definitions are a priori and thus transhistorical and undisputable. Accordingly, the Kantian social model embodies a legal state that emerges out of the state of nature and that by definition should serve as the model for all new constitutions. Reason prescribes that there should be constitutions and that these constitutions should be based upon the principles of freedom. Therefore, for constitutional legislators it remains only to "repeat the norms of natural law in the positive legislative acts," as worded by the Danish Kantian philosopher and law professor Johan Schlegel (1765–1836) (1805: 2:92–93). Accordingly, any constitutional legislator should follow the dictates of reason. Thus, the legislator's constitutional repeat is in a Kantian sense simply putting into text the constitution of reason and acknowledging that it (the constitution of reason) is the society's true constitution.

Does the Kantian understanding of reason's significant role demand that the modern constitution have a specific textual quality? Not quite. The work of Johan Schlegel illustrates how different perspectives on the connection between constitutions and texts were at work in the late Enlightenment. Schlegel was an important personality in the intellectual life of Denmark-Norway's capital, Copenhagen. In his influential writings, Schlegel combines the existing model of Danish-Norwegian absolutism, which for political reasons could not accept a modern constitution, with the discourse of modern constitutionalism, which insisted on a constitution's importance in securing citizens' freedom. To overcome the contradiction between absolutism and constitutionalism, Schlegel attempts to interpret an absolutist society as being in reality a constitutional and liberal one. In his discussion of natural law, *Naturrettens eller den almindelige Retslæres Grundsætninger* (1805), Schlegel distinguishes between interpreting the constitution concept broadly and narrowly (see also Holmøyvik in this volume). According to his broad interpretation, Schlegel understands the constitution concept as a Kantian interpretation of the original social contract, which, in turn, is based on the idea of reason. In his narrow interpretation, Schlegel defines the constitution concept as the written constitutional document of a particular state (1805: 76–80).[7] Thus, in Schlegel's discussion, the difference between the broad and narrow interpretations of the constitution concept is the difference between unwritten and written constitutions.

By relativizing the connection between constitutions and texts, Schlegel can state the following: "According to the judgment of Reason, the actual form of a constitution is not the main point; what is important is that the government is led in a democratic spirit, so that the general will becomes the basis for the running of the state" (1797: 360). Thus, Schlegel maintains that the modern constitution concept does not necessarily demand one exhaustive written document. As long as the state's actual practice conforms with the principles of constitutionalism—which means that it conforms with the democratic interpretation of the original social contract—such practice is an even better response to reason's demands than is the alternative understanding of the constitution concept as meaning one written document. Consequently, through this definition, the constitution concept becomes a fundamental nontextual phenomenon.

Intertextuality: The Constitution as Derivative Texts

When a constitution is adopted and put into practice, a number of derivative texts are produced. The state organs created by a constitution must continuously interpret the very same constitution whenever they apply a constitutional norm. Thus, the constitution becomes the foundation for a vast amount of legal documents that reflect aspects of it. Legal documents are, however, not the only texts produced in response to a constitution. Because a constitution is very much a political and ideological document as well, political and ideological texts that concern constitutional life constitute a significant category of derivative texts. In addition, any constitution that is important in a nation's life will become the object of many kinds of reflections. Therefore, countless texts will be produced that somehow address, discuss, and mirror the constitution.

Through social processes, these derivative texts become interwoven with the constitution. Put differently, constitutional practices transcend law and become a broader social practice embedded in cultural ideology and social structure. This transcending is apparent in the history of Norwegian constitutional practice. Soon after 1814, Norwegian constitutionalism became part of the program of Norwegian nationalism. This coupling is testified to in many nineteenth-century literary works. A proud connection between the nation and the Constitution ("self-adopted laws") was voiced already in the popular song that between 1820 and 1864 served as Norway's national anthem (Kydland 1995: 54–55). The fifth stanza reads:

> Frihedens Tempel i Nordmandens Dale
> Stander saa herligt i Lye af hans Fjeld;
> Frit tør han tænke, og frit tør han tale,
> Frit tør han virke til Norriges Held.
> Fuglen i Skove, Nordhavets Vove
> Friere er ei end Norriges Mand;
> Villig dog lyder han selvgivne Love,
> Trofast mod Konning og Fædreneland. (Bjerregaard and Blom n.d.)

> (The freedom temple in the Norwegian's valley
> stands so glorious, sheltered by his mountains;
> Freely dares he think and freely dares he speak,
> freely dares he work for Norway's good fortune.
> The bird in the forests, the North Sea wave
> are not freer than the Norwegian;
> Yet willingly he obeys the self-adopted laws,
> true to king and fatherland.)

The two most prominent literary authors coupling nationality and constitutionalism were probably Henrik Wergeland (1808–1845) and Bjørnstjerne

Bjørnson (1832–1910). Wergeland depicted national historical themes in a number of literary sketches (see H. Jæger et al. 1932). In addition, he wrote (H. Wergeland 1841–1843) the first historical account of the events leading up to the adoption of the Norwegian Constitution in 1814. In the introduction to this work, Wergeland writes:

> The fact that our country's constitution has been fruitful in benefactions for our people deserves a recorder. The record of them [the Constitution's benefactions] and its [the Constitution's] genesis by the people's own power should also make the Norwegian Constitution fruitful for other nations. (H. Wergeland 1841–1843: iv)[8]

Poet and dramatist Bjørnson discussed the Constitution on several occasions. A defining current in Bjørnson's work is the thematization of Norwegian identity, both historical and contemporary.[9] Moreover, he intervened directly in contemporary political debates, as in 1880 during the conflict over the (Swedish) king's right to veto (see Sand in this volume):

> Vor Grundlov er Kontrakt med det Land, som er vor Mor,
> vort Odelsbrev til Hjæmmet her i Norden.
> Paa det vi gaar med Ære til Folkeraadets Bord
> og bænkes blandt de Frieste paa Jorden. (Bjørnson 1880)

> (Our Constitution is the contract with the country that is our mother,
> our freehold document for our home here in the North.
> Based on it [the Constitution] we proceed with honor to Parliament's table
> and seat ourselves among the freest on earth.)

Both Wergeland and Bjørnson were instrumental in making 17 May Constitution Day, the national day for celebrating the adoption of the 1814 Constitution. In sum, by writing the Constitution into the center of Norwegian politics and cultural life, the Norwegian literary authors' achievement influenced the intellectual and popular understanding of the Constitution in ways that in turn influenced people's ideological and legal expectations of the Norwegian Constitution.[10]

Wergeland and Bjørnson are examples that illustrate the many derivative texts that in various ways and genres respond to and interpret the Constitution in social life. As a whole, these texts attain an identity that we may identify as the Norwegian constitutional tradition. This tradition may be characterized by three major elements. The first is the system of legal and other types of texts that any legal tradition must refer to. The second consists of those communicative fields within which the constitutional tradition involves politics, ideology, culture, and social structures; indeed, a constitutional tradition might be defined as an evolving system of communication between the above-mentioned entities. Last, the processes of innovations should be stressed. The importance of innovations is obvious when we consider the massive legal and political changes during the nineteenth and twentieth centuries. Norwegian constitutional law enabled changes that were as equally massive as those that Norwegian constitutional law underwent as part of social and political upheavals.

The 1814 Norwegian Constitution was adopted in a specific geopolitical situation and was formed by the modern constitution model. Simultaneously, the political elite harbored patriotic motives, and therefore a number of uniquely Norwegian features were written into the Constitution. For example, the farmer's role was reflected in Article 107: "The Odels- and Aasædes-Ret (Right of redeeming patrimonial lands and of dwelling on the chief mansion) must not be abolished."[11] Paradoxically, the 1814 Constitution failed to index the Norwegian language as a distinct national feature (see Madzharova Bruteig in this volume). Nonetheless, the Constitution's national dimension strengthened throughout the nineteenth century, as the writings of Wergeland and Bjørnson demonstrate. Increasingly, the Constitution was interpreted as an expression of the Norwegian nation. Conflicts beginning in 1814 concerning the union between Norway and Sweden, which culminated in that union's dissolution in 1905, only increased this national interpretation. Germany's occupation of Norway from 1940 to 1945 and the formation of the welfare state's ideology later in the twentieth century contributed to new forms of national interpretations of the Constitution. The Norwegian people's rejection of Norwegian membership in the European Community in 1972 and their rejection of Norwegian membership in the European Union in 1994 also had effects in that direction. Both rejections contributed to confirming the image of Norway as a "free, independent and indivisible Realm" (Article 1).

This excerpt from poet Arnulf Øverland's speech on Constitution Day (17 May) in 1945 is but one example of such twentieth-century interpretations:

> Today is the Day of our Constitution. It was the Constitution that our enemies tore up and trampled on. And it is the Constitution that we have got back.
>
> This old paper—inspired by America's freedom struggle and the innovative ideas of the French Revolution, written in Eidsvoll in the May days in 1814, when the Norwegians felt that now was time, now they had to proclaim their freedom if they would have it!—this old paper contains today the clearest expression of what we understand by human rights.
>
> The Constitution ensures freedom of opinion, conscience, and expression. It gives us the rule of law and equality before the law. And it gives us self-determination and popular sovereignty.
>
> On all counts, it was violated, all its guarantees were taken from us. Now we have got it back, now our Constitution is again in force. Indeed, today we have cause to celebrate Constitution Day! (quoted in Øverland 1946)[12]

Since about 1980, the unceasing process of nationalizing constitutions has been replaced by an internationalization trend (Koskenniemi 2011). The general political and cultural qualities of constitutions are no longer regarded as expressions of national states, but rather as the means for realizing values transcending national ones. This change from nationalization to internationalization is particularly apparent regarding the international regimes of human rights supplementing civil rights sections of national constitutions. The Norwegian Constitution has become connected to the vast new international (global and European) norm regimes that refer to an extraordinarily large number of texts and their heterogenic interrelations (see Sand in this volume). Administering popular sovereignty has been transformed by these new international regimes, such as that of the European Union.

This transformation is not exclusive to the Norwegian Constitution. In the new international order, debates continue about national constitutions (Moyn 2010: 176–210). Contemporary constitutions are no longer just part of national projects. Nevertheless, it would be wrong to assume that national constitutions, as they are practiced, deemphasize national references. National constitutions are not solely defined through international treaties and conventions, and international concepts such as the rule of law and human rights are not yet the sole raison d'être of national constitutions. Because they work in specific nationally defined societies, all of which have their own rhetorical, legal, and linguistic cultures, these constitutions have national dimensions in addition to the international ones. One can even claim that it now seems as necessary to pay attention to the national dimensions, that is, to pay attention to what has been called "constitutional patriotism," as to ensure the shared public democratic appreciation of the constitution (Müller 2007). Today, the political and social identities of a constitution exist in the tensions between nationalism and internationalism.

From Textuality to Visual Representations

From the early nineteenth century, the Norwegian Constitution transcended its quality as a written document and became known through the symbolic images of Constitution Day (17 May) celebrations. Surprisingly, these images remain undiminished in contemporary popular culture (see, e.g., Blehr 2000). There is also a connection between the Constitution and the Norwegian flag, and between the Constitution and Eidsvold Manor, where the Constitution was framed and adopted. Moreover, from the early 1830s until the end of the nineteenth century, reproductions of the Constitution decorated the walls of numerous Norwegian homes (Hemstad 2012). Even today, copies of the most popular reproduction still hang in many institutions, particularly schools (see figure 3.1). This poster reproduces the Constitution of 4 November 1814, and includes articles later repealed (for example, the banning of Jews in Article 2).

In other words, when interpreting the poster as a symbol of Norwegian democracy, people do not consider its actual, *out-of-date* wording. Instead, they regard the poster as a visual symbol of the *current* Constitution.

3.1. *Kongeriget Norges Grundlov* (The Constitution of the Kingdom of Norway). Poster printed in 1836 by Prahl in Bergen.

All these important dimensions illustrate the complex ways in which a constitution becomes a visual symbol for a nation-state or for an ideology. A constitution may even attain auditory dimensions, as demonstrated by music pieces by European composers of political Enlightenment music (Steinberg 2004). In the Norwegian case, the repertoire of songs, marches, and music pieces used on Constitution Day represents similar auditory references to the Constitution.

In his book *The Eye of Law,* the German legal historian Michael Stolleis (2009) analyzes the visual representations of constitutionalism and legality around 1800.[13] As discussed above, in the revolutionary epoch of modern constitutionalism, the general idea was that a constitution should be based upon natural law. Formulated in the vocabulary of the day, a constitution was the result of reason's insight regarding the best way of governing the state. In a number of images, reason's role was revealed in the imagery of the eye of the law. Particularly in the tumultuous period of the French Revolution, this new imagery was pushed to its extreme. Judges' clothing in the new French courts of 1795 included a band with an image of a silver eye symbolizing the ever-present reason and law (Stolleis 2009: 37–49). In legal parades, judges and other representatives of the law carried banners with the image of the eye of the law. As was stated in the language of the time, law should govern men, not the other way around, an attitude that was equally important to the drafters of the Norwegian Constitution.[14] Thus, the new French word *loyaume* (derived from *loi,* law), invented during the French Revolution, was intended to substitute *royaume* (kingdom); the law was understood as an abstract universal entity as defined in the constitutions and that replaced both God and king. The law was the sovereign that never slept and that kept an eye on everybody in society. The idea of law referred not only to constitutional law, but also to abstract law in general. At this time, the first codifications (systematic law books) emerged in Europe, with the French *Code civil* in 1804 as the prime example. Thus, constitution and codification were seen as closely connected because both legal forms were regarded as resulting from a constant legalization of society, a legalization based upon reason and socially visualized in the presence of the eye of the law.

The obsession with the law—metaphorically expressed in the eye—was a positive expression in constitutional thinking because it represented morality in politics and society. But during the nineteenth century, this attitude changed. As Stolleis emphasizes, the eye metaphor then attained the opposite function: the eye that watched was not necessarily the depersonalized abstract law of constitutional thinking around 1800. Rather, the eye expressed personal interests and power. This new interpretation coincided with the nineteenth-century social critique of the constitutional state. Later, this state was critically viewed as being transformed into an emerging surveillance society. In the metaphors of the philosopher Englishman Jeremy Bentham (1748–1832), the law was no longer something being seen; it had changed into a law that constantly sees. Law also became a symbol for the all-pervasive gaze of power, as in the hierarchical prison, the so-called panopticon, where one guard can watch all prisoners: "The essence of [the panopticon] consists, then, in the *centrality* of the inspector's situation, combined with the well-known and most effectual contrivances for seeing without being seen" (Bentham 1995: 43; italics in original). In this way, the controlling eye attained quite another function than the constitutional idea of the eye of the law, in which the eye secured the abstract character of law. The panopticon became a new metaphor for another and darker side of modern law.

Approaching constitutions as something more than institutional and normative products that are based on written documents requires a set of theories suited to studying the connections of law and visual representation. Most legal scholars have not fully accepted these connections' importance, presumably because few have seen the relevance of discussing the consequences that visual representations may have for understanding the functioning of law and constitutions in society. However, since about 1990, some studies on the impact of constitutions' visual representation on law and justice in modern society have been published (e.g., Modeer and Sunnqvist 2012). When law and constitutions are understood not only in the traditional terms of power, institutions, and hierarchy, but also as important means of communicating frameworks for human action, then the impact of law's and constitutions' visual representations gains relevance. Law and constitutions are being visually communicated in numerous ways, whether by legal institutions, powerful social groups, or stakeholders representing alternative political or cultural perspectives. In the public sphere, visual communication of law is continuously present, as actual court dramas or as TV series. As we enter a new era characterized by an expanding visual culture, new questions may arise about the textual identities of constitutions. Additional questions arise because of the use of digital technology. Today, the Norwegian Constitution exists, in one of its several forms, as a website. With its many links and its continual amendments, the website challenges the 200-year-old idea of a constitution as a single, exhaustive, written document.

NOTES

1. Tone Brekke, Karen Gammelgaard, and Eirik Holmøyvik contributed to this chapter.
2. For more complete analyses of the character of the modern concept of constitutions, see Holmøyvik (2012: 78–102) and in this volume. Regarding general constitutional history, see Michalsen (2011: 289ff.).

3. The database is accessible at http://www.modern-constitutions.de/.

4. Definitions quoted from the entry "constitution" in the *Oxford English Dictionary* (http://www.oed.com/, accessed 29 November 2012).

5. The acts were Crewe's Act (1782), Clerke's Act (1782), Fox's Libel Act (1792), the Conspiracy Act (1794), the Treasonable and Seditious Practices Act (1795), the Seditious Meetings Act (1795), the Suppression of Radical Societies Act (1799), the Act of Union between Britain and Ireland (1800), the Regency Act (1811), the Repeal of the Test and Corporation Act (1828), Roman Catholic Emancipation Act (1829), the Great Reform Act, England and Wales (1832), the Great Reform Act, Scotland (1832), the Great Reform Act, Ireland (1832), and the Municipal Reform Act (1835).

6. I thank Professor Heinz Mohnhaupt (Frankfurt) for this quotation. Quote translated by Eirik Holmøyvik.

7. In legal terminology, "positive constitution" means the current and most often written constitution.

8. All literary texts quoted were translated by Karen Gammelgaard. Storsveen (1997) discusses Wergeland's account of the Norwegian Constitution.

9. Keel (1999: 35–85) analyzes the interactions of constitutional politics and literature in Bjørnson's work.

10. The nexus between constitutionalism and Norwegian nationalism resonated in what was in the nineteenth century still regarded as one shared Danish-Norwegian literature. In Hans Christian Andersen's fairy tale "The Rags," a personified rag says: "'I am Norwegian,' said the Norwegian, 'and when I say that I am Norwegian, I believe I've said enough! I am firm in my threads as are the primary rocks in ancient Norway, the country that, just like the free America, has a constitution!'" (Andersen [1868] 1967: 113).

11. The parenthetical explanation of "The Odels- and Aasædes-Ret" is in the 1814 English-language translation of the Constitution.

12. Translated by Karen Gammelgaard.

13. See also Michalsen (2005: 222–228) and Lüsebrink and Reichardt (1997: chap. 4).

14. The influential draft by Adler and Falsen to the Constitution of 1814 includes the phrase "law should govern men" (*Riksforsamlingens forhandlinger* 1914–1918: 3:14).

▶• Part II •◀

TRANSNATIONAL CONVERSATIONS

The Norwegian Constitution and the Rhetoric of Political Poetry

Ulrich Schmid

Introduction: Constitution as Poetry in Hegel's Sense

The Norwegian Constitution of 1814 is not only a legal, but also a rhetorical phenomenon of its time. It uses a certain style of political rhetoric that mainly stems from the revolutionary movements in the United States and France. Drawing on *The Philosophy of Right* by the German philosopher Georg Wilhelm Friedrich Hegel (1770–1831), I conduct a comparative rhetorical analysis of selected constitutions of the late eighteenth and early nineteenth centuries, most of which proved to be quite short-lived: the constitutions of the Batavian Republic (1798), the Helvetic Republic (1798), Poland (1791), and Spain (1812). The Norwegian Constitution of 1814 can be interpreted against this background as a successful attempt to incorporate not only political, but also rhetorical lessons from the past.

Hegel has the reputation of being a staunch assertor of the authoritarian Prussian state. One of the most prominent critics of Hegel as a totalitarian philosopher and as a predecessor to fascism is the Austrian philosopher Karl Popper. He created the notion of an "open society," which he presented as the exact opposite of the Hegelian state (Popper 1945). Adherents of Popper's allegation most often quote the famous sentence from the introduction to Hegel's *The Philosophy of Right*: "What is rational is actual and what is actual is rational" (Hegel 1952: 6). This statement serves as a legitimation for a strong state: once the authoritarian Prussian state came into being, it was justified by the spirit of reason. This interpretation is at least problematic, if not wrong. Arguably, Hegel built his philosophy around the notion of freedom. The French Revolution was undoubtedly the most important historical event in his life (Ritter 1965: 18). According to Hegel, the consciousness of freedom necessarily entailed freedom itself. Hegel perceived his time as a liminal period in which freedom became the core of human society. Hegel claimed in another famous passage from the introduction to his *The Philosophy of Right* that philosophy "is its own time, apprehended in thoughts" (1952: 8). He constructed his own philosophy to live up to this aspiration. The importance of the French Revolution for Hegel is that it not only brought freedom about as a political reality, but also formulated freedom as a human right. The text that pronounces and thereby grants the right to freedom is of course the constitution. The state that is based on such a constitution becomes "the actuality of concrete freedom" (Hegel 1952: 82).

Hegel's philosophy sums up the predominant ideas about constitutionalism in his time. Most important is Hegel's universal approach: he saw law and ethics as one, embedded the individual in society, and endowed aesthetics with consciousness. Hegel was generally preoccupied with the relation of content and its formal representation. Constitutions and their rhetorical expression of so abstract a notion as freedom are a case in point. I will argue that constitutions can be understood as poetry in Hegel's sense. They do not belong to the prosaic genres, which are constructed around logical argumentation. Poetry does not need reasoning because its truth derives directly from its utterance. Once the poetic truth is formulated, it becomes valid and enters into being.

In his "Lectures on Aesthetics," Hegel defines poetry as the original mode of presenting truth:

> Poetry is older than skillfully elaborated prosaic speech. It is the original presentation of truth, a knowing which does not yet separate the universal from its living existence in the individual, which does not yet oppose law to appearance, end to means and then relate them together again by abstract reasoning, but which grasps the one only in and through the other. Therefore it does not at all take something already known independently in its universality and merely express it in imagery. According to its immediate essential nature it abides by the substantive unity of outlook which has not yet separated opposites and then related them purely externally. … With this way of looking at things, poetry presents all its subject matter as a totality complete in itself and therefore independent; this whole may be rich and may have a vast range of relations, individuals, actions, events, feelings, sorts of ideas, but poetry must display this vast complex as perfect in itself, as produced and animated by a single principle which is manifested externally in this or that individual detail. Consequently the universal and rational are not expressed in poetry in abstract universality and philosophically proved interconnection, or with their aspects merely related together as in scientific thinking, but instead as animated, manifest, ensouled, determining the whole, and yet at the same time expressed in such a way that the all-comprising unity, the real animating soul, is made to work only in secret from within outwards. (1975: 2:973)

Constitutions are poetry in the sense that they possess a totality wherein causes and effects are not separated, but rather exist as a whole. From Hegel's perspective, constitutions are not individually drafted texts, but rather expressions of a consciousness of freedom. In a way, there is only one constitutional macro-text, which cannot be altered—it integrates freedom and civil rights into the organization of the state. The constitutions that came into being after the path-breaking foundational documents in the United States and France are for Hegel but recastings of this ideal master plot that gravitates toward formulation once it has been thought. The striking resemblance of most constitutions finds its explanation in this peculiarity: constitutions are variations on a theme that is not at the disposal of the framers of the constitutional text. There is a certain spectrum of possible phrasing, but the main lines are predetermined. Hegel calls the constitution a "building" in which the "fate" of a people lives (1935: 5). In his treatise on the end of the German state after the Treaty of Lunéville (1801), he praises the ideal state not as a legal construction, but as a natural phenomenon:

> The German Reich is a kingdom like the kingdom of nature with its productions, unfathomable in the large and inexhaustible in the small, and this capacity fills him who is intimate with the infinite details of rights with amazement for the venerability of the German state body and with admiration for this system of most perfect justice. (Hegel 1935: 9)

Drawing on Hegel, the prominent German constitutional scholar Ernst-Wolfgang Böckenförde (1991: 92–114) claimed that the modern, secularized state lives on preconditions that cannot be guaranteed by that very state. He surmises that the constitutional state has to live on "inner bonding forces" that resemble religious belief. For this reason, constitutional prose often uses formulas of self-evidence. The fundamental norms of constitutions are anthropological norms. In the US and French cases, these anthropological norms were formulated in a special foundational document that preceded the constitution: the US Declaration of Independence and the French Declaration of Human Rights, respectively. In both texts, mankind is defined in its assumed essence, and departing from these definitions, the legal design of a state can be described in the subsequent constitutions.

The rhetorical genre of declaration belongs to so-called performative speech acts. Such speech acts achieve their effect by the mere fact of enunciation. In the title of his famous book from 1962, the British philosopher of language John L. Austin called this relation, "How to do things with words." It is obvious that various legal rituals are performative speech acts. The Swedish legal philosopher Karl Olivecrona (1971: 218–230) drew attention to the performative, quasi-religious, and even magical character of many constitutional provisions that create norms just by being uttered and not by being proven.

The famous formulation in the US Declaration of Independence of 4 July 1776 explicitly draws its legitimation not from an external source but from "self-evident truths":

> We hold these truths to be self-evident, that all men are created equal, that they are endowed by their Creator with certain unalienable Rights, that among these are Life, Liberty and the pursuit of Happiness.—That to secure these rights, Governments are instituted among Men, deriving their just powers from the consent of the governed. (Vile 1997: 255)

The claimed self-evidence of the principles enunciated in this document opens up an ideological vacuum. Since this rhetoric of truth cannot be based on an argument (truth is already itself the basis), the lack of reasoning in the constitution has to be compensated for by a quasi-religious pathos. It is quite interesting to note is that God occurs in this famous phrasing not in a Christian guise. The "creator" is a notion from civil religion. By referring to this entity, the Declaration of Independence defines a very specific anthropology: man is not just an accidental animate being, but acts as a dignified subject of a creation. Man's dignity encompasses eternal and unalienable rights that must be secured by men themselves. The "creator" does not actively participate in this process, but he gives hints to show mankind that it is on the right path. The US statesman and founding father James Madison (Hamilton et al. 2009: 202) noted that the success of the US Constitution suggests the presence of "a finger of that Almighty hand which has been so frequently and signally extended to our relief in the critical stages of the revolution." The revolutionary Thomas Paine ([1791] 1894: 431) even called the US Constitution the "political bible of the state." As several scholars have pointed out, the norms written down in the US Declaration of Independence and the US Constitution form the core of US civil religion (Bellah 1976: 55–73; Hase 2001). Still, in 1952, Justice William O. Douglas wrote in the Supreme Court decision for *Zorach v. Clauson* (343 U.S. 306 [1952]: 312–313): "We are a religious people whose institutions presuppose a Supreme Being" (quoted in De Wolfe Howe 1965: 13).

In these argumentations, Hegel's totality of causes and effects in poetry can be detected very clearly: man possesses dignity, this dignity encompasses eternal rights, and finally the protection of these rights in the form of a good government becomes one of the main tasks of mankind. The US Declaration of Independence states its beliefs not so much as the result of a political decision, but as a metaphysical right. This argumentation explains the excess of pathos that is present in its text. The French Declaration of Human Rights explicitly acknowledges its own poetic dimension. It defines its own rhetorical mode as "solemn" and calls the rights "sacred":

> The representatives of the French people, organized in National Assembly, considering that ignorance, forgetfulness or contempt of the rights of man, are the sole causes of the public miseries and the corruption of governments, have resolved to set forth, in a solemn declaration, the natural, unalienable, and sacred rights of man, in order that this declaration, being present to all

the members of the social body, may unceasingly remind them of their rights and their duties; ... and in order that the demands of the citizens, grounded henceforth upon simple and incontestable principles, may always take the direction of maintaining the constitutions and the welfare of all. (Blaustein and Sigler 1988: 83)

According to this declaration, human rights are neither invented nor constructed. They exist already before they have been acknowledged—but in the act of their enunciation and recognition, they become real. The performative speech act of declaring the human rights is simultaneously the institution of those rights. This conception is very close to Hegel's philosophy of right: the consciousness of freedom is a revolutionary act. Anyone who dares to think freedom is free. Man is thus endowed with a higher dignity that is based not merely on his new legal status as a citizen of a free nation, but also on the consciousness of this freedom. The French Declaration of Human Rights is not just a contract; it is also almost a holy scripture that is granted "in the presence and under the auspices of the Supreme Being." There is a significant Masonic line of tradition that leads to this formulation. Masonic rhetoric is already present in the US Constitution. The first president of the United States, George Washington, had been a Mason since 1753, the Capitol resembles a Masonic temple, and Washington laid its foundation stone according to the Masonic rite. In a famous contemporary painting representing the French Declaration of Human Rights, the painter Jean-Jacques-François Le Barbier placed the Masonic symbol of the eye of God above the stone tablets of the law (see figure 4.1).

The Declaration of Human Rights itself elicits in its rhetorical form the Catholic catechism, especially the Apostles' Creed: "I believe in God, the Father almighty, creator of heaven and earth. I believe in Jesus Christ, his only Son, our Lord. He was conceived by the power of the Holy Spirit and born of the Virgin Mary. He suffered under Pontius Pilate, was crucified, died, and was buried" (Catechism of the Catholic Church 2006).

The Declaration of Human Rights could also put the performative formula "I believe that ..." at the beginning of each article:

Art. 1. Men are born and remain free and equal in respect of rights. Social distinctions shall be based solely upon public utility.

Art. 2. The purpose of all civil associations is the preservation of the natural and imprescriptible rights of man. These rights are liberty, property, security and resistance to oppression.

Art. 3. The nation is essentially the source of all sovereignty; nor shall any body of men or any individual exercise authority which is not expressly derived from it. (Peaslee 1956: 2:20)

As in the Catholic catechism, these elements are not just part of a personal belief that might be true. The truth of these sentences cannot be contested, because they form the ideological basis of two important institutions: the Roman Catholic Church and the French Republic. Rhetorically, the presence or

4.1. Jean-Jacques-François Le Barbier's 1789 representation of the French *Déclaration des droits de l'homme et du citoyen.*

absence of the performative formula "I believe" matters little, because the veridiction in both cases makes an absolute claim: neither believer nor citizen is free to decide upon the truth of the text. Rather, they are part of the text. Their task is not to discuss or even criticize the content, but instead to acknowledge its validity.

A similar rhetorical gesture can be observed in the Constitution of the Batavian Republic from 1798. It created a state in the Netherlands that was completely under Napoleon's control and was therefore heavily influenced by the French Constitution of 3 September 1791. However, there are national specifics that already become clear in the very first articles of the Constitution of the Batavian Republic (Elias 2001: 43–52):

> Article 1: The happiness of a people resides principally in the wisdom of the laws that it gives itself.
>
> Article 2: The laws must always be the result of experience, and have to be adapted as much as possible to the genius, the manners of the Nation, and the peculiar circumstances of the land.
>
> Article 3: The main principle of social freedom consists in the fact that the law guarantees the same rights to and imposes the same duties on all citizens regardless of their rank or birth. (*Constitution de la République Batave* 1805: 3; my translation)

The Batavian Constitution preserves the declarative character of the French foundational documents. But at the same time, it underlines the fact that the Netherlands were a client state of the French Republic. The Batavian Constitution must serve a double purpose: it must implement the general rhetoric inspired by the French Declaration of Human Rights and in addition insist on the national sovereignty of the Dutch people. From this perspective, Article 1 even gains a subversive meaning: if the happiness of the Dutch people depends on the wisdom of its laws—and of course the Batavian Constitution is the most prominent case in point—then these laws must not aim for an absolute, but rather for a relative good. In the given situation, the Dutch had to express their patriotism within the narrow framework of French hegemony—and they pushed their political aspirations to the limits. Article 2 explicitly relativizes the universality of laws—the Batavian Constitution is much more prominently a *national* constitution than is the French Constitution.

The Constitution of the Helvetic Republic (1798) emerged in a similar historical situation to that of Batavia. After Prussia and Austria had lost the War of the First Coalition (1792–1797) against revolutionary France, Napoleon instigated revolutionary movements in the tributary regions of the old Swiss Confederation. The French army invaded Switzerland and created a new political order, which required a constitution. The text clearly draws on the French example and states the unalienable rights of man. The author, the Mason Peter Ochs, added a moral provision that had basically nothing to do with human rights or political order:

> Article 14: The citizen is indebted to his fatherland, his family, and the unhappy. He cultivates friendship, but he does not sacrifice any of his duties. He abjures all personal resentments and any motif of vanity. He wants only the moral ennoblement of the human race; he invites incessantly the mellow sentiments of brotherhood; his glory is the esteem of the good people, and his conscience knows how to reward him for the refusal of this esteem. (Quoted in Salamin 1969: 17–19; my translation)

There is, however, a difference from the French model. The normativity of the Constitution of the Helvetic Republic is not derived from a higher being, but resides in the text. This is a more radical solution: whereas the French Declaration of Human Rights invokes a "Supreme Being" and thus introduces an external element to a poetic text in Hegel's sense, the Helvetic text relies completely on itself and mirrors Hegel's poetic totality. The constitutional validity is couched in the Masonic ethics of self-perfection—the constitutional state shall be the community of free citizens whose behavior is governed by their moral self-control.

Finally, the Polish Constitution of 1791 voices its own historical experience when it calls for a strong executive authority, namely, the king: "The most perfect government cannot exist without an effectual executive power. Experience has taught us that the neglecting of this essential part of government has overwhelmed Poland with disasters" (Blaustein and Sigler 1988: 75).

Authority and the Authorial Voice

Because the early constitutions claim to establish a new political order, their main task is to speak with authority. The most famous case in point is the formula "We the People" in the preamble to the US Constitution. The authorial voice here serves simultaneously as the object of the text. The enunciation of the will of the people constitutes not only the state, but also the people itself. In a performative speech act, the people become a community: saying "we" means becoming "we."

Constitutions do have authors—in the United States the founding fathers, in France the Constitutional Assembly, in Norway the deputies at Eidsvold. But the rhetorical structure of constitutions requires the effacement of personal authorship. Self-evidence of values is the presupposition of the texts— and therefore constitutions may not be presented as the work of one or many authors. The norms in a constitution are not legitimized by personal authority, logical argument, or even the vote of a majority. Their validity has to be detached rhetorically from personal invention or construction. The authorship of a constitution must be concealed; the text itself takes up the place of the author. The constitutional authorial voice does not allow for objections—with ultimate authority, it states the new political order and purports to speak for all citizens. Even stylistically, there should not be a trace of the author's literary preferences. The Constitution of the Helvetic Republic could be too easily recognized as the work of Peter Ochs (Kopp 1992), and was hence ridiculed as *Ochsenbüchlein* (booklet of an ox).

The subject of enunciation of a constitution is the people. This does not mean that the constitution is deprived of any style. The style of the people is the pathos of self-empowerment. The people speak with the full consciousness of their own political weight and therefore make neither demands nor claims, but ascertainments. The general mode of the constitutional text is the indicative and the general tense is the present. These grammatical categories, however, have a special dimension in the constitutional context. The indicative does not mirror reality, but rather creates the political reality in a performative speech act. The present tense claims to be an eternal tense. The articles of a constitution come without an expiry date—if they had one, their "self-evident truth" would be quite dubious (Bastid 1985: 187; see also chapters by Visconti; Gammelgaard; Jordheim; Warner et al. in this volume).

The real authors hide behind the lyrical subject of the constitutions. They have every reason to do so: in the US case, the authorial statement "We the People" is obviously an exaggeration, because the Federal Convention in Philadelphia consisted of merely fifty-five persons; the Constitution itself was signed by only thirty-nine founding fathers (Parent 2011: 42). The Norwegian Constitution was decided upon by 112 men. The printed version of the document featured the signatures of 104 deputies.

The Norwegian Constitution is a document that is clearly based upon the US and French models (N. Höjer 1882). However, the authors of the Norwegian Constitution do not engage in a pathos of human rights, and the reason for this becomes clear in Article 2: "Jesuits and Monastic orders shall not be tolerated. Jews are furthermore excluded from the Kingdom" (*The Constitution of the Kingdom of Norway* 1814: 3). With these restrictions, the Norwegian Constitution reflects European reservations against Jews and Jesuits, who allegedly conspired against the freedom of democratic states. This was a widespread prejudice in the eighteenth century. Even the French Enlightenment knew this form of discrimination: the philosopher and writer Denis Diderot authored a highly negative entry on the Jesuits for the *Encyclopédie* (Diderot 1766).

Conversely, the characteristics of the Norwegian nation were accurately defined in Article 93: "In the offices of the state must only be employed those Norwegian citizens who profess the Evangelical-Lutheran religion, have sworn obedience to the Constitution and the King, [and] speak the language of the country." Interestingly, the Norwegian Constitution does not define the "language of the country" linguistically. The Constitution itself is written in Danish—in the language of the former colonial power (see also Berge; Madzharova Bruteig in this volume).

As in the Batavian example, the Norwegian Constitution is not a universal, but a national document. Whereas the United States and the French Republic understand themselves as states that are based on universal principles, Norway states its national peculiarity from the outset. Of course, the formulations "We the People" and the French "Nation" also allude to an imagined community with culturally defined characteristics. But the US and French nations are held together in their constitutions by common values that are taken for granted (liberty, equality, welfare, etc.). The Norwegian Constitution laid the groundwork for the independent national state that eventually came into being in 1905. From the very beginning, Norwegian nationalism was opposed to Swedish Scandinavianism (Parent 2011: 103; see also Ringvej in this volume).

A similar orientation toward nationality can be found in the Spanish Constitution of 1812, which carefully defines the Spanish nation in the first chapter:

> Article 5. The following are Spaniards:
> 1. All free men born and resident in the Spanish dominions, and their children;
> 2. Foreigners who have obtained certificates of naturalization from the Cortes;
> 3. Foreigners who, without such certificate, reside ten years in a district, may obtain it, according to law, in any town of the monarchy;
> 4. Freedmen as soon as they obtain their liberty in Spain.
>
> Article 6. Love of his country is one of the principal obligations of all Spaniards, as well as justice and beneficence. (Blaustein and Sigler 1988: 118)

There is quite a spectrum of authorial voices in the early constitutions. The US Constitution engaged in a pathos of human rights but extended them only to white males. Quite telling is Section 2 of Article I, which regulates the political representation of the member states: "Representatives and direct taxes shall be apportioned among the several states … by adding to the whole number of free persons, including those bound to service for a term of years, and excluding Indians not taxed, three-fifths of all other persons" (Vile 1997: 29). "Other persons" meant slaves from the Southern states—this issue was suspended at the Philadelphia Convention for twenty years and remained controversial until after the Civil War and the adoption of the Thirteenth Amendment, which eventually abolished slavery in 1865. The authorial voice of the US Constitution can aptly be defined as the revolutionary consciousness of the Republican Party as it was later most prominently incarnated by the abolitionist Abraham Lincoln.

The French Constitution of 1791 is probably the most universalistic document among the early constitutions. The French revolution was primarily a social, not a national revolution. The independence of the nation was not at stake in 1789, but social justice and economic welfare were. The lyrical subject of the French Constitution is the *citoyen* (citizen), not the *Français* (Frenchman). Most clearly, the difference between the French and other cases may be observed in the slogan *liberté, égalité, fraternité,* which was modified in the newly established Swiss canton of Vaud in the year 1803 to *liberté et patrie* (freedom and fatherland) in order to stress the independence from the occupants of Bern. The text of the Vaud Constitution, however, does not reflect this patriotic dimension—it just soberly organizes the separation of powers (*Constitution du canton de VAUD* 1803).

The Dutch, Spanish, and Norwegian constitutions are very much preoccupied with the national independence of their states. In all three cases, "freedom" meant not only civil freedom in the sense of habeas corpus, but freedom as national self-determination. The authorial voice of these constitutions belongs, therefore, to the patriotic people that acknowledge their own freedom. However, in all three cases the independence was quite conditional: the Netherlands and Spain had been invaded by the French army and had to accept a king who was appointed by Napoleon. Half a year after the adoption of its constitution, Norway had to agree to a personal union with the Kingdom of Sweden. However, we must not forget the fact that most European constitutions were a revolutionary export from France, just as were the Bonaparte family members who ascended European thrones by appointment of their mighty relative, the French emperor (Hawgood 1939: 40). In Germany, many principalities granted their people a constitution because they feared a revolution like that in France. In 1866, Otto von Bismarck (then prime minister of Prussia) maintained that if there was to be a revolution, it would be better to make it than to suffer it (Pflanze 1998: 317).

The poetics of a constitution mainly relies on authority. The constitutional text emanates from an instance of expression that has three main features: the authorial voice does not have a name, it promises a high degree of authenticity, and it is monologic. The namelessness allows for identification: ideally, every citizen may recognize his own dignity in the constitution and perceive himself as a revolutionary hero. Authenticity is important because it enhances the truthfulness of a constitution: the validity of the articles is highlighted by a sincere voice that claims unconditional credibility. Finally, constitutions may not be debated or contested. They consist of statements, not of proposals for discussion. Therefore, they are deeply monologic—and can be likened to the expression of a lyrical subject who speaks for himself and does not expect an answer.

Positivity and Negativity

Most constitutions must not only be read with respect to their positive state-ments. Even more important is the explicit or implicit image of the negative political order that is presented as a bogey if the constitution is not respected.

The US Declaration of Independence is rhetorically modeled upon a dis-tinction between the "good" colonists and the "evil" British (Lucas 1989: 67–130). Thereby, this text inverted the cliché of the "dangerous nation," as the United States was seen to be by the British (Kagan 2006). The US Constitution developed the principles of the Declaration of Independence further. Not de-duction, but finality is the main argument in the US Constitution from 17 September 1787. The preamble starts with an enumeration of goals that are to be achieved:

> We the People of the United States, in Order to form a more perfect Union, es-tablish Justice, insure domestic Tranquility, provide for the common Defence, promote the general Welfare, and secure the Blessings of Liberty to ourselves and our Posterity, do ordain and establish this Constitution for the United States of America. (Peaslee 1956: 3:582)

This text must also be read against the odious traditional order of the British colonial regime. Every noble political principle that is solemnly named in this preamble is the sheer opposite of what is allegedly customary in the British kingdom. The implicit message points to the danger of not adopting this con-stitution—if the constitution fails, the population in the new territories will fall back to the status of British colonialists, with the duty of paying taxes but without political rights.

The US Constitution establishes legitimacy by not posing the problem, but by performing a speech act in which the nation is virtually present: the for-mula "We the People" does not evoke the legitimacy of a political representa-tion, but instead points to a *volonté générale*. The general volition of the people is an abstract entity that is supposedly there, but needs to be recognized and formulated. The lack in number of representatives at the Philadelphia Conven-tion is compensated by a surplus of pathos: justice, tranquility, welfare, and lib-erty are among the common goods that the Constitution is about to produce. The US Constitution enumerates the positive effects in order to stress the vital importance of its own text.

The same metaphysical goal can be achieved by other rhetorical means. The French Constitution of 1791 has a preamble that is ripe with negative formulations:

> The National Assembly, wishing to establish the French Constitution upon the principles which it has just recognized and declared, abolished irrevocably the institutions that have injured liberty and the equality of rights.

> There is no longer nobility, nor peerage, nor hereditary distinctions, nor distinctions of orders, nor feudal regime, nor patrimonial jurisdictions, nor any titles, denominations, or prerogatives derived therefrom, nor any order of chivalry, nor any corporations or decorations which demanded proofs of nobility or that were grounded upon distinctions of birth, nor any superiority other than that of public officials in the exercise of their functions.
> There is no longer either sale or inheritance of any public office.
> There is no longer for any part of the nation nor for any individual any privilege or exception to the law that is common to all Frenchmen.
> There are no longer jurandes, nor corporations of professions, arts, and crafts.
> The law no longer recognizes religious vows, nor any other obligation which may be contrary to natural rights or to the constitution. (Blaustein and Sigler 1988: 85)

By pointing out the negative sides of the ancien régime under the absolutist king, the French Constitution highlights the enormous progress achieved with the adoption of the new political order. The negative formulations enhance the contrast between the gloomy past and the bright future to come.

Positivity and negativity may also be mixed, as this example of the Polish Constitution of 3 May 1791 shows:

> Convinced, by a long train of experience, of many defects in our government, and willing to profit by the favourable moment which has restored us to ourselves; free from the disgraceful shackles of foreign influence; prizing more than life the external independence and internal liberty of our nation; in order to exert our natural rights with zeal and firmness, we do solemnly establish the present constitution, which we declare wholly inviolable in every part, till such period as shall be prescribed by law; when the nation, if it should think fit, may alter by its express will such articles therein as shall be found adequate. (Blaustein and Sigler 1988: 73)

The Norwegian Constitution—unlike the French and US constitutions—does not point to the evils to be avoided or to the goods to be achieved. Even though the first section is entitled "Form of Government and Religion," the Constitution starts with the definition of the territory and the assertion of sovereignty: "The Kingdom of Norway is a free, independent, indivisible and inalienable Realm" (*The Constitution of the Kingdom of Norway* 1814: 3). This seemingly undramatic formulation has a deeper meaning. The excess of adjectives only superficially hides the fact that in May 1814, all of these characteristics were far from being obvious. Norway had been under Danish rule for the last three hundred years, the hitherto Norwegian islands Iceland, Faroe, and Greenland were lost, and the kingdom itself could hardly maintain its autonomy—already in November 1814 the Constitution had to be modified and Norway had to accept a personal union with Sweden.

The first article of the Norwegian Constitution presents as self-evident what was by no means clear. The real political danger was compensated with a surplus of rhetorical confidence. Positivity in the Norwegian case is repelled negativity.

Conclusion

The end of the eighteenth century saw a rise of constitutions in the Western world. This process was triggered by a global crisis that had economic, political, and social aspects. The prominent German historian Reinhart Koselleck (1979: xv) called this period *Sattelzeit* (saddle time) and defined it as a paradigm change in European history. The time between 1750 and 1850 was characterized by the emergence of a new type of citizenship, a new system of production, and a new culture that was not confined to aristocratic circles. After the US Revolutionary War and the French Revolution, the Napoleonic wars served as the main medium of export of republican ideas to Europe. A veritable wave of constitutions followed in many states in Europe at the beginning of the nineteenth century. As a rule, authoritarian rulers hastened to turn their principalities into constitutional monarchies in order to avert revolutionary movements. In most European countries, constitutional movements were suppressed during the nineteenth century. Norway is an exception to this rule. The explanation for this special position goes back to the institutional economy of the situation: both neighboring imperial powers, Denmark and Sweden, were in a period of transition. They had limited economic and military resources and faced the problem of how to govern the rebellious Norwegians without too many expenditures. The chosen solution (a Norwegian constitution with an eventual personal union with Sweden) lasted for almost one hundred years.

A special rhetoric was needed to shape the new political design of the time. Hegel, a very astute observer of these developments, tried to combine political, anthropological, and aesthetic aspects in his universalistic philosophy. The early constitutions belong to the genre of poetry as it was defined by Hegel: they do not engage in prosaic arguments about the relation of cause and effect or means and end, but instead state their ideals as self-evident truths that not only do not need, but even would be compromised by a logical proof. The constitutions create authority by using the rhetoric of a collective "we." The new state, founded on a constitution, is an imagined community of people and ultimately offers membership to every citizen. The dignity of this process must not be underestimated: on 19 May 1814, the Danish crown prince Christian Frederik answered the Constitutional Assembly, which had offered the Norwegian crown to him, thusly:

> Norwegians! The high calling, to which you are elected by the trust of your fellow Citizens, is finished. The Constitution of Norway is founded; the Norwegian people has maintained its rights through you, its selected Deputies; it has maintained them for futurity, and, by a sage distribution of the power, secured civil Liberty and that public order which the executive power is obliged and able to preserve. (*The Constitution of the Kingdom of Norway* 1814: 39)

The pathos in this answer implies that by the force of the Constitution, not only is the king crowned, but also every man is elevated to the rank of Norwegian citizen, which is of no lesser importance than the throne itself.

The solemn inauguration of the national citizen does not work for every constitution: while the US Constitution had social reservations about Native Americans and slaves, the Norwegian and Spanish constitutions carefully defined their national citizens.

Constitutions explicitly or implicitly draw a picture of their enemy. They may use positive or negative rhetorical devices in order to persuade their audience. In all cases, constitutions perform speech acts that call a political order into being.

►• 5 •◄

Constitution as a Transnational Genre

Norway 1814 and the Habsburg Empire 1848–1849

*Karen **Gammelgaard***

Introduction

Following the American and the French revolutions in the late eighteenth century, a revolutionary understanding of "constitution" began to spread in Europe. "Constitution" began to be regarded as having the form of a written document, as having its genesis in popular sovereignty, as including protection of human rights, and as describing the separation of powers and popular participation in government (Grimm 1990; Holmøyvik 2012). The understanding of "constitution" as a written document allows considering "constitution" as a genre: a category of texts similar in form, style, content, and the social actions they represent.

To contribute to identifying characteristics of the constitution genre, in this chapter I compare the Norwegian Constitution of 4 November 1814 with three constitutions for the Habsburg Empire that were framed from 1848 to 1849. Some of the framers of the Habsburg Empire constitutions knew the Norwegian Constitution. Rather than tracing direct influences, however, I deal in a comparative analysis, with the selected constitutions as instantiations of a shared transnational genre. A shared genre does not mean that all texts adhering to that genre have identical end results. The Habsburg Empire constitutions led to authoritarian restoration. Identifying the characteristics of these constitutions may contribute to clarifying how the constitutional genre may be used to achieve aims very different from those pursued by the framers of the Norwegian Constitution in 1814.

The constitutions for the Habsburg Empire include the so-called Pillersdorf Constitution promulgated on 25 April 1848, the so-called Kremsier Draft framed between 2 August 1848 and 7 March 1849, and the so-called Stadion Constitution promulgated on 7 March 1849. These three constitutions reflect a year of turmoil when the Habsburg Empire experienced a social (mainly agrarian) revolution and a number of national revolutions in addition to the constitutional revolution (and reaction against it) focused on here.[1]

The Pillersdorf Constitution (named after Interior Minister Franz von Pillersdorf) was the Crown's attempt at framing a constitution, meeting demands from Vienna revolutionaries in March 1848. It was meant as a preliminary constitution only. The task of framing a lasting constitution was given to the Constituent Assembly, elected in the early summer of 1848. Its 383 deputies convened on 10 July 1848 in Vienna. Negotiations in the assembly were interrupted in October when revolutionaries staged a new insurrection in Vienna and the Crown's brutal repressions followed. On 22 November 1848, the assembly reconvened in the small town of Kremsier,[2] from which the Kremsier Draft takes its name. Negotiations in Kremsier continued until 7 March 1849, when in the early morning the Crown's troops surrounded the assembly's meeting place. The assembly was declared dissolved and, at the same time, the Stadion Constitution (so named after Interior Minister Franz Stadion) was issued by imperial authority alone.

All three 1848–1849 Habsburg Empire constitutions were written first in German and then translated into the main languages of the multiethnic empire. However, only the German and Czech versions of the constitutions are preserved.[3]

Naturally, the languages used to frame the Habsburg Empire constitutions differed from the language of the Norwegian Constitution. The 1814 Norwegian Constitution was written in Danish, the administrative language of Denmark-Norway (see Madzharova Bruteig in this volume). Yet, despite linguistic differences, the Norwegian Constitution and the Habsburg Empire constitutions shared discursive patterns that enabled framers and readers to identify the documents as instances of the constitution genre. In this chapter, I trace these patterns by focusing on how framers turned the principle of popular sovereignty into text, how they segmented texts and connected text components, how they selected words, how they expressed that constitutions were actions with legal force, and how they reflected their knowledge of their historical context.

Analysis of the Norwegian Constitution is based on the 4 November 1814 edition adopted by Storthinget on the occasion of the union between Norway and Sweden. In that edition, some articles of the 17 May Constitution were changed. Most prominently, the first sentence in Article 1 now stated, "Norway is a free, independent, indivisible, and inalienable Kingdom, united with Sweden under one king."[4] The 4 November Constitution is used here because this version gained fame abroad. As we shall see, international interest stemmed partly from how the 4 November Constitution combined the central features of modern constitutions with governance in a multiethnic state.

Analyses of the Habsburg Empire constitutions are based on their versions in the contemporary press. In most cases, analysis of the Kremsier Draft is based on the version agreed to by the Constituent Assembly's Constitutional Committee on 2 March 1849. This version did not contain the articles on human rights (called "Fundamental Rights"), although articles 7–32 were reserved for them. However, only the first thirteen articles were approved in their final form. Conventionally, when the Kremsier Draft is published, the human rights articles are printed in the form approved by the Constitutional Committee. They are placed as an appendix and numbered articles 1–27. When quoted below, these articles are numbered in the same way and referred to as Kremsier Draft–Rights (KD–R).

Genre

People spontaneously categorize texts into genres, deducing each text's genre from its discursive pattern. Most often, such categorizing is done for texts in the same language. However, some texts display similar discursive patterns across languages. Such texts represent instances of transnational genres.

Genres are understood here as typified social actions that are mediated by discourse (see Miller 1984). This understanding implies that when people are acting by framing a text, they are applying the discursive patterns that correlate with the patterns of the relevant genre. In turn, the genre's discursive patterns enable people to recognize which action is carried out through the individual text. For example, when deputies were framing the Norwegian Constitution in 1814 at Eidsvold and in Christiania, they knew that they were doing just that, framing a constitution, because they were applying the discursive patterns of the constitution genre. Similarly, when, in 1848 and 1849 in Vienna and Kremsier, the Habsburg Empire ministers and Constituent Assembly deputies were framing constitutions, they knew they were doing just that because they were applying the discursive patterns of the constitution genre. The discursive patterns are the keys to the framers' actions and to the political choices and compromises contained in those actions.

Similar or identical features recur in a particular genre's individual texts. If a genre is transnational, these features may be expected to be relatively stable across languages. These stable features secure the genre's identity. Yet, when people create new texts within a particular genre, they use their competence and creativity to meet the demands of the specific situation. Therefore, genres are dynamic as well (see van Dijk 2008: 44). Every genre changes by every new text produced in that genre.

The transnational character of the constitution genre is reflected in the fact that to name the genre, people in many linguistic communities use loanwords based on the Latin *constitutio*. The famous US and French documents that established the modern constitution genre were titled "constitution." In the first half of the nineteenth century, in the three languages relevant for the analyses here, the genre was often named *Constitution* (Danish and German) or *konstituce* (Czech). These names, however, competed with names of domestic or other origin. Moreover, people continually negotiated the meanings of "constitution," negotiations that reflected different knowledge of constitutions and different views on government. In addition, negotiations concerned the very question of whether "constitution" meant a written document (see Michalsen in this volume).

In Norway by 1814, most political actors had arrived at an understanding of *Constitution* as a written constitution in its revolutionary form, an act of the sovereign people represented by an elected constituent assembly. *Constitution* had become synonymous with the until then prevalent term *Grundlov*, and the meaning of coexisting terms *Forfatning* (equivalent of the German *Verfassung*), *Statsforfatning*, and *Regieringsform* were transformed by this shift in meaning (see Holmøyvik 2012; Holmøyvik in this volume).

In the Habsburg Empire, the situation was more complex. In the nineteenth century, public debate was conducted in several national languages following the geographical distribution of the multiethnic population. Throughout the empire, only German served all functions of justice, legislation, and government (Hlavačka 2005). German also predominated in advanced learning. Accordingly, representatives of the national elites spoke and wrote German in addition to their mother tongue. Presumably, their understandings of "constitution" developed hand in hand with the understandings developing in the German linguistic community.

In Germany in the first half of the nineteenth century, relatively few participants in public debate understood "constitution" in line with the revolutionary understandings spreading from the United States and France and adopted in Norway. Instead, many debaters understood *Verfassung* in a more evolutionary way, as an "expression of a concrete and historical existence" (Grimm 1990: 882). They toned down popular sovereignty as a requirement for the genesis of *Verfassung* and paid little attention to *Verfassung* as a document. In the Frankfurt Assembly, the first freely elected constituent assembly for all of Germany in May 1848, the revolutionary understanding of *Verfassung* prevailed for the first time.

In the Habsburg Empire, public debate on constitutions heated up after freedom of the press was proclaimed on 14 March 1848 (Oleschowski 2006). The number of newspapers and other periodicals greatly increased (Höbelt 2006). Many shared an interest in constitutions. Vienna daily *Die Presse* followed closely and critically the negotiations in the Constituent Assembly and reported on the course of events abroad, particularly in Germany. Inspiration was sought from afar, too. Thus, *Die Presse* described the political and economic situations in Norway in a series of articles called "Über der Verfassung Norwegens" (On the Norwegian Constitution). On 27 July 1848, the editors of *Die Presse* explained their reasons for printing the series, citing Norway's unique constitutional situation:

> But what gives us the right to direct the reader's attention to a distant rocky country and its institutions, the reader who is busy at this moment with the constitutional activity of his own country? Norway is in these moments the only democracy in Europe. In the awareness of the Austrian people, the essence of democracy has taken root so deeply that he who would give Austria a constitution other than a democratic one, would need first to create a different nation. That is why we point to Norway.

In the Czech lands, too, constitutions were a hot issue. In the wave of hope and enthusiasm in early 1848, "a constitution polka was danced, people greeted each other by a constitution greeting, and one could even satisfy one's hunger with constitution bread rolls" (Efmertová and Savický 2009: 33). While the Constituent Assembly began work, the Prague weekly *Kwěty a plody* printed a translation of the Norwegian Constitution of 4 November 1814. The Czech political elite's dual interest in a new constitutional order for the Habsburg Empire—democracy *and* national emancipation—appears in how the editors justified their printing of the Norwegian Constitution. On 5 August 1848, they explained:

> Having in mind to submit in this journal some of the most important constitutions, we began with the Norwegian one because its democratic tendency matches the predominant mood best, and because here the undertaking of fusing two realms under one crown is solved very carefully in an extraordinary way.

For "constitution," the Czech linguistic community had the word *ústawa*. In the early nineteenth century, jurisprudence was not conducted in Czech at any university. In the Czech lands, as elsewhere in the Habsburg Empire, most advanced learning was conducted in German. Therefore, the meanings of central legal and political terms, such as *ústawa,* were vague. The authoritative 1835–1839 Czech-German dictionary explained that *ústawa* spanned meanings such as "regulation," "statute," "resolution," and "*constitutio*" (quoted in Jungmann [1838] 1989–1990). Czech coinages of *constitutio* were used in the press, albeit not in any strict way. The Pillersdorf Constitution appeared both as *Konstituční zákon* (constitutional law) and as *Ústawní listina* (constitutional document). The editors who printed the Norwegian Constitution entitled it

Konstituce norwežská (Norwegian Constitution), subtitling the articles of the constitution proper *Základní zákon říše norwežské* (Fundamental law of the Norwegian realm).[5]

Many debaters tried to explain "constitution" to the Czechs. For example, on 19 March 1848 in *Pražské nowiny* political leader František Palacký explained "constitution" as a right and system of government, according to which the ruler "is required in all important matters relating to general law and order in the country, to hear first the entire nation's request and respect it." On 6 April 1848, again in *Pražské nowiny*, Wládař Pomoří (probably a pseudonym) summed up the meaning of "constitution" in four points: (1) deputies as popular sovereignty, (2) law of finances, (3) freedom of expression, and (4) freedom of national guards. In sum, Czech understandings of "constitution" reflected ideas on popular sovereignty, separation of powers, and human rights. The idea of constitutions as written documents emerged when editors named the constitutions they published.

In the Constituent Assembly, many deputies acknowledged inspiration from foreign constitutions. A particularly popular source of constitutional knowledge was Karl von Rotteck and Karl Theodor Welcker's multivolume *State Encyclopedia*. In Volume 11 (1841), an entry on Norway included a detailed description of the Norwegian Constitution, emphasizing its genesis in popular sovereignty. Perhaps a deputy recalled this entry when, during discussions on the proposed article on religious freedom, he argued, "I remember that one of the most liberal constitutions, namely the Norwegian one, tolerates no monasteries" (Fischel 1912: 119). Other foreign constitutions inspired deputies even more. For example, the chairman of the subcommittee responsible for framing the articles on human rights explained that "the North American, the Belgian, the Prussian, and other constitutions in addition to Robespierre's Human Rights had hovered before the subcommittee" (Fischel 1912: 7).[6] Deputies also referred to the French constitutions and to the Frankfurt Assembly's "Fundamental Rights." Essential for the analysis here is that the framers in the Habsburg Empire in the period 1848–1849 as well as the framers in Norway in 1814 used foreign constitutions not only as inspiration for which rights should be introduced and how government should be regulated; they were also inspired (perhaps without realizing it) by how rights and government could be framed in text.

Putting Popular Sovereignty into Text

Popular sovereignty underpins the revolutionary understanding of "constitution." Yet, how do framers put this principle into text? In perhaps the most famous declaration of popular sovereignty, that of the Constitution of the

United States of 1787, the principle was placed in the preamble and phrased thus: "We the people … do ordain and establish this constitution." In the Norwegian Constitution, the principle of popular sovereignty was included in Article 49—"The people shall exercise the legislative power through a Storthing"—and in Article 112, which through Storthinget gave the people the right to constitutional amendments.

The deputies of the Habsburg Empire's Constituent Assembly attempted to phrase the principle of popular sovereignty directly in the constitution's articles. On 26 September 1848, the Constitutional Committee presented its proposal on the human rights section. In Article 3 of this proposal, the principle of popular sovereignty was phrased as follows: "All state powers emanate from the people and are applied in the manner specified in the Constitution."[7]

However, after the Crown's troops had quelled the Vienna insurrection in October, many deputies lost all hope of reforming the empire, and their support faded for the human rights articles. Before the first reading, a majority of the Constitutional Committee deleted Articles 1 and 2 and the first sentence in Article 3. However, they kept the core phrasing of the principle of popular sovereignty quoted above. That phrasing now became Article 1. With this Article 1, the human rights articles had their first reading in the Constituent Assembly on 21 December 1848. Deputies met many articles with loud cheers and approved entering the human rights articles into the second reading without comments (Fischel 1912: xxiv).

The second reading began on 4 January 1849. Yet, before deputies could begin negotiations, Interior Minister Stadion interrupted them. Referring to Article 1, he rejected it as "abstract theory," and declared that "in the form of government of constitutional monarchy, the hereditary monarchical right appears as the sacred and inalienable source of supreme power" (*Offizielle stenographische Berichte* 4 January 1849). After a few confused speeches, further negotiation was postponed. When negotiation resumed on 8 January 1849, most deputies yielded to the pressure from the Crown and discarded the principle of popular sovereignty. In so doing, they discarded an essential feature of a revolutionary constitution.

Deputies continued to work with the aim of presenting a constitution before 15 March 1849. Yet, they had lost enthusiasm. Deputy Adolf Fischhof lamented, "I do not know if these articles are gravestones, on which the inscription says: 'Here lie the wishes of the Austrian peoples,' or if they are the cornerstone of our future freedom" (*Offizielle stenographische Berichte* 29 January 1849). His first alternative proved to be right. Even stripped of the article on popular sovereignty, the draft constitution was too revolutionary for the Crown. It soon became apparent that while the deputies had been working on framing a constitution, central ministers of the emperor's government had been framing *their* constitution, the Stadion Constitution. This constitution lacked any phrasing concerning popular sovereignty and represented a step toward the authoritarian rule that was to characterize the empire's public life in the following decades.

Segmentation and Connectedness

Although only the Norwegian Constitution contains phrasing concerning the principle of popular sovereignty, all four selected constitutions share other discursive patterns. Noticeably, all are segmented into numbered articles, marked by section signs (§). Apart from visually marking the constitutions as texts of legal language, the section signs enable splitting the texts into relatively independent articles. In other words, the section signs render unnecessary many means used to refer to words used earlier in the text, such as personal pronouns. Only the hastily framed Pillersdorf Constitution uses means to refer to the same word across article boundaries (pronouns in the German version and finite verb endings in the Czech version).

The Norwegian Constitution is divided into 112 articles, the Pillersdorf Constitution into 59 articles, and the Kremsier Draft into 160 articles. The Stadion Constitution consists of 123 articles. Just shortly before publication of the Stadion Constitution, its framers decided to publish articles on human rights as a separate law, the so-called *Grundrechtspatent* (Basic Patent Law) (Brauneder 2000: 122). Its thirteen articles are included in the analysis here.

Subdivision of a text reifies a specific order, and order significantly partakes in creating a genre's discursive patterns. All four analyzed constitutions place first those articles that specify the entity for which the individual constitution is to be in force and place last those articles that specify amendment procedures. In addition, similarities exist in the order of sections about the respective powers. First, the executive power is addressed, second, the legislative power, and third, the judicial power. This shared subdivision and order indicate that all four constitutions reflect ideas regarding the separation of powers.

However, similar textual subdivision does not equal identical *balance* of powers. The case of popular participation in government exemplifies differences in balance. In Rotteck and Welcker's *State Encyclopedia* (1834–1843), the entry on Norway emphasized that the Norwegian Constitution's Article 49—"The people shall exercise the legislative power through a Storthing"—and Article 79, which prevents the king from vetoing, "undeniably stamp the Norwegian Constitution as democratic." However, after having discarded the principle of popular sovereignty, the framers of the Kremsier Draft abstained from including phrasing similar to that of the article on popular sovereignty. Even more blatantly undermining the autonomy of the legislative power, the

Stadion Constitution stated that "accordance" between the emperor and the lawmakers was "necessary" on every law (Article 66).[8]

In all four analyzed constitutions, most articles consist of one to three clauses. All articles have a high ratio of main clauses. This simplicity runs counter to the generally acknowledged character of legal language, namely, "the formal and written style coupled with considerable complexity and length" (Cao 2009: 21).

Within articles, all four constitutions move from the whole to parts, from the general rule to exceptions. Accordingly, means frequently used are conjunctions meaning "except," nouns meaning "exception" and "condition," and word order expressing condition. For example, the Norwegian Constitution states: "Nobody shall be punished for any writing ... *unless* he has willfully and openly manifested or caused others to manifest disobedience to the laws" (Article 100). The Habsburg Empire constitutions apply the same pattern: "No one may be arrested, *except* by virtue of a judicial, reasoned command" (KD–R, Article 2).[9] Another way of expressing exceptions consists of using modifiers, as in the Stadion *Grundrechtspatent*: "Any *legally recognized* church and religious community has the right" (Article 2).

Framers may use this relation between general rules and their exceptions to in effect restrict human rights. A telling case concerns the revisions of the human rights articles done by deputies in the Habsburg Empire Constituent Assembly in late 1848 and early 1849. During these revisions, exceptions were added and strengthened. For example, in the first proposal on human rights, the article on the death penalty simply stated: "The death penalty is abolished." After the Vienna insurrection had been quelled in October 1848, the revised version stated: "Death penalty *for political crimes* is abolished." Even more exceptions were added after the Crown's intervention in early January 1849. For example, framers supplemented as follows the general rule about citizens having no limitations for exercising their religion: "as far as this exercise is neither legally nor morally offensive, nor opposes civil or civic obligations" (Article 11). Again, however, even with these added exceptions the Kremsier Draft was more liberal than the Stadion Constitution, which contained comprehensive exceptions. For example, Article 12 of the *Grundrechtspatent* stated that the restricted human rights could be suspended "in the event of war or unrest in the interior."

Vocabulary

Any genre correlates with a particular diction. The analyzed constitutions contain between two thousand and six thousand words.[10] The words most clearly expressing what the texts are about (their topoi) are the so-called autosemantic words, words whose meanings depend least on context.[11] Unsurprisingly, the shared semantic feature of the constitutions' autosemantic words is that they reflect topoi related to the general realm of law. They concern "prescriptions … defining and enforcing the arrangements, relationships, procedures and patterns of behaviour that are to be followed in a society" (Jenkins 1980: 98).

The Norwegian Constitution and the Kremsier Draft show many parallels in their most frequent autosemantic words, particularly the nouns. In the Norwegian Constitution, the most frequent noun is *Storthing*. The Kremsier Draft has *Reichstag* (diet) as the second most frequent noun, topped only by *Gesetz* (law). That both constitutions deal thoroughly with the legislative power appears also from the frequent nouns *Medlem* (member, most often referring to members of Storthinget) in the Norwegian Constitution and *Abgeordneter* (deputy) and *Kammer* (chamber) in the Kremsier Draft. Other frequently applied nouns relate to the executive power: *Konge, Statsraad, Regjering* (king, cabinet, government) in the Norwegian Constitution and *Kaiser, Minister* (emperor, minister) in the Kremsier Draft.

The Stadion Constitution differs from these patterns. Its two most frequent nouns are *Kronland* (crown land) and *Reich* (realm). *Kronland* often combines with the adjectives *einzelen* (single) and *übrigen* (remaining), an expression of the fact that most attention was being given to subdivision of the empire.

The words used in the four constitutions share many specific ways of combining with other words and grammatical forms. For example, the nouns denoting the potentate occur in identical combinations: *Konge* (king) and *Kaiser* (emperor) occur always in the definite form, and in most cases, these nouns function as the grammatical subject. An interesting case concerns the nouns denoting the legislative assemblies. In the Norwegian Constitution, *Storthing* occurs in many different combinations, as does *Reichstag* in the Kremsier Draft. *Storthing* and *Reichstag* function as grammatical subjects and objects, they modify other nouns (when used in the genitive case), and they occur after different prepositions. These varied combinations thoroughly model *Storthing* and *Reichstag* and enrich their meaning. Moreover, in both the Norwegian Constitution and the Kremsier Draft, frequent verbs are those describing activities related to legislative assemblies: *holdes* (assemble) and *møde* (meet) in the Norwegian Constitution, and *wählen* (elect) and *zusammentreten* (meet) in the Kremsier Draft. These verbs further model the legislative power in the texts.

All four analyzed constitutions include many means of expressing completeness. High frequency of these means reveals framers' intention to cover all activities in the area they address. This semantic feature is most often expressed by synsemantic words (words whose meaning stems primarily from context). The constitutions teem with pronouns and prepositional phrases that express completeness. To mention a few: "*Every* citizen shall … be equally bound to perform military service" (Norwegian Constitution, Article 109); "*All* ethnic groups are guaranteed sanctity of their nationality and language" (Pillersdorf Constitution, Article 4);[12] "*Everyone* has the right to freely express his thoughts" (KD–R, Article 18); "The right to petition is available to *everyone*" (Stadion Constitution *Grundrechtspatent*, Article 6). Sometimes completeness is expressed by nominal phrases with definite articles: "*The Austrian citizens* are guaranteed religious liberty" (KD–R, Article 11). Because Czech has no definite articles, in the Czech version, the same right is expressed by the pronoun *každý* (every).

Frequently, completeness appears as negated quantity: "Land and inheritance shall *in no case* be subject to forfeiture" (Norwegian Constitution, Article 104); "*No* religious community (church) enjoys state privileges over others" (KD–R, Article 12). Negated quantity is considerably less frequent in the Stadion Constitution than in the Kremsier Draft.

Performativity

In Visconti's introduction to speech acts in legal language, she states that "[o]ne of the most striking pragmatic properties of legal documents concerns their performative character. Besides norms laying out duties and norms conferring rights, every legal system contains rules productive of legal effects by the very act of being uttered" (Visconti 2009b: 393). Mindful of Visconti's claim, let us first address the relation between the four constitutions and the instances that utter them. The Norwegian Constitution contains an explicit performativity formula in the preamble: "We, representatives of the Norwegian realms assembled at an extraordinary Storthing on 7 October 1814 in Christiania, do hereby proclaim."[13] That the representatives of the sovereign people are the "uttering authority" is thus expressed by the first person plural pronoun "we."

Performativity is very different in the Habsburg Empire constitutions. The Kremsier Draft lacks explicit performativity formulas. This lack reflects the messy situation after the Constituent Assembly deputies discarded the principle of popular sovereignty but nonetheless continued framing a constitution. Their draft of 2 March 1849 prescribes a "Law establishing the Constitution," postponing thus the question of the uttering authority. In the Pillersdorf and the Stadion constitutions, preambles express the authority with the power to establish them, namely, the emperor. The preamble to the Pillersdorf Constitution is perhaps most revealing: "We, Ferdinand the First ... permanently tending to accept that the nations entrusted to us are not left behind ... have secured them by the patent of 15 March to grant a constitution." Similarly, the Stadion Constitution begins with the formula, "We, Franz Joseph the First, Grace of God Emperor of Austria ... prescribe ..." Both constitutions conclude with formulas containing the verb *gegeben* (given) and the names of the emperor and central ministers. The uttering authority is named with all due clarity. Moreover, both constitutions were "given" in advance of publication. The Pillersdorf Constitution was in force from 15 March 1848 but was first published on 25 April. The Stadion Constitution was in force from 4 March 1849 but was published first on 8 March. Therefore, both constitutions refer to actions that have already been taken. Authority was thereby removed from the "very act of uttering" and located in the text-external sovereign. Evidently, the framers of these constitutions did not regard them as documents with a performative character.

On the other hand, what links the Norwegian, the Pillersdorf, and the Stadion constitutions is the so-called thetic speech acts instantiated by the verbs "proclaim," "grant," and "prescribe." In contrast to mere acting through words, when framers utter thetic verbs, they produce a state of affairs. They change an extant situation. Most often, speech acts (including thetic speech acts) are not communicated by means of explicit performativity markers. Instead, the present tense of verbs signal that speech acts are being performed. For example, Article 1 in the Norwegian Constitution states: "Norway is a free, independent, indivisible, and inalienable Kingdom." The present tense ("is") signals a thetic speech act that can be paraphrased thus: "We, deputies of the National Assembly, hereby sanction that the Kingdom of Norway is a free, independent, indivisible, and inalienable Kingdom." In all four analyzed constitutions, almost all verbs are in the present tense and signal speech acts. The generic convention of present tense verbs is unaffected by the character of the uttering authority (see also Warner et al.; Visconti; Schmid; Jordheim in this volume).

In many instances, equivalents of "is" link sentences' grammatical subjects with the subject complements. In those cases, meaning is carried by the complements: "Whoever is chosen representative is *in duty bound to accept the office*" (Norwegian Constitution, Article 63); "Science and its teaching are *free*" (KD–R, Article 16). Consider also Article 1 of the Kremsier Draft: "The Empire of Austria is *an indivisible constitutional hereditary monarchy.*" This wording is similar to that in Article 1 of the Norwegian Constitution. By being uttered, both opening articles change the extant character of the relevant entities. Therefore, the constructions with equivalents of "is" represent powerful thetic speech acts. The Pillersdorf and Stadion constitutions use descriptive verbs in their opening articles: "All countries belonging to the Austrian Empire *make up* an indivisible constitutional monarchy" (Pillersdorf Constitution); "The Empire of Austria *consists* of the following Crown lands" (Stadion Constitution). These articles do not change the world in the same way the opening articles of the Norwegian Constitution and the Kremsier Draft do. Rather, they sanction that what they describe is the case.

Specific kinds of thetic speech acts are communicated by the relatively frequent so-called anairectic verbs. Anairectic verbs (defined by Conte 2002; see also Visconti 2009b) are verbs that by being uttered *undo* an extant state of affairs, such as "Death penalty *is abolished*" (KD–R, Article 4). In the Norwegian Constitution and in the Kremsier Draft, anairectic speech acts are often represented by modal verbs combined with negations: "Torture *shall not* be inflicted" (Norwegian Constitution, Article 96); "*No* religious society *may* be given leading influence on public schools" (KD–R, Article 17). Similar constructions, as well as anairectic verbs, are less frequent in the Stadion Constitution. Presumably, this difference stems from the fact that the Stadion Constitution's framers intended to continue a tradition. By contrast, the framers of the Norwegian Constitution and the Kremsier Draft intended to undo traditions. These constitutions are revolutionary not only in being written documents with performative force, but also in the sense that their framers intended to change extant governments.

Information Structure

Many thetic speech acts may be understood as such only in the light of their historical situation. For example, the Kremsier Draft states, "The right of petition and of collecting signatures on petitions is unlimited" (KD–R, Article 7). Historical knowledge allows us to understand that until then, the right to petition may have been restricted. Similarly, in a literal translation, the Norwegian Constitution states, "Liberty of the press shall take place" (Article 100).[14] The thetic character of this statement may be understood best in contrast to the situation up to that point, when liberty of the press did not exist (see Berge; Ringvej in this volume).

The dynamics of historical situations are reflected in the constitutions' information structure, too. Information structure reflects the framers' knowledge at the time of framing and what they considered to be the knowledge of their readers. Consider again the introductory articles quoted above. All begin with expressions that denote geographical entities that contemporaries knew. Then, new information is added about those entities. That is to say, these articles follow a general rule of structuring information in texts, namely, that in single utterances, known information tends to be placed first and new information tends to be placed last. Articles concerning the executive power give other clear examples of this rule. Most of these articles begin with the known information ("king" or "emperor") and then add new information about the potentate's specific powers and their limitations.

This distribution of known and new information enables us to elucidate how constitutions are situated historically and locally. Human rights articles demonstrate this situatedness most clearly. They are mostly structured so that a specific punishment or right comes first. Then, as new information, its status is specified. For example, "Torture shall not be inflicted" (Norwegian Constitution, Article 96) and "Death penalty is abolished" (KD–R, Article 4). Information structure in these articles shows that when the constitutions were framed, torture and the death penalty were known phenomena to members of the Danish-Norwegian and German linguistic communities. Other cases show differences between the communities. For example, the Norwegian Constitution states, "The right of search in dwellings shall exist only in criminal cases" (Article 102) and "No on shall be arrested, except in the case and mode prescribed by law" (Article 99). By contrast, the Kremsier Draft and the Stadion Constitution apply terms known in German legal tradition, such as *Hausrecht* and *Freiheit der Person*.[15] These terms needed no explanation by means of paraphrasing. They could simply be followed by information on their new status: "*Das Hausrecht* is inviolable" (KD–R, Article 5) and "*Die Freiheit der Person* is guaranteed" (KD–R, Article 2).

Put differently, differences in information structures stem from what framers considered general knowledge in their respective linguistic communities at the time of framing. The framers of the Kremsier Draft and the Stadion Constitution could use many terms as known information.[16] On the other hand, regarding freedom of expression, it is the Norwegian Constitution that refers to a known entity. Article 100 begins with the term *Trykkefrihed* (liberty of the press). The corresponding article in the Kremsier Draft (Article 18) first explains freedom of expression and then declares that this right may not be limited. The framers communicating with their linguistic communities must have considered explanation of this right necessary. By contrast, the framers of the Norwegian Constitution could rely on knowledge of freedom of expression in the Danish-Norwegian 1814 linguistic community (see also Berge; Ringvej in this volume).

Conclusions

Analysis in this chapter has shown that all four selected constitutions follow these discursive patterns:

- Articles are arranged in sections according to the branches of government. Sections reflect separation of powers. Articles demarcating the constitutional entity come first, and articles on amendments come last.
- Text connectedness is characterized by additive structures and by relations between general rules and exceptions.
- Most autosemantic words include semantic features relating to the general realm of law.
- Means expressing completeness are frequent.

- Nouns denoting the potentate appear as grammatical subject and in the position of known information.
- Verbs are in present tense.

Presumably, these discursive patterns recurred in many European nineteenth-century constitutions. They contributed to defining the transnational constitution genre.

Inclusion of the principle of popular sovereignty distinguishes the Norwegian Constitution from the Habsburg Empire constitutions. Deputies of the Habsburg Empire Constituent Assembly were forced to remove popular sovereignty from their constitution. Nonetheless, the following set of discursive patterns distinguishes the Kremsier Draft and the Norwegian Constitution on the one hand from the Pillersdorf and Stadion constitutions on the other hand:

- Few exceptions from general rules.
- Frequent use of verbs describing activities related to legislative assemblies and rich modeling of nouns denoting legislative power.
- Relatively high presence of anairetic speech acts (expressed by anairetic verbs or modal verbs with negations).

Accordingly, the Norwegian Constitution and parts of the Kremsier Draft stand out particularly in those aspects that are related to the content matter of the constitutions and to the situation of uttering them. Similarities with authoritarian constitutions, such as the Stadion Constitution, mostly concern formal matters.

In other words, in a constitutional text, it is possible to adhere to the revolutionary understanding of "constitution" only formally and to use these formal patterns to pursue authoritarian goals. Increasing exceptions to general rules may undermine the protection of human rights typical of revolutionary constitutions. Separation of powers may be undermined when the constitutional text lacks an adequate modeling of the legislative power. And popular sovereignty may fail to materialize if not explicitly phrased in the constitutional text. In sum, using general discursive patterns of the transnational constitution genre does not guarantee constitutional democracy. To ensure application of the revolutionary understanding of "constitution," discursive patterns reflecting core values of modern constitutionalism should be put into text—as the Norwegian framers did in 1814.

NOTES

1. For general historical accounts of the Habsburg Empire around 1848 see, for example, Kann (1974) and Rumpler (1997).
2. Today, Kremsier (Kroměříž) is located in the east of the Czech Republic.

3. In the Constituent Assembly, German was pragmatically recognized as the language of negotiation (Rumpler 1997: 285).

4. Quotes from the 4 November Constitution stem from its translation into English in 1895 (*The Constitution of the Kingdom of Norway* 1895).

5. Unlike the Constitution of 17 May, the version of 4 November had a preamble. Its first sentence stated, "Given by the Constituent Assembly at Eidsvold on May 17th, and now, on the occasion of the union between the Realms of Norway and Sweden decreed by the Storthing in an extra Session at Christiania, revised and affirmed on November 4th, 1814." (Translated by the author. The preamble is not included in the 1895 translation into English.)

6. Probably, the "North American Constitution" was the US Constitution of 1787. The "Belgian Constitution" was that of 1831. The "Prussian Constitution" was the so-called *Charte Waldeck*, a liberal constitution draft of July 1848.

7. This phrasing quoted almost verbatim Article 25 in the Belgian Constitution of 1831. The first articles also echoed phrasings on popular sovereignty in the Texas Constitution of 1845. Its translation appeared in Rotteck and Welcker's *State Encyclopedia* (1834–1843). Translations from the Habsburg Empire constitutions and parliamentary recordings are the author's. All italics in quotations are the author's.

8. Quotes from the Stadion Constitution (including the *Grundrechtspatent*) stem from *Wiener Zeitung*, 8 March 1849. A Czech version of the Stadion Constitution appeared in *Pražské nowiny*, 9 and 11 March 1849.

9. Quotes from the Kremsier Draft stem from *Entwurf der Constitutions-Urkunde*. 1849. A Czech version of the Kremsier Draft (human rights articles not included) appeared in *Národní nowiny*, 8, 10, 13, and 14 March 1849.

10. The Norwegian Constitution contains about 4,300 words; the Kremsier Draft contains about 5,800 words; and the Stadion Constitution (including the *Grundrechtspatent*) contains about 4,600 words (as measured in the German version). The preliminary character of the Pillersdorf Constitution corresponds to about 2,000 words only.

11. Čermák (2010) describes the theoretical basis for the approach to vocabulary used in analysis in this section.

12. Quotes from the Pillersdorf Constitution stem from *Wiener Zeitung*, 25 April 1848. A Czech version of the Pillersdorf Constitution appeared in *Pražské nowiny*, 27 April 1848.

13. Translated by the author. The preamble is not included in the 1895 translation into English.

14. The 1895 translation into English says, "The liberty of the press shall remain inviolate."

15. Exactly because these terms stem from the specific German legal tradition, they are difficult to translate. *Freiheit der Person* covers the right to move freely. *Hausrecht* covers the right to decide on what happens in a building. In Czech contemporary translations, German terms were adopted as loan translations.

16. The Pillersdorf Constitution used few established terms. Probably, the lack of terms was partly due to haste.

⊢• 6 •⊣

Discursive Patterns in the Italian and Norwegian Constitutions

Jacqueline Visconti

Introduction

The magical nature of legal texts, that is, their capacity of producing extra-linguistic effects, is particularly evident in constitutional texts, which have as their function to constitute, to create, the normative foundation of a state.[1] This property may be one of the reasons underlying the "power" of the genre, as highlighted by Gammelgaard (in this volume). If two historically related constitutional texts are found to share a number of discursive patterns, their commonality may be attributed to their proximity and influence. Yet if two texts, such as the Norwegian and the Italian constitutions, which are set over one hundred years and one thousand miles apart and are written in (relatively) unrelated linguistic and legal settings, nevertheless share a set of discursive patterns, then the hypothesis that such features may be distinctive of the genre is worth pursuing. Using a comparative perspective in this chapter allows for highlighting some of these patterns and for testing the hypothesis that they may be related to a specific textual type. In what follows, I compare the 2012 form of the Norwegian Constitution (on its archaic language and amendments procedures, see Madzharova Bruteig in this volume) with the current Italian Constitution that came into force on 1 January 1948. When the language of the original is not essential for the analytical points, I quote official English-language translations.

The Italian Constitution

"How much blood and how much pain to get to this Constitution! Behind every article, o youth, you must see young people like yourselves, who fell in war, shot, hanged, tortured, starved in concentration camps, who died in Russia, died in Africa, died on the streets of Milan, on the streets of Florence, who gave their lives so that freedom and justice could be written on this charter." Those were the words spoken by one of the fathers of the Italian Constitution, the jurist Piero Calamandrei (1889–1956), in a 1955 speech at the Società Umanitaria (Humanitarian Society) in Milan.[2] As reflected in those words, the dominant attitude among the 556 deputies in the Assemblea Costituente (Constituent Assembly), elected by universal suffrage on 2 June 1946, was deeply antifascist. The election of the Constituent Assembly was held simultaneously with a referendum on abolishing the monarchy. The *Costituzione della Repubblica italiana*, enacted by the Constituent Assembly on 22 December 1947 and which came into force on 1 January 1948, thus aimed at regulating the newborn republican state, one century after the previous constitutional text, the *Statuto Albertino* (Albertine Statute)—which had remained in force till then, though devoid of substantive value—had been granted to the Kingdom of Piedmont and Sardinia by King Carlo Alberto. The Italian Constitution, therefore, evolved in a historical setting very different from that of Norway in 1814. In addition, the introduction of a republican system distinguishes the Italian Constitution from the Norwegian Constitution. If, despite such differences, similarities exist in how the constitutions were put into text, these similarities may help us understand the characteristics of constitutional texts.

The elegant simplicity and clarity of the Italian Constitution's language has inspired numerous linguistic analyses.[3] Ninety percent of the lexicon consists of a simple vocabulary (De Mauro 2006, 2011; Leso 2012); the sentences are short, averaging twenty words, with prevalent parataxis, that is, simple juxtaposition of clauses with rare instances of complex subordination (for details, see Cignetti 2005: 89–92; Korzen 2010: 180–190). Such linguistic features are the result of a long and careful drafting process by the deputies of the Constituent Assembly, which aimed at making the constitutional text as accessible as possible to the majority of citizens (bearing in mind, however, that Italian literacy was estimated to be around 38 percent in 1931, falling to 13 percent in 1951; see De Mauro 2011: 185).[4]

One of the characteristics shared by all normative texts, but particularly important in constitutional texts, is the hierarchical disposition of their content, explicitly organized in partitions. Such a disposition, as we shall see in the section on connectives below, has an important cohesive function.

The Italian Constitution has no preamble (unless one considers as such the twelve articles of the "Fundamental Principles" concerning the democratic foundation of the republic, citizens' equality before the law, etc., as does, e.g., Korzen [2010]). The structure is similar to that of the Norwegian Constitution in that the Italian deputies also defined the executive, the legislative, and the judicial power in separate sections (the executive power is addressed in two sections, one on the president and one on the government). As argued by Holmøyvik (in this volume), separation of powers lies at the heart of modern constitutionalism. Notably, in the Italian Constitution a comprehensive section on citizens' rights and duties precedes the sections on institutional settings.

Textual Features

Given that they define a state's legal foundations, constitutional texts are destined to last over time. This durability is reflected in a set of textual features concerning, first, the explicitness and completeness of the outlined norms. Indeed, constitutional norms are often introduced by universal quantifiers, whether positive, such as "every" and "all," or negative, such as "nobody" and "nothing": "All inhabitants of the Realm shall have the right to free exercise of their religion" (NC, Article 16);[5] "No restriction may be placed on a person's liberty save for as provided by law" (IC, Article 25).[6]

Unlike articles in other normative texts, such as codes or statutes, articles of constitutions almost invariably open with one main clause expressing a general provision, as shown by this example:

> Kongens Myndighetsalder fastsættes ved Lov.
> Saasnart Kongen har opnaaet den lovbestemte Alder, erklærer han sig offentligen at være myndig. (NC, Article 8)[7]

> (The age of majority of the King shall be laid down by law.
> As soon as the King has attained the age prescribed by law, he shall make a public declaration that he is of age.)

Framing adverbials, if present, such as "Saasnart Kongen har opnaaet den lovbestemte Alder" (As soon as the King has attained the age prescribed by law), which frame the main clause, "erklærer han sig offentligen at være myndig" (he shall make a public declaration that he is of age), by specifying more specific circumstances, are located within the body of the article. This textual structure, that is, an opening main clause containing a general provision, optionally followed by a framing adverbial on specific circumstances and their consequence(s), is equally present in the Italian Constitution:

> The President of the Republic is elected for seven years.
> Thirty days before the expiration of the term, the President of the Chamber of Deputies shall summon a joint session of Parliament and the regional delegates to elect the new President of the Republic.
> During dissolution of Parliament or in the three months preceding dissolution, the election shall be held within the first fifteen days of the first sitting of a new Parliament. (IC, Article 85)

Such a textual configuration represents a specific text-typological trait of constitutions, as argued regarding the Italian Constitution by Luca Cignetti (2005: 103). Indeed, in other types of normative texts, a framing adverbial is often found at the very beginning of the article. This is shown in an example from the Italian Criminal Code, where the opening framing adverbial ("In the cases foreseen by Articles 361, 362, 363, etc.") introduces a set of intratextual references:

> In the cases foreseen by Articles 361, 362, 363, 364, 365, 366, 369, 371 bis, 372, 373, 374, and 378, a person is not guilty if forced to commit the offence to defend himself or a close relative from grievous and inevitable damage to their freedom and honor. (*Codice Penale italiano*, Article 384; my translation)

As noted by Cignetti, this configuration would not be typical of a constitutional text. Indeed, examples of intratextual references in the Norwegian Constitution (such as in Articles 17, 44, 80, and 81) are typically found within the body of the article.

To sum up, the Italian and the Norwegian constitutions share two distinctive textual features, the presence of universal quantifiers and the opening of articles by using a main clause. These features set apart constitutions from other normative texts.

Tenses and Types of Norms

When we move further inside the (micro)structure of the constitutional text, we notice the overwhelming prevalence of the present indicative tense in both the Italian and the Norwegian constitutions. Such a formal feature corresponds to a set of important functional distinctions within the realm of normativity. As noted by some scholars of both legal and linguistic backgrounds (see, e.g., Visconti 2009b for an overview), the traditional dichotomy between descriptive and prescriptive discourse fails to account for legal products such as constitutions and other normative texts. Besides norms laying out duties and norms conferring rights, such texts contain rules that produce legal effects by the very act of being uttered, such as: "Den udøvende Magt er hos Kongen" (NC, Article 3; The Executive Power is vested in the King); "Arvefølgen er lineal" (NC, Article 6; The order of succession is lineal); "L'Italia è una Repubblica democratica, fondata sul lavoro" (IC, Article 1; Italy is a democratic Republic founded on labour); "La libertà personale è inviolabile" (IC, Article 13; Personal liberty is inviolable).[8] In a constitutional text, as in other normative texts, such as statutes or codes, utterances like those above neither describe a state of affairs nor prescribe any behavior; rather, they bring about, or, to use a technical term, "constitute," such states of affairs.

One of the first scholars to notice this phenomenon was the philosopher Herbert Spiegelberg (see Di Lucia 1997: 35). In his 1935 *Gesetz und Sittengesetz* (Law and Morality), Spiegelberg identified certain norms, such as those contained in the examples above, that neither have as an object a behavior nor concern a legal obligation or the attribution of rights pertaining to the future. Through these norms, he argues, "a state of affairs is realized that does not allow or need further realization" (Spiegelberg 1935: 54).[9] He called such statements "constitutive norms" (*Gestaltungsgesetze*), as in his example: "Rechtsfähig ist jedermann" (*Schweizer Zivilgesetzbuch,* Article 11; Everyone has legal competency).

Referring to John L. Austin's theory of performative utterances, Gaetano Carcaterra (1994: 228) argues that such constitutive or "dispositive" performatives belong to a previously unforeseen class of performatives, cutting across the five categories envisaged by Austin himself. Underlying constitutive norms would be a performative utterance of the following kind: "By the present norm it is enacted that ..." Constitutive norms are opposed to prescriptive norms. Whereas the former, as said, produce the effect, which is their aim and content, by the very act of being stated, the latter aim at producing an event by exerting pressure on someone's behavior.

Both types of norms are present in the two constitutions analyzed here. Consider the following example of a prescriptive norm from the "Transitional and Final Provisions" section of the Italian Constitution:

> La Repubblica, entro tre anni dall'entrata in vigore della Costituzione, adegua le sue leggi alle esigenze delle autonomie locali e alla competenza legislativa attribuita alle Regioni. (IC, Transitional and Final Provisions, IX)

> (The Republic, within three years of the implementation of the Constitution, shall adjust its laws to the needs of local autonomies and the legislative jurisdiction attributed to the Regions.)

The behavior in question is not brought about by the norm, as in constitutive norms; indeed, as noted by the linguist Bice Mortara Garavelli (2001: 60), such a state of affairs has not been enforced yet.

In Italian, both types of norms can be expressed by the present tense. In prescriptive norms such as that contained in the above example, the present tense verb *adegua* (adjust) can be paraphrased by a modal verb construction, such as *deve adeguare* (must adjust, "shall adjust" in the official translation). Italian models of legal drafting, however, encourage the legislator to use the present tense instead of the modal verb construction whenever such use is unambiguous (see Mortara Garavelli 2001: 114–115). The modal verb construction, including an active or passive infinitive, occurs approximately fifteen times in the Italian Constitution (Mortara Garavelli 2011a). For example: "Ogni altra legge che importi nuove o maggiori spese deve indicare i mezzi per farvi fronte" (IC, Article 81, 4; Any other law involving new or increased spending shall detail the means therefor).

As prescriptive utterances concern states of affairs that are not yet in force, future reference tenses are also well suited for expressing them. Simple future used to be the prevalent tense in older Italian constitutions (Mortara Garavelli 2011b: 4), such as the 1848 *Statuto Albertino* mentioned above, which features twenty-six occurrences of prescriptive future in eighty-four articles, such as: "Il potere legislativo sarà collettivamente esercitato dal Re e da due Camere" (*Statuto Albertino*, Article 3; The legislative power will be jointly exercised by the King and two Chambers).[10] In the current Italian Constitution, on the other hand, the future form occurs just three times, as, for example, in: "La Costituzione, munita del sigillo dello Stato, sarà inserita nella Raccolta ufficiale delle leggi e dei decreti della Repubblica" (IC, Transitional and Final Provisions, XVIII; The Constitution, bearing the seal of the State, shall be included in the Official Records of the laws and decrees of the Republic).

In the Norwegian Constitution, too, prescriptive norms, as well as constitutive norms, can be expressed by the present tense: "Saasnart Kongen har opnaaet den lovbestemte Alder, erklærer han sig offentlig at være myndig" (NC, Article 8; As soon as the King has attained the age prescribed by law, he shall make a public declaration that he is of age). Yet the modal verb construction with the modal verb *skulle* (present tense *skal*) is also used, as in: "Kongen skal bo inden Riget" (NC, Article 11; The King shall reside in the Realm).

The fact that the present tense can be employed in both types of norms, constitutive and prescriptive, explains the high frequency of this tense in both the Italian and the Norwegian constitutions.

Interestingly, in the English-language translation of both constitutions, many instances of present tense indicative are rendered by *shall,* which, as shown, for example, by Garzone (2001), can have both prescriptive and constitutive functions. As well as the Italian example above with *adegua* (translated as "shall adjust"), notice, just to quote a few initial instances in the Norwegian Constitution, Article 8 (*fastsættes,* "shall be laid down"), Article 13 (*afgjøres,* "shall be decided"), Article 14 (*handler,* "shall act"), Article 19 (*vaager,* "shall ensure"), Article 20 (*har,* "shall have"), Article 32 (*udfærdiges … og undertegnes,* "shall be drawn up … and be signed"), and so forth.[11]

Other Modals

Another shared feature in the two constitutions concerns the use of modal "may" forms. Italian modal *potere* ("may," "can") in the present tense indicative *può* corresponds to a set of pragmatic functions: confer a power, grant a right, as in:

> Ogni cittadino può circolare e soggiornare liberamente in qualsiasi parte del territorio nazionale. … Nessuna restrizione può essere determinata da ragioni politiche. (IC, Article 16)
>
> (Every citizen has the right to reside and travel freely in any part of the country. … No restriction may be imposed for political reasons.)

In the negative form, *può* is used to convey a prohibition: "Con la legge di approvazione del bilancio non si possono stabilire nuovi tributi e nuove spese" (IC, Article 81; The budget may not introduce new taxes and new expenditures). Prohibitions are mainly realized by such negative "may not" constructions. Only a handful of passive forms of the verb *vietare* (forbid) or *proibire* (prohibit) are found (see Mortara Garavelli 2011a): "Sono vietate le pubblicazioni a stampa, gli spettacoli e tutte le altre manifestazioni contrarie al buon costume" (IC, Article 21; Publications, performances, and other exhibits offensive to public morality shall be prohibited); "Sono proibite le associazioni segrete e quelle che perseguono, anche indirettamente, scopi politici mediante organizzazioni di carattere militare" (IC, Article 18; Secret associations and associations that, even indirectly, pursue political aims by means of organisations having a military character shall be forbidden).

In the Norwegian Constitution, we find a similar pattern: the modal verb *kunne* (present tense *kan*) is used to grant a right or to confer a power: "Under Kongens Reiser inden Riget kan han overdrage Rigets Bestyrelse til Statsraadet" (NC, Article 13; During his travels within the Realm, the King may delegate the administration of the Realm to the Council of State). The negative present tense forms of the modal verb *maatte* (may), *maa ikke* or *maa ei*, but also negatives occurring with *kan*, are used to convey a prohibition: "Kongen maa ikke modtage nogen anden Krone eller Regjering uden Stortingets Samtykke, hvortil to Trediedele af Stemmerne udfordres" (NC, Article 11; The King may not accept any other crown or government without the consent of the Storting, for which two thirds of the votes are required); "Ægtefæller, Forældre og Børn eller to Søskende maa ei paa samme Tid have Sæde i Statsraadet" (NC, Article 12; Husband and wife, parent and child or two siblings may never sit at the same time in the Council of State); "Ingen kan vælges til Repræsentant uden at være stemmeberettiget" (NC, Article 61; No one may be elected as a representative unless he or she is entitled to vote).

Notice how the English-language translation differs from the original text in the following examples, in which *maa ikke*, literally, "may not," is rendered as "must not" (Article 96); *maa gives* as "must be given" (Article 97); and *maa ikke finde Sted* as "shall not be made" (Article 102):[12] "Ingen kan dømmes uden efter Lov, eller straffes uden efter Dom. Pinligt Forhør maa ikke finde Sted" (NC, Article 96; No one may be convicted except according to law, or be punished except after a court judgment. Interrogation by torture must not take place); "Ingen Lov maa gives tilbagevirkende Kraft" (NC, Article 97; No law must be given retroactive effect); "Hus-Inkvisitioner maa ikke finde Sted, uden i kriminelle Tilfælde" (NC, Article 102; Search of private homes shall not be made except in criminal cases). In these cases, the translation makes explicit the inference from "not permitted to" to "obliged to not" that is associated with the original examples in the ambiguous *maatte* (Vinje 2002: 140).

Having identified a set of similar patterns within the realm of modality, I shall now compare clause-linkage devices in the two constitutional texts.

Connectives

Connectives, that is, expressions such as "because," "if," and "unless," which mark the semantic relationships between a text's propositions (cause, condition, exception, etc.), play a crucial role in the interpretation of legal documents by providing the interpreter with the necessary instructions to reconstruct the corresponding legal facts (see, e.g., Visconti 2009a). However, coherence in constitutional texts is chiefly realized by topic relationships and by the content's hierarchical disposition; thus, fewer connectives are found in constitutional texts than in other types of normative texts (see, e.g., Cignetti 2005: 107–113). As noted above, adverbial clauses introduced by such connectives are almost exclusively located within the body of the article.

Among the most frequently expressed semantic relationships are foreseeable conditionals, expressed in the Italian Constitution by *se,* as well as by *quando* followed by the subjunctive mood:

> Le deliberazioni di ciascuna Camera e del Parlamento non sono valide se non è presente la maggioranza dei loro componenti, e se non sono adottate a maggioranza dei presenti, salvo che la Costituzione prescriva una maggioranza speciale. (IC, Article 64)

> (The decisions of each House and of Parliament are not valid if the majority of the members is not present, and if they are not passed by a majority of those present, save for those instances where the Constitution prescribes a special majority.)

> In tali casi, quando vi sia assoluta urgenza e non sia possibile il tempestivo intervento dell'Autorità giudiziaria, il sequestro della stampa periodica può essere eseguito da ufficiali di polizia giudiziaria, che devono immediatamente, e non mai oltre ventiquattro ore, fare denunzia all'Autorità giudiziaria. (IC, Article 21)

(In such cases, when there is absolute urgency and timely intervention of the Judiciary is not possible, a periodical may be confiscated by the criminal police, which shall immediately and in no case later than 24 hours refer the matter to the Judiciary for validation.)

In the Norwegian Constitution, conditional semantic relationships are expressed by *hvis* and by subject-verb inversion. Both occur in the following example:

Er ingen arveberettiget Prinsesse eller Prins til, kan Kongen foreslaa sin Efterfølger for Stortinget, der har Ret til at bestemme Valget, hvis Kongens Forslag ikke bifaldes. (NC, Article 7)

If there is no Princess or Prince entitled to the succession, the King may propose his successor to the Storting, which has the right to make the choice if the King's proposal is not accepted.)

An interesting pattern is constituted by relations of exception, which are in both constitutions expressed and translated by a variety of—not always semantically equivalent—connectives. In the Norwegian Constitution, the connective *medmindre,* for instance, is translated as "unless" but also as "otherwise":

I de Sager som af Stortinget foranstaltes anlagte for Rigsretten, kan ingen anden Benaadning, end Fritagelse for idømt Livsstraf, finde Sted, medmindre Stortinget har givet sit Samtykke dertil. (NC, Article 20)

(In proceedings which the Storting causes to be brought before the Court of Impeachment, no pardon other than deliverance from the death penalty may be granted, unless the Storting has given its consent thereto.)

Kongen skal bo inden Riget og maa ikke uden Stortingets Samtykke opholde sig udenfor Riget længere end sex Maaneder ad Gangen, medmindre han for sin Person vil have tabt Ret til Kronen. (NC, Article 11)

(The King shall reside in the Realm and may not, without the consent of the Storting, remain outside the Realm for more than six months at a time, otherwise he shall have forfeited, for his person, the right to the Crown.)

Yet "unless" is also used to translate *uden* (Articles 41, 61) or *naar ikke* (Article 27), while *uden* also corresponds to "except" (Articles 96, 99, 102) and "without" (Articles 11, 22, 25, 35), as well as to more peculiar translations, as in Article 100 ("only") and Article 109 ("irrespective of").

Similarly, in the translation of the Italian Constitution, *salvo* corresponds to "except" (Articles 16, 68, 97) and "unless" (Articles 59, 73, 88, 118, 122), but also to more surprising solutions, such as the conditional "subject to" (Articles 35, 117), "save" (Article 64), or the concessive "notwithstanding" (Article 86).

Overall, nevertheless, connectives have a less prominent role in constitutional texts, where, as said, cohesion is ensured by their content's hierarchical organization: the opening of articles by using main clauses distinguishes constitutional texts from statutes or codes.

Conclusion

Clearly, national legal traditions influence how framers select linguistic and discursive means when writing constitutions. However, the converging discursive patterns identified in the Italian and Norwegian constitutions lend support to the idea that single national constitutions may be considered as instances of a shared, transnational genre, although in most cases, it should be noted, the difference with respect to other types of normative texts, such as statutes or codes, is not a categorical one but rather one of gradience.

An interesting topic for further investigation concerns the translations of constitutional texts. Some examples discussed in this chapter highlight the tension between a faithful translation and unfaithful renderings: although official translations of constitutional texts are not meant to have binding value, cases such as the original "may not" translated into "must not," or the variety of connectives used to render exceptions, raise the issue of the semantic equivalence between the original text and its translation.

NOTES

1. This was not always the meaning of the concept, as shown in Holmøyvik (in this volume); see also Bambi (2011) on the evolution of the Latin *constitutio* from "form of government" in Cicero to "emperor's law" in Vulgar Latin, and the Italian *costituzione* from "law of the sovereign" to "fundamental law of the state."
2. The quote stems from Calamandrei (2008). Quote translated by the author.
3. I shall mainly refer to Cignetti (2005), De Mauro (2006, 2011), and Mortara Garavelli (2001, 2011a, 2011b); see references in those works for an extensive bibliography.
4. These characteristics, that is, the elegant simplicity and clarity, are not shared by subsequent amendments, as highlighted, for example, by Cignetti (2005: 121–128).
5. The English-language translation, here and in subsequent examples, is from *The Constitution—Complete Text: The Constitution, as Laid Down on 17 May 1814 by the Constituent Assembly at Eidsvoll and Subsequently Amended* (2013). At the time of writing (2014), no official English-language translation exists that reflects the amendments approved in May 2014.
6. The English-language translation, here and in subsequent examples, is from *Constitution of the Italian Republic* (n.d.).
7. Quotes in Norwegian stem from *Kongeriget Norges Grundlov, given i Rigsforsamlingen paa Eidsvold den 17de Mai 1814* (2012).

8. Quotes in Italian stem from *Costituzione della Repubblica italiana* (n.d.).

9. Translated by the author. German original: "durch die Festsetzung kann z. B. auch unmittelbar ein Sachverhalt geschaffen werden, der einer weiteren Verwirklichung weder fähig noch bedürftig ist."

10. All quotes from the *Statuto Albertino* come from the 1898 version edited by Domenico Zanichelli (*Statuto Albertino 1848* 1898). All translations are by the author.

11. See Williams (2009) for the observation of a rise of the present indicative form over "shall" in English legislative texts.

12. This may have been prompted by the semantics of the Danish modal verb *maatte*, which differs from its contemporary Norwegian formal equivalent in that it refers to both necessity and permission. However, the shift from discretion to obligation is a recurrent feature in normative texts, regardless of the original language (see, e.g., Charnock [2009] for a discussion of English statutes cases in which the holder of a legal discretion may be under an obligation to exercise it).

➤• **Part III** •◄

HISTORICAL TRANSFORMATIONS

Timing the Constitutional Moment

Time and Language in the Norwegian Constitution

Helge Jordheim

Introduction

The Norwegian Constitution owes its existence to one of the most dramatic and fateful moments in Norwegian history, which culminated during a few weeks in April and May 1814. After the Treaty of Kiel in January 1814 but before the Swedish king had taken possession of the country ceded to him by the Danish crown, an opportunity arose and Norwegian elites seized it, led by the Danish prince Christian Frederik. Time was short, and within just a few weeks, the deputies at Eidsvold succeeded in giving Norway a constitution.

Reading the constitutional text, however, we find few traces of this historical drama. Instead, the text is written in typical legal prose, in which dramatic events or actions that will change the face of Norway forever are made more or less invisible by the use of the present tense, for example, in Article 1: "The Kingdom of Norway is a free, independent and indivisible Realm."[1] To use a recurring phrase from legal criticism, the law—in this case the Norwegian Constitution—is "continually speaking" (Williams 2007: 85). Although it is situated in the present, the prescriptive legal text is not an integral part of the historical moment or the event, but refers to actions that will take place in the future and—to the extent that it is relevant—that have already taken place in the past. In this way, the state is removed from the complex and highly contingent narratives of national awakening and emancipation and relocated in a continuous, stable, and more or less immutable present: the present of the law. In her book *The Anatomy of National Fantasy,* the Anglicist Lauren Gail Berlant discusses how the law "transforms the temporal frame in which people experience social life into a new synchronic space, a juridical present tense." But, she continues: "The present tense of the law, like all synchronic moments, actually condenses a number of diverse temporalities" (Berlant 1991: 200).

Taking my cue from Berlant, I will in this chapter discuss what I refer to as "the two presents" involved in the writing of the Norwegian Constitution. As indicated earlier, the Norwegian Constitution, just as the US Constitution of 1787 and the French Constitution of 1791, is in itself an event, a rather dramatic and even potentially revolutionary one. In the constitutional text, however, this historical present is controlled, hidden, even tamed, by the use of legal prose, more precisely, by the use of the grammatical present of juridical language, what Berlant referred to as "the present tense of the law." In the first part of the chapter, I will discuss the tension between these two presents—the historical and the grammatical—and how they affect the actual constitutional text.

Second, I analyze the diverse temporalities that are condensed and synchronized in the constitutional text, and trace the conflict between what I like to call "monarchical time" and "republican time." On the one hand, I investigate to what extent references to the king, the royal persona, invest the constitutional text with a particular temporality, which can be described as biological and generational. The state's continuity is secured in discussions of birth, death, inheritance, education, and so forth, that is, practices having to do with the king's body and the royal family. On the other hand, and opposed to "monarchical time," the Norwegian Constitution also construes or adheres to another temporal regime, which might be referred to as "republican," according to the way the term has recently been used by the intellectual historians J.G.A. Pocock (1975) and Quentin Skinner (2001) as well as by the political philosopher Phillip Pettit (1996). In their view, "republican" means a form of government that does not accept any form of arbitrary power and is based on the participation of the citizens. Hence, "republican time" is the temporal regime of elections and electoral periods, in terms of repetitive and repeatable institutional structures designed to anticipate and control the potentially risky and contingent republican practices of participation and representation. According to these two temporalities, "monarchical time" and "republican time," the relationship between contingent event and institutional structure as well as between disruption and continuity is organized in very different ways.

The methodological inspiration for the following discussion is taken from Reinhart Koselleck's "historical semantics" (2004), which, however, will be expanded with a strong pragmatic element, often underestimated by the German historian and theorist himself. Historical semantics is concerned with the changing meanings of certain words, concepts, and expressions, especially to the extent that these meanings contain specific temporal relations and structures. As a result of his work on historical semantics, Koselleck has developed "a theory of historical times" ([1972] 2000: 302; Jordheim 2012), to which the following analysis of the Norwegian Constitution owes a substantial debt. In my analysis, I seek to identify words, concepts, passages, or topoi where different and conflicting temporal experiences, structures, or regimes are at stake. To get at the rhetorical and pragmatic level in the Norwegian Constitution I use some insights from Quentin Skinner, who strives to pinpoint the passages in texts where conventions are accepted or rejected (2002). In this combination of semantic and pragmatic elements there is already latent a conflict between the singularity of a speech act and the repetitive structures—words, concepts, and utterances—that constitute linguistic meaning. In the following, this conflict, discussed in depth in two comparative studies of Koselleck and Skinner (Palonen 1999; Jordheim 2007), will be used for analytical purposes: to pinpoint and describe the oscillation between dramatic and sudden change and the ideal of stability in the Norwegian Constitution.

Constitutional Moment and Constitutional Text

In the speeches held and the diaries and letters written by the deputies at Eidsvold, there are many references to what is often called "the fateful moment of the realm" (*Rigets kritiske Øjeblik*; Nicolai Wergeland, quoted in Fure 1989: 39) or "the moment of danger" (*Farens Øjeblik*; Valentin Sibbern, quoted in Fure 1989: 40), referring to the immediate present unfolding in the spring of 1814. By contrast, the Norwegian Constitution itself bears almost no traces of this dramatic moment of origin. Instead, the political drama of this particular historical moment, of the days, weeks, and months of the early spring of 1814, which Norwegian priest and diarist Claus Pavels famously called Norway's annus mirabilis (Dyrvik 2005: 7), is neutralized and transformed into the juridical present of the law. Hence, Article 1 reads: "The Kingdom of Norway is a free, independent and indivisible Realm. Its form of government is a limited and hereditary monarchy." In the following I will ask what real historical temporalities are invested in the present tense "is" (*er*), what kind of temporal experiences are hidden in this conspicuously inconspicuous form of the verb.

There is a tension between the Norwegian Constitution as a dynamic, dramatic intervention in history, cleanly breaking with the past, changing the future, and responding to the present exigency, and the wholly abstract, atemporal, ahistorical, apolitical, and quasi-eternal "is," which posits a permanent juridical present. In direct contrast with the actual historical events leading up to 1814, nothing really seems to happen in the constitutional text itself—as if Norway had always been "a free, independent and indivisible Realm," as if there was no contingency, no historical transformations to deal with at all. This claim to continuity, part of a rhetoric of playing down the constitutional moment's drama and insisting on the realm's stability, is reinforced by Article 2, which says that the Evangelical-Lutheran religion shall be "maintained" (*forbliver*) as the "Church of the Kingdom" (*Statens offentlige Religion*) and that Jews are "furthermore" (*fremdeles*) excluded from the kingdom. Though there is a revolution in the political system, which might lead to war with Sweden, the moral fundament of the realm and its citizens remains the same, not only before and after the constitutional moment, but even in the foreseeable and the unforeseeable future, ensured by the continuity of generations: "The inhabitants who profess the said religion are bound to educate their children in the same." In this way, in the shift from Article 1 to Article 2 and by the use of words like "maintain" (*forbliver*) and "furthermore" (*fremdeles*), the "is" is extended not only forward into the future, but also—and just as importantly—backward into the past. In the words of Koselleck, the "space of experience" and the "horizon of expectations," *Erfahrungsraum* and *Erwartungshorizont*, which are disconnected and have become too asymmetrical due to dramatic political events and changes, are rejoined to a continuous history (2004: 255–275).

This way of understanding the constitutional text's role and function corresponds well with the famous definition of politics found in Pocock's republican tradition: politics, he claims, in reference to Machiavelli's concept of *fortuna*, is "the art of dealing with contingency" (1975: 156). In Machiavellian terms, the claim evokes the prince's ability to seize the opportunity when it presents itself and to act accordingly in order to establish or strengthen his rule. According to Pocock, however, it serves as a definition of politics in general, independent of the system of government. The Norwegian Constitution deals with contingency, with the contingent historical and political event, by suppressing and denying it. Hence, the new nation is relocated into an eternal present, weaving together past and future without having to deal with the potential instability of the present. Indeed, the opening sentence of the Norwegian Constitution successfully hides the fact that every act of foundation, in the realm of politics, is also an act of coercion, at least potentially. There is no before or after, just the eternity of the law.

However, to understand the Norwegian Constitution as a text, we must know more about what kind of temporal experiences are invested in this seemingly neutral and temporally indistinct "is," in reference to *Rigets kritiske Øjeblik* (the fateful moment of the realm). The stabilized, almost immobile grammatical present is contrasted with the real historical present that has everything that the constitutional text seems to lack: events, actions, dramatic circumstances, even a war.

The Fateful Moment of the Realm

To get an impression of the historical present that the deputies at Eidsvold were part of and intervened in, there is no better place to look than in the newspapers and letters that were read and discussed by the deputies themselves. Prior to 16 April 1814, when the Constitutional Assembly was due to discuss the eleven basic statements suggested by the Constitutional Committee, the political implications of this singular historical moment at the end of the Napoleonic Wars made themselves felt in newspapers and letters. In the diaries and reports from the deputies at Eidsvold, there are innumerable references to "heaps of newspapers" (Jacob Aall, quoted in Fure 1989: 49) present in the building, "newspapers left in the assembly room, such as *The Times,* Swedish papers until 6 April, newspapers from Aalborg, the already mentioned *Statstidende*" (Frederik Schmidt, quoted in Fure 1989: 49). Additionally, there were many letters, both official and private, that reached the deputies and were thoroughly read and discussed. The feeling of immediacy must have been somewhat tempered by the fact that the newspapers were mostly around two weeks old, but still the medium, the bristle paper, broadsheets, and headlines reporting from Continental Europe, strongly testified to the historical drama unfolding in real time around them.

At stake was Norway's future. Responding to the Norwegian people's declaration of independence, which occurred in seventy-five churches across Norway on 25 February 1814, as well as to the machinations of the Danish prince Christian Frederik, proclaiming himself regent of Norway, the victors in the Napoleonic Wars, England and Sweden, answered threateningly: if Norway and the prince did not immediately give up their reckless and illegal ambitions, they risked embargo, bankruptcy, famine, and even invasion by Swedish troops. In this situation, rumors of plots and conspiracies, involving both the Danish prince and his opponents, were making the rounds. On 13 April 1814, just three days before discussions about the Constitutional Committee's draft were due to begin, deputy, ironworks proprietor, and later historian Jacob Aall describes how the Constitutional Assembly received several papers from Prince Christian Frederik. In one of them was reprinted a letter from "the Prince of Ponte Corvo" (Carl Johan, heir to the Swedish throne) to General Hans Henrik von Essen, commander of the Swedish military forces at Norway's border. In this letter, the future Swedish king insists that "it had never been England's and the allied forces intention to support Norway's reckless claim to independence" and promises that "no man shall be withdrawn from Norway" (Aall, quoted in Fure 1989: 49). The reprinted letter is accompanied by official documents wherein English and Russian support for the Swedish claim to Norway is promised and "Norway's course of action is condemned in the most harsh ways" (Aall, quoted in Fure 1989:

49). That even the newspapers might be part of a political plot, or even a conspiracy, is suspected by deputy, theologian, and poet Fredrik Schmidt, who wonders "how this magazine was printed in Norway and who brought it here" (Schmidt, quoted in Fure 1989: 49). He also refers to a Swedish paper carrying an article about how badly deputy, businessman, and politician Carsten Anker, owner of the Eidsvold Manor housing the Constitutional Assembly, had been received in London when he went there to gather support for Norway's cause and to try to put the interests of the Great Powers against Sweden's.

However, more serious than the lack of international support for Norway's freedom struggle was the attempt to embargo the export of food and supplies to Norway. In a letter to Prince Christian Frederik, residing in the capital Christiania, his aide-de-camp Johan F.W. Haffner at Eidsvold writes how news arrived on the morning of 16 April that Swedish privateers were setting to sea to seize corn transports sailing for Norway (Haffner, quoted in Fure 1989: 50). Similarly, upon arriving at Eidsvold in the morning, "on a warm and tumultuous day," as he puts it, Fredrik Schmidt learns that Carl Johan had decided to sail up the fjord to the Norwegian capital Christiania with twenty thousand Swedish soldiers and ten thousand Russian soldiers, and that two ships had returned from Denmark empty, reporting that export to Norway was now forbidden (Schmidt, quoted in Fure 1989: 50). The information was false, of course, but testifies to the amount of rumors and half truths that circulated at Eidsvold and contributed to the feeling of "crisis," in the original Greek sense, meaning a decisive moment. In a similar tone, Jacob Aall refers to 16 April as "a nervous day," in which there were reports both of newly arrived ships full of corn and of ships put under embargo. And he adds: "This news had different effects and gave occasion to the most brave and the most desperate political constellations" (Aall, quoted in Fure 1989: 51).

As the deputies gathered to discuss the eleven propositions for a Norwegian constitution, the immediate temporal framework was a dramatic, fateful, and highly unpredictable present. Undoubtedly, other temporal regimes were in play, too: Norway's glorious and heroic pasts and its possible futures, either under the Swedish yoke or as a free and autonomous nation. However, at least in the sources, they were overshadowed by more immediate concerns, such as the approaching Swedish and Russian troops and the hijacking of the corn transports. The first proposition to be discussed on this day was: "Norge bør være et indskrænket og arveligt Monarchie" (Norway shall be a limited and hereditary monarchy) (Fure 1989: 47). In the Norwegian Constitution's final version, the modal form *bør være* (shall be) was replaced by the present tense *er* (is). In the draft, the propositions were all expressed in the modal form *bør* (shall), whereas in the final version most of them—to the extent that they kept the same wording—were changed to simple present. In other words, the modal verb's future meaning seemed to point only as far ahead as to the moment when the constitutional text would be passed by the Constitutional Assembly and thus would change from a draft to an official document—if it had a future meaning at all, and not merely a modal one (Williams 2006: 45–47). Thereafter, the use of the modal verb is dropped. The most famous exception to this rule is Article 100, which states, "There shall be freedom of print"—and in which the modal verb has a normative rather than a prognostic or even prophetic meaning.

In light of the highly dramatic and fateful historical moment, the juridical present tense, the "is" of Article 1, changes character. In an article from 2009, Jacqueline Visconti argues that all juridical language has a strong performative character. Thus, in legal documents, such as the Norwegian Constitution, "the legislator's utterance neither *describes* nor *prescribes* a behavior; rather it brings about, or to use a technical term, *constitutes,* a new state of affairs" (Visconti 2009b: 393; italics in original). In the case of Norway in 1814, this understanding corresponds to the historical drama of the situation. According to Visconti, it lies in the nature of juridical language to bring about "a new state of affairs." In other words, the entire drama of liberating Norway from foreign domination, against the will of the Great Powers of Europe, is contained in the use of the present tense "is," which on one level is just an equation sign, but which also signals performativity. Until the words were put to paper and accepted by the Constitutional Assembly, Norway was not a "free, independent and indivisible Realm." Afterward it was. Simultaneously, a work of synchronization takes place between "monarchical time," to which "the Kingdom of Norway" belongs and conforms, and "republican time," which manifests itself in the idea of a "free, independent and indivisible Realm."

The temporal reference of the constitutional text is the immediate historical present, the rhetorical and political situation, in which the Constitution is discussed, put to paper, and adopted. Deciding upon the wording in a constitution is a political action and a political event in the same way as troop movements and diplomatic exchanges are—only often more important. In the following, I present one example of a text, more precisely, a speech, given at Eidsvold that aims to express the constitutional event's decisive elements in terms of a fateful moment that must be seized.

Seize the Moment: Nicolai Wergeland

At Eidsvold, one of the most heated debates concerned the actual mandate of the Constitutional Assembly and the plans to appoint a committee not only for law and finance, but also for foreign affairs. In this debate, deputy Nicolai

Wergeland, a priest from Kristiansand in southern Norway, who was a member of the Constitutional Committee and an active debater and speaker, gives a fiery speech defending Norway's right to have its own foreign policy—in a rhetorical form completely devoted to the moment:

> For old Norway, a time has come, which is rarely seen in a thousand years, a moment, for which many nations have waited for centuries, a moment, of which many nations on the globe are deeply envious, at least to a certain extent—a moment when the sons of *Nor* will regain a free and independent people's absolute right to decide the constitution of its own government, to select the means and methods to secure the civic fortune of children and grandchildren—and possesses this right, without having won it through fierce efforts and painful convulsions. (Wergeland, quoted in Fure 1989: 75; italics in original)

In his speech, Wergeland uses the word *Øjeblik,* literally, "the blink of an eye," to evoke the moment, and compares it with the hundreds and thousands of years, the *Sekler* (centuries) and the *Aartusinde* (millennia) that have gone by, without such a moment presenting itself. Many nations of the world, Wergeland points out, shifting from a diachronic to a synchronic perspective, never get to experience such a moment, when they are in a position to give themselves their own constitution and thus arrange for the future of their children and grandchildren. In a sense, what we encounter in Wergeland's speech is the Greek notion of kairos, referring to a particular and exceptional moment, a rupture or a turning point, a particularly decisive, fateful, or dangerous situation, "the opening of a discontinuity in a continuum" (Balibar et al. 2004: 815). Almost in a metaphysical sense, the kairos situation is produced by history itself. Wergeland continues with a series of rhetorical questions:

> Can any moment be more solemn, more important than this, on which depends the prosperity of the fatherland now and in the future! Can any duty be more precious, more holy, more religious, than that which is entrusted in our hands? Will it not be the greatest responsibility towards God and men how we take care of it? And will it not depend on the perseverance, the loyalty, and the conscientiousness, which inspire us from the beginning to the end, if our fellow citizens and our descendants will curse or bless us, scorn or praise our memory? (Wergeland, quoted in Fure 1989: 75)

As in the quotation above, Wergeland begins with an appeal to the moment, as something sacred and fateful, as a metaphysical, almost theological kairos, but then he slightly revises his argument, evoking the moment as something that can be "used" to secure the well-being "of the fatherland" in the present as well as in the future. All of a sudden, the moment has become a "duty," "entrusted in our hands," that we should manage. This double meaning echoes both the rhetorical tradition, going back to the Sophists, and Hippocratic discourse.

On the one hand, kairos refers to the situation or occasion itself, its inherent possibilities and dangers; on the other hand, it refers to the proper way to act or, mostly, to the proper things to say in this situation. It is "a decisive moment that must be caught in passing" (Balibar et al. 2004: 815), often represented in art as a young man, shaved bald at the back, but with a long lock of hair at the front by which the swift or foresighted could catch him (Kinneavy and Eskin 1998: 841).

To use Pocock's (1975) expression, one way to "deal with contingency" is to stabilize the present, transform it from a dynamic and complex historical present of actions and events to the continuous abstract and thus constant and stable present of the law. The other way is to tame contingency and change it into patterns and structures of repetition, to social and political rhythms. The task of a constitution is to do both, to stabilize the present and to create a rhythm for the future. In the Norwegian Constitution, there are two competing rhythms, two competing temporal regimes, the monarchical and the republican.

Monarchical Time

At Eidsvold, none of the deputies questioned the form of government: "a limited and hereditary monarchy." Much more salient were the role and the title of the monarch. Depending on how this role was framed, both the immediate and the long-term fate of the Norwegian independence struggle could change dramatically. Not least, two actual possible monarchs were making their presence felt, though differently, to the framers at Eidsvold: the Danish prince Christian Frederik, representative of Danish absolutism but also champion of Norwegian independence, and Carl Johan, the future Swedish king and hence the king of Norway, according to the Treaty of Kiel.

In the Norwegian Constitution's final version, there are in all thirty-nine articles that concern the person of the king and the royal family, the succession to the throne, the king's whereabouts, his faith, his education, his health, his death, and so forth. In these articles, we find an attempt to deal with perhaps the biggest predicament of any constitutional monarchy: the intentions, actions, and movements, indeed, the very life and death of that most contingent person, the king. The entire Section B (Articles 3–48) deals with "executive power, the king and the royal family," starting with the following declaration: "The executive power is vested in the King. His title shall be: We N.N., by the Grace of God and the Constitution of the Kingdom, King of Norway." In Article 4, we learn that "the King is sacred; he cannot be blamed or accused. Responsibility lies with his Council." The question of the regent's title gave rise to the first major controversy among the deputies at Eidsvold, between those who wanted the regent's title to be added to the article stating that Norway is a monarchy and those who saw it as an attack on the possibility of a union with Sweden. If it was stated in the Constitution that the regent should be called king, as suggested by the jurist and historian Christian Magnus Falsen (Fure 1989: 54), it would be impossible for Norway to legally accept the Swedish king as the Norwegian king, the opponents argued (Fure 1989: 54–56). In the debate, Nicolai Wergeland took the opportunity to lecture the other deputies at length on the different forms of government, quoting from Rousseau and Montesquieu (Schmidt, quoted in Fure 1989: 53).

The king, or at least a strong pretender to the Norwegian throne, was very much part of the Eidsvold deputies' historical present. When the Constitutional Assembly met in the big room on the second floor of Eidsvold Manor, the Danish prince Christian Frederik had installed himself on the first floor, where he slept, ate, and met with the deputies who came to see him and to discuss the events happening upstairs. His stay was interrupted only by some shorter visits to Christiania, for example, prior to the meeting on April 16, which he undertook to avoid putting undue pressure on the deputies (Fure 1989: 49). Nevertheless, the prince, or rather the regent (*Regenten*), as he was referred to, was a prominent and indeed physical presence at Eidsvold, which added to the feeling of drama and insecurity and posed a threat to the openness, freedom, and rationality of the discussion. Even though Christian Frederik had positioned himself as the champion of Norwegian independence, he was nevertheless the embodiment of Danish absolutist rule, and his original idea had been to claim the Norwegian throne for himself before his Norwegian friends advised him otherwise. For obvious reasons, this royal presence, along with the other historical contingencies (the news from the Continent, the letters from politicians and heads of state) interfering in the deliberations at Eidsvold, had to be controlled by the constitutional text—a work that takes thirty-nine articles.

More than half of these articles constitute a list of what the king does, what he "shall," "may," or "must not do." He "may issue and repeal Ordinances concerning Commerce, Duties, Trade and Police" (Article 17), he "elects and appoints all civil, ecclesiastical and military functionaries" (Article 21), he "has the supreme command of the land and naval forces of the Kingdom" (Article 25) as well the "right to assemble troops, declare war, and conclude peace" (Article 26). In other words, in the Norwegian Constitution of 1814, the king is a person who acts, often symbolically and not always with great effect, but he is nevertheless defined through his actions, which by definition take place in the temporal regime of the moment, of the now, as opposed to the eternal present of the law. This wide range of possible actions that the king might perform, often of an immediate and sudden character, makes the state liable to arbitrary power, unless these action are systematically defined and limited by law (Skinner 2001; Pettit 1996). Hence, in each case, the action performed by the king must be in accordance with the Constitution or be approved by Storthinget (the parliament, referred to as the "National Assembly" in the 1814 English-language translation) or by the king's council. The king may do only what is granted him in Article 17, provided these actions "do not infringe upon the Constitution and the laws given by the National Assembly," or in Article 21, "after hearing the declaration of his Council of State." In this way the temporality of individual action and of the historical moment are kept in check by the temporality of the law.

In Norway in 1814, however, the royal person, incarnate in the Danish prince Christian Frederik, was not only a symbol of historical contingency; he also represented a possibility to stabilize and give durability to the state founded by the revolutionary act at Eidsvold. As demonstrated by the debates on 16 April, the king, the figure but also the title, was perceived as a bulwark against a union with Sweden. As long as Norway had its own king, some of the deputies argued, it remained the "free, independent and indivisible Realm" described in Article 1 of the Constitution.

In some constitutional articles, the king also has the function of a temporal trope, which connects the possibly unstable and fateful present, the now, with the past and the future and thus serves to stabilize it. Despite the change of regents, representatives, or executives, there must be a principle that guarantees the continuous existence of the state (Skinner 2009). In the Norwegian Constitution, this principle is the king, whose powers are limited by law but who still is able to represent the state from the past, through the tumultuous present, and into the future.

An interesting example of how this temporal logic works on both a textual and a historical level can be found in Article 15, which says, "The King shall always have professed and actually profess the Evangelical-Lutheran Religion." At Eidsvold, the word *stedse* (always) prompted a heated debate among the deputies, mainly because the Swedish pretender to the Norwegian throne, Carl Johan, was a Catholic until, in 1810, he accepted the Swedish throne and converted to Protestantism. In the discussion, other arguments were also raised against Article 15, for example, that "if there had been another Henri IV, we could not get him as a king, because of these words" (Wilhelm Frimann Koren Christie, quoted in Fure 1989: 130) or "it would exclude everyone from the throne, because it presupposed of the candidate that his first scream, when he was born, was a confession of the Lutheran faith" (Gustav Peter Blom, quoted in Fure 1989: 131). Henri IV, one of the most popular kings in French history and the king who ended the Wars of Religion, was born a Catholic, converted to Protestantism, and finally had to abjure his Protestant faith to become king of France in 1589. Ultimately, however, Article 15 was passed in its original form, and thus the legitimacy of the Norwegian constitutional monarchy was founded on the idea of something that had "always" existed, even if it was only the religious conviction of the king.

The most obvious example of the introduction of "monarchical time" into the Constitution's juridical present is the idea of heritage and hereditary succession. Already in Article 1, it is stated that Norway is a "hereditary monarchy," and in Article 5, we learn that this "hereditary succession is lineal and agnatical," as well as which hereditary lines should be preferred. The reason for this succession model, Article 6 says, is that the kingdom shall remain "for ever undivided." In this way, the principle of hereditary succession makes it both legally and rhetorically possible for the Constitution's authors to project their vision of the indivisible Kingdom of Norway into eternity.

It is interesting to note how the succession of articles follows the life cycle of the king. The succession illustrates to what extent the idea of kingship and its particular temporalities guide the Norwegian Constitution: Articles 7–9 are concerned with the king's birth, Articles 10–12 with his coming of age and his accession to government, Articles 13–35 with his actual reign, and Articles 36–48 with his death. In the way they succeed each other, the articles of Section B in the Norwegian Constitution introduce a narrative movement into the constitutional text's continuous present; moreover, this movement has the shape of a specific narrative, well-known in that period from the popular genre of the *Bildungsroman*. It is the narrative of an individual's life, from cradle to grave, through the stages of childhood, youth, maturity, and old age, which in this case gives rhythm and predictability to the state's life.

Most striking is this narrative's last part, which is concerned with the king's death. As is well-known from the works of German historian Ernst Kantorowicz and his French student Ralph Giesey, the king's death is the most perilous moment for a monarchy, when the body natural collapses and the body politic must be upheld through ceremonies and rituals until a new king is crowned (Kantorowicz 1997; Giesey 1987). Similarly, in the Norwegian Constitution, the legal issue of the king's death is introduced concerning the succession question. The "heir to the crown," his title, his place in the Council of State, what he should do when the king dies, what happens if he is underage, and so forth, are discussed in much detail in several articles before the moment of succession is actually introduced; hence, when the actual event of "the King's death" is brought up, in Article 46, the successor is already in place, textually. Again, the individual's life rhythm, this time the crown prince's, is brought to bear on the state's political rhythm, inscribed into the more general rhythm of monarchical time, which can continue forever and thus secure the state's permanent existence. Monarchical time is the life rhythm both of the king and of hereditary succession; there can be no gaps or stops, moments when the state risks collapse.

Republican Time

In Section C of the Norwegian Constitution, "Of Burghership and the Legislative Power," another way of dealing with the contingency of the historical moment or the political event is presented, and with it another temporal regime. Because this way of experiencing and organizing time is not linked to the king's life or to hereditary succession, but rather to a vision of the political life of citizens and of their participation in a state, I will refer to it as "republican," in accordance with Quentin Skinner's recent use of the term (2001). As mentioned, none of the deputies at Eidsvold spoke out in favor of a republican form of government. Nevertheless, republicanism as a tradition of political thought, in which the well-being of the state and the citizens was given priority over the ruler's absolute sovereignty, significantly influenced the Norwegian Constitution. Section C is a representation of "republican time" that, similar to the "monarchical time" of Section B, serves to control the eruptive force of the historical present, of the 1814 Norwegian Constitution's rhetorical situation, by stabilizing it and extending it indefinitely.

In his book on parliamentarism, *The Politics of Limited Times,* the Finnish political scientist Kari Palonen argues that "the entire parliamentary procedure is … arranged around items that succeed each other in time" (2008: 17); "the rhythm of regular and recurrent choices in both elections and the parliaments appears at the crux of politics" (2008: 14). To orchestrate a shift from monarchical government's more durable form, including lifetimes, generations, and genealogies, to constitutional democracy's scarce times, extending no longer than from one election, or even one parliamentary session, to the next, a "rhetorical conversion," a change of terminology and figures of speech, is needed (Palonen 2008: 19). Undoubtedly, the Norwegian Constitution of 1814 is the scene of such a rhetorical conversion. In monarchical time, there is still the risk of power being performed arbitrarily, which, according to Skinner and Pettit, is the main threat to republican freedom; therefore, the king's potentially arbitrary actions, to "issue and repeal Ordinances" (Article 17), to "pardon criminals" (Article 20), and to "declare war" (Article 26), have to be controlled meticulously. In republican time, however, whose main function is to allow citizens to participate in the government of the Norwegian state, there is no such risk, because all political actions and events that potentially have consequences for the state and the citizens are performed according to a specific political rhythm. Section C's role in the Norwegian Constitution, on legislative power, is to organize this republican time.

Whereas monarchical time follows the king's natural life rhythm and is structured according to biological periods, childhood, maturity, and old age, delimited by birth and death, republican time is imposed by means of specified intervals defined by the Constitution. The most important interval is defined in Article 68: "The Sessions of the National Assembly generally begin every third year on the first work-day of the month of February." However, even at this most crucial point in the Constitution, in which the realm's social and political rhythms are established, concessions to monarchical time are made. For example, the next article grants the king the right to convoke Storthinget "out of ordinary time," thus reiterating the link between arbitrary power and the suspension of the intervals specific to republican government. However, this royal convocation of Storthinget can happen only "on extraordinary occasions." In this particular linguistic device, the old Sophist appeal to the kairotic moment survives in the Norwegian Constitution, in terms of a legally circumscribed break with the republican political rhythm. Republican time is seemingly reserved for ordinary days, whereas the extraordinary is the king's domain.

The intervals of republican time are not found or observed. Instead, they are produced. To install a specific rhythm in a people and in a political system requires significant work, which includes tools, like political calendars and estimates of the time required to complete specific tasks. This work is described at length in the Norwegian Constitution. Hence, every third year the inhabitants of a town or parish choose their electors by vote. If they are in a town, the electors "meet within eight days after" the election (Article 57); in a parish they "meet within a month" (Article 58). These electors choose the deputies who shall take a seat at Storthinget. These elections must happen "before the end of the month of December" (Article 54). It is important that no time be wasted, that the rhythm of the nation not be disturbed by delay of any kind, which risks creating a nonsynchronicity between various political processes and thus jeopardizing the republican regime as such. In monarchical time, we observed the fear of a time gap opening between one king's death and the crowning of another, during which monarchical power and thus the political order might become unstable or even collapse; the same fear of empty, uncontrolled time, outside the carefully controlled rhythm of constitutional government, is found in the republican framework. According to Article 64, the transfer of power to deputies must happen "immediately" after their election, to avoid any brief instability or contingency that might interrupt the regularity of republican time. Similarly, Article 74 states that the opening of Storthinget—which is performed by the king "or whom he appoints in his place" by means of a speech— shall follow "immediately" after Storthinget is constituted.

Finally, in contrast to monarchical time, which has as its primary function in ensuring stability and permanence in all matters of the state, republican time aims for permanence only through change. Indeed, it is the recurring, rhythmic changes, the three-year election cycles when deputies to Storthinget can be reelected or replaced, and the swiftness, even the immediacy, of these transitions that guarantee the republican state's stability. Personal continuity in positions of power, which is the sole aim of monarchical time, is eclipsed by the insistence on shorter and rationally construed intervals. Hence, even Storthinget is allowed to assemble only for "the prescribed time," which is three months; if it wants to remain sitting longer, it must have the king's consent (Article 80). Paradoxically, according to the separation of power doctrine, the king, who is not bound by the periods and intervals of republican time, is made the guardian of the republican temporal regime.

Conclusion

The law speaks—or rather is "continuously speaking"—in the present tense. This also goes for the Norwegian Constitution of 1814. The aim of this chapter has been to take a close look at this grammatical present, so typical of legal texts, and to ask what other times, temporal experiences, and temporal regimes might be contained in it. I found, on a first level, a tension between the dramatic historical present, the constitutional moment, and the abstract, stabilizing, and stabilized grammatical present of the constitutional text, and, on a second level, another tension between "monarchical time" and "republican time," the time of the king and the time of the people. To negotiate these tensions is one of the primary, though rarely acknowledged, tasks of the Norwegian Constitution.

NOTES

1. All English-language quotes concerning the Norwegian Constitution of 17 May 1814 are from *The Constitution of the Kingdom of Norway* (1814). All English-language quotes from Norwegian sources other than the Constitution are translated by the author.

▶• 8 •◀

The Norwegian Constitution and Its Multiple Codes

Expressions of Political and Legal Change

Inger-Johanne Sand

Introduction

In a highly condensed form, constitutional texts express the most vital prin-ciples and competences of state governance and human rights. In addition, constitutional texts construct the most authoritative institutions for dealing with central political and legal conflicts in society. Simultaneously, constitu-tions are caught in the crossfire of conflicting demands: constitutions express consensual values, but they may also be the object of societal and political conflict. As texts and as state practice, constitutions are meant to stabilize in-stitutions as well as political and societal relations, but they should also be able to respond to relevant societal change. Furthermore, constitutions' political and legal functions pose different and sometimes contradictory demands. For example, in legislatures, constitutions have the status of *lex superior,* but in the political realm, this status may be challenged if political needs run contrary to the constitution. These conflicting demands highlight the need of addressing matters of constitutional change.

Constitutional change is unavoidably complex and often happens out of sync with its context. Changes in society, politics, state practice, and the con-stitutional text may occur in different tempi and under different institutional conditions. Changes in society, politics, and state practice may occur for dif-ferent reasons, in different situations, and following different paths. Their very function requires constitutional texts to comply with societal and political val-ues and with state practice. Yet to change, most constitutional texts require the fulfillment of specific amendment procedures. Typically, amendments require a qualified majority among legislators, and amendments often must pass some kind of delay mechanism.

Changes in constitutional texts may be analyzed and explained in many ways, depending on perspective, discipline, and methodology. In this chapter, I apply a combination of legal, sociolegal, and semantic methodologies. I track changes in the Norwegian Constitution by identifying the main values, principles, and concepts expressed in the Constitution's text and by identifying how they are practically applied over time. Such a specific cluster of main values, principles, and concepts, in conjunction with semantic patterns, I will refer to as a *code*. Constitutions consist primarily of a political and a legal code. The two codes interact and interdepend. The codes may coincide but they may also be interpreted differently. Functionally, the two codes are deeply intertwined (Luhmann 1995: 59–82, 137–150; 2005: 381–422). The political code is vitally present in legal interpretations, and it may dominate political and symbolic interpretations. The legal code always predominates in legal cases. Additionally, constitutions are coded in values that differ according to themes (Tuori and Sankari 2010; Sand 2010: 49–67). Therefore, the individual sections of the constitutional text may have different codes. Finally, constitutions are historically coded; they can be seen as palimpsests of historical situations, as layer upon layer of bygone contexts.

To illustrate these points, I focus on three cases of change in the Norwegian Constitution. The first case concerns the relation between the legislative and the executive branches of government. The second case concerns Norway's international obligations. The third case concerns the scope and ambitions of human rights.

The Norwegian Constitution's text is characterized by the absence of general reform during its 200-year life span. Instead, amendments stem from very different periods, and many amendments lag behind state practice and acceptance of relevant political ideas. Interpretation of the Constitution's text has been challenged by the fact that amendments have often been approved long after changes in state practice and in political ideas. In addition, the Constitution's authoritative and symbolic status may have resulted in delayed amendments and conservative interpretations. Last, the sheer complexity of the many and often conflicting demands on constitutional norms and on the Constitution's articles may account for some of the disagreements over interpretation.

Because constitutions contain historical layers where different norms and ideas are promoted, I argue that we should see the Norwegian Constitution not only as one unified text, but also as a text that may be deconstructed into different historical, political, and legal codes and layers of meaning. This deconstruction illustrates the general forms of change that constitutions may take. In focusing on how the Norwegian Constitution's main codes have changed over time, I will first survey the evolution of the Constitution's text. My second purpose is to illustrate the dynamics between social and political change, state practice, and the Constitution's text. My third purpose is to illustrate the many different conflicts between its codes.

The Evolution of the Norwegian Constitution

The primary purposes of the liberal nation-state constitutions emerging late in the Enlightenment era were to formalize sovereignty and to institute a contract between the people and the government on how government should be constituted and organized. Authoritarian rule became more difficult to uphold as ideas emerged of more differentiated social and economic spheres and of an increasingly comprehensive citizenship involving more human rights. The Norwegian Constitution can be seen both as a political declaration of sovereignty (see Warner et al. in this volume) and as an expression of valid law. In this section, I give a brief, general account of the Norwegian Constitution's evolution. The changes mentioned will be more specifically commented on and analyzed in the following sections.

The Norwegian Constitution has a unique history, starting with its foundation in 1814. The Treaty of Kiel meant that Norway was transferred from the King of Denmark-Norway to the King of Sweden. In response, and in an attempt to declare Norwegian sovereignty, deputies gathered at Eidsvold and adopted the Constitution of 17 May 1814. However, Norway lacked military power and financial means to maintain its own sovereignty and therefore had to accept a union with Sweden under the Swedish king. Thanks to the 17 May Constitution, Norway was nevertheless able to retain its independence, and the Constitution was accepted by the Swedish king on 4 November 1814 with only a few amendments. Following the 4 November Constitution, the executive branch of government in Norway was in the hands of a king who also ruled Sweden.

Because of the events in 1814 and the Constitution's role in safeguarding Norwegian sovereignty, the Constitution gained an exceptional symbolic and authoritative standing. The union with Sweden was dissolved in 1905, but still in 2014, significant parts of the 1814 text and its structure function as the framework for the current Constitution. Even an archaic linguistic coloring was retained until the reforms of 2014 (see Madzharova Bruteig in this volume). Since 1814, many amendments have been adopted, but no general reform or rephrasing of the Constitution's text has taken place. Amendments follow the procedures of Article 121 (Article 110 in the version of 17 May 1814, later Article 112): first, the proposed amendment is presented before Stortinget (the Norwegian parliament) either by one of its members or by the government. Then—after the next regular general election has taken place—Stortinget decides whether to adopt the amendment. A two-thirds majority is required for adoption.

The Norwegian Constitution is remarkable in having remained in effect since 1814, albeit with several significant amendments. The Constitution's main principles and much of its structure have been retained. Changes have been made concerning relations between the king and his government and between the government and Stortinget, the most vital change being that the parliamentary system has been introduced (see details below). The election system has been reformed several times. New human rights statutes have been added. Some changes are reflected in the Constitution's text (amendments), whereas others are changes in interpretation or practice. Amendments include the introduction of new human rights first in Articles 110–110c, then in 2014 in a new chapter E, Articles 92–113, Article 93 (1962), in 2014 changed to Article 115, on transferring sovereignty to international organizations, the new Article 15 (2007) on the vote of no confidence in the parliamentary system, and many changes in Articles 49–85 on voting rights, parliamentary elections, the royal veto on legislation, abolishing the two-chamber system, and so forth.[1] Many other more gradual changes could be mentioned. In addition to formal amendments to the Constitution's text, articles have been interpreted differently over time. The most striking examples are of key articles concerning the executive branch and relations between the king and the government, such as Articles 12 and 30 (Articles 28 and 32 in the 1814 text) (see details below). Here the formulation has allowed a flexible interpretation consistent with changing views on the king's personal role in the government. Finally, some articles have remained, but are decreasingly applied or not applied at all. Some of these articles were abolished in 2014. Articles 78–79, on the king's right to veto legislation, are no longer applied, but are still seen as valid law. Article 17 on royal ordinances is decreasingly applied. Different views exist on the interpretation and the validity of some rarely used and more silent articles, and on the relations between the Constitution's text and historical practice (Smith 2012: 122–132, 247–253).

These different forms of change to the Norwegian Constitution illustrate that a written constitution may be changed by amendments, by new interpretations, and by changes in the relevance and the use of its articles.[2] The Norwegian Constitution exemplifies an emphasis on the symbolic value of retaining a text over time rather than making statutory changes when changes occur in political views, values, or relevance. Increasingly, however, Stortinget has resorted to making formal amendments in the Constitution's text. Since about 1990, an increasing number of constitutional amendment proposals have been made, and Stortinget has adopted several. Vital examples of such substantive amendments are (1) the introduction of the parliamentary system, which was not explicitly referred to in the text until 2007, when Articles 15 and 82 were completely reformulated; (2) the abolishment of the two-chamber system, by changes to Articles 49 and 76 in 2007; and (3) in 1994, the general constitutional acknowledgment of Norway's human rights obligations in Article 110c and later in 2014 by the inclusion of a more comprehensive chapter on civil and political rights.

The 1814 Constitution's structure reflected the era's conception of constitutional competences and institutions. It is probably not coincidental that the section on the executive branch, including the king's position, is placed first, before sections on the other two main branches of government, the legislative and the judicial branches. Moreover, in the section on the executive branch, the king is given predominance over the government. In the twentieth century, new aspects of the constitutional principles were emphasized, such as fundamental human rights, universal suffrage in parliamentary elections, and the parliamentary system. Irrespective of the various amendments, the 1814 text's main structure has been kept, along with some of the 1814 Constitution's main ideas. Consequently, the present Norwegian Constitution can simultaneously be seen as a unified document and as a text consisting of codes from different periods of the Constitution's history.

Coding the Relation between the Legislative and the Executive Branches: The Parliamentary System

The core function of constitutions is in defining the highest state authorities' competences and in defining fundamental human rights. In the Norwegian Constitution, defining the executive branch is one of the most complex operations regarding the relation between the Constitution's text, constitutional amendments, and state practice. The section concerning the executive branch is one of the most significantly changed over time. In the text of 1814, the king had the executive power formally and substantively: "The executive power is vested in the King" (Article 3). The government was merely his council. Its members were given the duty to voice their opinions, but the decision-making responsibility was still the king's:

> Every body who has a seat in the Council of State is obliged to declare his opinion freely, to which the King shall attend; but it is left to the King to take a resolution according to his own judgment. (Article 32 in the 17 May 1814 Constitution, Article 30 from the 4 November 1814 Constitution on)

Initially, the king also appointed council members of his own choosing: "The King himself elects a Council of Norwegian citizens whose members must not be younger than thirty years" (Article 28 in the 17 May 1814 Constitution, Article 12 from the 4 November 1814 Constitution on).[3] During the nineteenth-century union with Sweden, government members increasingly often proposed new members to the king, but the decision was ultimately his, real as well as formal, until the gradual introduction of the parliamentary system following a decisive Court of Impeachment case in 1884 (Andenæs and Fliflet 2006: 41–45). Government members also increasingly often made proposals and acted politically on their own, but generally, they remained within a political framework in accordance with royal predominance.

Over time, the executive power was effectively transferred from the king's person to the government. Yet this substantive change in the law has left few changes in the Constitution's text. Its relevant articles have allowed for different interpretations and practices. One significant change in the text was made in 1911, when Article 31 was amended so as to require the prime minister's countersignature for any executive decision to be valid: "All decisions drawn up by the King shall, in order to become valid, be countersigned." This amendment formalized the executive power's transfer from the king's person to the government.

There has also been a crucial change in the relation between the executive and the legislative branches of government, from a relation predominantly based on the separation of powers principle to one predominantly based on the parliamentary system, with more direct democratic rule. Here, too, there have been relatively few amendments, given the many and significant changes in state practice and in the substantive relations between the two branches of government.

According to the 1814 text, government ministers were not members of Storthinget, and they refused to appear before Storthinget to answer any questions concerning their proposals for legislative acts and constitutional amendments, their recommendations concerning the king's right to veto, and other actions they would take as part of the executive. Thus, they maintained a clear and real separation of powers between the legislative and executive branches of government. This separation of powers was a vital code of the 1814 Constitution's text. The king also had, and formally in the text still has, the right to veto proposals for legislation, thereby postponing them (Articles 78–79).[4] He often used this right in the nineteenth century, until 1884. That year saw the Court of Impeachment decide the case concerning the king's right to veto constitutional amendments. The Court of Impeachment in 1884 had twenty-six members, nine Supreme Court judges and seventeen members from Storthinget. The Court of Impeachment majority (the members from Storthinget) held that the king's right to veto ordinary legislation did not include the right to veto constitutional amendments. The minority, the Supreme Court judges, held that the Constitution gave the king the right to veto constitutional amendments.

The background for the 1884 Court of Impeachment decision was a constitutional amendment proposal establishing a constitutional obligation for government ministers to appear before Storthinget. The king and the government did not approve the amendment, but following the court's decision rejecting an executive veto of constitutional amendments, the amendment was adopted. Disagreement on this point had long been one of several disagreements between the king and the government on the one hand and Storthinget on the other hand. The case before the Court of Impeachment in 1884 came to symbolize a more comprehensive conflict concerning executive-legislative relations. After the court's decision, and having failed to appoint an effective government of his own choosing, the king appointed a new government, headed by the majority party's leader, Johan Sverdrup, as prime minister. Over the next few years, the king gradually accepted that as a general rule, the prime minister and the government should come from the majority parties of Storthinget, thus reflecting its political composition. The decision was still, for some years, the king's. Yet, he and his advisors accepted that a changing society demanded closer operational relations between the executive and the legislative branches, the government and Storthinget, respectively.

These events were the starting point on the path toward a more stabilized parliamentary system. The process of change involved a three-way conflict between Storthinget, the government, and the king. The parliamentary system as a state practice and as the constitutionally defining relation between the legislative and the executive branches was incrementally accepted by politicians and constitutional lawyers. The code was changed, step by step, from the separation of powers toward a parliamentary system. Included in the changes were those in the above-mentioned relations in the executive branch, between the government and the king. The Court of Impeachment case of 1884 was only part of a long process of democratic development that involved many other parts of the Constitution. Separation of powers remains one of the Constitution's codes, but it has another meaning today than it had in 1814.

The change from separation of powers to a parliamentary system did not result in vital amendments to the Constitution until 2007. Only then were fundamental formulations on the parliamentary system added to the Constitution's text, such as the government's obligation to resign following a vote of no confidence in Stortinget (Article 15; see *Dokument 12:2 [2003–2004]*). Parliamentarians and government ministers accepted, explicitly or implicitly, that the Constitution's text was flexible enough to include the changes in state practice and in the political constitutional codes.

A similar discrepancy exists between the Constitution's text and practice regarding the king's position as head of the executive branch. A superficial reading of today's Constitution text leaves the impression that the king plays an active role in the executive branch, although he no longer does. The text still emphasizes the king's formal power in Articles 3, 12, 30, 31, and 78 (Articles 3, 28, 32, 35, and 78 in the 1814 text), which mainly concern the power and the duty to sign (approve) the government's decisions.[5] The same overemphasis of the king's role applies to the executive prerogatives in Articles 16–26, as illustrated by Article 25: "The King is Commander-in-Chief of the land and naval forces of the Realm." Moreover, in parts of the 2014 Constitution's text, the government is still treated more as the king's council than as what it in political fact and constitutional state practice is—the government of the elected Storting.

A telling illustration of the effects of keeping the 1814 Constitution's text is that the word *demokrati* (democracy) was not used in the text until 2004. In that year, *demokrati* was included in Article 100 as an evaluative principle for the freedom of expression (see Kalleberg in this volume). In 2012, Article 2 was changed to: "The basic values remain our Christian and humanistic heritage. This Constitution shall secure democracy, rule of law and human rights." Democracy had otherwise been only represented as a code in Article 49 since 1814: "The people exercises the legislative power at the National Assembly." Articles 50–67 concern the precise definitions of the right to vote and of regulations on how members of Stortinget are elected. In these articles, democracy as a form of government for Norway is defined, specified, and explained. These articles have undergone significant changes since 1814, but these changes have nevertheless been kept within the 1814 text's structure. There are many other examples of the same tendency to maintain the basic structure of the Constitution's text. Article 1 from the 17 May 1814 text on the form of government states: "The Kingdom of Norway is a free, independent and indivisible Realm. Its form of government is a limited and hereditary monarchy."[6] As a result of the dissolution of the union with Sweden in 1905, "inalienable" was added to the qualities of the "Realm" in Article 1. A similar example concerns Article 3. In the 1814 text, it states, "The executive power is vested in the King." In 1990, "or the Queen" was added to Article 3 so as to reflect changes in the view on gender equality.

These examples show that the old structure and many old words, concepts, and semantics remain in the Constitution's text, thus seemingly giving a preference to old codes and principles. Arguably, insufficient textual representation has been given to more recent codes and principles that are in fact applied, and that could be considered more representative of current constitutional practice and law. Stortinget, the main interpreter of the Constitution, has presumably seen the Constitution's text and its words and concepts as flexible enough to include several codes of constitutional law and several interpretations.

In summary, in the Constitution's articles on the executive branch and also in other articles on the relation between the executive and the legislative branches, different codes coexist in the text, albeit with a precarious balance struck differently over time between democracy, separation of powers, parliamentarism, accountability, human rights, and rule of law. These different codes and the formulations of the articles have, however, been interpreted flexibly so as not to violate each other. In fact, keeping much of the Constitution's text in its historical form, including previous constitutional codes, has been preferred as long as it has also seemed possible to include new codes and state practices within the text. One may argue, however, that the code of democracy could and should have been more explicitly represented in the Constitution's text long before 2012, given democracy's constitutional and factual prominence. Arguably, even the amendment in Article 2 in 2012 does not fully repair the weak representation of the code of democracy.

Coding International Cooperation

Today, international cooperation between states is much greater than it was in the nineteenth century, because of the founding of the United Nations (UN) in 1945 and the adoption of the Universal Declaration of Human Rights in 1948, and because of several international treaties and organizations, such as the General Agreement on Tariffs and Trade, the International Monetary Fund, the World Bank, and the Geneva Convention Relative to the Treatment of Prisoners of War. Most constitutions have initially included regulations on the competence to enter into association and treaties with other states as a vital element defining sovereignty's external side.

In the Norwegian Constitution, Article 26 states: "The King has the right to call up troops, to engage in war in defense of the Realm and to make peace, to conclude and denounce treaties, to send and receive diplomatic envoys."[7] The article continues with a 1931 amendment: "Treaties on matters of special importance, and, in all cases, treaties whose implementation, according to the Constitution, necessitates a new law or a decision by the Storting, are not binding until the Storting has given its consent thereto." The king's right to call up military troops to defend the state mirrors both the view on sovereignty and the view on the international situation from 1814 to 1945. These views focused on both internal and external aspects of states' sovereignty, on the competences of state authorities, and on voluntary international cooperation through treaties. Internal state authorities were presumed to take care of governing states and their citizens and all operations necessary to do so. International cooperation was presumed to take care of interstate affairs only.

The year 1945 marks a paradigmatic change in defining the tasks of international legal and political cooperation and in defining the scope of such cooperation. This change resulted from the establishment of the UN, the International Court of Justice, and other vital international organizations such as those mentioned above. The themes and tasks of international cooperation began transcending boundaries between states (Sassen 2006: 223–242). The following human rights conventions emerged: the Universal Declaration of Human Rights in 1948; the International Covenant on Civil and Political Rights (ICCPR) and on Economic, Social, and Cultural Rights (ICESCR) in 1966; and the European Convention on Human Rights (ECHR) in 1950, including the European Court of Human Rights. Political views decisively changed concerning the necessity of increased international cooperation on a broad spectrum of themes. The main purpose of the international treaties and organizations was to achieve a more stable peace through more active forms of cooperation and increased respect for human rights. A major tool for increasing respect for human rights was the creation of a comprehensive international catalog of human rights. This catalog has had both a strong symbolic impact and, over time, legally binding and effective operational impacts. With human rights recognized by a large number of states, acceptance is emerging for aspects of a more cosmopolitan legal regime across the boundaries of autonomous state regimes. The idea and practice of universal human rights create a different foundation for international cooperation and different codes for both domestic and international law. The European Economic Community (EEC) (1957), later the European Union (EU) (1993), emerged as the first comprehensive supranational treaty. The latest EU reform treaty, known as the Lisbon Treaty (2009), included a human rights chapter.

However, democratic European states' constitutional texts have not been sufficiently influenced by the comprehensive internationalization of law and politics. At the constitutional level, the traditional distinction between the national and the international has, predominantly, been kept. In the Norwegian Constitution, the new Article 93, introduced in 1962 (from 2014 Article 115), has been the main new contribution concerning the internationalization of law and politics (*Dokument 3 [1961–1962]*). Article 115 (93) allows Norway, by a three-quarter majority of Stortinget, to join an international organization, even when joining includes transferring "the right, within specified fields, to exercise powers which in accordance with this Constitution are normally vested in the authorities of the state, although not the power to alter this Constitution." Article 115 thus allows for the transfer of sovereignty to international organizations, which may then make decisions directly affecting the state and its citizens. To use Article 115 requires purposes of safeguarding international peace and security or promoting the international rule of law and cooperation. However, requirements are broad and unclear. Particularly, the meaning of "within specified fields" has been widely debated. In 1992, Article 93 (115) was applied for Norway's entry into the European Economic Area (EEA), which allows Norway, Iceland, and Lichtenstein to participate in the EU's internal market without being EU members. There have been heated discussions regarding whether EU membership, and its scope, at the historical stages of the EU treaties is compatible with this condition.

Considering the emphasis on national sovereignty in the rest of the Constitution's normative pattern and in its constitutional codes, Article 115 is remarkable because it allows for increasing internationalization of nation-state governing and consequently increasing the quality and the code of international cooperation, blurring the boundaries between states and international organizations (Sassen 2006: 378–390). Given the general challenges of internationalizing law and politics, the new code of international constitutionalism that Article 115 signifies should be seen as highly appropriate. Yet as mentioned above, Article 115's formulation is insufficient and its scope is inadequate to fully realize this new code.

The boundaries between national and international competences are increasingly overlapping and unclear, creating new institutions and new concepts (Sassen 2006: 404–423). Surprisingly, European democratic states' constitutional texts are little marked by the new code of and the significant increase in international cooperation, both of which have led to increasingly binding international obligations for states. The constitutions of some EU member states, such as Germany and Finland, have articles referring to EU membership, but in very short formulations. National sovereignty has prevailed as the main code of nation-states' constitutional texts. In addition, EU membership, and for Norway EEA membership, has resulted in transferring significant parts of the executive and legislative processes of member states to supranational levels. In addition, the Court of Justice for the European Union, the European Free Trade Area (EFTA) Court, and the European Court of Human Rights function as operative courts for member states. State practice is much more influenced by the vastly increased international cooperation than the member states' constitutional texts imply. In summary, the new international code is insufficiently represented in the member states' constitutional texts.

Coding Human Rights

The 1814 text of the Norwegian Constitution contained several articles on human rights, but fewer than planned. Because of time constraints and legal disagreements, Eidsvold deputies withdrew proposals for a more comprehensive human rights catalog (Smith 2012: 359; Tønnesson 1990: 30). The main human rights included were the protection against imprisonment or detention without statutory basis and court order (Article 96), prohibition against retroactive legislation (Article 97), freedom of expression (Article 100), and protection of private property (Article 105). These rights are core human rights in a rule-of-law system. Of these, only Article 100 has been substantively changed in the Constitution's text (see Kalleberg in this volume).[8] All these human rights have been actively applied by the Supreme Court when reviewing legislation and administrative acts.

Norway's accession to the European and international human rights treaties for a long time did not significantly affect debates on including more operative human rights in the Constitution's text. Norway maintained a dualistic system regarding including in Norwegian law relevant articles from international treaties. In 1954, Article 110 on the right to work was included, but in the form of a recommendation, not in the form of a legal right enforceable by the courts. The human rights in the Constitution's text were later extended by Article 110a on the rights of the Sami population to preserve and develop their language, culture, and way of life (1988) (in 2014 Article 108) by Article 110b on the right to an environment conducive to health and to a natural environment whose productivity and diversity can be maintained (1992) (in 2014 article 112); and by Article 110c on the state authorities' general responsibility to respect and ensure human rights (1994) (in 2014 Article 92). The rights given under Articles 110 to 110b are social, cultural, and environmental rights and are thus a later generation of rights than those included in 1814. They are formulated generally, and are arguably mostly symbolic in the sense that their rules are nonsanctionable by the courts.

The formulation of Article 110c in 1994 was a compromise after a long discussion about Norway's international treaty obligations concerning better protection of human rights. In 1999, a statute on human rights was passed, fully incorporating into Norwegian law the international treaties on human rights referred to above (ICCPR, ICESCR, and ECHR). This statute also contained a clause of preference relative to any other conflicting Norwegian laws. Subsequently, more treaties were included in the human rights statute.

Recently this trend has reached the Constitution. In January 2012, a commission of previous members of Stortinget and experts appointed by Stortinget delivered a report recommending a comprehensive modernization of human rights protections in the Constitution (*Dokument 16 [2011–2012]*). In September 2012, the commission's recommendations were formally proposed as constitutional amendments by members of Stortinget (*Dokument 12:30 to 12:36 [2011–2012]*). The amendment proposals were deliberated on in the spring term of 2014 and decisions were made just in time for the Constitution's bicentenary in May 2014. The proposals were largely influenced by international treaties, particularly the ECHR, and include strengthening of human rights protection of humans' basic integrity; explicitly banning the death penalty, torture, and slavery; improving formulations of the right to trial before independent courts; and better protection of equality before the law. Including such rights directly in the Constitution can be seen as both a continuation of a rule-of-law code and a strengthening of a fundamental freedom and of an individual rights-oriented code of human rights. Other rights in the constitutional amendment proposals include social, cultural, and economic rights such as the right to education, to protection of cultural identity, and to a reasonable standard of living. It was not possible to get the two thirds majority that was necessary for all the proposals made. The civil and political rights (from the ECHR) were adopted. Of the social rights proposed, the protection of the rights of children and the rights to education were adopted. Additionally, a proposal for modernizing language of existing provisions was adopted.

Conclusion: Between Stability and Change

Just like many other constitutional texts, the Norwegian Constitution's text reflects normativity and operative multifunctionality, as well as the duality of stability and change. Relative to their comprehensive functions, constitutions are short texts. They are furthermore subject to authoritative interpretation by both politicians and lawyers. Constitutional changes may be necessary, but they are nevertheless often subject to more controversy than are changes in other legal and political texts because of constitutions' status as *lex superior* and their complex amendment procedures. Moreover, constitutional judicial review may result in interpretations that the parliamentary majority disagrees with. Complex balancing may be necessary between the constitutional text's stability on the one hand and responsive textual change and political relevance on the other hand. Constitutional texts hold significant political and legal power while also being complex legal texts.

The main structure of the Norwegian Constitution's text has been preserved throughout periods when political and state practice have changed significantly and despite several amendments. In some cases, the Constitution's text has been formally amended. In other cases, interpretative changes have emerged incrementally. Additionally, the gradual nonuse of constitutional powers has occurred, leaving open whether they still exist. The significant change toward a parliamentary system instead of a strict separation of powers is one example of gradual change in state practice, and one in which changes in the Constitution's text have come at a very late stage. Arguably, these late textual changes have only partially covered the actual legal and political implications of the change toward a parliamentary system. The Constitution's stability has been emphasized further by the tradition of writing amendments in a nineteenth-century language form, until this tradition was ended by the 2014 reforms (see Madzharova Bruteig in this volume).

Choosing to keep the main structure and vital parts of the 1814 Norwegian Constitution's text—even beyond what could and should have been more explicitly changed—confirms the symbolic power and functions of the Constitution's text. Because the articles and single formulations refer to different codes from different periods, the Constitution's text of 2014 may appear more fragmented than a fully reformed text would. The king clearly has a more prominent place in the present Constitution's text than he would if the text were to reflect current constitutional state practice and current values. Articles concerning the executive branch and the king's personal role in it have not been fully harmonized, or updated, but instead point in slightly different directions, partly because they have been written in different historical situations, but always respecting monarchical traditions. Several aspects of current de facto constitutional state practice are either too modestly or too insufficiently presented. Democracy, parliamentarism, and the government's constitutional responsibility are insufficiently presented in the text, given their importance in state practice. Human rights obligations are also arguably underrepresented, given Norway's international obligations and their legal, ideological, and political significance, even after the 2014 reforms with a new chapter E on human rights. Article 115, on the transfer of sovereignty to international organizations, is formulated briefly and unclearly, but has led to de facto significant transfers of state authorities' competences in the form of the EEA Agreement. The EEA Agreement's unusual construction as an international treaty—in many respects it functions as a supranational treaty because of its close dependence on the more operative EU Treaty—clearly has de facto constitutional consequences. These consequences are not apparent in the Norwegian Constitution's text. Additionally, Norway has signed and is obliged by several other comprehensive international treaties in a wide variety of areas.

The Norwegian Constitution illustrates how a constitutional text may include several different, even conflicting, constitutional codes that reflect historical processes. The Norwegian Constitution still seems to have maintained a high degree of both political and legal consensus and a popular acceptance of its symbolic function. One could argue that the Constitution's historical and symbolic functions as a unifying political text above other texts have been prioritized over continuous relevant change and precise statutory operability. Relatively few complaints exist about the Constitution's lack of precision and its inoperability, but given the increasing and complex international obligations that are constitutionally relevant, that situation is changing. The Constitution's text has generally proven to be flexible and inclusive of several constitutional codes. Articles 26 and 115 illustrate, however, the text's inability to represent and account for the enormous increase in international political cooperation and legal obligations.

The Norwegian Constitution's text is thus part of the ambiguity of power that exists even in a relatively transparent democracy. As the supreme, authoritative text concerning the distribution of political and legal power in a transparent democracy, it should lead the way rather than follow behind other political and legal texts in conveying as precisely as possible all forms of public and accountable power and their procedures. As shown above, it lacks precision concerning the executive branch, the parliamentary system, the comprehensive forms of international cooperation, and human rights. There are still vital inconsistencies between the Constitution's text, constitutional practice, and current political ideas. One may argue that textual precision has lost to pragmatism and to symbolic and historic power. This is not necessarily a wrong choice, but in some above-mentioned examples, one could have expected more relevance and realism from legislators. Depending on one's perspective, the Constitution's text may be seen as insufficiently relevant and lacking in transparency, or as sufficiently robust and well-functioning, given its many codes.

NOTES

1. In this chapter, references will be made to the 1814 and later editions of the Norwegian Constitution. In quotes from the 1814 edition, the official English-language translation (*The Constitution of the Kingdom of Norway* 1814) is used. In quotes from later editions, English-language translations are the author's.
2. On unwritten constitutions, see Michalsen; Holmøyvik in this volume.
3. In 1975, the text in Article 12 concerning an age limit for ministers was exchanged for one concerning citizens entitled to vote.
4. Since an amendment in 1938, Article 79 in the Norwegian Constitution allows the king to veto legislation only once, meaning that if the proposed legislation is adopted by the Storting following a general election, the legislation is put into force. Until 1938, the king could also veto the second adoption by the Storting, and only the adoption by a third Storting following another general election could finally override the royal veto.
5. I disregard here the above-mentioned 1911 amendment of Article 31.
6. The word "limited" (*indskrænket*) is a first hint of democracy.
7. Here I quote the current text of article 26. Apart from the 1917 addition of "in defense of the Realm," this is the same as the 1814 text.
8. The scope of Article 100 was increased in 2004 when "liberty of the press" was replaced by "freedom of expression" (see also Ringvej; Berge in this volume).

9

Norwegian Parliamentary Discourse 2004–2014 on the Norwegian Constitution's Language Form

Yordanka Madzharova Bruteig

Introduction

Language form is an important aspect of any modern constitution's textuality.[1] This chapter investigates how members of the Norwegian parliament, Stortinget, perceive the Norwegian Constitution's language form. The reason for investigating this matter is that until May 2014, the Norwegian Constitution and its amendments were written in a language form corresponding to the written language of juridical and administrative genres in Norway in the last third of the nineteenth century (Vinje 2002). This language form of the Constitution's text was established in a thorough linguistic revision in 1903. The Norwegian language has evolved considerably since the 1903 revision was done, however, and the Constitution's language form resembled Danish more than modern Norwegian. Thus, there was a vast gap between the Constitution's language form and the modern Norwegian language. In May 2014, just before this book went into print, Stortinget finally modernized the Constitution's language form.

In Norway, the Constitution and all its amendments since 1903 are considered an evolving text: an amendment replaces the original phrasing of the relevant article, and dates of each amendment are entered into the constitutional text. In other constitutions, amendments do not replace the original constitutional text, but instead are added at its end. The Norwegian Constitution does not specify the language form of constitutional amendments. Yet, since the revision in 1903, the practice has been to write all constitutional amendments in the language form of that revision. This practice is unique in an international context. In addition, it differs from that used in ordinary Norwegian legislation. Despite its unique position, however, the Constitution's language form has rarely been a topic in Norwegian parliamentary discourse. Between 1906 and 2008, Stortinget did not discuss complete renovation of the Constitution's language form, instead only correcting language errors.[2]

In 2008, a complete renovation of the Constitution's language form was proposed (*Grunnlovsforslag nr. 16 [2007–2008]*). The proposal was eventually rejected by Stortinget in May 2012 mainly (but not only) because it did not take into account both official Norwegian languages, *bokmål* (a modified form of Danish) and *nynorsk* (a nineteenth-century literary form devised from the country dialects). Shortly thereafter, Stortinget's presidium appointed a panel of legal and linguistic experts to draft a proposal for a modernized constitutional text in both languages (*Dokument 19 [2011–2012]*), which resulted in *Grunnlovsforslag nr. 25 (2011–2012)*. The presidium's plan was to have the new language versions of the Constitution adopted before the Constitution's bicentennial on 17 May 2014. As this chapter will show, modernizing the Constitution's language proved to be more difficult and complicated than Stortinget's presidium envisaged.

The main question in this chapter concerns how in the period 2004–2014 members of parliament (MPs) have perceived the Constitution's language form. In the Constitution's Article 112, MPs are given the power to amend the Constitution. Moreover, MPs are key users of the Constitution because they must relate to the Constitution in their legislative work. I look at the MPs' arguments and positioning as expressed in the discourse and at how procedural, political, and institutional factors influence discourse.

This investigation is one of the first studies of Norwegian parliamentary discourse, and builds on approaches developed for analyzing parliamentary discourses as institutional communication (Madzharova Bruteig 2010). The investigation concentrates on what I call "parliamentary discourse on the Constitution's language form," which I define as everything considered relevant to forming discourse (parliamentary discourse in this case) on this topic (for arguments concerning this way of selecting discourse for analysis, see Teubert [2010: 8–24]). Sources include constitutional amendment proposals, official stenographic reports and video records from Stortinget's chamber meetings, Stortinget's committee reports and other parliamentary printed matter, other materials from Stortinget's official website, and selected responses in Norwegian print media.

Constitutional Amendments and Language Form

Only since 2006 have changes in the Constitution's language form been considered amendments. The draft for the language revision in 1903 was worked out by Stortinget's presidium and approved by the Constitutional Committee (*Kontroll- og konstitusjonskomiteen*) without being debated in the chamber (Hylland 1989: 349–350). Apparently, MPs in those days did not consider mere language corrections to be constitutional amendments per se, so they did not use the formal amendment procedure specified in the Constitution's Article 112.

The 1903 revision mainly changed the orthography of the Constitution's text. The revised edition of the Constitution was published as a book (*Kongeriget Norges Grunnlov og øvrige Forfatningsdokumenter* 1903) and the language form used in this book established the language norm for subsequent editions. The next official editions of the Constitution, including newly accepted amendments, were printed in 1914 and 1921. In these two editions, changes of the Constitution's language form were not treated as constitutional amendments, either. The 1914 edition established the praxis of proposing constitutional amendments in the language form of the 1903 revision. Up to 2012, this praxis has been adhered to in all revised editions of the Constitution. Since 1967, such revised editions are published every fourth year.

However, MPs have experienced increasing difficulties in complying with the 1903 language form when writing constitutional amendment proposals. A proposal must include the exact phrasing of the proposed amendment. MPs' difficulties stem mainly from the vast difference between today's Norwegian and the Constitution's language form. For example, nouns are no longer written with initial capitals, verbs today have the same form in the singular and the plural, and many words have undergone changes in meaning. One example concerns Article 17, which allows the king (in reality the government) to pass provisional legislation concerning, inter alia, *Politi* while Stortinget is not in session. *Politi* literally means "police," which in today's Norwegian, like in English, refers to the police as an institution for law and order. In 1814, however, this term referred to public regulation and welfare in general, and this is still the legal meaning of *Politi* in the Constitution. It is a safe guess that this meaning will escape most modern readers other than lawyers and other specialists. Finally, legal and administrative language and the language in parliamentary practice have become less formal.

An article by professor in social economy and political science Aanund Hylland (1989) sparked new interest in the Constitution's language form by pointing out that it did not, as was widely believed, date from the 1814 Constitution. The language form of the 1989 edition represented that of the renovated 1903 edition. His article was followed by a monograph by Finn-Erik Vinje (2002) on the Constitution's language form from a historical perspective, a monograph ordered and published by Stortinget. Vinje was professor of Norwegian language until 2006. He also served as a language consultant for Stortinget.[3] These studies may have been instrumental in later attempts to renovate the Constitution's language. As the Constitution is venerated because of its symbolic significance for Norway's independence in 1814, there is less symbolic power in the 1903 language form.

In recent years, MPs have taken a greater interest in the role of the Constitution's language form. When, in February 2006, Stortinget's chamber debated a set of language corrections, MPs unanimously voted for a presidium proposal that stated that "even mere language changes in the constitutional text [require] submission of formal proposals for constitutional amendment and processing in accordance with Article 112" (*Stortingets presidentskap til professor Finn-Erik Vinje* 2004). Therefore, since 2006, corrections of language errors are considered formal constitutional amendments.

The practice of writing constitutional amendment proposals only in the 1903 language form changed in 2008. In a letter specifically about the language correctness of constitutional amendment proposals, then Stortinget president Thorbjørn Jagland expressed willingness to consider having new proposals written in modern language, too, if those making such proposals insist (*Stortingets presidentskap ved Thorbjørn Jagland* 2008). In addition, the letter explained that an arrangement with language consultants had been established to secure the language correctness of constitutional amendment proposals. Only proposals that had undergone language proofing would be announced in print. Already in September 2008, seven out of twenty-five submitted constitutional amendment proposals were written in both the 1903 language form and the modern language form.

Despite MPs' clearly increased interest in language matters, as reflected in the procedural changes in 2006 and 2008, it should be noted that generally most MPs are far less concerned with language changes per se than with substantive changes (*realitetsendringer*). It is a recurring phenomenon that those arguing in favor of changes in the Constitution's language form guarantee that the proposed changes will not lead to substantive changes in the Constitution itself.

Debates on Constitutional Amendment Proposals in the Chamber

Traditionally, debates on constitutional amendment proposals happen in the chamber twice yearly: once in the spring session and once in the autumn session. When considering most constitutional amendment proposals, MPs debate less actively than they do during routine legislative work (exceptions are a few debates on some recurrent, very controversial proposals). Normally, MPs debate several constitutional amendment proposals during one meeting. Voting takes place after all constitutional amendment proposals have been debated, not separately after debate on each proposal.[4] Presumably, the tendency to debate constitutional amendment proposals less actively and postponing votes until after debates on all constitutional amendment proposals strengthen the debates' *consensual character*. In debates on these proposals, MPs express agreement rather than disagreement.

Indeed, debates on constitutional amendment proposals in the chamber often consist of consensus-oriented utterances. For example, MPs begin speeches by expressing recognition of and agreement with the previous speaker's point. When a case can be presented as positive or negative, MPs avoid the negative. *Rejection* of a proposal may be announced by the president by emphasizing that the Constitutional Committee's report was *approved*: "Voting: In a vote between the Committee's report and the proposal from the Socialist Left Party, the report was approved by 153 votes against 11 votes" (*Referat Stortinget* 2012).

That all questions must be submitted through the president during debates in the chamber contributes to these debates' consensual character. Speakers do not address each other directly, but via the president. Finally, each constitutional amendment proposal is presented to the chamber by the Constitutional Committee's rapporteur for that specific proposal. The proposal is not presented by its author.

Architectonic features and MPs' seating order further support the consensus-oriented interactions. Because of the chamber's rotunda shape, MPs sit in almost a full circle open to the presidium's seats and the speaker's tribune. Seating is alphabetical by district name. Unlike the seating in many other parliaments, the seating in Norway's is not by party affiliation. Also unlike in many other national parliaments, in Norway's many MPs use their local dialect when debating. Thereby, they emphasize their regional affiliation, perhaps sometimes so that party affiliation is toned down.

Regarding eventually *accepted* constitutional amendment proposals, they are debated briefly and by only a few speakers. Generally, a more lively debate occurs on eventually *rejected* constitutional amendment proposals, such as those proposing separation of church and state or those proposing a republican form of government. These two proposals have been regularly presented to Stortinget since 1870 and 1905, respectively. The first one was finally approved after intense debate on 21 May 2012.

The consensual character of debates on constitutional amendment proposals is perhaps also linked to *grunnlovskonservatisme* (constitutional conservatism) (see Warner et al. in this volume), a notion that Norwegian scholars, political scientists, and legal scholars often use to describe Stortinget's alleged reluctance to amend the Constitution. The notion of constitutional conservatism is alive despite the fact that three-quarters of the Constitution's articles have been amended one or more times since 1814.

Perhaps the decoration of Stortinget's chamber accentuates to MPs their connectedness with the Eidsvold framers and their veneration for the 1814 Constitution. The Constitution is always present through the only painting in the chamber, Oscar A. Wergeland's *Eidsvold 1814*. The painting forms the visual background for all work in the chamber. It hangs behind the presidium's seats and the speaker's tribune so that it is in front of all MPs (see figure 9.1). Painted in 1885, it captures the historic moment when, on 17 May 1814, deputies signed the Constitution at Eidsvold. It was painted to hang in this exact place in the chamber.[5] Wergeland's painting is perhaps the most common visual symbol of the Constitution; it receives special attention in relation to Constitution Day, 17 May. In addition, it has become a frequent symbol of Stortinget. For example, it is often seen in televised chamber debates.

However, one reason that the notion of constitutional conservatism is alive and well may also stem from the Constitution's language form. For example, political scientist Bjørn Erik Rasch states, "The myth about constitutional conservatism is still alive, most likely because of the archaic language in which the Constitution and all recent constitutional amendment proposals are phrased" (Rasch 2000).

Proposals for Partial Language Renovation 2004–2012

Constitutional language matters are perceived as changes of an administrative character that are the responsibility of Stortinget's presidium. Therefore, pre-

9.1. Oscar A. Wergeland's painting *Eidsvold 1814* in Stortinget's chamber.
Copyright: Stortinget

sidium members have made almost all constitutional amendment proposals for changes of the Constitution's language form. MPs have paid little attention to partial language renovation. Such renovation typically concerns correcting language errors.

If in the chamber MPs mention such corrections, they typically do so only in passing. For example, in a chamber debate on the important Article 100, which concerns the freedom of speech, the Constitutional Committee's rapporteur Svein Roald Hansen said, "Hereby, a thorough debate and a broad hearing on freedom of speech will hopefully be brought to a final agreement on Article 100 of the Constitution, with the exception of possible language errors" (*Referat Stortinget* 2006a).

Constitutional amendment proposal number 8 (*Grunnlovsforslag nr. 8 [2003–2004]*) concerned language corrections in fifteen articles. When the proposal was debated in the chamber on 2 February 2006, only one speaker was on the agenda, the chair of the Constitutional Committee. In his first sentence, he guaranteed that the constitutional amendment proposal would not lead to substantive changes: "This is a constitutional amendment proposal that does not change the Constitution's substance, but that suggests correcting language errors" (*Referat Stortinget* 2006b). The proposal was accepted by unanimous vote after this short presentation. The whole consideration took four minutes.[6]

The next Storting constituted for October 2009–October 2013 debated four constitutional amendment proposals on 27 May 2010. Proposal number 15 (*Grunnlovsforslag nr. 15 [2007–2008]*) suggested some small, mostly orthographic, changes in four articles. In the Constitutional Committee's report, the committee guaranteed that these language corrections did not cause substantive changes. Therefore, the committee approved the corrections: "The Committee would like to underline that the proposals did not evoke any substantive changes, but only correction of obvious language mistakes" (*Innstilling 254 S [2009–2010]*). MPs voted, without debate (no MP made a speech, not even the Constitutional Committee's rapporteur), to approve the proposal after Stortinget's president had read it.

Debates in the chamber concerning language corrections, therefore, have often been merely formal, even after such corrections were given the status of constitutional amendment proposals.

Proposals for Complete Renovation of the Constitution's Language Form

In his monograph on the Constitution's language form from a historical perspective, Vinje (2002: 150–160) listed five possible variants for the Constitution's future language form: (1) restore the language form of the 1814 Constitution (based on either the 17 May edition or the 4 November edition), and write new amendments in that same language form; (2) keep the status quo, that is, the language form of the 1903 edition; (3) do not revise the present form, but write new constitutional amendments in modern language—as is the praxis of ordinary legislation; (4) translate the Constitution into present-day Norwegian; and (5) carefully modernize the language form.

Vinje followed up his work by authoring, in 2008, a constitutional amendment proposal for complete renovation of the Constitution's language form. The proposal included the entire constitutional text in the renovated language form. The renovation followed the fifth variant above and, according to Vinje, the proposed changes were only "language adjustments."[7] The proposed changes consisted mainly of orthographic changes (for example, *aa* would change into å, *th* would change into *t*), as well as single morphological, syntactical, and lexical adjustments. The proposed renovation would not modernize the Constitution's language form into contemporary Norwegian. The Constitution would still have an archaic language form. Moreover, some realities that had ceased to exist would nevertheless be maintained in the constitutional text. The Constitution's language form would still display traces of the Norwegian language's evolution so that readers could appreciate the text's historical significance.

Vinje's constitutional amendment proposal presented the constitutional text only in *bokmål*. This presentation conforms to the Norwegian tradition of approving new legislation only in *bokmål* or *nynorsk*. Decisions concerning which language laws should be submitted in are in praxis made by the MP who is the case's rapporteur in Stortinget's relevant committee.

Because since 2006 changes in the Constitution's language form are considered constitutional amendments, this complete language renovation must follow constitutional amendment procedures as regulated by Article 112. The former vice president of Stortinget Carl Ivar Hagen submitted the constitutional amendment proposal on behalf of Vinje (*Grunnlovsforslag nr. 16 [2007–2008]*).

In subsequent debates conducted in newspapers, participants argued that the Constitution's position as a national symbol should not be weakened. For example, some argued that the Constitution is a ceremonial document with representative and symbolic dimensions and that these are perhaps best served by an elevated archaic language form. Others argued that improving the understandability of the Constitution required renovating its language form because many of its articles are written in language that is difficult to understand today.

As testament of the importance placed on the Constitution's language form, the Constitutional Committee held its first ever open hearing on constitutional amendment proposals to discuss this very proposal for complete renovation of the Constitution's language form. Normally, the Constitutional Committee's meetings are closed to the public. Thus, the hearing on 1 March 2012 was characterized by its chair, Anders Anundsen, as "historic" ("Åpen høring i Stortingets" 2012).[8] The following experts spoke before the Constitutional Committee: professors Vinje and Hylland, professors of law Eivind Smith and Mads T. Andenæs, ombudsmann Arne Fliflet, and representatives from the Norwegian Language Council, Arnfinn Muruvik Vonen (director) and Åse Lill Kimestad (deputy chair of the board). All argued in favor of renovation to remove inconsistencies and language errors from the Constitution, which was characterized as "a national treasure." The Constitution, they argued, has a unique importance and a consolidating and unifying function. Several speakers (experts and Constitutional Committee members alike) referred to the proposed renovation of the Constitution's language form as a "translation." Andenæs emphasized that the significant distance between the Constitution's current language form and contemporary Norwegian creates a tension between the antiquated language form and the Constitution's living content. Smith called the Constitution's 1903 language form an "unnecessary screen" between the people and the Constitution's text. He argued that if the Constitution's language form is renovated, people will understand the Constitution better and perhaps debate it more. Therefore, he concluded, renovation could influence the functioning of Norwegian democracy.

For Constitutional Committee members, the most significant issue was whether the proposed renovation of the Constitution's language form would allow new interpretations of the content and therefore substantive changes. They feared that the proposed renovation would not be a purely linguistic change.

The Norwegian Language Council representatives emphasized two aspects as most important: the Constitution must exist in a language understandable for all, and both official Norwegian languages, *bokmål* and *nynorsk,* should be treated equally. It was also mentioned that perhaps a version in the Sami language (the language of the Sami minority) should be considered.

Official Norwegian state policy is that state institutions should use both *bokmål* and *nynorsk* in public documents (*Lov om målbruk i offentleg teneste* 1980). The practice for other important texts is similar. For example, in 2011, two translations of the Bible were published simultaneously, one volume in *bokmål* and one in *nynorsk*. However, until 2012, the only proposal for renovating the Constitution's language form in both *bokmål* and *nynorsk* was submitted in 1906. This proposal (by Nikolaus Gjelsvik) was not approved (Hylland 1989: 356; see also Holmøyvik 2010). It included changes to content, such as numbering of articles, and some substantive changes.

Mainly because of the unsolved issue of *bokmål* and *nynorsk,* on 21 May 2012 Stortinget adopted the Constitutional Committee's report rejecting the constitutional amendment proposal for complete renovation of the Constitution's language form. Eight MPs spoke prior to the voting (including both the rapporteur for the proposal and the committee's chair), and the consideration in the chamber was unusually lengthy, nearly an hour. In their speeches, most MPs praised the work of the committee's rapporteur and of Vinje. On the other hand, they emphasized the need to have the Constitution in a renovated language form and in both official languages. A minority consisting of MPs from the two biggest rightist parties supported adopting the proposal (the proposed renovation only in *bokmål*) because, as voiced by MP Per-Kristian Foss (of the Conservative Party), "We have managed without a *nynorsk* version for nearly two hundred years" (*Referat Stortinget* 2012). However, after the roll call vote, the constitutional amendment proposal was rejected 95–69. In a new vote, 151–12, Stortinget accepted the following proposal for further work on complete renovation of the Constitution's language form: "Stortinget asks the presidium to see that updated language editions of the Constitution, in *bokmål* and *nynorsk*, are prepared. In this work, the two editions should have equal positions and linguistic modernization should not change the substance of the old (current) Constitution" (*Referat Stortinget* 2012).

Shortly after, Stortinget's presidium appointed an expert committee (*Grunnlovsspråkutvalget*) charged with working out the proposals for renovations in both *bokmål* and *nynorsk*. The committee's report became a main part of the constitutional amendment proposal presented on 28 September 2012 (*Grunnlovsforslag nr. 25 [2011–2012]*). This proposal consists of two complete renovations of the Constitution's language form: one in *bokmål* and one in *nynorsk*.

Despite Stortinget's decision in 2012 to have an expert committee prepare updated language versions of the Constitution was made with a huge majority (151–12), Vinje and his supporters in Stortinget were not satisfied with the outcome. Consequently, MPs of the Conservative Party and the Progress Party also put forward Vinje's language version as an amendment proposal in 2012. As a result, in May 2014 Stortinget had to choose between two variants either the *bokmål* and *nynorsk* versions of the expert committee appointed by the presidium, or the *bokmål* version of Vinje joined by the *nynorsk* version of the expert committee (*Grunnlovsforslag nr. 21 [2011–2012], Grunnlovsforslag 22 [2011–2012]*).

When the two proposals came up for discussion in the Constitutional Committee in February 2014, it quickly became apparent that the language reform would not pass the Committee smoothly. This time, the main point of dispute was not the *nynorsk* edition of the Constitution, but the *bokmål* edition. The political parties could not agree on the choice between the more conservative language style in Vinje's *bokmål* edition and the more modern language style and more comprehensive modernization in the *bokmål* edition prepared by the expert committee. Language is a sensitive issue in Norway, and the choice between language styles can be of historical, cultural and social significance. In this case, the language is of particular importance as it concerns the Constitution, with its own deep historical, cultural and political significance in Norway.

After another public hearing on 19 February, members of the Committee argued in the media for quite different outcomes of the proposed language reform. A majority still supported the language version prepared by the expert committee on the request of the presidium. They argued that a language reform would strengthen Norwegian democracy and the Constitution itself since the reform removed the linguistic barrier between the Constitution and the citizens. However, the rightist Progress Party still supported Vinje's language version, while the Christian Democratic Party and the Conservative Party eventually opposed all the amendment proposals for language reform. On one hand, the opponents to the language reform stressed that the archaic language symbolized the Constitution's historical and cultural roots, and on the other hand they were worried that the language reform might lead to unintended substantive changes. Even though these parties were in a minority in the Committee, they could still block a reform of the Constitution's language as they held more than 1/3 of the votes in Stortinget. In Norway, constitutional amendments require a 2/3 majority.

In the end the political deadlock was broken when the Progress Party and the Christian Democratic Party reached an agreement with the parliamentary majority only a few days before the vote on 6 May. At that time the media reported that the language reform was doomed. The prospect of a failed language reform, intended as a symbolic act of giving the Constitution back to the people for the bicentenary, was probably instrumental in turning the tide. The end result was a compromise which few were happy with. The majority reluctantly agreed to Vinje's language version as the *bokmål* edition of the Constitution, while the Progress Party and the Christian Democratic Party agreed to a *nynorsk* version. When the Conservative Party realized they were left alone in their opposition to the language reform, they too abandoned all their arguments against the reform and joined ranks with the other parties. In the end, the language reform was passed on 6 May 2014 with a convincing 168–1 vote. The large majority provides a formal veil of consensus over the harsh rhetoric and the disputes between MPs and between the political parties in the months before and indeed also in the parliamentary debate on the day of the vote. The two new and quite different language versions of the Constitution, a *bokmål* version in a conservative language and a *nynorsk* version in a modern language and with modernized concepts and structure, was an unforeseen outcome when Stortinget in 2012 decided to modernize the Constitution's language. In 2014 the outcome was considered by the parliamentary majority to be an unhappy but necessary compromise. Therein is the germ for future discussions of the Constitution's language.

Conclusions

Since 2006, significant procedural changes have occurred regarding the Norwegian Constitution's language form. These changes are unique in the Constitution's 200-year history. MPs have become more aware of the need for language correctness in the Constitution's text and more aware of the general role of language form. Because of their increased awareness, Stortinget gave language corrections the status of constitutional amendments (in 2006) and approved writing new constitutional amendment proposals in modern language (in 2008). The first open hearing in the Constitutional Committee (on 1 March 2012) was held specifically to hear expert opinions concerning the constitutional amendment proposal for complete renovation of the Constitution's language form. On 21 May 2012, the Constitution's language form was explicitly debated when Stortinget agreed to require complete renovation into both *bokmål* and *nynorsk*. The constitutional amendment proposals of 28 September 2012, which presents two such renovated editions, and the intense debates on the language reform in the months before its adoption on 6 May 2014, reflects an increased sensitivity to the Constitution's language.

Debates on constitutional amendment proposals in Stortinget's chamber are characterized by greater consensus and fewer voices than are debates concerning commonplace legislative work. This consensus may stem from veneration of the Constitution as well as from discursive features and procedural praxis. Yet by renovating the Constitution's language, Stortinget has now taken steps toward making the Constitution more accessible to the MPs and the people alike. And in its new language forms, the Constitution may appear more modern and more relevant to public debates. In the long term, Stortinget's language renovations may thus have prepared the ground for more debate and less consensus on the Constitution's contents. For the advanced Norwegian democracy and the Constitution itself, this development can only be a good thing.

NOTES

1. Karen Gammelgaard and Eirik Holmøyvik contributed to this chapter. Quotes from parliamentary documents and discussions were translated by the author.
2. Between 1906 and 2008, Stortinget did not discuss complete renovation of the Constitution's language form, but only corrected language errors, except for the brief consideration of the Liberal Party's general proposal (*Representantforslag 87 S [2010–2011]*) for complete renovation of the Constitution (language and content). This proposal was rejected by all other parties after a very short debate.
3. In addition to contributing to public debate on the Constitution's language form, professors Hylland and Vinje have also been involved directly in writing constitutional amendment proposals. However, because they are not MPs, they do not have the right to formally make constitutional amendment proposals.

4. Voting on constitutional amendment proposals proceeds by roll call vote. The president reads out the MPs' names alphabetically by district, and each MP has to answer yes or no to the proposal.

5. Parliamentary chambers in Europe have no standard solution as to the decoration of the wall behind the presidium. To use only neighboring Denmark and Sweden as examples, the Danish Parliament Folketinget and the Swedish Parliament Riksdagen have modern neutral large textile works behind the chambers' presidium. Many other chambers have the state emblems behind the presidium.

6. This proposal was debated at the same meeting as the change in Article 100 on the freedom of expression (*Grunnlovsforslag nr. 21 [2003–2004]*). The change in Article 100 was approved after two speeches (concerning committee work on this proposal, see Kalleberg in this volume).

7. "Linguistically adjusted" articles were also the so-called sleeping articles that "may continue to sleep—however in a newer nightgown" (*Grunnlovsforslag nr. 16 [2007–2008]*).

8. Other committees in Stortinget sometimes hold open hearings to gather information on topics of particular importance. During three months, from March to June 2011, thirty-nine open hearings were held in the other committees in Stortinget.

▸• Part IV •◂

FREEDOM OF EXPRESSION

10

Article 100 and the Evolution of a Public Opinion Text Culture in Denmark-Norway 1770–1799

Kjell Lars Berge

Introduction: Communication Spheres of Late Eighteenth-Century Denmark-Norway

Which ideas and experiences enabled deputies at Eidsvold in 1814 to frame Article 100 in the Norwegian Constitution? In this chapter, the relatively progressive Article 100 stating that "an intire liberty of the press shall take place" will be accounted for by the development of a fresh, intense, and fertile communication culture of public opinion in Denmark-Norway during the eighteenth century's last three decades. We shall see how a new rhetoric mediating the ideas of the 1814 Constitution was created in an interaction between the communication spheres in Copenhagen, Denmark, and Trondhjem, Norway.[1] These communication spheres consisted of a complicated growth and interplay of different text cultures such as belles lettres and science, of genres such as essays, dialogues, and private letters, and of formats such as pamphlets, journals, books, and newspapers. The most prominent space for these new communication spheres was the capital, Copenhagen. It was the dominant center of the twin kingdoms until 1814 and by far its most populous city. There, too, resided the king, the central administration, and the kingdom's only university, and most of the kingdom's trade was conducted there. For the development of Norwegian intellectual life, Copenhagen was relevant because until 1811, all young men aspiring for higher education and a position in the state had to take their exams at the university there. These young men in exile formed an important cultural group, Det norske Selskab (the Norwegian Society), where new ideas on how the kingdoms should be governed were imported and discussed.

Still, some important alternative intellectual and political centers developed in Norway, too, especially in the old religious center of Trondhjem, where the cathedral built over the grave of the most important Nordic saint, St. Olav, was a reminder of Norway's historical past and consequently of the possibility of a more independent Norwegian state. During the eighteenth century, Trondhjem developed as an important economic center because of the king's sale of old properties originally belonging to the Catholic Church and to the archbishop of Nidaros (i.e., Trondhjem). Young and dynamic entrepreneurs, most of them emigrants from the duchies of Slesvig and Holsten in the southern part of the Danish-Norwegian kingdoms, bought these properties. Trondhjem also developed as an intellectual center thanks to the establishment of Det kongelige norske Videnskabers Selskab (the Royal Norwegian Society of Sciences and Letters) in 1760. Therefore, it was not accidental that it was in Trondhjem that some of the most radical thoughts in the kingdoms were developed, profoundly influencing the 1814 Constitution's Article 100 and its interpretation (Berge 2010).

But how was this development toward a liberal constitution based in the new communication sphere of public opinion possible? The development can be explained by presenting the evolution of a public opinion text culture in Denmark-Norway constituted primarily by the announcement of the important, and in its era almost sensational, *Kongelig Reskript af 14. September 1770* (1786) (freedom of writing rescript of 14 September 1770).

Textual, Cultural, and Political Consequences of the Freedom of Writing Rescript

In 1771, a pamphlet, written as a letter to King Christian VII of Denmark-Norway, was published in Copenhagen. The letter opened as follows:

> You Monarch of virtue! Despite being born to despotic Government, do YOU believe, from the position of YOUR Baltic shores, that you also govern me? Am I one of YOUR subjects, that YOU therefore act toward me, as towards them? That YOU soften my life and make me happy?
>
> There are only a few Kings, such as YOU, who transgress the borders that nature has established for their holy power. The Emperor of China, to whom I often write, has to this date not given me any compliments. I am more satisfied with the praiseworthy amazon[2] that has challenged the imperial throne of the fat Mustapha,[3] and the wise Stanislaus[4] and the great Friedrich[5] (that I for some time was an enemy of) that have sent, in my humble solitude, some graceful greetings that Switzerland[6] decorates its newspapers with. I am not a good friend of Ganganelli.[7] He believed that I was not a good Christian, because I visited Prussia. But this Pope was wrong; even he is infallible.[8]

> But still, without examining what one owes the Bible, whether it is better in this world to be a Pope or a king, or whether it is more comfortable to live as an unknown such as I, my old age allows me to let me be heard from the remote deserts of Jura[9] to YOUR wise youth. And free, still respectful, bold without pride, I fall on me knees before YOU in the name of all mankind. It speaks through my voice. It blesses YOUR mildness. YOU return mankind its rights, and YOU allow thinking. Sermons, novels, natural science, odes, history, opera: everything might be written by anyone. Let everyone who wants to whistle, do so. (Voltaire 1771)[10]

The author of the letter was the famous French philosopher Voltaire. Translated from French into Danish, the letter was published under the title *Hr. F.A. de Voltaires Brev til Hans Majestet Kongen af Danmark angaaende den udi hans Stater forundte Tryk-Frihed* (Mr. F.A. de Voltaire's Letter to His Majesty the King of Denmark Concerning the Allowed Freedom of Print in His States). The letter is important and interesting for at least three reasons.

First, it points to the fact that a new communication realm in society had been constituted by the king of Denmark-Norway. This new communication realm is the institution of *public opinion* in a so-called *public sphere*.

Second, it points to the prospect that a new pact between the people and the king of Denmark-Norway, building on the *universal right of free thoughts and opinions for all human beings,* might be established.

And third, the letter points to the possibility that all utterances and texts—from the text culture of opera to the text culture of natural science—might represent this universal pact of freedom of thought and opinion in the institution of public opinion. Thus, Voltaire indicates the necessity of a specific text culture consisting of *a new rhetoric* that mediates public opinion.

In his open letter, Voltaire praises the unconditional and therefore sensational freedom of writing rescript by the king of Denmark-Norway. On 14 September 1770, the king had announced that the censorship of all writing should end. Virtually overnight, the constitutive norms of communication through writing in society were transformed. The possibility of a new communication order, the public sphere, could no longer be considered exclusively a utopian ideal or goal, but an actual political possibility, challenge, and reality. Internationally, this potential communication order was considered a sensation, and something fundamentally new and unheard of. It is this sensation that Voltaire's letter to the king expresses.

We see from how Voltaire expresses his opinions that he clearly thinks that censorship's end, and with it the establishment of the institution of public opinion, implies a new legal pact between those with absolute power, the kings, and the people serving them. In Voltaire's words, the Danish-Norwegian monarch did no more than return to the people freedoms of thoughts and expressions that already rightfully belonged to them. And we can see from the letter's proud positioning that Voltaire boldly speaks to the king on everyone's behalf. Consequently, the king can no longer be considered as the one and only individual or institution determining what is true and right in society. Power and truth must be distinguished from each other. In this way, a new communication sphere must be developed, where truth and the rights of the society are discussed without intervention by an absolute ruler, the king. This ancient but recently reestablished pact implies—according to Voltaire—that every man is born free and that his opinions must be respected in their own right. In Voltaire's letter, we find traces of the classic Enlightenment ideas of universal human rights. Therefore, freedom of speech and writing is the fundamental warrant of a possible new pact of how relations between society's members should be constituted, for instance, in the state's constitution.

Today, Voltaire's reasoning is universally known and recognized. The ideas of a public sphere and of public opinion on the one hand and of universal human rights on the other hand have been thoroughly studied and discussed in academic literature ever since their post-Renaissance development. Moreover, Voltaire's argumentation is warranted in the fundamental ideas of the Enlightenment program to which he prominently contributed.

The third reason that Voltaire's letter is important is less often discussed in literature on the Enlightenment, and even less often in literature discussing the 1814 Norwegian Constitution. In his letter, Voltaire explicitly refers to the new text cultures of the Enlightenment that may flourish through this new freedom granted by the king, a freedom creating a new situation for all mankind. This third argument, referred to in Voltaire's letter by the words "sermons, novels, natural science, odes, history, opera: everything might be written by anyone. Let everyone that wants to whistle do so," in fact indicates a need for *new text norms* adapted for this newly constituted communication sphere where free men might express their thoughts in writings and in printed texts freely and without fear of being censored or punished. As we understand from Voltaire's probably hastily collected catalog of genres, these new text norms were not yet established as a stable genre system for opinion makers. Huge differences existed in how the belles lettres genre of "odes" on the one hand and the religiously founded "sermons" on the other hand may represent independent individuals' free thinking and publically formulated viewpoints in political matters.

The Evolution of a New Rhetoric and Constitutive Text Norms for Public Opinion

How were these new text norms established as a resource for developing public opinion? A rhetoric using these new text norms as a resource enabled the intellectual climate that laid the groundwork for and fertilized the ideas of the 1814 Constitution. As indicated in this chapter's introduction, Trondhjem's communication sphere has been chosen as representative of the development in Norway because of the sphere's rich diversity of rhetorical activities. It has also been chosen because quite a few of its most active authors were prominent in the communication sphere of Copenhagen, too. However, no direct causal link exists between this new rhetoric and the making of the 1814 Constitution. The 1814 Constitution must be understood as a result of complex intentions and events and above all must be understood as internationally founded.[11] Still, *without* the evolution of this new rhetoric after 1770 that mediated freely expressed information and opinions by individuals who did not fear absolute rulers, the 1814 Constitution would probably not have come into being. Consequently, the 1814 Constitution should not be understood as accidental.

The freedom of writing rescript of 1770 stimulated immense text cultural changes in Denmark-Norway. The rescript was the most important reason why the common Danish-Norwegian text cultures so rapidly changed direction and shape. Politically, the rescript enabled young and ambitious men to find new arenas for intellectual, political, and rhetorical cultural education. A new public habitus was created, adapted to these young aspiring writers' interests.

Until the rescript was published, professors at the University of Copenhagen had to read and sanction all publications before they were printed. If printing was considered a theological matter, the publications had to be approved by the bishops in Denmark, Norway, and the duchies of Holsten and Slesvig. Most of this *printed* literature was bought and read by people belonging to the classes of noblemen, clergy, civil servants, officers of the armed forces, or the growing class of entrepreneurs and capitalists. The common man, on the other hand, was obliged to use a *Sorenskriver* (a sworn writer), appointed by the king, if he wanted to put his views and complaints forward to society's authorities in a *written* document. In general, lower and local civil servants dealt with such petitions. Sometimes, however, peasants were allowed to personally present petitions to the king at his Copenhagen castle on special weekdays. Absolutist communication between king and subject, whether written or printed, was thereby heavily regulated and controlled in all society's estates. In principle, until the rescript of 14 September 1770, the king was the addressee of all written texts regardless of medium, format, and genre. Every written and/or printed text had the king as its targeted model reader.

From a political as well as a juridical viewpoint, that a text was printed was secondary to the fact that it was written. This is why the king's announcement is called the freedom of *writing* rescript. Of course, even in an autocratic society such as that of Denmark-Norway, printed texts were more easily controlled and censored than were written texts that were not printed. An interesting example of this differentiation of the printed and the written is provided by the development from the seventeenth century onward of the newspaper's development as a medium for freely circulating information and opinion (Berge and Riiser Gundersen 2010). Until the 1814 Norwegian Constitution, with few exceptions printed newspapers were called *Adresseaviser* (address newspapers). They carried the king's proclamations, information about the arrival of ships and goods, information about weddings and deaths, excerpts of (mostly) scientific literature on sale in bookstores, and so forth. The address newspapers' publishers were required to have a royal permit to print their papers. Only one such permit was granted in each cathedral city. Often, the same individual was granted a royal permit to run both a bookstore and a print shop. Newspapers written by hand, in contrast, were so-called *politiske Aviser* (political newspapers). They published information about the government. These handwritten political newspapers were often created by a town's postmaster and distributed by him to subscribers all over the vast area of Denmark-Norway. These handwritten newspapers were neither controlled nor censored. Thus, as printed texts, the address newspapers belonged to the official communication sphere of the era prior to the freedom of writing rescript, while the handwritten newspapers belonged to the private sphere. The quality that distinguished handwritten newspapers from private letters was that these political handwritten newspapers were products intended for sale. Private letters constituted a text culture of their own, enabling families and friends to inform each other and keep in contact, especially families of civil servants and clergy. Both the written and the printed newspaper transformed everyday information, rumors, gossip, talk, and chattering between people into a new kind of merchandise: *the news*.

Before proceeding, it is important to differentiate between the act of expressing the truth about nature on the one hand and the act of expressing opinions on how society should be governed on the other hand. This difference between free information of truth and freely distributed opinions was not always considered in the late eighteenth century. The differences of and dynamics between the two kinds of expression might often explain why the king and his administration gradually lost power to new social groups, especially the rising class of manufacturers and their political associates. In the freedom of writing rescript, censorship was not abolished to allow free opinions from free men. Instead, it was abolished *primarily* to meet the king's need for true information about "prejudices" and "abuse" in order to react to possible "delusions." Fundamentally, the king intended to stimulate the industries of Denmark-Norway. What the king and supporters of the absolute monarchy's traditional values did not recognize—before it was too late—was that distributing free information led to distributing public opinions. For instance, if you knew that the king's centralized financial politics toward Norwegian entrepreneurs exporting goods from Norwegian ports was ineffective economically, you might also formulate an opinion on how financial politics should change. In such ways, differences between the king's economic interests and political opinions on the one hand and the manufacturers' economic interests and political opinions on the other hand surfaced in society. Such differences became visible as well as serious in the 1793 conflict over a Norwegian university, which soon became a national conflict. In this case, the conflict could only be curbed with the help of the ideology of patriotism. Patriotism enabled supporters of the Norwegian university to formulate common interests between different social groups competing for power, but open conflicts such as this created a juridical problem because according to the existing law, the king could not be criticized.

To understand public opinion characteristics at the end of the eighteenth century and the conditions participants worked under in the existing communication spheres, it should be emphasized that the evolution of the institution of public opinion was achieved as a process. Relevant text norms and genres did not exist as already developed resources. The text norms had to be consecutively invented through active communication in specific situations. It took years before the institution of public opinion could be considered a settled and stable text culture. Also in this case, the newspaper's development exemplifies the processual and dynamic nature of the late eighteenth century's new text cultures. In principle, every printed newspaper was an underdeveloped textual marketplace presenting and selling news, that is, information from the king and his officials, information about goods for sale in the city, and information about books for sale in bookstores, most of them related to science, technology, and didactic moral narratives. The printed newspaper did not carry any other news. As we have seen, in a printed newspaper, a reader would never find the so-called political news about what happened at the governmental level nationally and internationally. An interested reader would need access to handwritten newspapers. Even in these handwritten newspapers, the news, as it were, often involved spreading rather trivial information. Not until the end of the eighteenth century did printed newspapers start more systematically carrying news such as report-like texts informing citizens of spectacular events such as murders or fights in the harbor between local boys and foreign sailors. And even then, it was impossible to find in printed newspapers even superficial reports on how society was governed. In sum, officially sanctioned printed newspapers covered only business related to the market or conveyed information about births, marriages, deaths, and so forth that occurred among dignified citizens. Completely absent were genres and themes such as politically oriented reports, comments on political events, or public opinions—even of the more trivial kind. Therefore, it is anachronistic to understand the eighteenth-century newspaper as a phenomenon that eventually developed into an alternative power in the state (the so-called fourth estate).

So how could freely expressed information and opinions be distributed? And how did a more stable institution of public opinion develop, creating a reliable resource for creating politics? To answer these questions we must look to other formats for textual production besides the newspaper, primarily the pamphlet (Berge 1998). The pamphlet represented an old-fashioned format used extensively in conflicts leading to the division of Christianity into Catholic and Protestant, and the more modern formats developed into journals. Also, the traditional format of the book might be relevant. The dynamic uses of the pamphlet and the book developed the public sphere and created the background of the new text culture forming the idea of freedom of printing reflected in Article 100 of the 1814 Norwegian Constitution.

Some Democratic Challenges and Deficits in the Evolving Public Sphere

To understand the development of the text cultures of the public sphere and the implementation of experiences with it in Article 100, one must consider two prominent challenges that emerged as soon as the freedom of writing rescript of 1770 was implemented. Both challenges were related to the fundamental question of ownership of and inclusion in the public sphere (Sandvik 2010). Who should define relevant themes and participants in the newly established public sphere? In other words, did this public sphere evolve as a truly democratic communicative realm open for all groups, individuals, and topics?

The first challenge concerned features of the opinions expressed in the public to debate. Were the opinions directed to the king and were they answers to his wish for open-mindedness, or were they directed toward a new audience, forming a possible public opinion about the case presented? If so, what were the topics considered relevant by participants?

The second challenge concerned textual qualities of the opinions expressed publicly, that is, the textual norms or the ethics of the rhetoric of the unrestricted utterances. What rhetorical qualities characterized the new public opinions? Were they traditional humble requests for the king's attention, or were they distinguished as new forms suited to a new rhetorical situation and a new rhetorical culture?

Let us consider the first challenge. The freedom of writing rescript of 1770 was, as Voltaire makes clear in his letter to the king, at its core based on Enlightenment principles. However, seen from the viewpoint of the later consequences of open public debate, particularly the 1789 French Revolution, the reform was characterized by a rather naïve understanding of how an absolute monarchy could exercise power unchallenged. Originally, the rescript's writer and instigator, the king's head of government Johann Friedrich Struensee, justified his radical reform by the idea that in allowing public debate, the king would have access to information that was more honest and true on the economic situation and on the local administration of his public servants in the twin kingdoms of Denmark-Norway. But Struensee could neither foresee nor understand that establishing public opinion would have consequences for society's power relations, even the most essential of all, the relation constituting the basis for the absolute monarchy: the contract between the holder of absolute power—the king—and his subjects—the people.

In texts written from the perspective of the third estate, forming the overwhelming majority of the people, the so-called *almuen* (common man), the relation between the king and the people was clear. It was one between a "father" and his "children." This conservative and traditional idea was expressed in a pamphlet written by two Norwegian peasants and published anonymously in Copenhagen in 1771 ([Bie] 1771; Berge 1991). In this pamphlet, the two Norwegian peasants accuse the king's civil servants of corruption in their local district in Norway. Written, printed, published, sold, and read in Copenhagen, this pamphlet contributed to the development of the new text culture of public opinion. Nevertheless, the authors explicitly pointed out its model reader. It would be "alle tiders" (marvelous),[12] the pamphlet authors exclaim, if "han Far skiøl i Kiøpenham" (father himself in Copenhagen) would examine and inspect the case. Although the peasants write in the new public sphere based on the principles of free public opinions, they still consider the king as the model reader of the text. This viewpoint is in accordance with the law: in the absolute kingdom of Denmark-Norway, the king was the model reader of every text written and/or printed in the twin kingdoms. As mentioned, according to the king's law, peasants could complain through the king's local official, the *Sorenskriver*. According to the 1771 pamphlet, the fundamental change after the freedom of writing rescript was that peasants could write directly to the king without mediation of the *Sorenskriver*. As we will later see, this understanding of the concept of public opinion as primarily written and not printed leads to a difference in the discussion on how to formulate Article 100 in the 1814 Constitution between the peasants' representatives on the one hand and those of civil servants and the bourgeoisie on the other hand. At the 1814 Constitutional Assembly at Eidsvold, peasants insisted on the formulation "freedom of writing" in addition to freedom of printing, while civil servants and the bourgeoisie insisted on "freedom of printing" only (Langeland 2005; see Ringvej in this volume). In this way, the peasants' interpretation of the freedom of writing rescript was identical with the king's—in reality his head of government, Struensee's—explicit intentions. Unfortunately for the peasants and other representatives of the common man, the civil servants and the bourgeoisie's formulation was preferred.

Nevertheless, even if the peasants' 1771 pamphlet in no way formally diverged from the king's intentional and expressed will, their pamphlet represented something sensationally new and radical. It was an omen of a new form of authority whereby public opinion was formed through open and democratic debate. This authority was increased by the fact that all public opinions could be expressed, written, and published in total anonymity both for author and for printer. Therefore, the king and his civil servants could not investigate the motivation and social background of the criticism put forward in published texts, nor could they prosecute author and printer.

Moreover, the peasants' pamphlet illustrates how utterances should be composed. Genres for the new institution of public opinion were not constituted. Nevertheless, the authors did not create out of the blue a rhetoric adapted to the institution of public opinion. Well-established genres existed that defined how public opinion could be uttered in the public sphere.

Of course, there existed the old tradition of school rhetoric or *progymnasmata,* in which most young men attending the university were schooled. The status of this tradition was disputed, not least by the intellectual elite, for being a degenerate and antique form without relevance for new philosophical and political theories and the development of public opinion. The establishment of public opinion resulted in a renaissance of political rhetoric coined in the classical tradition of Marcus Tullius Cicero. Crucial for understanding the genres of the institution of public opinion is the revival of rhetoric in the so-called Scottish Enlightenment, primarily through Hugh Blair's famous book *Lectures on Rhetoric and Belles Lettres* (1783). It came to influence important and prominent participants in Danish-Norwegian society. A local Danish-Norwegian version of Blair's work was developed and published by the Norwegian Jacob Rosted in 1810. The title was *Forsøg til en Rhetorik* (Attempt at a Rhetoric).

Another strong text cultural tradition was that of the language of the church and of the various congregations developing in the shadow of the state church's Lutheran orthodoxy. As often before, the genre traditions of the Bible and of text norms built on those traditions represented a potential for political opposition, and consequently a resource for public opinion. Often the genres of religious life were used, such as sermon or prayer.

Moreover, authors participating in the public sphere had to choose rhetorical strategies as individuals. Authors often used traditional forms from other and more conventionalized text cultures, such as the didactic dialog, well-known from antiquity, and often used for religious purposes in Christian tradition. Alternatively, they could use the genre resources developed in the more liberal and advanced public spheres that had evolved in Great Britain and France. For instance, several authors used means of genres associated with the journals *The Tatler* and *The Spectator,* imported from London, or they used the essay genre often associated with a French tradition beginning with Montaigne. Authors could also use genres we today associate with the belles lettres or even the opera, such as the ode or the aria.

The Norwegian peasants' 1771 pamphlet is a typical example of the rhetorical challenges of expressing public opinion. In accord with the conservative understanding of the situation, the peasants wrote the text as a letter to the king. To be able to put forward their complaints to the king, they composed the letter as a dialog between two peasants. One, called Reiar, appears as more informed about the political situation after the publication of the freedom of writing rescript than the other, called Einar. Therefore, the letter to the king exploits didactic dialog means. Moreover, the pamphlet uses the conventions typical of oral intercourse. When informed by Reiar, the dialog partner Einar tells stories of how the king's foreign civil servants cheat peasants, in ways similar to how the king is cheated by foreign moneylenders in the free city of Hamburg. Einar's stories follow the standardized pattern of oral narratives.

A graphic presentation of how the text culture of public opinion between 1770 and 1799 integrated different, more or less established, text cultures and genres such as religious texts, poetry, scientific texts, and mostly private letters is given in figure 10.1 below. The king's texts governing the kingdoms are not included in the public sphere. Neither the king nor his public servants discussed the government of the society publicly. The king did not lower himself to being involved in politics. Not even what later became the prominent text culture of literature is included in the sphere of public opinion in 1770. In the eighteenth century, novels, stories, and fictional texts were generally considered unserious texts. Not until the nineteenth century was literature successively included in the public sphere. Its authors (such as the playwright Henrik Ibsen) created at the end of that century what became called a "poetocracy."

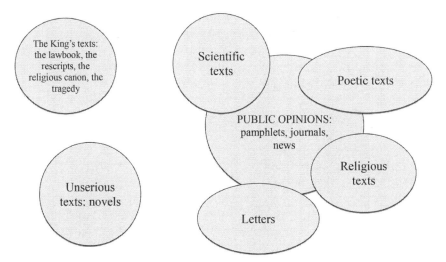

10.1. The text culture of public opinion in Denmark-Norway 1770–1799 in relation to other text cultures.

Accordingly, the authorities in Denmark-Norway experienced some of the same challenges of public debate as the citizens of Athens in 500 BC experienced when democracy based on public debate was implemented as an institution for executing power. As is well-known from the writings of, among others, Plato, Aristotle, and Isocrates, public debate leading to publically accepted decisions and actions had to follow some textual norms defining ethical standards. Only debate following these norms was considered acceptable. Consequently, the Greeks established schools where new generations of citizens could learn how public debate should be executed to be considered acceptable (Yunis 1996). The Greeks' challenges were repeated in Denmark-Norway after 1770 following the freedom of writing rescript. Article 100 in the Norwegian Constitution of 1814 should be interpreted as an answer to these challenges.

The Evolution of a Public Opinion Text Culture in Norway: The Case of Trondhjem

The Norwegian city of Trondhjem emerged as a melting pot for developing a public sphere in eighteenth-century Denmark-Norway. This sphere was local and provincial, but still connected to the kingdom's undisputed center, Copenhagen. Thanks to the strong capitalistic development in the city and in its hinterland, a strong interest for scientifically based knowledge and public opinion had been established. As presented earlier, the first Norwegian society for the promotion of science was established in Trondhjem. Prominent entrepreneurs and landowners supported and often became members of the society. Some of the founders also started journals in the fashion of international trends, such as Peter Frederik Suhm's journal *Throndhiemske Samlinger* (Trondhjem Collections). Suhm established an important connection with the elite in Copenhagen. When he returned to Copenhagen in 1765, he became an influential figure in the liberal and modernization-oriented Danish opposition to Struensee.

Another indication of the significance of the text cultures developing in late eighteenth-century Trondhjem was the fact that the city's bishop, Johan Ernst Gunnerus, was invited to Copenhagen to reform the university there. A young student, Johan Nordahl Brun, followed Gunnerus as his secretary. Nordahl Brun wrote the first tragedies in Danish, thus contributing to making theater an important text culture. Significantly, Nordahl Brun's second tragedy, *Einar Thambeskjælver*, first staged in 1772, raised the sensitive and potentially dangerous question of the cultural and political differences between Danes and Norwegians. Thereby, Nordahl Brun's tragedy demonstrated the potential of the belles lettres genres to express public opinions. A less prominent, but still relevant, indication of Trondhjem's status as a text cultural melting pot in

Denmark-Norway was that in 1756, the city's mayor, Niels Krog Bredahl, was invited to Copenhagen to write the libretto and stage the first Danish opera.

Still, for developing public opinion, establishing an address newspaper in the city was more important. Establishing the newspaper *Tronhiems kongelig allene privilegerede Adresse-Contoirs Efterretninger* (Trondhjem Royal and Only Privileged Address Office Intelligences) in 1767 did not initially indicate anything radically new. In fact, the paper's founder and first editor, a young lawyer, Martinus Nissen, in the first edition explicitly distanced himself from public debate generally. Nevertheless, the paper represented and functioned as a publication presented to and read by citizens, as the city's textual meeting place or marketplace. Therefore, a possible agora for public opinion was created. Perhaps, Nissen's establishing the paper reflected more than the interest of the city's civil servants and the capitalistic entrepreneurs to coordinate their economic and private activities, such as importing and selling goods or announcing marriages and births. In addition, despite his opposition to public debate, Nissen's establishing the paper perhaps reflected the interest in public debate of individuals from his social strata. Considered from this angle, a quite significant debate was instigated by a young and eager law student from Trondhjem. Under the pseudonym Philopatreias, Jacob Christian Bie published several pamphlets directly criticizing the foundations of the autocratic government of Denmark-Norway. His pamphlets immediately created shock waves in Copenhagen (see, e.g., [Bie] 1771). Bie's opinions were strongly challenged by a professor, Ove Høegh-Guldberg, at the important noble academy of Sorø near Copenhagen. He also was the teacher of the king's children. Høegh-Guldberg became the de facto prime minister of Denmark-Norway after Johann Friederich Struensee was driven from power and executed in 1773.

It is against this background that Matthias Conrad Peterson's emergence as a pioneer of public opinion must be understood and explained. When Nissen died in 1795, Peterson succeeded him as editor of Trondhjem's only newspaper. As a symbolic act of his explicit political agenda, he changed the paper's name to *Throndhjemske Tidende* (Throndhjem News). From 1795 to 1799, Peterson edited both *Throndhjemske Tidende* and the important journal *Qvartbladet* (Quarto Paper). From 1815 to 1819, he published the journal *Den lille Trondhjemske Tilskuer* (Little Trondhjem Spectator). Peterson developed *Throndhjemske Tidende* into a modern newspaper, inspired by the experiences of public debate in Denmark-Norway after 1770 and by the events of the French Revolution. He not only opened the newspaper's pages for public debate, but also quite enthusiastically urged citizens to express themselves honestly and without fear in the paper. Peterson's efforts to create an uncensored local public sphere, where public opinions might be expressed, were frowned upon by local authorities that reported to the king and his administration in Copenhagen. Because of a decree published in

1799 that radically restricted possibilities of public opinion (*Trykkefrihets-forordningen av 27. september 1799* 1800), Peterson was forced to resign as editor of Trondhjem's newspaper. But he did not do so without thumbing his nose at the king, publishing the king's decree in its entirety in a series of copies of *Throndhjemske Tidende* as a sort of insult and as an implicit comment on the stupidity of autocratic government.

From Public Opinion to Article 100: The Constitutive Text Norms of Public Speech

Peterson was not the only pioneer of public opinion in Norway in the two last decades prior to the 1814 Constitution. Yet he was the most radical and inventive. It was not a coincidence that he was the first to take Article 100 seriously and to use it to legitimate free and open social debate. In 1821, at the newly established Norwegian Supreme Court, he won an important and decisive freedom of printing trial against King Carl Johan of Sweden-Norway. The verdict established a relatively progressive understanding of the political debate in Norway.

At a general level, the case and fate of Peterson illustrate some of the political and juridical constraints and democratic limits of what became Article 100. First, Peterson represented a social class that during the decades after the announcement of the 1770 freedom of writing rescript—that Voltaire so vigorously cheered—had developed text norms that excluded other ways of expressing public opinion, especially the text traditions of the common man. By Peterson's rhetorical norms, the peasants' 1771 pamphlet would be considered naïve and silly, and accordingly an utterance not to be taken seriously. Peterson's reaction to lay preachers' political agitation using the traditional genres of the religious text culture is symptomatic of a class conflict between the educated liberal classes and the common man. When in 1799 the influential lay preacher Hans Nielsen Hauge visited him wanting to publish an article in his paper, Peterson refused to publish the text (Berge 2010). He felt that Hauge represented naïve and stupid prejudices and a childish approach to modern society. Consequently, Hauge and people like him could not be considered participants in the public sphere, but instead potentially dangerous religious rebels who could undermine society's liberal values. Coincidently, a majority of the deputies at Eidsvold in 1814 wished to consider illegal any religious meetings among laypersons if such meetings lacked the consent of an ordained state priest. In addition, participants in the public sphere needed to have access to the resources of classical rhetoric taught at the secondary school preparing young men for university. Consequently, the "intire liberty of the press" in Article 100 actually evolved as a freedom for the educated. Article

100 became a vehicle for opinion making for Peterson and his kind of people, not for the plebeian Hauge and his followers.

Second, and related to the first restriction, Article 100 speaks of liberty of "the press," not of liberty of "writing." The few peasants who were represented at Eidsvold in 1814 reacted to this wording. The educated deputies in their turn reacted to the peasants' opposition with arrogance and a patronizing attitude. For them, public opinion was printed, not written. Thereby, common men, used to the conventions of writing complaints to the king through the *Sorenskriver*, were in principle excluded from taking part in the public sphere. Not only were they not properly educated, but they also lacked access to the relevant formats, that is, the papers and journals where written public opinions were printed in a manner that was in accord with the rhetorical standards and textual norms of the educated, that is, the ruling class in the newborn Kingdom of Norway.

To sum up, Article 100 in the Norwegian Constitution of 1814 was phrased similar to how liberal ideas were phrased in Voltaire's open letter to King Christian VII of Denmark-Norway after the publication of the freedom of writing rescript in 1770. The subsequent public debate in Denmark-Norway challenged these liberal ideas and developed them further. The public debate also led to the evolution of communicative and textual norms defining how public opinion should be expressed. It was this normative cultivation and formation of the public sphere that enabled deputies at Eidsvold in 1814 to phrase and define Article 100 at all. Therefore, Article 100 presupposed specific constitutive norms for how public speech should be uttered by the free and autonomous members of "all mankind" that Voltaire spoke on behalf of in 1771. After 17 May 1814, these norms defined the understanding of a free and autonomous Norwegian citizen participating in the public sphere.

NOTES

1. Since 1931, the official name is Trondheim.
2. Catherine the Great of Russia.
3. The Sultan of the Ottoman Empire, Mustapha III.
4. Stanisław Leszczyński, King of Poland and Grand Duke of Lithuania.
5. King Frederick the Great of Prussia
6. Voltaire had lived in exile in Switzerland since 1758 in fear of persecution from, among others, the French king.
7. Ganganelli was the family name of Pope Clemens XIV.
8. Voltaire refers to the fact that King Frederick the Great of Prussia was a Protestant, and refers the Catholic doctrine of the Pope's infallibility.
9. The Swiss Republic.

10. Translated by the author. Capitalization of words and words written entirely in upper-case letters are per the original.
11. For example, N. Höjer (1882: 195) lists the French Constitution of 1791 among the direct sources of Article 100.
12. The pamphlet uses *altir*. The pamphlet is written in a Norwegian dialect. The publication is the first instance of written Norwegian language used for serious purposes since the Middle Ages.

To Speak What the Hour Demands

Framing the Future of Public Speech at Eidsvold in 1814

Mona Ringvej

The Norwegian Constitution declared on 17 May 1814 at Eidsvold was a speech act uttered in an environment that could not guarantee its performative power: would foreign powers accept Norway as a sovereign state? After a few months of international diplomacy and skirmishes with the Swedes, it became clear that this speech act did have performative power. It was a so-called happy speech act.[1] Norway was acknowledged as a sovereign nation after 1814, although in union with Sweden, sharing the same king.

How do we identify the forces behind the success of this speech act, seemingly performed without the circumstances one would expect necessary for its validation? It was certainly not a powerful people who declared this sovereignty, either in economic, infrastructure, or any other terms. Nevertheless, the Norwegians found strength in seeing themselves as a nation, a people in their own right. In so doing, they gained momentum from the ideological winds of revolutionary Europe, primarily from the principle of popular sovereignty. The force of the speech act must therefore lie in the way that the Norwegians managed to adopt such principles, indeed, in that they reached an agreement on such a detailed text of 110 carefully designed articles *by speaking in one voice*.

Before arriving at Eidsvold, the deputies had found themselves plagued by uncertainties. Since January 1814, when the Treaty of Kiel had made Norway a nation without a state, a people without a king, and disposables of the absolutist twin state of Denmark-Norway, debate raged in streets, marketplaces, dinner parties, and the papers. Until this point, discussants had been loyal subjects of one of the most absolutist states of Europe, a state that since 1799 had little free speech (see Berge in this volume). The disturbing news of the peace treaty, however, made the Norwegians feel that they had been "given away like cattle," causing debate to take center stage (Platou 1871: 6).

When the international tables were turned by the Treaty of Kiel in January and this nation was separated from its king, a situation of rumors and talk followed. It was a crisis with no soldiers, no invasion, and no revolt, only this: words. People hardly talked of anything but news, strategic analysis, and constitutional theory. In this situation of words and rumors, the question was not so much what to do but rather what to say. An extensive use of freedom of expression unfolded after news of the Treaty of Kiel, despite restrictions on public speech. These public and private discussions of the spring of 1814 occurred despite the severe laws that had since 1799 restricted public debates, at least in print. Moreover, these debates and their political implications exceeded the scope of the freedom of expression that would be defined and adopted in the Constitution as Article 100, "There shall be freedom of print."[2] It was thus an extensive practice of freedom of expression that unfolded in the spring of 1814 had, paradoxically, both absolutist as well as liberal origins.

The spontaneous outbreak of such extensive public debate was due to the confusing, bewildering, and provocative situation. For this people to find its way, discussions were needed. Debate seemed necessary to enable the Norwegians, along with their former governor, Prince Christian Frederik, to synchronize their sentiments, so that they eventually would be able to powerfully perform a speech act. This precarious situation demanded decisive action. Norwegians and their prince had to seize the rhetorical moment.[3] Thereby, when the 112 deputies finally met at the Constitutional Assembly in April at Eidsvold, they were able to decide quickly upon 110 articles and how each of them should be framed, word by word. Quite a few articles were thus adopted without debate, as self-evident principles. Some articles still caused debates, surely, but never was the time schedule threatened by disturbing dissent.

Among the self-evident principles, we find stated in Article 100: "There shall be freedom of print." This was one of the first principles to force its way forward as constitutive of the new constitution, and to be formalized already at the outset of the Constitutional Assembly at Eidsvold. Ultimately, this principle would also be adopted as Article 100 without discussion. In general, freedom of expression seems to have been a force behind the whole process. The assembly itself was an improvised and novel arena for the exercise of free, political speech, as it was decided that nobody would be held responsible outside the assembly for anything said within it (N. Wergeland 1830: 10). One may wonder what had caused such self-assured faith in this principle, so decidedly forbidden since 1799, among these deputies who had lived their lives as subjects of absolutist silence. Where did this awareness of the situation come from? How did they so clearly perceive that the hour demanded exactly this: performing a powerful speech act, allowing a variety of voices in order to be able in the end to speak in one voice?

Christian Frederik's Journey

The situation had as much tension as a Greek drama, very much like Aeschylus's *Seven against Thebes*, where the city of Thebes finds itself surrounded by an attacking army. This causes panic within the walls, which forces the king, Eteocles, to speak his voice. As leader, he must speak what the moment requires in order to direct actions to the best outcome. He pictures himself as captain of a ship, with the serious task of steering it through troubled waters. Thereby, the panic in the city subsides.

In Norway, the ship's captain was Prince Christian Frederik. Since May 1813, he had been governor of Norway. He was immensely popular, insisting on strong ties to the Norwegians. In the situation that had occurred with the Treaty of Kiel, he felt he could not leave the Norwegians to themselves, like disposables of the Danish dynasty, as his cousin King Frederik VI had done, and he did not intend to obey the king's orders, following the Treaty of Kiel, to leave the country immediately, thereby abandoning it to the Swedes. To the contrary, he would be king, was king already in his own mind, as he reflected when he wrote in his diary on 17 January 1814:

> [My] first duty is by no means to betray the interests of the people, which interests the king has entrusted me, not due to my own personal merits, but because I am the only one of royal lineage who rests with them and who really has the ability to hold the helm of this ship which is thrown around in the sea of its future destiny. (quoted in Raabe 1914: 141)[4]

Christian Frederik noted this before he had received news of the Treaty of Kiel. His plan was to proclaim himself king of Norway as heir to the Danish throne. Thereafter, he would give the nation a constitution, with the help of a council of advisors.[5] However, he soon came to understand that he would have to let people speak out much earlier in the process. In fact, people were already talking. He was surprised to find that the city of Christiania and the rest of the country were completely embroiled in speculation and patriotic speeches, and that much of the talk was at odds with his initial plans.

Christian Frederik, in fact, had encouraged some of the talk by instructing priests to fill their preaching with patriotism and comments on the situation. However, he did not manage to control the situation as he had planned to. Awaiting news that would spark action, he found himself surrounded by debates on serious subjects: separation from Denmark, possible war with foreign states, economic issues, avoiding famine, and, last but not least, constitutional issues. When the first news of the Treaty of Kiel was announced in the papers, separation from Denmark was not mentioned. Christian Frederik himself was behind the vagueness of the announcement, in his initial attempt to control and direct discussions. Rumors, however, fairly accurately reflected the situation and immediately sparked a mental climate of constitutional planning in Christiania (Platou 1871: 9). Later, in February, the Christiania paper *Tiden* (Time) invited the public to write constitutional drafts.

Despite Christian Frederik's attempt to control the news, he was eager to find out people's sentiments, outside Christiania as well. He decided to travel to Trondhjem, a smaller but important town and administrative center in the northern part of Norway. He undertook this journey to win time and to find out where the loyalty and hopes of the Norwegians lay. The answer would turn out to be: in future sovereignty under his kingship or in Swedish rule.[6] It was, for him and the people, a journey of words, of expressing wishes and hopes, through speeches, questionings, demands, and written petitions. Tears, of both listeners and speakers, accompanied the speeches, especially Christian Frederik's own tears. He was, and would continue to be, moved by the situation. Emotions were also expressed through the many hurrahs of hope and consent accompanying the speeches.

The journey was about coming to a common understanding of the situation, including voices from high and low. From peasants at Aamot, a rural area north of Christiania, he received a petition on the current relationship with England. On 26 January, he noted in his diary, "This is what trade brings with it. The common people lose their simple ways and innocence. They talk politics. In other words, they are not peasants anymore" (quoted in Raabe 1914: 160). However, the prince seems to have found it necessary to listen to such voices as well in planning the way forward. For the prince and the Norwegians alike, the situation was open and required much discussion before deciding how to keep this nation, without king and constitution, together.[7]

Minds were changed in this process, not least Christian Frederik's own mind. His initial plans were changed in two very important ways. First, he soon understood that he could not claim the throne of Norway as heir of the Danish dynasty. Norway no longer belonged to that family. Therefore, he would have to be chosen by a sovereign people. Second, he would have to assemble representatives from this sovereign people and ask *them* to write a constitution. The constitution would have to come first, before the king.

On his journey to Trondhjem, Christian Frederik listened to many disparate voices: loyal adherents within the elite of public officials, peasants along the route, and others approaching him on the way. For example, at a dinner reception in Trondhjem in February, he was made familiar with a petition signed by fifty-eight citizens of the city suggesting that he convene an assembly of deputies from around the country with the task of making a constitution (Faye 1863: 19). Nothing suggests that Christian Frederik liked the idea at the time. He does not mention it in his diary. A week later, however, he would give in to all these voices when, at Eidsvold, he met his loyal friends and Norwegian notables to discuss strategies for winning the autonomy and throne of Norway. He gave in to the idea of popular sovereignty when the notables assured him that public opinion would accept no other way (Raabe 1914: 16). The self-confidence of this public opinion is suggested by the fact that observers in Christiania predicted that Christian Frederik would change his mind in this very matter before he actually did.[8]

Christiania was a city of words and Norway a nation of participants in this situation. Christian Frederik could not, as King Eteocles of Thebes had done, instruct his subjects to shut up in the hour of crisis. Christian Frederik was not king. He was the former governor in a country with no legitimate power structures outside those built on trust, loyalty, and hope for the future. He was himself thrown around on a sea of destiny, or rather, of intense thinking and speaking. He moved the situation, but was also moved by it, moved to tears like so many of these actors and moved to change his mind. One such move, concerning an issue that was on everybody's mind, and that only gradually came to Christian Frederik's attention, was freedom of expression as a constitutional principle.

Defining Is Restricting

Some weeks after Christian Frederik had changed his mind on how to win the Norwegian throne, he had to deal with yet another issue: actors around him were preoccupied with the question of freedom of the press. He initially rejected it, seeing no need for constitutional protection of such a principle. The prescript of 1799 would work fine, in his mind, and true enough, the severe restrictions of the 1799 prescript, which forbade criticism of king, government, and officials, had not seemed to prevent important discussions in 1814. The discussants, however, thought otherwise. Again, the prince was confronted with the power of speech: he was told that public opinion would demand constitutional protection of free speech. He decided to think about it (Raabe 1914: 173). Similar incidents occurred until Christian Frederik changed his mind on this question and noted in his diary: "[T]his principle forces its way forward, and I have nothing against it" (quoted in Raabe 1914: 184).

Discussions on freedom of expression had been going on for a while. In one of the many public activities in Christiania, a meeting of the association Bond-evennen (the Peasant's Friend), participants had decided that freedom of print should be among the constitutional laws (Riis 1864: 158). In the *Trondhjems Avis* (Trondhjem Newspaper), readers could find a lengthy text on the blessings of freedom of print. An important source for these discussions, the priest Claus Pavels, fully agreed on the importance of the freedom of the press, adding that had not the Danish king so keenly suppressed the pen and the press, the Danish-Norwegian kingdom would have survived the troubled times that had caused its split (Riis 1864: 162).

At the time, understandings of what the principle of freedom of expression entailed were fluctuating in extensive, undefined practices. Unformulated, it was a practice without formal borders. Consequently, a variety of ideas of free speech were expressed. We find some examples in the petitions to the Constitutional Assembly at Eidsvold. These were formulated by different local communities, expressing gratitude to Christian Frederik and making constitutional suggestions. A petition from the community in Eidsvold pleads for what they call freedom of *writing*, understood as the liberty to write documents to the authorities, which such communities had hitherto been forbidden to write themselves (Olafsen 1914: 119, Berge in this volume). Such documents had, until then, to be written by authorized officials and were very costly. What the authors of this petition expressed in their plead for freedom of writing was a hope to be relieved of a hindrance in their communication with official powers.

Concepts of freedom of expression were central in almost all the constitutional drafts at Eidsvold, such as the one by a rich peasant and deputy, Anders Lysgaard, who stated that freedom of *opinion* should be shared by all (see Olafsen 1914: 164). A draft from the common people of the county of Modum holds that "freedom to write and print is a blessing that no free citizen will easily give up" (quoted in Olafsen 1914: 217). A petition from the county of Hedemarken states that freedom of *print* benefits country and king alike because it enables the king to be informed of the people's sentiments (see Olafsen 1914: 404). Such sentiments were widespread, testifying to strong agreements on the importance of freedom of expression.

Many of these conceptions differed significantly from the liberal principle of freedom of expression that would eventually be adopted. For example, a petition from the county of Gudbrandsdalen stated:

> Freedom of religion, as well as freedom of thought and writing, are liberties naturally belonging to a nation, and we expect that the prince regent secures these liberties for the well being of himself as well as for the nation, and that we should really not have to ask for it. *The regent and the people are very closely connected to each other,* and *freedom of writing* is the most powerful way to unite them. By freedom of writing the regent and his people are able to inform each other on their meanings, actions, and texts on any subject *without long and costly journeys.* (quoted in Olafsen 1914: 375; italics added)

This notion of freedom of thought and writing was one of direct communication between the people and kingly power. It was not a product of imagination, however, but rather a product of the experience of absolutist institutions. The peasants were referring to the institution of supplication, a means by which ordinary subjects had the opportunity to approach the king, either by the written word or by delegations to Copenhagen to meet with him during his meeting hours (Supphellen 1978: 167).

The institution of supplication was especially valuable for the lower strata of society, because they had few other means by which to be heard. One may, of course, question the reality of such connections between kingly power and subjects. Obviously, the king did not personally answer the supplications, at least not many of them. However, the force of supplication was primarily symbolic. It was an expression of the absolutist king as a ruler of justice, above the law; for example, the king could pardon as an answer to such supplication. Supplication legitimized absolutism by enabling such access to the king. It kept up hopes of a higher justice. In fact, the percentage of actual kingly pardons was rather high, continually strengthening the symbol (Supphellen 1978; Bregnsbo 1997).

The peasants of Gudbrandsdalen conceived freedom of expression as direct communication between king and subjects, which was a natural inference given their experience of absolutist rule. However, this conception was also related to the republican tradition of eighteenth-century constitutionalism. Similar conceptions are represented in General (*Overkrigskommissær*) Wincents Sebbelow's constitutional draft, which describes freedom of *writing* as a human right, as "the most effective means by which the regent and the people may influence each other" (quoted in *Riksforsamlingens forhandlinger* 1914–1918: 3:184). Freedom of expression is thus a kind of parliament addressing the king. Another example of this conception presented to the Constitutional Assembly is present in "Count F. A. Holstein-Holsteinborg's Thoughts on a Constitution for Norway." Count Holsteinborg discusses freedom of expression at length as a human right under the heading, "On the unrestricted use of Reason" (see *Riksforsamlingens forhandlinger* 1914–1918: 3:130). He states that reason is something given us by providence. It should and must be used and refined. Such refining may be done, he says, orally as well as in writing. Reason itself demands freedom of speech *and* freedom of print. At one point, he singles out freedom of *print* as particularly important, as the most efficient means that enables every man in the country to participate in government, by the people informing those in power. Enlightenment is the reward of freedom of print, scientific enlightenment as well as the light that will be shed on the will of the people. Therefore, he concludes thus: "The voice of the people is the voice of God!" (quoted in *Riksforsamlingens forhandlinger* 1914–1918: 3:134).

The Silence in the Constitutional Assembly

Freedom of expression seems to have had an all-embracing presence before as well as during the Constitutional Assembly at Eidsvold. It was adopted as one of eleven general principles decided upon already in the preparatory phase of the first days. After a few weeks of work, the Constitutional Committee presented their draft to the assembly for discussions and adoption in the plenary sessions. The proposal for the article on freedom of expression was worded as follows:

> There shall be freedom of print. No one should be punished for any writing [*noget Skrivt*] of any content, which has been printed and published, unless he deliberately and openly has invited [*tilskyndet*] lack of obedience for the law, or lack of reverence for religion and morality [*sedelighet*], or the constitutional powers, to oppose the prescriptions of these or for inviting actions against the law, or for having presented false and defamatory accusations against anyone. Free speech concerning the authorities and whatsoever other subject is allowed for everyone. (quoted in Fure 1989: 373)

This wording would be adopted with only minor linguistic adjustments in the Constitution of 17 May. This silent approval of the article on freedom of print, adopted without further discussions, is somewhat odd among an assemblage of deputies that had adopted absolute free speech as a guiding principle for its own debates.

The reason for deciding that nobody should be held responsible for their opinions at the assembly at Eidsvold must have been that participants felt the need to allow as many different voices as possible to speak up, that is, they felt the need to avoid silencing dissenting voices. Political theorist Hannah Arendt, who has contributed some valuable thoughts on how politics is made powerful, holds that such plurality of voices is a precondition for the fruitfulness of any political process. She states that power is first and foremost produced when people meet and are expressing their diversity of opinions. Plurality is necessary for making deliberations powerful because discussants will be moved by each other's diversity. In such deliberations, one will find out where the common interests are, and that is where power resides. "Power is what *inter-est*" (Arendt 1963: 86). We have already seen examples of such movement in Christian Frederik's mind. We should remember that the speeches, with all the tear shedding, should not be seen as merely emotional movement, but indeed as rational movement, as changing of minds.

Christian Frederik must have sensed something about this power of plurality, because he had decided that the deputies at Eidsvold should represent four strata of Norwegian society, including the peasants. Such power of plurality is also a plausible motivation for inviting local communities to submit petitions and constitutional drafts. Political participation was at the core of this activity, which had started in January. As priest and diarist Ludvig Stoud Platou noted in those early days: "Everything politicizes now" (1871: 8). Norway in the spring of 1814 and at the Constitutional Assembly at Eidsvold was revolutionary in this sense. It was a moment of political freedom, and what participants were aiming at was exactly what Hannah Arendt sees as the difficult task, namely, to make this moment of political action a permanent state of freedom. The Norwegian example fits Arendt's theory in several ways, except for the seemingly unconditional approval of freedom of expression (see also Fure 1989: 218). How could this principle be adopted without debate? One would expect some kind of negotiation, tacit or open, to have preceded the adoption of this article that defines a principle so differently understood by so many different actors.

Negotiations

In defining something, people necessarily mark out borders, restrictions. Such restrictions are described in Article 100 as certain kinds of utterances that are unwanted, such as inviting lack of obedience to the law, religion, morality, and constitutional powers. These restrictions are matters of content. What about form, media? *The printed word* is the one protected by Article 100: "There shall be freedom of print." Access to the free word is thereby restricted in several ways: by education, leisure, access to printing technology, and so on. Thus, the term "freedom of print" (*Trykkefrihed*) automatically directs this freedom somewhat up the social ladder. What about the spoken word? The article states that everybody is allowed free speech on any matter whatsoever, on the authorities particularly. However, the way that this free speech is defined shows a clear breach with concepts of communication represented in the constitutional drafts prepared for the Constitutional Assembly at Eidsvold—the direct line (link) between power and people. One may speak freely *about* the authorities, according to Article 100. The direct link *to* the authorities, however, is broken.

This liberal freedom was what later theorists have called a *negative* freedom to criticize the authorities from the outside, as opposed to a positive freedom to participate in political debate within the political institutions (see Berlin 1969). This liberal conception of freedom of expression as something outside political institutions has, since the nineteenth century, become almost self-evident. However, it was not self-evident for the men at Eidsvold. Their conception of freedom of expression was to a certain extent grounded in experiences from absolutism, in which the connection between power and people had been an important element. This connection had been staged in several ways as *direct* communication between king and people. Although we must not forget the main monologist character of everything involving communication with kingly power, these communications also staged the possibility, slight as it was, for contact. Therefore, we find dialogic elements even in the most top-down messages from the king. For instance, in an order from May 1755, the king changed the time schedule for the local *thing*s in Bergen (*Anordning, angaaende Sommer- og* Høste-Tingenes Holdelse udi Bergens Stift 1755).[9] Phrased as an order, nonetheless, it was an answer to several supplications asking for these very changes. Initiative came from below. The supplications were phrased by the common people, and the king's resolution was a positive answer to their demand. Surely, the king would not have done so if it had been at odds with his own interests, but that is beside the point. Subjects of Denmark-Norway perceived the king as an approachable power, a notion that was manifestly present still in 1814.

It should also be mentioned that such communication had an oral character. Laws and declarations from the king were primarily announced orally, in the churches or at the *thing*. These *thing*s are important markers of the way absolutist subjects perceived of powerful speech: laws and declarations from the king proclaimed in assemblies of local communities, followed by reactions, discussions, perhaps even the phrasing of an answer. For instance, a community could answer something like this, "No, we cannot pay these taxes." The *thing* was an important public arena where the subjects themselves acted as judges, served as witnesses, and had the opportunity to discuss matters of common interest (Tretvik 2000). To receive the printed word in silent reading was far from their notion of freedom of expression. Speech was oral, in contact with power. These *thing*s were present in the mind of those at Eidsvold: already during the first days of the Constitutional Assembly, the parliament about to be designed for the new state was spoken of as the Storthing, that is, the major or supreme *thing*. In due time, Norwegians would also have to design how the Storthing should be connected to these local communities. In the process, which lasted for several decades, the *thing*s would disappear, except as judicial organs, when the local administration was finally settled in 1836 (Lauten 2010).

Despite their figurative presence in the choice of the term "Storthing," the local *thing*s were thus ignored as local public arenas for the future at Eidsvold. Could we not have expected them to have been discussed there as possible arenas for a newly decided freedom of thought, speech, or print? Suggestions had been made at Eidsvold that clearly had their origin in experiences of such local institutions of communication with power where perhaps the term "freedom of *speech*" would have been more appropriate and include a broader segment of the people than "freedom of *print*." Nevertheless, we find few references to discussions of these topics, no solid traces of any negotiation arguing why the final definition would have to be freedom of *print*, only this: laughter. When the petition from the peasants in the county of Eidsvold was read aloud, the whole assembly burst into a relieving laughter after a hard day's discussions on other subjects (N. Wergeland 1830: 35).

This laughter possibly silenced humbler members of the assembly and other dissenting voices. Scholars have noted the existence of techniques of domination in the assembly. Consequently, many have assumed that the status of the deputies was equal to their influence at Eidsvold, often assuming that the peasant deputies were quiet, not daring to speak their mind.[10] One may question the sweeping generalization of such observations, but there are traces of controlling behavior and lack of free atmosphere for those belonging to the lower strata of society, not least the recurring instances of laughter when petitions and constitutional drafts from the common people were read aloud.

Is it likely that the elite at Eidsvold simply rejected notions primarily belonging to the common people, silencing with laughter or other techniques at their disposal any dissenting voices? Perhaps, but the communicative concepts of freedom of expression did manifestly also belong to discourses that the educated elites had engaged in for several decades, as will be discussed below. Such notions were central parts of the very debates, revolutions, and literature that had surrounded the educated elites of the eighteenth and early nineteenth century, during their youth in particular. They were even present in the very texts and ideals they were at this point using as guidelines for their work, namely, in the constitutions of the revolutionary Enlightenment.

Constitutionalist Ideals

Signs of those discourses are patently present among the texts at the Constitutional Assembly's disposal, such as in Count Holsteinborg's learned thoughts. His draft fed on theories that had flourished in former decades, theories concerning republican ideas of government. Count Holsteinborg states that freedom of expression (in print) is a valuable means that makes it possible for "every man in the state" to partake in government and to inform the government of the voices of the people, in order to make open a flowering of information and a transparency between the government and people (*Riksforsamlingens forhandlinger* 1914–1918: 3:131). Freedom of expression was here to function as an indirect means for people outside political institutions to participate in politics despite being far away from governmental circles. Public opinion seen in this way represented a radical feature at the time, although some stated that such mechanisms in fact already existed within absolutism.[11] Within this discourse, freedom of expression was seen as a blessing for the king because he could be informed by his people: an instrument of good governance. We saw echoes of such ideas in Claus Pavels's diary: if King Frederik VI had not been a ruler so deaf to the voices of his people, he would not have lost Norway. This understanding of the need for a communicative link between power and people was not new. It had boasted both kingly and popular spokesmen throughout the former century (Ringvej 2011).

In the United States, such direct communication had found its way into constitutional textuality. The First Amendment (adopted in 1789) prohibits abridging freedom of speech in general and forbids infringing on freedom of the press. What is more, it prohibits interfering with the right to peaceably assemble and the right to petition for governmental redress of grievances. Citizens were not only allowed to speak their minds freely; they could do so within contexts where their words could lead to actions, in freely assembled meetings. Moreover, they could address the authorities directly. In addition, the French Constitution of 1793 proclaims that people could express their opinions in peaceful assemblies.[12]

No article in the Norwegian Constitution of 1814 secured freedom of assemblage, or freedom of petitioning, for that matter. How could these freedoms, so clearly present among the petitions sent from the lower strata of Norwegian society and in the US Constitution, a source of inspiration for the Norwegian framers, be so absent in the discussions at Eidsvold and in the Constitution? We could have expected some form of discussion on such subjects, not least because such experiences were central to emblematic conflicts in recent Danish-Norwegian history. One such conflict was the 1765 revolt against higher taxes in western Norwegian regions, a revolt that in fact resulted in a law prohibiting free assemblage. One could expect that the question of free assemblage would have been an issue among the deputies at Eidsvold in their efforts to put an end to absolutist repression: there had been strong traditions for unauthorized assemblies, despite the law of 1765. They had sparked new revolts, for example, the so-called Lofthus uprising in 1787.[13] Such revolts tended to be written protests rather than violent actions. Grievances and discussions could be and were transformed into political action toward the government by petitioning and sending delegates to Copenhagen. Thereby, the commons made provocative use of this primarily symbolic channel to the king.

Few words were spent on such practices at Eidsvold, although the US Constitution addressed such issues directly. That the French Constitution of 1793 was ignored on this matter is not as surprising. It was a radical constitution of the bloodiest era of the French Revolution, and a symbol of the Reign of Terror. It was never adopted, nor was it used as an inspiration elsewhere. Its value in this connection lies in its presentation of freedom of expression in a seemingly radical but in fact very absolutist way. It had made constitutional law of practices that subjects of absolutism were familiar with. The US Constitution, on the other hand, was among the most important ideals for the deputies at Eidsvold. Nevertheless, the wording of Article 100 ignores, perhaps deliberately rejects, principles that had been high on the agenda in these times of constitutional thinking, such as freedom of assemblage and the right to petitioning.

Only one example of such highly relevant topics is attested in documents from Eidsvold. It appears in the constitutional draft by one of the members of the Constitutional Committee, Nicolai Wergeland, in an article draft declaring that all assemblies of the people should be illegal and all decisions adopted at such meetings considered invalid (*Riksforsamlingens forhandlinger* 1914–1918: 3:268). No further discussion on these topics is to be found, and they were ignored in further work on the Constitution. One might have expected some of the peasants to discuss such principles, but no peasants were members of the Constitutional Committee, and no records were kept. Therefore, we know nothing of the debates within this elite group of text producers. When they finally presented Article 100, it was quietly embraced as a concept of freedom of expression suitable for the liberal era to come, allowing the press to work independently and critically, as well as allowing private individuals the right to speak freely on any matter. This is the new liberal notion of negative freedom, a right to criticize from the outside, among outsiders. But the channel to the king, or to power, was closed. Article 100 allowed everyone to speak freely on any subject, but whether anyone with power was listening was now irrelevant.

Seizing the Moment

The deputies' joint speech act of uttering the Constitution was a document embedded in a rhetorical moment of great uncertainty. With uncertainty come disagreements. However, the representatives of the nation managed in the end to speak with one voice. Internal unity was an absolute necessity in this situation. On the question of freedom of expression, however, this entails an apparent paradox, since this unity must be accounted for by the spontaneous outbreak of freedom of cacophonic speech in the spring of 1814. Article 100 ignored this swarm of political activity that had moved Christian Frederik and other actors toward such strong arguments. The Norwegians would have to stand firm and in agreement. Any crack in this picture would have made the project of autonomy futile. Had there been strong enough dissent in the initial phases, such harmony might not have been achievable. Only sensitivity to public opinion of the broadest sort could enable Norwegians to identify the realities of this situation, which was exactly what Christian Frederik had done.

The deputies at Eidsvold, however, saw no need to institutionalize forms of freedom of expression that apparently had helped them give strength to this speech act. To determine the degrees of intent and rejection in the final phrasing of Article 100 is, of course, impossible. However, the history of

Norway in 1814 is a history of a chain of events where necessity and agency are intriguingly intertwined along the way. It would be wrong to simply assume that such an important principle, a subject on everybody's lips, should not have been surrounded by differences of opinion also in its final stage of constitutional phrasing. Several understandings of freedom of expression were patently circulating in the orbit of questions raised at Eidsvold, many of them coming to a closure by the phrasings adopted, such as the one on freedom of print. Christian Frederik's ability to listen to those around him is of great importance in this picture. Seeing himself as the savior of Norway, he came to learn that the people of this kingdom had a voice of their own. He let them speak, but never surrendered his conviction that he and the Constitution were one and the same. Just like King Eteocles, he fought for his kingdom, and like King Eteocles, he was unable to see that he and the kingdom were not one and the same. He did not see that the kingdom could exist on its own. The Norwegian Constitution of 17 May 1814 proved to be a powerful speech act, a happy speech act, because it was based on internal strength, the consent and agreement reached by an assembly of diverse opinions stimulated by Christian Frederik. The kingdom did not, as the summer of 1814 should prove, need the prince for its further existence. Christian Frederik was a tragic hero of a happy speech act.

NOTES

1. In the speech act theory of British philosopher of language John L. Austin, the speech act, if successful, would be labeled "happy," depending on whether it were pronounced under "appropriate circumstances." The declaration of a new state by a newly gathered assembly with no traditional authority lacks certain features that would make a statement like this "happy," such as being founded upon procedures with already defined rules and appropriate behavior. The apparent lack of appropriate circumstances highlights the drama of this speech act (see Austin 1962: 12). On constitutions as speech acts, see also Visconti in this volume.

2. The author's verbatim translation of the first sentence in Article 100: "Trykkefrihed bør finde Sted."

3. On the rhetorical moment—the kairos—see also Jordheim in this volume.

4. The diary was written in French, and was translated into Norwegian in 1914 by Jens Raabe. Except otherwise stated, all English-language translations from Norwegian are the author's.

5. In fact, such thought had already been discussed throughout the preceding year in letters to his friend and Norwegian dignitary Carsten Anker, the owner of the manor at Eidsvold and host to the Constitutional Assembly (see Anker 1904).

6. On 17 January, before he knew anything certain about the Treaty of Kiel, he received a visit from Bishop Bugge from Trondhjem, affirming that "the people of his region are firmly decided that they do not want to become Swedish" (quoted in Raabe 1914: 140).

7. This is also among the reasons for the journey to Trondhjem, as he relates in his diary on 26 January: "[M]y presence in this remote part of the country ... will strengthen the internal ties among this people and between the whole people to me" (quoted in Raabe 1914: 145).

8. On 15 February 1814, Platou writes, "Promising rumors are spread. ... The prince will declare himself as constitutional king, he will summon representatives of the nation ... he will share legislative powers" (Platou 1871: 17).

9. On *things*, see Warner, Holmøyvik, and Ringvej in this volume.

10. This focus on the elite at Eidsvold, as well as in the debates of spring 1814, is dominant, for instance, in Seip (2002). Originally published in 1974, this book has been a central and highly influential work for students of Norwegian history for several decades.

11. See, e.g., Peterson (1798) and Voltaire's 1771 letter to King Christian VII of Denmark-Norway (Voltaire 1771; see also Berge in this volume).

12. This constitution also established the right to assemble in primary assemblies, where the French people were to exercise their sovereignty directly, and from where they could communicate with the national, representative assembly containing the representatives chosen in these very primary assemblies (*Acte constitutionnel,* Article 2).

13. As for the tradition of unauthorized assemblies, they are not very frequently commented upon in the sources, but seem to have been common. I have found them described already in the *Kongsspegelen* (The King's Mirror), a book on kingly government, written about 1230 (see *Kongsspegelen* 1976). Here we find such *things*, arranged on the people's own initiative, described as "unruly things" (*sjølrådeting*). They were illegal, but apparently were a practice that the subjects would turn to if their king did not govern well.

12

Scholarly Texts' Influence on the 2004 Revision of the Norwegian Constitution's Article 100

Ragnvald Kalleberg

Introduction

Article 100, which concerns freedom of the press in the 1814 Norwegian Constitution, remained unchanged for 190 years. In 2004, the Norwegian parliament (Stortinget) unanimously adopted a revised article on freedom of expression. It had become desirable to harmonize the old article with international law and there was a need for a principled clarification of freedom of expression (NOU 1999: 15–16, 19–20). In the ten years prior to 2004, many contributions influenced Norwegian legislators, including scholarly texts from the humanities and the social sciences.

In this chapter, I concentrate on how texts by one scholar, the German sociologist and philosopher Jürgen Habermas, influenced the revision. The chapter opens with a general reflection on how scholarly texts from the socio-cultural disciplines can influence society. This is an important type of influence in modern societies, but studies of it are relatively rare. I then document Habermas's influence on the revision of Article 100, focused on the role of deliberation in constitutional democracies. In the last section, I discuss how such scholarly ideas about deliberation and democracy, now incorporated in the Constitution, can contribute to further develop the historical project of democracy.

Scholarly Texts Influencing Society and Culture

It is often taken for granted that the natural sciences much more strongly influence society than the social sciences and the humanities do. Such comparisons are, however, more complicated to perform than often assumed (Kalleberg 2005a: 287–292). The natural sciences influence typically through technologies. One must marvel at the achievements, for instance, in information technology. The social sciences and the humanities influence communicatively, stimulating new definitions of situations and of identities. Such influence is easy to overlook because insights and ideas from the sociocultural sciences may become part of cultures, institutions, routines, and self-definitions. They become common knowledge and their origins forgotten. Ideas incorporated in a constitution show how powerful such influence can become. A methodological reflection can illuminate this particular kind of power.

Scholars in social science, the humanities, and jurisprudence access their empirical fields communicatively. Typical examples are interviewing and interpreting texts produced by those studied. Natural scientists cannot communicate like this with their subject matter, be it chemical processes or insects. Social and cultural scientists have no other choice than to communicate. They relate to a sociocultural reality, designed and defined by human beings. "It is not merely the perception of facts that is symbolically structured, but rather the facts as such" (Habermas [1967] 1988: 92; see also Giddens 1976: 79, 146). To describe and explain social processes, the social and cultural scientist must document and analyze the reasoning of actors. Reasons, such as knowledge of facts and evaluations of states of affairs, are based on speech acts performed by knowledgeable, autonomous people (Habermas 1984–1987: 1:273–337).

Data collection in the social sciences and the humanities can be conceptualized as transforming experience of symbolically structured reality into texts. Three main strategies for collecting and constructing data are to (1) observe those studied, (2) interview them, and (3) interpret existing sources, such as newspapers and constitutions. Experiences and information based on observations, interviews, and interpretations of existing sources are transformed into texts, such as field notes and transcripts of interviews. For a long period, mainstream social scientists one-sidedly focused on the importance of quantifying experience. However, transforming experience into texts is a more basic operation than quantification in these disciplines, and a necessary condition for generating quantitative data (Kalleberg 2005b: 146–154). To call attention to this methodological insight, it is helpful to emphasize the fundamental importance of *textualizing experience*, that is of *putting experience into text*.

In the description, analysis, and explanation of sociocultural phenomena—for instance, to answer why Norway created a constitution in 1814, why Nazi Germany invaded Norway in April 1940, or why Norway in a 1994 referendum decided not to join the European Union—texts are essential. The Danish king Frederik VI lost Norway to Sweden in 1814 because he was on the losing side in the Napoleonic Wars. The subsequent political order was established also with the help of negotiations and texts, such as the Treaty of Kiel. German political and military texts document that two reasons for the 1940 invasion of Norway were to secure bases for ships and U-boats to fight the Allied forces in the North Atlantic and to secure iron ore from Sweden through the Norwegian port in Narvik (Beevor 2012: 70–78). The essential importance of speech acts and of all kinds of texts is obvious in the description and analysis of a referendum in a modern media society (Sejersted 2011: 476–83).

Emphasizing symbolically mediated communication in speech acts and texts does not imply that everything in society and culture can be reduced to communication. The Napoleonic Wars before 1814, the German occupation of Norway in 1940, and the expansion of the European Union highlight the importance of factors other than texts as well, such as military power and market forces. What is claimed is that communication is indispensable for coordinating human interaction, including (inter)action in contexts where brute force is of primary importance.[1]

The communicative relationship between sociocultural scholars and their subject matter, their empirical material, opens up for influence in two directions. Scholars are influenced by opinions, insights, and concepts from the social and cultural fields they are studying, such as business enterprises, parliaments, or social movements. Sometimes the influence is so strong that scholars "go native," as it is termed in social scientific fieldwork methodology, unwittingly identifying with one group's perspective. The communicative relationship also opens up for influence in the opposite direction. To exemplify by Norwegian history from the Middle Ages onward, scholarly texts have influenced institutions, policies, and mentalities. Naturally, such influences are interpreted and transformed by the readers, located in specific roles, institutions, regions, and traditions. The legal revolution in Western Europe during the twelfth and thirteenth centuries (Huff 1993: 119–148) influenced the shape of Norwegian society. The writings of Martin Luther influenced Norway's transformation from a Catholic into a Lutheran society. Other influential scholarly texts include those by, for instance, Hugo Grotius, Adam Smith, John Stuart Mill, Karl Marx, Sigmund Freud—and Jürgen Habermas.

Texts by Habermas That Influenced the Revision of Article 100

To document that Habermas's texts influenced the revising of Article 100, an official report (NOU 1999) is my main empirical source material. The report was written by the Commission on Freedom of Expression, appointed by the Norwegian government in 1996. According to the mandate, the report was to present "a thorough consideration of the status of freedom of speech in our society" and to clarify conditions for "the constitutional protection of free speech." Its main task was to propose to Stortinget a revised Article 100. The commission had sixteen members, including seven professors from five scholarly fields (history, law, media and communication, philosophy, and linguistics). In 1999, the group submitted its comprehensive report, quoting the first paragraph of the proposed revised article as its title: "There shall be freedom of expression" (NOU 1999).[2] After much public discussion and consideration of alternative phrasings, in 2004 Stortinget adopted a new text close to the one proposed in the report.

The commission's report contains ten references where Habermas is mentioned by name. These mentions cover direct references both to his works and to scholars using them.[3] Three references occur in chapter 2, where the principled arguments for freedom of expression are presented, two in the third chapter, which discusses the historical development of the Norwegian public sphere, and four references occur in the fourth chapter, oriented toward the analysis of public sphere institutions (such as education and media) and conditions stimulating deliberative quality in public forums. The last reference occurs in chapter six, on the limits of freedom of expression, for instance, to stop child pornography.[4]

Four of Habermas's texts are explicitly mentioned (Habermas 1962, 1981, 1992b, 1994). A central fifth text on law and democracy (Habermas 1996), establishing him as a major theorist of law (Baxter 2011), is not mentioned explicitly. Essential ideas from this book, such as the pivotal importance of enlightened public discourses among citizens for the legitimate circulation of democratic power, were incorporated in the report through an essay by commission member and professor of philosophy Gunnar Skirbekk (see below).

Of course, not only Habermas's texts influenced this report. Several others were used, such as by John Stuart Mill, Karl Popper, and Ronald Dworkin. I do not claim that the revised Article 100 could not have been worded the same way had Habermas's texts not been used. The report and the revised Article 100 are in accordance with strong Norwegian legal, political, and cultural traditions. But I do claim that central ideas in Habermas's oeuvre were incorporated in a source of Norwegian constitutional law, namely, the report by the Commission on Freedom of Expression (NOU 1999), influencing the revision of Article 100.

The Triple Grounding of Freedom of Expression: Truth, Autonomy, and Democracy

The Commission on Freedom of Expression stated that:

> The grounds for freedom of expression are normally explained by reference to three principles that correspond to the three characteristic features of the Age of Enlightenment. These are *the principle of truth, the principle of autonomy*

("the individual's freedom to form opinions") and *the principle of democracy.* (NOU 1999: 20; italics in original)

To clarify its argument, the commission variously speaks of "principles," "grounds," "processes," "concepts," "arguments," and "features." The basic idea is that freedom of expression is necessary to improve public opinion, to stimulate citizens' autonomy, and to facilitate the formation of enlightened democratic opinion. These principles refer not only to ideas and ideals of individuals, but also to social interaction (NOU 1999: 255), to institutions such as schools and mass media, and to the interrelationships between institutions, such as voluntary organizations and parliaments. The ambition is that freedom of speech shall facilitate open and enlightened public discourse, an idea at the heart of Habermas's oeuvre (Habermas 2006: 12–13).

The commission did not assume that it was introducing something wholly new in relation to existing scholarly literature. In a footnote to the statement about how the three principles are "normally explained," it refers to a similar typology in a comparative study of freedom of speech by British professor of media law Eric Barendt (NOU 1999: 20; see Barendt 2005). In the same footnote, the reader is informed that these three concepts—truth, autonomy, and democracy—"will be interpreted somewhat differently" on the basis of an essay by commission member Skirbekk (1998). In the 1998 essay, he presents a principled argument for freedom of expression, introducing, explaining, and justifying the three principles of truth, autonomy, and democracy. Skirbekk locates himself within the discourse theory of law and democracy as developed by Habermas (1996) and underlines the deliberative features of democracy, features that can improve the rationality of public decisions by stimulating enlightened opinion formation in civil society.

Regarding the *principle of truth,* a connection is made to the breakthrough of modern science in early modern Europe. The new institution of science demonstrated that "truth is arrived at by means of debate where assertions put forward can be corrected in confrontation with other opinions" (NOU 1999: 20). Scientists, as other human beings, are fallible and need the correction and inspiration of others to improve their knowledge and insights. It is argued that the deliberative strategy used in science, to improve knowledge by means of open discussions, was extended to other forums during the eighteenth century, even to the discussion of controversial political issues (NOU 1999: 21).

The *principle of autonomy* presupposes a liberal-democratic basis of free and equal citizens governing themselves. The second paragraph of the proposed article contains the phrasing "the individual's freedom to form opinions," which is connected to independent, reasoning persons. The Norwegian word used, *myndig,* is translated into English as "the mature human being" (NOU 2005: 29). The commission here alludes to Immanuel Kant's concept of autonomy (German *Mündigkeit*), a highly influential concept in Western political and cultural history. A modern democratic demos, comprising all adult inhabitants legally conceived as free and equal, can be developed only when autonomous and knowledgeable members actually have rights, competence, and opportunities to participate and learn in democratic processes (see Kalleberg 2011: 106). Such ideas and ideals can only be realized as part of a longer, historical project.

The interplay of the private and public spheres is essential for fostering individual autonomy and active citizenship. By using Habermas's discourse theory of law and democracy, the commission profits from this theory's breakthroughs in linking private and public autonomy. They are equally fundamental and presuppose each other. Citizens in a constitutional democracy shall have the same basic rights as *addressees* of the law. As *authors* of the law, through their representatives, citizens exercise their public autonomy (Habermas 1996: 104).[5]

The commission argues that its concept of a "mature human being" is not one-sidedly individualistic, as in mainstream Anglo-American liberal thought: "In a way society exists prior to the individual, and not the reverse as in Locke" (NOU 1999: 21). Individual and civic character are formed in interaction processes within basic institutions, such as family, local communities, education, and public forums.

The *principle of democracy* refers not only to basic structural arrangements for a society to be a democracy, such as the separation of legislative, executive, and judicial powers. The commission focuses especially on the importance of freedom of expression for the formation of public opinion in open forums in civil society. "This communicative or deliberative aspect of democracy is at least as important as the democratic decision-making procedures such as voting" (NOU 1999: 23). The commission does not try to introduce a new type of deliberative democracy in Norway. Rather, it tries to clarify an essential aspect in the Norwegian cultural and political tradition.

The crucial point about democratic deliberation could have been made even clearer by explicitly using Habermas's normative model of the legitimate, democratic circulation of power (Habermas 1996: 315–328, 341–387; 1998: 282–288; Kalleberg 2010: 192–199). Here, the informal forums in civil society are connected with the formal institutions in the constitutional state. Public opinion formed in civil society can be transformed into formal decisions and administrative power by legislative bodies and by cabinets forming and implementing political programs. This model makes it possible both to criticize actual political processes and to identify realistic improvements in existing practices and institutions.

The commission's principled, triple grounding of free discourse among autonomous citizens in an open society is expressed in the second paragraph of the proposed Article 100. In the article finally adopted by Stortinget in 2004, this way of thinking is used in both the second and the third paragraphs of Article 100:

> No person may be held liable in law for having imparted or received information, ideas or messages unless this can be justified in relation to the grounds for freedom of expression, which are the seeking of truth, the promotion of democracy and the individual's freedom to form opinions. Such legal liability shall be prescribed by law.
>
> Everyone shall be free to speak his mind frankly on the administration of the State and on any other subject whatsoever. Clearly defined limitations to this right may only be imposed when particularly weighty considerations so justify in relation to the grounds for freedom of expression.

The commission compares its proposed article with Article 10 in the European Convention on Human Rights and with Article 19 in the UN Convention on Civil and Political Rights. It is noted that the basic requirement about freedom of expression is articulated in all three, but it is claimed that the Norwegian wording is to be preferred because here individual and institutional aspects of freedom of expression are better balanced (NOU 1999: 240). The commission clearly presupposes that it will be useful for future lawmakers, courts, organizations, and citizens that these three arguments are incorporated into the revised Article 100.[6]

Publics in Civil Society: Forums Regulated by the Force of the Better Arguments

The commission first mentions Habermas by name in its discussion of the principle of democracy (in chapter 2.2.3). It uses a public radio lecture by philosopher Helge Høibraaten, who presented Habermas to the broad Norwegian public. Høibraaten focused on the democratic importance of a vibrant civil society and on the maintenance of public forums, where arguments are essential. The second reference is made in the same section, via media scholar Jostein Gripsrud, pointing to the permanent possibility of "refeudalization" of open societies, where discussions are taken out of public spaces to "closed rooms." The second main section in this chapter (2.3) concerns categorization of expressions and their status in relation to the three essential grounds for free speech. One of the themes discussed concerns regarding statements made in the public sphere versus those made in the private realm: "Such a 'public sphere' is not, as Jürgen Habermas reminds us, a matter of course, but an institutional *system* formed in a historical process" (NOU 1999: 28). A footnote refers to Habermas's (1962, 1989) historical-comparative study of the public sphere's emergence and transformation.

In the third chapter, important phases in the development of free speech in Norway are discussed. "The history of freedom of expression is first and foremost a history of how this institutional system developed" (NOU 1999: 36). The historical character of the phenomenon is emphasized: "The idea of communication free of constraints, and that this is something that can and should be aimed at, is new in history" (NOU 1999: 42). The somewhat unusual Norwegian expression used here, *tvangsfri kommunikasjon* (communication free of constraint), is an equivalent to German expressions often used by Habermas, such as *zwangfreie Kommunikation* (communication free of constraint) and *zwanglosen Zwang des besseren Arguments* (the forceless force of the better argument). The commission notes that such communication has long been institutionalized in Western societies.

The commission's central concepts and words, such as "open and enlightened public discourse" and public "seeking of truth," are clearly also influenced by Habermas. A subsection (chapter 3.5) concerns the institutionalization of "a public sphere." The Norwegian word used is *offentlighet*, the direct equivalent of the German Öffentlichkeit, the main concept in Habermas's book on the public sphere and a central concept in his discourse theory of law and democracy.

The basic claim supported by the commission, that human beings regularly coordinate their behavior also by unforced communication, is often interpreted as a kind of idealism, too good for the real world, something perhaps only to be dreamt of in a future, utopian world. Nonetheless, each of us experiences this peculiar kind of communicative power every day, the force of being convinced by the same arguments that convince others. This is an ordinary form of legitimate interpersonal influence in daily life, exercised in our everyday roles in society at large (Kalleberg 2010: 187–192). Interpersonal influence by means of reasoned dialogues is fundamental in a modern society. It is usually easy to identify the self-refuting reasoning of authors denying the existence of such deliberative power. Such authors argue at length to convince readers that argumentative influence is an illusion. They thereby, however, unwittingly confirm the existence of such influence (Kalleberg 2007: 151–152).

The commission illustrates its points by discussing nineteenth-century Norway and by referring to the increasing importance of newspapers, magazines, and critical journalism, as well as to all kinds of publications aimed to achieve public self-enlightenment by means of discussion. The analysis is summarized by quoting Habermas (1992b: 423): "[T]here sprang from the midst of the private sphere a relatively dense network of public communication" (NOU 1999: 44). Rational public discourse in the publics of civil society facilitated the emergence of reliable opinions about the facts of a situation, and improved the normative validity and legitimacy of evaluations. The ambition was that enlightened formation of opinion and will, formed in publics, should define the general lines of politics. The commission quotes an 1833 text by leading Norwegian politician Frederik Stang (1808–1884) insisting on the development of an enlightened "general will" through public deliberation, a will that must be "the moving force behind all directions taken by the organs of the state" (NOU 1999: 24). The quote illustrates a long deliberative tradition in Norwegian society. The commission's report demonstrates that this tradition can be adequately identified and analyzed with the help of the ideal type of "public sphere" originally developed to grasp historical developments in other parts of Europe (Habermas 1992b: 422–425).[7]

The commission characterizes the fourth chapter of its report as "primarily a sociological description of the conditions of freedom of expression in 'the public sphere,' which is not a single sphere, but consists of several publics or fields, such as science, art, the church … the labor movement's organizations, minority spheres etc." (NOU 1999: 11–12). It refers to a contribution by the Sami philosopher Nils Oskal, discussing the minority rights of Sami people, and mentions that he is inspired by Habermas (NOU 1999: 69). The institutions discussed include science, the universities, general education, the media, and art. A subsection of this chapter concerns "the information society and the digital revolution" (NOU 1999: 70–72). The commission argues that it is possible to document that Norway has changed from an industrial society into an information society. This new perspective implies that "to a much larger degree than before, one emphasizes communication as the essential society-constituting element." Two causes for the emphasis on communication are presented: real changes in society and the development of "new concepts to comprehend phenomena that have always been important, but which have been concealed because of the dominance of an economistic way of thinking" (NOU 1999: 70). A footnote points to the influence of social theorists "such as Arendt, Luhmann, and Habermas. The last one's book *Theorie des kommunikativen Handelns* is especially central."

The last explicit reference to Habermas occurs in chapter 6. It focuses on the limits of freedom of expression, partly in relation to individual interests, partly in relation to public interests. The commission recommends a maximum of freedom of expression in the private sphere: "It is only with a basis in such a private sphere that a relatively dense network of public communication emerges, to use the words of Habermas" (NOU 1999: 108).

The Infrastructure Requirement: The Essential Importance of Deliberative Institutions

The commission observes that today citizens have "acquired positive rights" and the state has an obligation to "actively provide for public discourse and free flow of information" (NOU 1999: 35). The establishment, maintenance, and development of a system of publics "cannot only be left to the market"

(NOU 1999: 250). Therefore, in fields such as education, research, and culture, state authorities must facilitate an open and enlightened public sphere, characterized by opinion and will formation adequate for solving common problems (NOU 1999: 36, 249–250). Such institutions cannot be regulated appropriately by adopting the values and mechanisms of markets and hierarchies.

The commission argues that there is an internal connection between the triple argument for freedom of expression and the state's broader democratic obligations:

> If we examine the three principal arguments in favor of freedom of expression … we quickly see that, in order to support freedom of expression, an extensive institutional structure is required. The generally educative school is … the most important public institution in the development of the public sphere and the mature human being. (NOU 1999: 36)

Other public and private institutions mentioned in this connection are universities, museums, libraries, public broadcasting, mass media, theaters, publishers, and cinemas. The commission is concerned with the "infrastructure requirement," and emphasizes that freedom of expression refers not only to the rights of individuals, but also to a set of institutions and practices where the democratic state is essential:

> This thus clearly states the responsibility of the state for ensuring that individuals and groups are actually given opportunities to express their opinions. Maintenance and development of the public sphere are invoked as major public responsibilities, consistent with the view long held by the Norwegian government. (NOU 1999: 10; see also 249–250)

The sixth paragraph proposed, and later accepted by Stortinget, is vital. It states: "It is the responsibility of the authorities of the State to create conditions that facilitate open and enlightened public discourse." The infrastructure requirement is crucial because it concerns how citizens can and should organize their self-enlightenment and develop a sustainable balance between civil society, market, and state in order to safeguard the rationality of public discourse and its institutional weight.

The commission makes no explicit reference to Habermas in the discussion of the infrastructure requirement, but this kind of institutional thinking is also typical for him. A recent illustration is a metaphor he uses when discussing quality newspapers as forums for opinion and will formation:

> When it comes to gas, electricity, or water, the state has an obligation to ensure the energy supply for the population. Shouldn't it have a similar obligation when it comes to supplying this other type of "energy," whose interruption causes disruptions harmful to the democratic state itself? (Habermas 2009: 136)

Challenges Raised by the Revised Article 100

The commission's report established rich intertextual connections between the revision of Article 100 and a broad range of scholarly texts. The report connected legal arguments with philosophical, historical, and social-scientific ones. This is in line with Barendt's (2005: 1–38) observation that it is neither possible nor desirable to isolate legal arguments from social-theoretical and philosophical ones. I have documented that central Habermasian insights have gained a foothold in a Norwegian source of law (NOU 1999), influencing the understanding of the Norwegian Constitution.

It is often commented that texts by Habermas are linked to an exceptionally large textual universe comprising the social sciences, humanities, jurisprudence, and theology, and even neurobiologists interpreting the nature of *Homo sapiens* (Habermas 2006: 151–180). Habermas has developed his theories in intensive dialogues with leading contributors from different disciplines and research traditions, such as the American political scientist Robert Dahl, perhaps the leading contemporary scholar on democratic theory.

I end with four reflections on challenges raised by the revised Article 100: democracy as a historical project that can be further developed; the dangers of institutional imperialism; the requirements for deliberative quality in the publics of civil society; and the essential importance of educational institutions for the future of democracy. I focus on the informal cultures and processes in civil society, not on the institutionalized deliberations in elected bodies.

The Unfinished Project of Democracy

Contemporary democracies have emerged over centuries. They are still unfinished historical projects (Kalleberg 2008: 18–20, 25–26). We can borrow a typology from Dahl to explicate the prospects for democracy. Dahl (1989: 213–224) distinguishes between existing "polyarchies" (governance by many) and future "democracies." According to this terminology, countries such as New Zealand, South Korea, Norway, Uruguay, and Canada are polyarchies, characterized by institutions like free, fair, and frequent elections and freedom of expression. "Democracy" refers to a future situation when standards defining "democratic processes" are realized to a much higher degree than they are today.[8] There are five standards characterizing a democratic process in any area and on any level: effective participation, voting equality, enlightened understanding, control of the agenda, and inclusion of all adults (Dahl 1989: 108–114).

A natural typology for further democratization is the following one. First, the number of polyarchies can be increased. Despite colonialism, world wars, and totalitarianism, the disastrous twentieth century also witnessed revolutionary democratic achievements. During the first decade of the twentieth century, 10 percent of the world's population lived in democratic polyarchies. Today, this is the case for half of the world's population. However, two-thirds of the world's 190 countries are still not democratic polyarchies (Dahl and Stinebrickner 2003: 83). Second, supranational institutions for democratic governance have been designed and can be further developed. Two examples are the Council of Europe and the European Union (Dahl 1994; Olsen 2010; Habermas 2012). Third, existing democratic polyarchies can be further democratized. Four examples are: (1) implementing democratic governance in new institutions, such as business enterprises ("economic democracy"); (2) improving the deliberative qualities of public discourses, as in mass media; (3) strengthening socialization and education of inhabitants as responsible and knowledgeable citizens; and (4) building mentalities and institutions to make polyarchies better able to form and implement long-term, knowledge-based policies for mastering collective problems, such as those related to climate change and sustainable development (Lafferty 2012).

Avoiding Institutional Imperialism

In social theory, it is common to conceptualize modern societies as being built on three societal orders: market economy, constitutional democracy, and civil society (Kalleberg 2008: 18–20). These orders and their institutions are constituted and regulated by different values. Primary values regulating well-functioning institutions such as business enterprises (profitability) in market economy, courts (justice) in constitutional democracy, and families (love, care) and sciences (truth) in civil society are incompatible. A basic challenge in a modern society is to find appropriate interinstitutional balances between such incompatible values, not to get rid of any them. In differentiated, pluralist societies, institutional imperialism is constantly a danger. Norms, values, and practices from one social order can invade another. For instance, state and market values can undermine, marginalize, or drive away traditional values in civil society (Habermas 1984–1987: 2:355). Values and norms from civil society can also invade institutional contexts where they do not belong. Nepotism can distort business life, and religious fundamentalism can deform politics. Civil society institutions can distort each other. For instance, social scientific market management thinking in universities can contribute to distortions in institutions such as hospitals and schools.

As in other contemporary polyarchies, Norwegian society today is heavily influenced by a neoliberal market management ideology (Olsen 2010: 152–155; Sandel 2012). This ideology makes it difficult to adequately comprehend institutions other than markets (exchange) and hierarchies (command). Such thinking stimulates conceptual misbehavior on the individual level, people seeing themselves mainly as employees, consumers, and clients instead of citizens. But public forums, for instance, in the mass media, cannot be adequately regulated as markets and hierarchies. Educational institutions cannot, without serious distortions, be (re)designed as business enterprises; scholars are not service providers; students are not consumers (Kalleberg 2011). In well-functioning deliberative forums, ordinary participants are not active in roles as employees, clients, or customers, but rather as citizens and members with rights and obligations.

Quality of Deliberation

In focusing on the informal deliberative aspects of democracy outside of elected bodies and their professional bureaucracies, the epistemic quality of deliberation in all kinds of forums is an essential challenge. It can be undermined by widespread scientific illiteracy (Kalleberg 2008: 17–18), and by mass media lacking sufficient independence and appropriate feedbacks from civil society (Habermas 2009: 174–181). It can be supported by academics taking their role as public intellectuals seriously. Challenges of this type have to be met with adequately designed institutions and maintenance of deliberative cultures.

There is much to learn from well-functioning scientific institutions. The ethos of democracy and the ethos of science are internally related. Fallible deliberation characterizes collective opinion formation in both fields (Kalleberg 2010: 192–199). Obviously, there are essential differences between general democratic publics and scientific publics. Majority decisions are a legitimate procedure in parliaments, but would be a perversion in science. A general lesson to be learned from science is the importance of institutions. The role of scientist is a public one, embedded in particular institutions, regulated by institutional imperatives that discipline individual scientists to conform to the norms of science (Kalleberg 2007; 2011: 94–97, 101–104). As rational but fallible beings, all of us also need to be disciplined by appropriate institutional imperatives in our roles within the forums of civil society. Some contributions in contemporary debates leave the impression that individuals only have a right to free speech, not also a corresponding obligation to answer criticism from others. Freedom of expression is a human right and an indispensible institution in constitutional democracies. It is, however, not a right and an institutional complex designed to cultivate closed minds deaf to the arguments, interests, and dignity of fellow citizens.

According to the analytical framework used here, also normative issues can be criticized and revised with reasons (Kalleberg 2009). The Commission that revised Article 100 also noted this (NOU 1999: 122). Habermas assumes that "suitable institutionalized deliberations" can mobilize, evaluate, and balance both descriptive and normative claims, so that the democratic process gets a "cognitive function" (2009: 146–152). According to the "democratic principle" articulated by him, only those standards and norms "may claim legitimacy that can meet with the assent of all citizens in a discursive process of legislation …" (Habermas 1996: 110). To move in this direction is a demanding challenge for institutional (re)design in contemporary polyarchic democracies.

The Importance of Educational Institutions

Too often, discussions of freedom of expression focus only on mass media. However, schools are the most influential institutions of general culture in a modern society. Their importance leads me to two concluding recommendations, one about the curriculum and one about discussion culture.

Education on all levels should include learning about constitutional democracy, about its honored and painful history, and about contemporary challenges. On Norwegian Constitution Day (17 May), the Constitution is celebrated as a symbol of Norwegian democratic tradition and national independence. Schools are heavily engaged in the annual meetings and parades. However, celebrations are often oriented toward the past and are vague regarding problems, dangers, and future possibilities. The day should also be oriented toward future tasks. Democracy is our only realistic, utopian vision for an egalitarian and solidary future, a vision that can also enthuse school children. Habermas once gave a wonderful expression of this vision: "The individual cannot be free unless all are free, and all cannot be free unless all are free in community" (Habermas 1992a: 146).

The school curriculum and Constitution Day celebrations should keep alive also the memory of those elements that we are not proud of, such as the Constitution's original Article 2 that excluded Jews from the country (until 1851). To achieve future progress, humility is important not only in science (Kalleberg 2011: 107–109), but also in general culture and democratic discourse. Most nations have something to learn from postwar Germany in this respect (Jarausch 2006; Specter 2010).

The educational system's knowledge base is provided by the scholarly and scientific disciplines. Therefore, in a constitutional democracy, educational institutions are the best settings for citizens to learn the skills of rational discussion: respect for facts, clarity, consistency, respect for opponents, and a sense of one's own fallibility. Such a discussion culture is an intrinsic part of the epistemic and ethical unity of all scientific and scholarly disciplines (Kalleberg 2011: 93–104).

In the Norwegian context, two recent official reports indicate the policy relevance of such general reasoning. An official report on integrating immigrants sought to determine "which common values should constitute the common basis in our multicultural society" (NOU 2011: 310). In answering, the report leans on an earlier official report on the main purposes of Norwegian schools (NOU 2007), where it was claimed that education should make visible and support a "scholarly way of thinking." The 2011 report suggests that a "scholarly way of thinking" deserves to be among the few common values of all citizens in an increasingly multicultural nation, together with human rights and democracy (NOU 2011: 325–326). This line of thought endorses a type of "constitutional patriotism" (Habermas 1996: 465; Habermas 2009: 106; Specter 2010: 133–170; Baxter 2011: 222–227), in accordance with the three basic arguments for freedom of expression. This is an essential insight, in accordance with the three basic principles for freedom of expression: truth, autonomy, and democracy. But instead of an individual "way of thinking" we should speak of a "discussion culture," the latter notion more clearly referring to social interaction where fallible participants can learn from each other.

NOTES

1. In his magnum opus on speech acts and communicative rationality in liberal democracies with market economies, Habermas (1981: 101) is unequivocal in rejecting linguistic idealism: "To avoid misunderstanding I would like to repeat that the communicative model of action does not equate action with communication."

2. Parts of the report are translated into English (NOU 2005). All page references are to the original Norwegian report. I use the English-language translation whenever possible (occasionally corrected by me); otherwise, the translation is my own.

3. Six authors referred to in the report present, use, or develop insights from Habermas. This mentioned by the commission for three of them (Gripsrud, Høibraaten, and Oskal), but not for Kalleberg, Sejersted, and Skirbekk.

4. The fourth paragraph of the revised Article 100 allows for "prior censorship ... in order to protect children and young persons from the harmful influence of moving pictures."

5. Dahl (2003: 122) expresses the same point about a constitution "enabling politically equal citizens to govern themselves under laws and governmental policies that have been adopted and are maintained with their rational consent."

6. Anine Kierulf (2012) studied the Norwegian Supreme Court's handling of twenty-four cases concerning freedom of expression in the first seven years after the revised Article 100 was adopted. She found that the Supreme Court had not yet used the revised article as an important source of law. Article 10 in the European Convention on Human Rights and cases from the European Court of Human Rights were clearly more influential.

7. Professor of history Francis Sejersted, who chaired the commission, recognized the "basic inspiration" (Sejersted 1997: 220, 223) from Habermas (1962) when he reflected on his own (1978) synthesizing study of Norwegian history during the first half of the nineteenth century.

8. The Norwegian Commission on Freedom of Expression contextualized freedom of expression in constitutional democracies, but did not succumb to self-defeating, relativistic contextualism: "The core of the three principles provides a *universal* defense of freedom of expression" (NOU 1999: 10; italics in the original). Rule of law, constitutional democracy, and democratic citizenship emerged historically in the West, but have universal relevance and validity when adequately contextualized and implemented. One example is the transformation of South Korea after 1948 (see Han 1998). An-Naʿim (2008) has persuasively argued that these ideas and ideals are also valid grounds for building secular, democratic states in Muslim societies.

Constitution for Kongeriget Norge

A. Om Statsformen og Religionen.

§ 1. Kongeriket Norge er et frit, uafhængigt og udeleligt Rige. Dets Regjerings-form er indskrænket og arvelig-monarkisk.

§ 2. Den evangelisk-lutterske Religion forbliver Statens offentlige Religion. De Indvaanere, der bekjende sig til den, ere forpligtede til at opdrage sine Børn i samme. Jesuitter og Munkeordener maae ikke taales. Jøder ere fremdeles udelukkede fra Adgang til Riget.

B. Om den udøvende Magt, Kongen og den kongelige Familie.

§ 3. Den udøvende Magt er hos Kongen, hvis Tittel er Vi N. N. af Guds Naade og efter Rigets Constitution Norges Konge.

§ 4. Kongens Person er hellig: han kan ikke lastes eller anklages. Ansvarligheden paaligger hans Raad.

§ 5. Arvefølgen er lineal og agnatisk, saaledes, at kun Mand af Mand kan arve Kronen. Den nærmere Linie gaaer for den fjernere, og den Ældre i Linien for den Yngre.

§ 6. Den udvalgte Konges, i lovligt Ægteskab avlede, mandlige Livsarvinger ere arveberettigede i den Orden, forrige § foreskriver, saa at Riget stedse bliver udeelt hos Een; hvorimod de øvrige Prindser, til hvilke Tronen ved Arv kan komme, bør nøies med den dem af Storthinget tilstaaende Apanage, indtil Ar-veordenen kommer til dem.

§ 7. Naar en, til Norges Krone arveberettiget, Prinds fødes, skal hans Navn og Fødselstid tilkjendegives førstholdende Storthing og antegnes i dets Protocol.

§ 8. Blandt Arveberettigede regnes ogsaa den Ufødte, der strax indtaget sit tilbørlige Sted i Arvelinien, om han end først efter Faderens Død fødes til Verden.

§ 9. Er ingen arveberettiget Prinds til, kan Kongen foreslaae sin Efterfølger for Storthinget, som enten antager eller forkaster Forslaget.

§ 10. Kongen er myndig, naar han har fyldt det 20de Aar. Saasnart han er indtraadt i det 21de Aar, erklærer han sig offentlig at være myndig.

§ 11. Saasnart Kongen, som myndig, tiltræder Regjeringen, aflægger han for Storthinget følgende Eed: "Jeg lover og sværger at ville regjere Kongeriget Norge i Overensstemmelse med dets Constitution og Love; saa sandt hjelpe mig Gud og hans hellige Ord!" Er intet Storthing paa den Tid samlet, nedlægges Eden skriftlig i Statsraadet og igjentages høitideligen af Kongen paa første Storthing.

§ 12. Kongens Kroning og Salving skeer, efterat han er bleven myndig, i Trondhjems Domkirke paa den Tid og med de Ceremonier, han selv fastsetter.

§ 13. Kongen skal stedse boe inden Rigets nuværende Grændser og maa ikke, uden Storthingets Samtykke, opholde sig udenfor dem længer, end 6 Maaneder af Gangen, medmindre han for sin Person vil have tabt Ret til Kronen.

§ 14. Kongen maa ikke modtage nogen anden Krone eller Regjering uden Storthingets Samtykke, hvortil 2/3 af Stemmerne udfordres.

§ 15. Kongen skal stedse have bekjendt og bekjende sig til den evangelisk-lutterske Religion, haandhæve og beskytte denne.

§ 16. Kongen anordner al offentlig Kirke- og Gudstjeneste, alle Møder og Forsamlinger om Religionssager, og paaseer, at Religionens offentlige Lærere følge de dem foreskrevne Normer.

§ 17. Kongen kan give og ophæve Anordninger, der angaae Handel, Told, Næringsveie og Politie; dog maae de ikke stride mod Constitutionen og de af Storthinget givne Love. De gjelde provisorisk til næste Storthing.

§ 18. Kongen lader i Almindelighed indkræve de Skatter og Afgifter, som Storthinget paalægger.

§ 19. Kongen vaager over, at Statens Eiendomme og Regalier anvendes og bestyres paa den af Storthinget bestemte og for Almeenvæsenet nyttigste Maade.

§ 20. Kongen har Ret til i Statsraadet at benaade Forbrydere, efterat Høiesterets Dom er falden og dens Betænkning indhentet. Forbryderen har Valget, om han vil modtage Kongens Naade, eller underkaste sig den ham tildømte Straf. I de Sager, som af Odelsthinget foranstaltes, anlagde for Rigsretten, kan ingen anden Benaadning, end Fritagelse for idømt Livsstraf, finde Sted.

§ 21. Kongen vælger og beskikker, efter at have hørt sit Statsraad, alle civile, geistlige og militaire Embedsmænd. Disse sværge Constitutionen og Kongen Troskab og Lydighed. De kongelige Prindser maae ei beklæde civile Embeder.

§ 22. Statsraadets Medlemmer og de Embedsmænd, som ere ansatte ved dets Comptoirer, Gesandter og Consuler, civile og geistlige Overøvrighedspersoner, Regimenters og andre militaire Corpsers Chefer, Comandanter i Fæstninger og Høistbefalende paa Krigsskibe kunne, uden foregaaende Dom afskediges af Kongen, efterat han derom har hørt Statsraadets Betænkning. Hvorvidt Pension bør tilstaaes de saaledes afskedigede Embedsmænd, afgjøres af det næste Storthing. Imidlertid nyde de 2/3 af deres forhen hafte Gage. Andre Embedsmænd kunne ikkun suspenderes af Kongen, og skulle da strax tiltales for Domstolene, men de maae ei, uden efter Dom afsettes, ei heller mod deres Vilie forflyttes.

§ 23. Kongen kan meddele Ordener til hvem han forgodtbefinder, til Belønning for udmærkede Fortjenester, der offentligen maae kundgjøres; men ei anden Rang og Tittel, end den, ethvert Embede medfører. Ordenen fritager Ingen for Statsborgernes fælleds Pligter og Byrder, ei heller medfører den fortrinlig Adgang til Statens Embeder. Embedsmænd, som i Naade afskediges, beholde deres hafte Embeders Tittel og Rang. Ingen personlige eller blandede arvelige Forrettigheder tilstaaes Nogen for Eftertiden.

§ 24. Kongen vælger og afskediger efter eget Godtbefindende sin Hofstat og sine Hofbetjente. Til at lønne disse og holde sit Hof tilstaaes ham af Storthinget en passende aarlig Sum.

§ 25. Kongen har høieste Befaling over Rigets Land- og Søemagt. Den maa ikke overlates i fremmede Magters Tjeneste, og ingen fremmede Krigsfolk, undtagen Hjelpetropper mod fiendtlige Overfald, maae inddrages i Riget uden Storthingets Samtykke.

§ 26. Kongen har Ret til at sammenkalde Tropper, begynde Krig og slutte Fred, indgaae og ophæve Forbund, sende og modtage Gesandter.

§ 27. Regjeringen er ikke berettiget til Militairmagts Anvendelse mod Statens Medlemmer, uden efter de i Lovgivningen bestemte Former, medmindre nogen Forsamling maatte forstyrre den offentlige Rolighed, og den ikke øieblikkelig adskilles, efterat de Artikler i Landsloven, som angaae Oprør, ere den trende Gange lydeligen forelæste af den civile Øvrighed.

§ 28. Kongen vælger Selv et Raad af norske Borgere, som ikke ere yngre end 30 Aar. Dette Raad skal i det mindste bestaae af 5 Medlemmer. Til at tage Sæde i Statsraadet kan Kongen foruden dem ved overordentlige Leiligheder

218 of Appendix A

tilkalde andre norske Borgere; kun ingen Medlemmer af Storthinget. Forret-
ningerne fordeler han blandt dem, saaledes som han det for tjenligt eragter.
Fader og Søn, eller to Brødre maae ei paa samme Tid have Sæde i Statsraadet.

§ 29. Alle Statsraader skulle, naar de ikke have lovligt Forfald, være nærværende
i Statsraadet, og maa ingen Beslutning tages der, naar ikke over det halve Antal
af Medlemmerne ere tilstæde.

§ 30. Forestillinger om Embeders Besettelse og andre Sager af Vigtighed—
diplomatiske og egentlige militaire Commandosager undtagne—skulle foredrages i Statsraadet af det Medlem, til hvis Fag de høre, og Sagerne af ham
expederes overensstemmende med Kongens i Statsraadet fattede Beslutning.

§ 31. Forbyder lovligt Forfald en Statsraad at møde, og foredrage de Sager, som
henhøre under hans Fag, skulle disse foredrages af en anden Statsraad, som
Kongen dertil constituerer. Hindres saa mange ved lovligt Forfald fra Møde i
Statsraadet, at ikke flere end Halvparten af det bestemte Antal Medlemmer ere
tilstæde; skulle andre Embedsmænd af Kongen constitueres til at tage Sæde i
Statsraadet.

§ 32. I Statsraadet føres Protocol over alle de Sager, som der forhandles. Enhver, som har Sæde i Statsraadet, er pligtig til med Frimodighed at sige sin
Mening, hvilken Kongen er forbunden at høre. Men det er denne forbeholdt
at fatte Beslutning efter sit eget Omdømme. Finder noget Medlem af Statsraadet, at Kongens Beslutning er stridende mod Statsformen eller Rigets Love,
eller øiensynligen er skadelig for Riget; er det Pligt at gjøre kraftige Forestillinger derimod, samt at tilføie sin Mening i Protocollen. Den, der ikke saaledes
har protesteret, ansees at have været enig med Kongen og er ansvarlig derfor,
saaledes som siden bestemmes.

§ 33. Den Statsraad, som forestaaer det udenlandske Departement, bør have
en egen Protocol, hvori de Sager indføres, som ere af den Natur, at de ikke bør
forlægges det samlede Statsraad. Forøvrigt gjelder i dette Tilfælde de samme
Bestemmelser som i 32te § ere fastsatte.

§ 34. Alle Regjeringens Beslutninger og Befalinger udstædes stedse i Kongens
Navn.

§ 35. Alle af Kongen udfærdigede Befalinger og officielle Breve—militaire
Commandosager undtagne—skulle contrasigneres af den, som ifølge sin Em-
bedspligt har foredraget Sagen, da han bør være ansvarlig for Expeditionens
Overensstemmelse med den Protocol, hvori Resolutionen er indført.

§ 36. Nærmeste Tronarving, om han er den regjerende Konges Søn, fører Tittel
af Kronprinds til Norge. De Øvrige, som til Kronen ere arveberettigede, kaldes
Prindser, og de kongelige Døttre Prindsesser.

§ 37. Saasnart Tronarvingen har fyldt sit 18de Aar, er han berettiget til at tage Sæde i Statsraadet; dog uden Stemme eller Ansvar.

§ 38. Ingen Prinds af Blodet maa forlade Riget, gifte sig eller begive sig i fremmed Tjeneste uden Kongens Tilladelse. Handler han herimod, forbryder han sin Ret til Kronen.

§ 39. De kongelige Prindser og Prindsesser skulle for deres Personer ikke svare for andre, end Kongen, eller hvem han til Dommer over dem forordner.

§ 40. Er Tronarvingen fraværende ved Kongens Død, bør han, hvis uovervindelige Hindringer ei forbyde det, inden 6 Maaneder, efterat Dødsfaldet er ham tilkjendegivet, indfinde sig i Riget, eller for sin Person have tabt Ret til Kronen.

§ 41. Er nærmeste Tronarving ved Kongens Død umyndig, fører Enkedronningen, om hun er Kongens kjødelige Moder, saalænge hun forbliver Enke, Regjeringen i Forening med Statsraadet, indtil Kongen vorder myndig. Er saadan Enkedronning ei til, da fører den nærmeste arveberettigede Prinds, som da er over 25 Aar gammel, Regjeringen paa samme Maade, under Tittel af Regent. Er Regentskabet tilfaldet en Fjernere i Arveordenen, paa Grund af, at den Nærmere ei var fuldmyndig, da skal den Første fravige det for den Sidstnævnte, saasnart denne har opnaaet 25 Aars Alder. I disse Tilfælde affattes Beslutningerne i Statsraadet efter de fleste Stemmer, og har Enkedronningen eller Regenten 2 Stemmer.

§ 42. Er ingen saadan fuldmyndig Prinds til, føres Regentskabet af Statsraadet i Forening med de Mænd, som Storthinget maatte finde fornødent at tilforordne, under Ansvar efter 45de §. Den første af Statsraadets Medlemmer har da Forsædet og 2 Stemmer.

§ 43. De i 42de § fastsatte Bestemmelser gjelde ligeledes i Tilfælde af, at Kongen ved Sinds- eller Legemssvaghed bliver uskikket til Regjeringen, eller er fraværende fra Riget.

§ 44. De, som ifølge Foranførte forestaae Regjeringen medens Kongen er umyndig, fraværende eller paa anden Maade ud af stand til selv at regjere, skulle for Storthinget, hver for sig, aflægge følgende Eed: "Jeg lover og sværger at ville forestaae Regjeringen i Overensstemmelse med Constitutionen og Lovene; saa sandt hjelpe mig Gud og hans hellige Ord!"

§ 45. Saasnart deres Statsbestyrelse ophører, skulle de aflægge Kongen og Storthinget Regnskab for samme.

§ 46. Ved Kongens Død, eller i de Tilfælde, i hvilke et Regentskab bør beskikkes, skal strax et overordentligt Storthing sammenkaldes af Statsraadet, eller andre Vedkommende. Opfylder Statsraadet ikke denne Pligt inden 4 Uger, besørges Sammenkaldelsen ved Justitiarius og Tilforordnede i Høiesteret.

§ 47. Bestyrelsen af den umyndige Konges Opdragelse bør, hvis hans Fader ei derom har efterladt nogen skriftlig Bestemmelse, betroes til visse, af Storthinget dertil udnævnte, Mænd i Forening med Enkedronningen, om hun er hans kjødelige Moder, med Udelukkelse af den nærmeste Tronarving, hans Livsarvinger, Statsraadet og Regentskabets øvrige Tilforordnede.

§ 48. Er den mandlige Kongestamme uddød, og ingen Tronfølger udkaaren, da sammenkaldes Storthinget strax, paa den i 46de § foreskrevne Maade, for at vælge en nye Kongeæt. Imidlertid forholdes med den udøvende Magt efter 42de §.

C. Om Borgerret og den lovgivende Magt.

§ 49. Folket udøver den lovgivende Magt ved Storthinget, der bestaaer af 2 Afdelinger, et Lagthing og et Odelsthing.

§ 50. Stemmeberettigede ere kun de norske Borgere, som have fyldt 25 Aar, have været bosatte i Landet i 5 Aar, og enten

a. ere, eller have været Embedsmænd,

b. paa Landet eie eller paa længere Tid end 5 Aar have byxlet matriculeret Jord,

c. ere Kjøbstadborgere, eller i Kjøbstad eller Ladested eie Gaard eller Grund, hvis Værdie i det mindste er 300 Rigsbankdaler Sølvværdie.

§ 51. Inden 6 Maaneder efter denne Constitutions Antagelse skal, i enhver Kjøbstad af Magistraten og i ethvert Præstegjeld af Fogden og Præsten forfattes et Mandtal over alle stemmeberettigede Indvaanere. De Forandringer dette efterhaanden maatte undergaae, anføres ufortøvet deri. Enhver skal, forinden han indføres i Mandtallet, offentligen til Thinge sværge Constitutionen Troskab.

§ 52. Stemmeret suspenderes:

a. Ved Anklage til Thinge for Forbrydelser,

b ved Umyndiggjørelse,

c. ved Opbud eller Fallit, indtil Creditorerne have erholdt fuld Betaling; medmindre Fallitten er foraarsaget ved Ildsvaade, eller andet utilregneligt og bevisligt Uheld.

§ 53. Stemmeret tabes:

a. ved at have været dømt til Tugthuus, Slaverie eller vanærende Straffe,

b. ved at gaae i en fremmed Magts Tjeneste uden Regjeringens Samtykke,

c. ved at erhverve Borgerret i en fremmed Stat, d. ved at overbevises om at have kjøbt Stemmer, solgt sin egen Stemme, eller stemt i flere, end een Valgforsamling.

§ 54. Valg- og Districtsforsamlingerne holdes hvert 3die Aar. De skulle være tilendebragte inden December Maaneds Udgang.

§ 55. Valgforsamlingerne holdes paa Landet i Præstegjeldets Hovedkirke, i Kjøbstæderne i Kirken, paa Raadhuset eller et andet dertil beqvemt Sted. De bestyres paa Landet af Sognepræsten og hans Medhjelpere, i Kjøbstæderne af disses Magistrater og Formænd. Stemmegivningen skeer i den Orden, Mandtallet viser. Stridigheter om Stemmeret afgjøres af Forsamlingens Bestyrere, hvis Kjendelse kan indankes for Storthinget.

§ 56. Førend Valgene begynde skal Constitutionen lydelig oplæses, i Kjøbstæderne af den første Magistratsperson, paa Landet af Præsten.

§ 57. I Kjøbstæderne udnævnes een Valgmand for hver 50 stemmeberettigede Indvaanere. Disse Valgmænd samles inden 8 Dage derefter, paa et af Øvrigheden dertil bestemt Sted, og udnævne enten af deres egen Midte, eller blandt de øvrige Stemmeberettigede i deres Valgdistrict 1/4 af deres eget Antal til at møde og tage Sæde paa Storthinget, saaledes, at 3 til 6 vælge Een, 7 til 10 To, 11 til 14 Tre, 15 til 18 Fire, som er det høieste Antal, nogen Bye maa sende. Har en Kjøbstad færre end 150 stemmeberettigede Indvaanere, sender den sine Valgmænd til nærmeste Kjøbstad, for at stemme i Forening med dennes Valgmænd, og ansees da begge Kjøbstæder som eet District.

§ 58. I hvert Præstegjeld paa Landet udnævne de stemmeberettigede vaanere, i Forhold til deres Antal, Valgmænd saaledes, at indtil 100 vælge Een, 100 til 200 To, 200 til 300 Tre, o. s. f. i samme Forhold. Disse Valgmænd samles inden een Maaned derefter paa et, af Amtmanden dertil bestemt Sted, og udnævne da, enten af deres egen Midte, eller blandt de øvrige Stemmeberettigede i Amtet 1/10 af deres eget Antal til at møde og tage Sæde paa Storthinget, saaledes, at 5 til 14 vælge Een, 15 til 24 To, 25 til 34 Tre, 35 og derover Fire, som er det største Antal.

§ 59. De i § 57 og 58 fastsatte Bestemmelser gjelde indtil næste Storthing. Befindes det da: at Kjøbstædernes Repræsentanter udgjøre mere eller mindre end 1/3 af hele Rigets, bør Storthinget til Følge for Fremtiden, forandre disse Bestemmelser saaledes, at Kjøbstædernes Repræsentanter forholde sig til Landets, som 1 til 2, og bør Repræsentanternes Antal i det Hele ikke være mindre, end 75 og ei større end 100.

§ 60. De inden Riget værende stemmeberettigede, der ikke kunne møde formedelst Sygdom, Militairtjeneste eller andet lovligt Forfald, kunne skriftlig sende sine Stemmer til dem, der bestyre Valgforsamlingerne, forinden disse ere tilendebragte.

§ 61. Ingen kan vælges til Repræsentant, medmindre han er 30 Aar gammel og har i 10 Aar opholdt sig i Riget.

§ 62. Statsraadets Medlemmer og de Embedsmænd, som ere ansatte ved dets Comptoirer, eller Hoffets Betjente og dets Pensionister kunne ikke vælges til Repræsentanter.

§ 63. Enhver, som vælges til Repræsentant, er pligtig at modtage Valget, medmindre han hindres derfra ved Forfald, der kjendes lovligt af Valgmændene, hvis Kjendelse kan underkastes Storthingets Bedømmelse. Den, som to paa hinanden følgende Gange har mødt som Repræsentant paa et ordentligt Storthing, er ikke forpligtet til at modtage Valget til det derpaa følgende ordentlige Storthing. Hindres en Repræsentant ved lovligt Forfald fra at møde paa Storthinget, træder den, som næst ham har de fleste Stemmer i hans Sted.

§ 64. Saasnart Repræsentanterne ere valgte, forsynes de med en Fuldmagt, underskrevet, paa Landet af Overøvrighederne og i Kjøbstæderne af Magistraten, saavelsom af samtlige Valgmænd, til Beviis for, at de, paa den i Constitutionen foreskrevne Maade, ere udnævnte. Disse Fuldmagters Lovlighed bedømmes af Storthinget.

§ 65. Enhver Repræsentant er berettiget til Godtgjørelse af Statskassen for Reiseomkostninger til og fra Storthinget og for Underholdning i den Tid, han der opholder sig.

§ 66. Repræsentanterne ere paa deres Reise til og fra Storthinget, samt under deres Ophold der, befriede fra personlig Heftelse, medmindre de gribes i offentlige Forbrydelser; ei heller kunne de udenfor Storthingets Forsamlinger drages til Ansvar for deres der yttrede Meninger. Efter den der vedtagne Orden er Enhver pligtig at rette sig.

§ 67. De paa forestaaende Maade valgte Repræsentanter udgjøre Kongeriget Norges Storthing.

§ 68. Storthinget aabnes i Almindelighed den første Søgnedag i Februarii Maaned hvert 3die Aar i Rigets Hovedstad, medmindre Kongen, paa Grund af overordentlige Omstændigheder, saasom fiendtlig Indfald eller smitsom Syge dertil bestemmer en anden Kjøbstad. Saadan Bestemmelse maa da betimelig bekjendtgjøres.

§ 69. I overordentlige Tilfælde har Kongen Ret til at sammenkalde Storthinget udenfor den almindelige Tid. Kongen udstæder da en Kundgjørelse, som bør være læst i alle Stiftsstædernes Kirker i det mindste 6 Uger, forinden Storthingets Medlemmer skulle møde paa det bestemte Sted.

§ 70. Et saadant overordentlig Storthing kan af Kongen hæves, naar han forgodtbefinder.

§ 71. Storthingets Medlemmer fungere som saadanne i 3 paa hinanden følgende Aar, saavel ved overordentlige, som ved det ordentlige Storthing, der imidlertid holdes.

§ 72. Holdes et overordentlig Storthing endnu paa den Tid, det ordentlige skal sammentræde, ophører det førstes Virksomhed, saasnart det sidste er samlet.

§ 73. Intet af Thingene kan holdes, medmindre 2/3 af dets Medlemmer ere tilstede.

§ 74. Saasnart Storthinget har constitueret sig, aabner Kongen, eller den, han dertil beskikker, dets Forhandlinger med en Tale, hvori han underretter det om Rigets Tilstand og de Gjenstænde, hvorpaa han især ønsker at henlede Storthingets Opmærksomhed. Ingen Deliberation maa finde Sted i Kongens Nærværelse. Storthinget udvælger blandt sine Medlemmer 1/4 Part, som udgjør Lagthinget, de øvrige 3/4 Parter danne Odelsthinget. Hvert Thing holder sine Forsamlinger særskilte og udnævner sin egen Præsident og Secretair.

§ 75. Det tilkommer Storthinget:

a. at give og ophæve Love, paalægge Skatter, Afgifter, Told og andre offentlige Byrder, som dog ei gjelde længere, end til 1ste Julii i det Aar, da et nyt, ordentlig Storthing er samlet, medmindre de af dette udtrykkeligen fornyes;

b. at aabne Laan paa Statens Credit;

c. at føre Opsynet over Rigets Pengevæsen;

d. at bevilge de, til Statsudgifterne fornødne, Pengesummer;

e. at bestemme, hvormeget aarligen skal udbetales Kongen til hans Hofstat, og at fastsette den kongelige Families Apanage, som dog ikke maa bestaae i faste Eiendomme;

f. at lade sig forelægge Statsraadets Protocol og alle offentlige Indberetninger og Papirer, egentlige militaire Comandosager undtagne;

g. at lade sig meddele de Forbund og Tractater, Kongen paa Statens Vegne har indgaaet med fremmede Magter, med Undtagelse af hemmelige Artikler, som dog ei maae stride mod de offentlige;

h. at kunne fordre Enhver til at møde for sig i Statssager, Kongen og den kongelige Familie undtagne; dog gjelder denne Undtagelse ikke ikke for de kongelige Prindser, forsaavidt de maatte være Embedsmænd;

i. at revidere midlertidige Gage- og Pensionslister, og deri gjøre de Forandringer, det finder fornødne;

k. at udnævne 5 Revisorer, der aarligen skulle gjennemsee Statens Regnskaber og bekjendtgjøre Extracter af samme ved Trykken, hvilke Regnskaber derfor skulle tilstilles disse Revisorer hvert Aar inden 1ste Julii;

l. at naturalisere Fremmede.

§ 76. Enhver Lov skal først foreslaaes paa Odelsthinget, enten af dets egne Medlemmer, eller af Regjeringen ved en Statsraad. Er Forslaget der antaget, sendes det til Lagthinget, som enten bifalder eller forkaster det, og i sidste Tilfælde, sender det tilbage med tilføiede Bemærkninger. Disse tages i Overveielse af Odelsthinget, som enten henlægger Lovforslaget, eller atter sender det til Lagthinget med, eller uden Forandringer.

Naar et Forslag fra Odelsthinget to Gange har været Lagthinget forelagt, og anden Gang derfra er bleven tilbagesendt med Afslag; træder hele Storthinget sammen og, med 2/3 af dets Stemmer, afgjøres da Forslaget. Imellem enhver saadan Deliberation maae i det mindste 3 Dage hengaae.

§ 77. Naar en, af Odelsthinget foreslaaet Beslutning er bifaldet af Lagthinget, eller det samlede Storthing, sendes den ved en Deputation fra begge Storthingets Afdelinger til Kongen med Anmodning om hans Sanction.

§ 78. Billiger Kongen Beslutningen, forsyner han den med sin Underskrift, hvorved den vorder Lov. Billiger han den ikke, sender han den tilbage til Odelsthinget, med den Erklæring, at han ikke fortiden finder det tjenligt at sanctionere Beslutningen.

§ 79. Beslutningen maa i dette Tilfælde ikke mere af det da samlede Storthing forelægges Kongen, som paa samme Maade kan forholde sig, om næste ordentlige Storthing paa nye foreslaaer samme Beslutning; men bliver den ogsaa af det 3die ordentlige Storthing, efter igjen at være drøftet, atter paa begge Thing uforandret antaget, og den da forelægges Kongen, med Begjering, at Hans Majestæt ikke vil nægte en Beslutning sin Sanction, som Storthinget, efter det modneste Overlæg, anseer for gavnlig; saa vorder den Lov, om end Kongens Sanction ikke paafølger inden Storthinget adskilles.

§ 80. Storthinget forbliver samlet saalænge, det finder det fornødent; dog ikke over 3 Maaneder uden Kongens Tilladelse. Naar det, efterat have tilendebragt sine Forretninger, eller efterat have været samlet den bestemte Tid, hæves af Kongen, meddeler han tillige sin Resolution paa de, ikke allerede forinden afgjorte Beslutninger, ved enten at stadfæste eller forkaste dem. Alle de, som han ikke udtrykkelig antager, ansees som af ham forkastede.

§ 81. Alle Love—de i § 79 undtagne—udfærdiges i Kongens Navn og under Rigets Segl i følgende Udtryk:

"Vi N. N., af Guds Naade og efter Rigets Constitution Norges Konge, gjør vitterligt, at Os er bleven forelagt Storthingets Beslutning af Dato, saalydende: (Her følger Beslutningen) Thi have Vi antaget og bekræftet, ligesom Vi herved antage og bekræfte samme som Lov; under vor Haand og Rigets Segl."

§ 82. De provisoriske Anordninger, som Kongen udgiver i den Tid, intet Storthing holdes, saavelsom de øvrige Anordninger og Befalinger, der vedkomme den udøvende Magt allene, affattes saaledes: "Vi N. N. etc. gjøre vitterlig, at Vi, i Kraft af den Os ved Rigets Constitution meddelte Myndighed, have besluttet, ligesom Vi herved beslutte o. s. v."

§ 83. Kongens Sanction udfordres ikke til de Storthingets Beslutninger, hvorved:

a. det erklærer sig samlet som Storthing efter Constitutionen;

b. det bestemmer sit indvortes Politie;

c. det antager eller forkaster de tilstedeværende Medlemmers Fuldmagter;

d. det stadfæster eller forkaster Kjendelser om Valgstridigheder;

e. det naturaliserer Fremmede;

f. og endelig, til den Beslutning, hvorved Odelsthinget sætter Statsraader eller andre under Tiltale.

§ 84. Storthinget kan indhente Høiesterets Betænkning over juridiske Gjenstænde.

§ 85. Storthinget holdes for aabne Døre og dets Forhandlinger kundgjøres ved Trykken, undtagen i de Tilfælde, hvor det Modsatte besluttes ved Stemmeflerhed.

§ 86. Den, der adlyder en Befaling, hvis Hensigt er at forstyrre Storthingets Frihed og Sikkerhed, gjør sig derved skyldig i Forræderie mod Fædrenelandet.

D. Om den dømmende Magt.

§ 87. Lagthingets Medlemmer tilligemed Høiesteret udgjøre Rigsretten, som i første og sidste Instans dømmer i de Sager, som af Odelsthinget anlægges, enten mod Statsraadets, eller Høiesterets Medlemmer, for Embedsforbrydelser, eller mod Storthingets Medlemmer for de Forbrydelser, de som saadanne begaae. I Rigsretten har Præsidenten i Lagthinget Forsædet.

§ 88. Den Anklagede kan, uden nogen dertil angiven Aarsag, forskyde af Rigsrettens Medlemmer indtil 1/3; dog saaledes, at Retten ei udgjør mindre end 15 Personer.

§ 89. Til at dømme i sidste Instans skal, saasnart mueligt, organiseres en Høiesteret, der ikke maa bestaae af færre, end Justitiarius og 6 Tilforordnede.

§ 90. I Fredstider er Høiesteret tilligemed 2 høie Officierer, som Kongen tilforordner, anden og sidste Instans i alle de Krigsretssager, som angaae enten Liv eller Ære, eller Friheds Tab for længere Tid, end 3 Maaneder.

§ 91. Høiesterets Domme kunne i intet Tilfælde paaankes eller underkastes Revision.

§ 92. Ingen kan beskikkes til Medlem af Høiesteret, førend han er 30 Aar gammel.

E. Almindelige Bestemmelser.

§ 93. Til Embeder i Staten maa allene udnævnes de norske Borgere, som bekjende sig til den evangelisk-lutterske Religion, have svoret Constitutionen og Kongen Troskab, og tale Landets Sprog, samt

a. enten ere fødte i Riget af Forældre, der da vare Statens Undersatter;

b. ere fødte i fremmede Lande af norske Forældre, som paa den Tid ikke vare en anden Stats Undersaatter;

c. eller som nu have stadigt Ophold i Riget, og ikke have vægret sig for at aflægge den Eed, at hævde Norges Selvstændighed;

d. eller som herefter opholde sig i Riget i 10 Aar;

e. eller som af Storthinget vorde naturaliserede.

Dog kunne Fremmede beskikkes til Lærere ved Universitetet og de lærde Skoler, til Læger og til Consuler paa fremmede Stæder. Ingen maa beskikkes til Overøvrighedsperson, førend han er 30 Aar gammel, eller til Magistratsperson, Underdommer og Foged, førend han er 25 Aar gammel.

§ 94. En nye, almindelig civil og criminel Lovbog skal foranstaltes udgivet paa første, eller om dette ikke er mueligt, paa andet ordentlige Storthing. Imidlertid blive Statens nugjeldende Love i Kraft, forsaavidt de ei stride imod denne Grundlov eller de provisoriske Anordninger, som imidlertid maatte udgives. De nuværende permanente Skatter vedblive ligeledes til næste Storthing.

§ 95. Ingen Dispensationer, Protectorier, Moratorier eller Opreisninger maae bevilges, efterat den nye, almindelige Lov er sat i Kraft.

§ 96. Ingen kan dømmes uden efter Lov, eller straffes uden efter Dom. Pinligt Forhør maa ikke finde Sted.

§ 97. Ingen Lov maa gives tilbagevirkende Kraft.

§ 98. Med Sportler, som erlægges til Rettens Betjente, bør ingen Afgiftter til Statskassen være forbundne.

§ 99. Ingen maa fængslig anholdes uden i lovbestemte Tilfselde og paa den ved Lovene foreskrevne Maade. For ubeføiet Arrest eller ulovligt Ophold staae Vedkommende den Fængslede til Ansvar.

§ 100. Trykkefrihed bør finde Sted. Ingen kan straffes for noget Skrift af hvad Indhold det end maatte være, som han har ladet trykke eller udgive, medmindre han forsetligen og aabenbar enten selv har viist, eller tilskyndet andre til Ulydighed mod Lovene, Ringeagt mod Religionen, Sædelighed eller de constitutionelle Magter, Modstand mod disses Befalinger, eller fremført falske og ærekrænkende Beskyldninger mod nogen. Frimodige Yttringer om Statsstyrelsen og hvilkensomhelst anden Gjenstand ere Enhver tilladte.

§ 101. Nye og bestandige Indskrænkninger i Næringsfriheden bør ikke tilstædes nogen for Fremtiden.

§ 102. Huusinqvisitioner maae ikke finde Sted, uden i criminelle Tilfælde.

§ 103. Fristed tilstædes ikke dem, som herefter fallere.

§ 104. Jord- og Brugslod kan i intet Tilfælde forbryes.

§ 105. Fordrer Statens Tarv, at Nogen maae afgive sin rørlige eller urørlige Eiendom til offentligt Brug, saa bør han have fuld Erstatning af Statskassen.

§ 106. Saavel Kjøbesummer, som Indtægter af det, Geistligheden beneficerede Gods, skal blot anvendes til Geistlighedens Bedste og Oplysningens Fremme. Milde Stiftelsers Eiendomme skulle blot anvendes til disses Gavn.

§ 107. Odels- og Aasædesretten maa ikke ophæves. De nærmere Betingelser, hvorunder den, til største Nytte for Staten og Gavn for Landalmuen, skal vedblive, fastsettes af det første eller andet følgende Storthing.

§ 108. Ingen Grevskaber, Baronier, Stamhuse og Fideicommisser maae for Eftertiden oprettes.

§ 109. Enhver Statens Borger er i Almindelighed lige forpligtet i en vis Tid at værne om sit Fædreneland, uden Hensyn til Fødsel eller Formue. Denne Grundsetnings Anvendelse og de Indskrænkninger, den bør undergaae, overlades til første ordentlige Storthings Afgjørelse, efterat alle Oplysninger ere erhvervede ved en Committee, der udvælges inden denne Rigsforsamlings Slutning. Imidlertid vedblive de nugjeldende Bestemmelser.

§ 110. Naar Rigsforsamlingen har antaget denne Constitution, vorder den Rigets Grundlov. Viser Erfaring, at nogen Deel af den bør forandres, skal

Forslaget derom fremsettes paa et ordentlig Storthing og kundgjøres ved Trykken. Men det tilkommer først det næste ordentlige Storthing at bestemme, om den foreslaaede Forandring bør finde Sted, eller ei. Dog maa saadan Forandring aldrig modsige denne Grundlovs Principer, men allene angaae Modificationer i enkelte Bestemmelser, der ikke forandre denne Constitutions Aand, og bør 2/3 af Storthinget være enig i saadan Forandring.

Paa Rigsforsamlingens Vegne

C. M. Falsen	H. M. Krohg	Christie
Præsident.	Vice-Præsident.	Secretair.

Vi undertegnede Kongeriget Norges Repræsentanter, erklære herved denne Constitution, som af Rigsforsamlingen er antaget, for Kongeriget Norges Grundlov, hvorefter alle og enhver sig have at rette. Dets til Bekræftelse under vor Haand og Seigl.

Eydsvold d: 17de May 1814.

Peder Anker. (L. S.)[1]	C. M. Falsen. (L. S.)	Christensen. (L. S.)		V. C. Sibbern. (L. S.)
F. W. Stabell. (L. S.)	Z. Mellebye. (L. S.)	Alexand. Chr. Møller (L. S.)		Motzfeldt. (L. S.)
H. Haslum. (L. S.)	W. F. K. Christie. (L. S.)	J. Rolfsen. (L. S.)	F. Meltzer. (L. S.)	J. Rein. (L. S.)
A. v. W. S. Koren. (L. S.)	G. B. Jersin. (L. S.)	B. A. S. Gierager. (L. S.)	Irgens. (L. S.)	N. Nielsen. (L. S.)
P. Hiermand. (L. S.)	O. E. Holck. (L. S.)	N. J. S. Loftesnæs. (L. S.)	F. Schmidt. (L. S.)	Johan Collett. (L. S.)
Christopher Hoen. (L. S.)	Løvenskiold. (L. S.)	P. J. Cloumann. (L. S.)		Tallev Olsen Huvestad. (L. S.)
G. Sverdrup. (L. S.)	Omsen. (L. S.)	N. Wergeland. (L. S.)	O. C. Mørch. (L. S.)	L. Weidemann. (L. S.)
Stabel. (L. S.)	A. Lysgaard. (L. S.)	John Moses. (L. S.)	Nicolaj Scheitlie. (L. S.)	C. A. Dahl. (L. S.)

Anders Michael Heiberg. (L. S.)	Bendeke. (L. S.)	A. Kønig. (L. S.)	O. O. Evenstad. (L. S.)	H. H. Nysom. (L. S.)
H. Wedel-Jarlsberg. (L. S.)	G. P. Blom. (L. S.)	O. R. Apeness. (L. S.)		A. Sibbern. (L. S.)
P. Steensgrup. (L. S.)	C. Hersleb Hornemann. (L. S.)	Diriks. (L. S.)		I. Hesselberg. (L. S.)
And. Grønneberg. (L. S.)	O. Amundsrød. (L. S.)	Gabriel Lund, junior. (L. S.)		Erichstrup. (L. S.)
T. J. Lundegaard. (L. S.)	Osmund Lømsland. (L. S.)	Erich Jaabech. (L. S.)		Sywert Eeg. (L. S.)
F. Motzfeldt. (L. S.)	G. Wulfsberg. (L. S.)	J. Aall, junior. (L. S.)		Grøgaard. (L. S.)
Thor R. Lilleholt. (L. S.)	Prydz. (L. S.)	Helge Waagaard. (L. S.)		Fleischer. (L. S.)
N. Dyhren. (L. S.)	D. Hegermann. (L. S.)	Sergeant Haraldstad. (L. S.)		Jørgen Aall. (L. S.)
Thomas Bryn. (L. S.)	E. T. S. Lande. (L. S.)	Ole Knudsen Tvedten. (L. S.)	H. M. Krohg. (L. S.)	I. Stub. (L. S.)
Elling Walbøe. (L. S.)	Richard Floer. (L. S.)	P. Hount. (L. S.)	John Hansen. (L. S.)	Did. Cappelen. (L. S.)
P. V. Rosenkilde. (L. S.)	Oftedahl. (L. S.)	C. Mølbach. (L. S.)		A. Regelstad. (L. S.)
J. S. Fabricius. (L. S.)	T. Konow. (L. S.)	P. Johnsen. (L. S.)	Even Thorsen *med ført Pæn* (L. S.)	D. Petersen. (L. S.)
Ole Svendsen. (L. S.)	P. Ramm. (L. S.)	P. Balke. (L. S.)	E. Høyum. (L. S.)	G. Røed. (L. S.)

A. Rogert. (L. S.)	Peter Schmidt, jr. (L. S.)	J. H. Darre. (L. S.)	A. Rambech. (L. S.)
L. L. Forsæth. (L. S.)	Christian Midelfart. (L. S.)	Hjeronymus Heyerdahl. (L. S.)	Sivert Bratberg. (L. S.)
Wasmuth. (L. S.)	Daniel Schevig. (L. S.)	Jacob Lange. (L. S.)	Helmer Giedeboe. (L. S.)
F. Heidmann. (L. S.)	P. J. Ertzgaard. (L. S.)	Carl Stoltenberg. (L. S.)	Just Ely. (L. S.)

O. B. Bercheland.   H. Carstensen.[2]
(L. S.)   (L. S.)

Vi Christian Frederik af Guds Naade, og efter Rigets Constitution Norges Konge, Prinds til Danmark, Hertug til Slesvig, Holsteen, Stormarn, Ditmarsken og Oldenborg, Giøre vitterligt: At Vi, kaldet til Norges Throne ved Nationens Beslutning, have i Overensstemmelse med den Os underdanigst overrakte Addresse af Rigsfors amlingen paa Eidsvold den 17de May 1814, antaget Norges Krone, og i Dag høytideligen udi Rigsforsamlingen besvoret at regiere Kongeriget Norge overensstemmende med denne af Nationens udkaarede Mænd affattede Grundlov; hvilket herved saaledes af Os paa den originale Constitutions Akt bekræftes.

Under Vor Haand og Rigets Seigl
Givet paa Eidsvold, d. l9de May 1814
Christian Frederik

Notes

1. The Latin phrase logus sigilli, *abbreviated L.S., means "place of the seal."*
2. The Constitutional Assembly protocols did not include electoral districts in the list of framers. Electoral districts are included in some later printed versions.

The Constitution of the Kingdom of Norway

Translated pursuant to order of government

A. Of the form of Government and the Religion.

§. 1.
The Kingdom of Norway is a free, independent and indivisible Realm. Its form of government is a limited and hereditary monarchy.[1]

§. 2.
The Evangelical-Lutheran Religion shall be maintained and constitute the established Church of the Kingdom.

The inhabitants who profess the said religion are bound to educate their children in the same. Jesuits and Monastic orders shall not be tolerated.

Jews are furthermore excluded from the Kingdom.

B. Of the Executive Power, the King and the Royal Family.

§. 3.
The executive power is vested in the King. His title shall be: We N.N., by the Grace of God and the Constitution of the Kingdom, King of Norway.

§. 4.
The King's person is sacred, he cannot be blamed, nor accused. The responsibility is incumbent on his council.

§. 5.
The hereditary succession is lineal and agnatical, in such a manner that only male descending from male may inherit the crown. The nearer line shall be preferred to the remoter, and the elder to the younger.

§. 6.
The elected King's male issue, begotten in lawful matrimony, is entitled to the succession, in the order prescribed in the foregoing §., so that the Kingdom remains for ever undivided; whereas the other Princes, to whom the crown may devolve by inheritance, shall be contented with such appanage, as shall be granted them by the National Assembly (called Stor-Thing), until the order of succession devolves to them.

§. 7.
When a Prince, entitled to succession to the throne of Norway, is born, his name and birthtime shall be communicated to the next Session of the National Assembly and be entered in its records.

§. 8.
Among those entitled to succession is also reckoned the unborn, who shall immediately assume his due place of succession, when born after the death of his father.

§. 9.
If there should be no Prince entitled to succession, the King may propose his successor to the National Assembly who either consents to the proposal or rejects it.

§. 10.
The King is of age when he has filled his twentieth year. As soon as he has entered his twenty first year, he shall publicly declare himself to be of age.

§. 11.
When the King is of full age he accedes to the Government after having made the following oath to the National Assembly: I promise and swear to govern the Kingdom of Norway according to its Constitution and laws; so help me God and his holy word.

 If there be no National Assembly sitting at that time the oath shall be deposited in writing in the Council of State, and the King shall repeat it solemnly in the next Session of the National Assembly.

§. 12.
When the King has attained to full age, his Coronation and Unction shall be performed in the cathedral of Trondhjem (Dronthem) at the time and with the ceremonies which he himself may appoint.

§. 13.
The King shall always reside within the present frontiers of the Kingdom, and he must not abide beyond them longer than six months at a time, without the consent of the National Assembly, unless he will, for his own person, forfeit his right to the crown.

§. 14.
The King must not accept of any other crown or government without the consent of the National Assembly, for which consent two thirds of the votes shall be required.

§. 15.
The King shall always have professed and actually profess the Evangelical-Lutheran Religion, which he shall maintain and protect.

§. 16.
The King ordains all public worship and divine service, all meetings and congregations concerning religion and superintends the public teachers adherence to the norms prescribed them.

§. 17.
The King may issue and repeal Ordinances concerning Commerce, Duties, Trades and Police, provided they do not infringe upon the constitution and the laws given by the National Assembly. Such ordinances are provisional and remain in vigour untill the next Session of the National Assembly.

§. 18.
The King generally levies the taxes and duties imposed by the National Assembly.

§. 19.
The King superintends the management and employment of the proprieties and regalia of the state conformably to the manner appointed by the National Assembly and tending most effectually to the public good.

§. 20.
The King, being in his Council of State, has a right to pardon criminals, after the Sentence of the High Court of justice has been pronounced and its Opinion heard. The criminal may choose whether he will accept the King's pardon or submit to the punishment imposed.

In the law-suits caused to be commenced by the Section of the National Assembly called Odels-Thing before the Court of State, no other pardon but dispensation from pain of death must be granted.

§. 21.
The King, after hearing the declaration of his Council of State, elects and appoints all civil, ecclesiastical and military functionaries. These shall swear to be faithful and obedient to the Constitution and the King.

The royal Princes must not be invested with civil offices.

§. 22.
The Members of the Council of State and the functionaries appointed in its offices, embassadors and consuls, the superior civil and ecclesiastical magistrates,

the chiefs of regiments and of other military bodies, governors of fortresses and commanders of ships of war may be discharged by the King, without any previous judgment, after hearing the declaration of his Council of State. How far pension or annuity may be allowed the functionaries thus discharged shall be decided by the National Assembly next sitting. In the mean time they shall enjoy the two thirds of their former salary. The other functionaries may only be suspended by the King, after which they shall immediately be prosecuted at law; but they must not be discharged without a previous sentence, nor must they be removed against their will.

§. 23.
The King may confer orders upon whom he chooses, as a reward for distinguished merits, which shall be made known to the public, but no other rank or title than what every office implies. The order exempts nobody from the common duties and burdens of Citizens, nor does it imply a peculiar right of preferment to any office in the Kingdom.

Functionaries discharged with the King's favour retain the title and rank of the offices they have borne. No personal or mixed hereditary prerogatives shall be granted to anybody for the future.

§. 24.
The King appoints and discharges, according to his own will, his household and the functionaries at his court. For the pay of these and the sustenance of his household a suitable sum shall be allowed him every year by the National Assembly.

§. 25.
The King has the supreme command of the land and naval forces of the Kingdom. They must not be left to the disposal or service of foreign powers, and no foreign soldiers, except auxiliaries against hostile invasion, must be called into the Kingdom without the consent of the National Assembly.

§. 26.
The King has right to assemble troops, declare war and conclude peace, to make and dissolve alliances, to send and receive embassadors.

§. 27.
Government has no right to employ military power against members of the state, except in cases determined by the law, unless any assembly should disturb the public tranquillity and it should not instantly be dissolved after the articles of the civil law concerning riot have been thrice audibly read by the civil magistrate.

§. 28.

The King himself elects a Council of Norwegian citizens whose members must not be younger than thirty years. This Council shall consist of five members at least. Besides them the King may, on extraordinary occasions, call other Norwegian citizens, except members of the National Assembly, to take place in the Council of State. He distributes the affairs among them in such a manner as he thinks most proper.

Father and son or two brothers must not at the same time take seat in the Council of State.

§. 29.

All the counsellors of state shall be obliged, if there be no lawful hinderance, to be present in the Council of State, and no resolution must be taken there if there be no more than half the number of the members present.

§. 30.

Presentations concerning the appointments to offices and other affairs of importance, except diplomatic matters and special affairs of military orders, shall be laid before the Council of State by the member to whose office they belong, and the affairs shall be dispatched by him according to the resolution taken by the King in the Council of State.

§. 31.

If a lawful hinderance should prevent a counsellor of state from meeting and exposing the affairs relating to his department, they shall be exposed by another counsellor of state, whom the King may constitute.

If so many members should be prevented by a lawful hinderance from meeting in the Council of State, that no more than half of the appointed number of members are present, other officers shall be constituted by the King to take seat in the Council of State.

§. 32.

A register shall be kept in the Council of State of all the matters which shall be discussed there.

Every body who has a seat in the Council of State is obliged to declare his opinion freely, to which the King shall attend; but it is left to the King to take a resolution according to his own judgment.

If any member of the Council of State should think the King's resolution inconsistent with the form of government or the laws of the Kingdom, or evidently prejudicial to the Kingdom, he shall be obliged to make forcible remonstrances against it and to insert his opinion in the register. He who has not thus protested shall be looked upon as being of the same opinion as the King and shall account for it in such a manner as shall be determined hereafter.

§. 33.

The counsellor of state who presides the department for foreign affairs shall have his own register wherein those matters shall be entered which are of such a kind as not to be laid before the assembled Council of State.

§. 34.

All Decrees and Ordinances of Government shall always be issued in the King's name.

§. 35.

All ordinances and official letters issued by the King, except matters concerning military orders, shall be counter-signed by him who has exposed the matter pursuant to his office, as being responsible of the expedition's conformity with the register in which the decree has been inserted.

§. 36.

The next heir to the crown, if he be a son of the reigning King, shall have the title of Kronprinds til Norge (Crown-Prince of Norway). The King's other sons who are entitled to the crown shall have the title of Princes and the King's daughters that of Princesses.

§. 37.

As soon as the heir to the crown has attained to an age of eighteen years, he is entitled to take seat in the Council of State; but he shall have no vote, nor shall he be responsible.

§. 38.

No Prince of the royal blood must leave the Kingdom, marry or enter into foreign service without permission from the King. If he act against this he forfeits his right to the crown.

§. 39.

The royal Princes and Princesses shall, as for their persons, not be responsible to others than to the King or to whom he may appoint their judge.

§. 40.

If the heir to the crown be absent at the King's death, and he be not prevented by insurmountable obstructions, he shall be obliged to repair to the Kingdom within a space of six months, after the death has been made known to him.

§. 41.

When the next heir to the crown be under age at the King's death, the Queen-dowager shall reign, if she be his german mother, as long as she remains widow, together with the Council of State, till the King be of age. If there be no Queen-dowager, the Prince next to succession who is above twenty-five years old, shall reign in the same manner, and he shall have the title of Regent. If the Regency should fall to a remoter heir in the line of succession, because the proper one was not yet of full age, the former shall resign it to the latter as soon as this has attained to an age of twenty-five years. In these cases resolutions shall be taken in the Council of State according to majority of votes, and the Queen-dowager, or Regent, shall have two votes.

§. 42.
If there be no Prince of full age, the Regency shall be conducted by the Council of State together with the persons whom the National Assembly may think necessary to appoint, under the responsibility prescribed in §. 45. The first member of the Council of State shall then preside and have two votes.

§. 43.
The regulations prescribed in §. 42 shall also have effect if the King should be unable to reign by weakness of mind or body or he should be absent from the Kingdom.

§. 44.
Those who, pursuant to the above mentioned articles, administer the government, while the King is under age, absent, or otherwise unable to reign, shall be obliged singly to make the following oath to the National Assembly:
I promise and swear to administer the government conformably to the Constitution and the Laws; so help me God and his holy word.

§. 45.
As soon as their government discontinues, they shall give an account of it to the King and the National Assembly.

§. 46.
At the King's death, or in the cases, in which a regency ought to be appointed, the Council of State, or others concerned, shall immediately convoke an extraordinary National Assembly. If the Council of State do not perform this duty within the space of four weeks, the convocation shall be done by the chief judge (Justitiarius) and the members of the supreme court of justice.

§. 47.
The care of the King's education while he is under age shall, if his father has not left any written appointment, be committed to some persons, selected for that purpose, by the National Assembly and the Queen-dowager if she be his german mother, excluding the next heir to the crown, his offspring, the Council of State and the other members of the regency.

§. 48.
If the King's male issue be extinct and no successor be elected, the National Assembly shall immediately be convoked in the manner prescribed in §. 46,

in order to elect a new line of Kings. In the mean time the same rules shall be observed concerning the executive power, as are prescribed in §. 42.

C. Of Burghership and the Legislative Power.

§. 49.
The people exercises the legislative power at the National Assembly, consisting of two sections, viz. the Lag-Thing (Court of Law) and the Odels-Thing (Court of Allodiality).

§. 50.
Voting members are only those Norwegian Citizens who have filled their 25th year, have been settled in the Kingdom for five years and who either
a) are or have been employed in any public office;
b) possess in the country, or have taken a lease of, any matriculated ground for more than five years;
c) are citizens of towns, or possess in a town or port a house or piece of ground amounting at least to the value of three hundred Rigsbank-Dollars Silver-Value.

§. 51.
Within six months from the sanction of this Constitution a register of all the voting members shall be drawn up in every town by the Magistrate, and in every parish by the Foged (Collector of the taxes) and the parson, wherein shall immediately be inserted all the changes which it might undergo by process of time. Everybody is obliged, before he is entered in the register, publicly to swear obedience to the Constitution before a court of justice.

§. 52.
The right of voting is suspended
a) by an accusation of crimes before a court of justice; b) by being reduced to a state of minority; a) by stopping of payment or failure 'till the creditors have received full payment, unless the failure may be occasioned by fire or by any other unforeseen or proveable misfortune.

§. 53.
The right of voting is forfeited
a) by having been condemned to work in a House of Correction, to the Slavery or to any infamous punishment;
b) by entering into the service of any foreign power without the consent of Government;
c) by acquiring burghership in a foreign state;

d) by being convinced of having bought votes, sold his own vote, or voted in more than one Elective Assembly.

§. 54.

The assizes of the Elective Assembly and those of the Districts are held every third year. The transactions shall be finished before the end of the month of December.

§. 55.

The Elective Assemblies are held in the country in the principal church of the parish, in the towns in the church, in the town-house, or at any other place convenient for that purpose. They are presided in the country by the parson and his coadjutors, in the towns by their Magistrates and Aldermen. The act of voting is performed in the order appointed in the register. Disputes concerning the right of voting are decided by the directors of the Assembly from whose judgment there may be appealed to the National Assembly.

§. 56.

Before the elections begin, the Constitution shall be audibly read, in the towns by the chief Magistrate, in the country by the parson.

§. 57.

In the towns one elector is chosen for each 50 voting inhabitants. These electors meet within 8 days after, at the place appointed by the Magistrate, and elect either from among themselves or among the other voting members in their respective district of election a fourth part of their own number, to meet and take seat at the National Assembly, in such a manner that 3 to 6 choose one, 7 to 10 two, 11 to 14 three, 15 to 18 four, which is the greatest number a town is allowed to send. If a town have less than 150 inhabitants entitled to vote it sends its elector to the next town, in order to vote together with the electors of this, in which case both the towns are regarded as one district.

§. 58.

In each parish in the country the inhabitants entitled to vote choose in proportion to their number electors in the manner following: A number from 1 to 100 choose one, from 100 to 200 two, from 200 to 300 three and so on in the same proportion. These electors meet within a month after that time, at a place appointed by the Amtmand (Chief Justice of the bailiage), for that purpose, and then either choose from among themselves, or among the other voting members in the bailiage a tenth part of their own number, to meet and take seat at the National Assembly, in such a manner that 5 to 14 choose one, 15 to 24 two, 25 to 34 three, 35 and upwards four, which is the greatest number.

§. 59.

The rules prescribed in §. 57 and 58 have their effect 'till the next meeting of the National Assembly. If then it be found that the number of the Deputies from the towns amount to more or less than 1/3 of the Deputies of the whole Kingdom, the National Assembly shall alter these articles, to serve as a norm for the future, in such a manner, that the Deputies of the towns correspond with those of the country at the rate of one to two, and the number of the Deputies in general shall not be less than 75, nor above 100.

§. 60.

The voting members residing within the boundaries of the Kingdom, and impeded by sickness, military service or any other lawful hinderance from meeting, may send their votes in writing to those who preside the Elective Assemblies, before these are concluded.

§. 61.

Nobody can be elected a Deputy unless he has filled his 30th year and has lived 10 years in the Kingdom.

§. 62.

The members of the Council of State and the functionaries employed at its offices, or at court, as well as its pensioners can not be elected Deputies.

§. 63.

Every one who is elected Deputy is obliged to accept of the election, unless impeded by any hinderance declared a lawful one by the electors, whose declaration may be submitted to the decision of the National Assembly. Whoever has met two times one after another at an ordinary meeting of the National Assembly is not bound to accept of the election for the ordinary National Assembly next following. If any Deputy be hindered by lawful impediment from meeting at the National Assembly, he who, next him, has the greatest number of votes, takes his place.

§. 64.

Immediately after the election the Deputies are provided with a full-power, signed in the country by the superior Authorities and in the towns by their respective Magistrates as well as by all the Electors, as a proof of the election being made in the manner prescribed by the Constitution. The legality of these full-powers is decided by the National Assembly.

§. 65.

On their journey to and from the National Assembly, as well as during their stay there, the Deputies are exempted from being personally arrested, unless they should be caught in public crimes, nor are they bound without the assizes of the National Assembly to account for opinions uttered there. Every one is obliged to submit to the order established there.

§. 67.
The Deputies elected in the manner above mentioned form the National Assembly of the Kingdom of Norway.

§. 68.
The Sessions of the National Assembly generally begin every third year on the first work-day of the month of February in the Capital of the Kingdom, unless the King, on account of extraordinary circumstances, such as a hostile invasion or a plague, might choose an other town for that purpose. In such cases the alteration must be timely published.

§. 69.
On extraordinary occasions the King has right to convoke the National Assembly out of the ordinary time. The King then issues a proclamation which shall be read in all the churches of the capital towns at least six weeks before the members of the National Assembly are to meet on the place appointed for that purpose.

§. 70.
Such an extraordinary meeting of the National Assembly may be dissolved by the King whenever he pleases.

§. 71.
The members of the National Assembly keep their charges as members of the said Assembly for three years together at the extraordinary as well as at the ordinary assizes which may be held in the mean time.

§. 72.
If an extraordinary Assembly be sitting at the time when an ordinary one is going to meet, the former is dissolved as soon as the latter is assembled.

§. 73.
Neither of the Assemblies can hold their assizes unless two thirds of its members are present.

§. 74.
Immediately after the National Assembly is constituted the King, or whom he appoints in his place, opens its transactions with a speech, in which he informs the Assembly of the state of the Kingdom and of the subjects on which he particularly desires to draw its attention. No deliberation must take place in the King's presence.

The National Assembly selects from among its members one fourth part to constitute the Lag-Thing; the other ¾ form the Odels-Thing.

Either of the Things holds its assizes separately and elects its own President and Secretary.

§. 75.

It belongs to the National Assembly:

a) to give and repeal laws, to impose taxes, duties, customs and other public burdens, which, however, have no longer effect than 'till the Ist of July in the year when an other ordinary National Assembly is sitting unless expressively renewed by it;

b) to open loans on the credit of the State;

c) to superintend the monetary system of the State;

d) to allow the sums necessary to defray the expences of the State;

e) to determine the sum allowed the King for the maintenance of his court, and to appoint the appanage of the Royal family, which, however, must not consist in possessions of grounds;

f) to order the records of the Council of State and all other public intelligences and papers, except military orders, to be laid before them;

g) to order a communication of the alliances and treaties, concluded by the King in the name of the state with foreign powers, except secret articles, which, however, must not be contrary to the public;

h) to summon any one, except the Royal family, to appear before it in state-affairs; yet this exception does not regard the Royal Princes in case they should be invested with any office;

i) to review the provisional lists of military pay or allowances, and to make the alterations in them which they should think necessary;

k) to appoint five Reviewers whose duty shall be every year to review the state-accounts and publish extracts of it in print, for which purpose the said accounts shall be communicated to the reviewers every year before the Ist of July;

l) to naturalize foreigners.

§. 76.

Every law shall previously be proposed at the Odels-Thing, either by its own members, or by government through a counsellor of state. When the bill is past there, it shall be sent to the Lag-Thing which either consents to it or rejects it, and in the latter case, it is sent back with remarks added to it. These are taken into consideration by the Odels-Thing which either may put aside the bill or send it a second time to the Lag-Thing with or without alteration. When the Odels-Thing has twice laid a bill before the Lag-Thing and the latter has a second time refused to confirm it, the whole National Assembly meets, and decides of the bill with two thirds of its votes. Between each such deliberation three days must pass at least.

§. 77.

When a bill proposed by the Odels-Thing is confirmed by the Lag-Thing or by the whole National Assembly, it shall be sent to the approbation of the King by a deputation from both the houses of the National Assembly.

§. 78.

If the King consents to the bill he adds his signature to it, by which it is made a law. If he do not consent to its he returns it to the Odels-Thing with the declaration, that he does not for the present think it proper to give his sanction to the bill.

§. 79.

On such occasions the National Assembly then sitting must no more present the bill to the King who may act in the same manner if the next ordinary National Assembly brings in the same bill again. But if the bill, upon a repeated and stricter examination, should again pass in the third ordinary National Assembly without any alteration at both courts, and it should then be presented to the King, with the desire that His Majesty will not refuse his sanction to a bill which the National Assembly, upon the maturest deliberation, judges to be useful, it shall be made a law, if even the sanction of the King should not follow before the National Assembly breaks up.

§. 80.

The National Assembly remains sitting as long as it should think necessary, though not above three months without the King's consent. When, after having finished its transaction, or after having been assembled the prescribed time it is dissolved by the King, he communicates it at the same time his resolution concerning the bills which have not yet been determined, by either sanctioning or rejecting them. All the bills, to which he does not positively consent, are looked upon as being rejected by him.

§. 81.

All the laws, except those mentioned in §.79, are issued in the King's name and under the seal of the Kingdom, in the following terms: We — —, by the grace of God and according to the Constitution of the Kingdom, King of Norway, make known, that, having received the resolution of the National Assembly of the following date and purport (here the resolution follows) We have Consented to and sanctioned the said resolution, as by these Presents We do actually consent to and sanction it as a law under our hand and the seal of the Kingdom.

§. 82.

The provisional ordinances, issued by the King while no National Assembly is sitting, as well as the other ordinances and orders, belonging only to the executive power, shall be drawn up in the following manner: We — — &.c, make known that, by virtue of the authority allowed Us by the Constitution of the Kingdom, We have decreed as by these Presents We do decree &.c.

§. 83.

The sanction of the King is not required for the Decrees of the National Assembly by which it

a) declares itself sitting as National Assembly pursuant to the Constitution;
b) regulates its interior police;
c) consents to or rejects the warrants of the members present;
d) confirms or rejects judgments in disputes concerning elections;
e) naturalizes foreigners;
f) and lastly the King's sanction is not required to the decree by which the Odels-Thing declares counsellors of state under accusation.

§. 84.

The National Assembly may receive the cognizance of the High Court of Justice concerning matters of law.

§. 85.

The National Assembly shall be kept at open doors and its transactions be published in print, except in the cases where the contrary is decreed by majority of votes.

§. 86.

Whoever obeys an order tending to disturb the freedom and safety of the National Assembly is guilty of treason against his native country.

D. Of the Judicial Power.

§. 87.

The members of the Lag-Thing together with those of the High Court of Justice constitute the Rigs-Ret (Court of State) who in the first and last instance shall judge in the causes, commenced before the Odels-Thing, either against members of the Council of State or of the High Court of Justice on account of crimes in the performance of their offices, or against members of the National Assembly, on account of crimes they commit in such a quality. In the Rigs-Ret the President of the Lag-Thing shall preside.

§. 88.

The Defendant may reject, without alledging any reason, even to a third part of the members of the Court of State, yet in such a manner that the court do not consist of less than fifteen persons.

§. 89.
In order to judge in the last instance a High Court of Justice shall be established as soon as possible, which must not consist of less than a chief judge and six members.

§. 90.
In times of peace the High Court of Justice together with two high military officers, whom the King appoints, constitute the second and last instance in all the affairs of court martial, concerning either life or honour or the loss of freedom for more than three months.

§. 91.
The judgments of the High Court may on no occasion be appealed or submitted to revision.

§. 92.
Nobody may be appointed member of the High Court of Justice before he is thirty years old.

E. General Rules

§. 93.
In the offices of the state must only be employed those Norwegian citizens who profess the Evangelical-Lutheran religion, have sworn obedience to the Constitution and the King, speak the language of the country, and
a) either are born in the Kingdom of parents who at that time were subjects of the Kingdom; or
b) are born in foreign countries of Norwegian parents who were not at that time subjects of an other state;
c) or who have at present a steady residence in the Kingdom and have not refused to make the oath to maintain the independence of Norway;
d) or who live in the Kingdom for ten years;
e) or who are naturalized by the National Assembly.
   Foreigners, however, may be appointed teachers at the University and the high schools, physicians and consuls on foreign places.
   Nobody must be appointed chief magistrate before he is thirty years old, or magistrate, inferior judge and collector of the taxes before he is twenty-five years old.

§. 94.
A new general civil and criminal law shall be caused to be published by the first, or, if this be not possible, by the second ordinary National Assembly. In

the mean time the present laws of the Kingdom shall remain in vigour, as far as they are not inconsistent with this fundamental law or the provisional ordinances which in the mean time might be issued. The present permanent taxes shall likewise remain untill the next National Assembly.

§. 95.
No dispensations, no bills of protection, no letters of respite or restitutions must be granted after the new general law has been published.

§. 96.
Nobody may be judged but by virtue of a law, or be punished but pursuant to a judgment. Torture must not be inflicted.

§. 97.
No law must be retroactive.

§. 98.
Perquisites due to the officers of the courts of justice must not be attended with taxes to the treasury.

§. 99.
Nobody must be imprisoned but in cases appointed by the law and in the manner determined by the same. Whoever thus, without any reason or sanction of the law, imprisons or detains anybody shall be obliged to account for it.

§. 100.
An intire liberty of the press shall take place. Nobody must be punished for any writing, of what argument soever, which he has published or caused to be printed, unless he has either willingly and evidently shown himself disobedient to the law or animated others to disobedience against the same, to contempt against religion, morality or the constitutive powers, to resistance against their orders, or uttered false and injurious accusations against anybody.

It is allowed everybody freely to deliver his opinions of government or any other subject.

§. 101.
New and constant restrictions on the liberty of trades must not be allowed to anybody for the future.

§. 102.
Inquiries in private houses are not permitted, unless in criminal cases.

§ 103.
No refuge is allowed to those who turn bankrupts hereafter.

§. 104.
Lands and moveable heritages cannot be forfeited in any case.

§. 105.
If the public welfare should require the sacrifice of anybody's moveable or unmoveable propriety to public use he shall be indemnified out of the public treasury.

§. 106.
The produce of the sale as well as revenues of glebelands (benefices of clergymen) shall only be employed to the benefit of the clergy and to the promoting of arts and sciences. The propriety of institutes of charity shall only be employed to the advantage of these.

§. 107.
The Odels- and Aasædes-Ret (Right of redeeming patrimonial lands and of dwelling on the chief mansion) must not be abolished. The further conditions, under which they shall continue to the greatest advantages of the state and benefit to the peasantry, shall be determined in the session of the first or second following National Assembly.

§ 108.
No Counties, Baronies, Fee-simples and Fidei-Commisses (feoffments in trust) must be erected for the future.

§. 109.
Every citizen of the state is in general equally bound to defend his native country during a certain time, without any regard to birth or fortune. The application of this rule and the restrictions it ought to suffer is left to the determination of the next ordinary National Assembly after having acquired all the informations possible by a committee, elected before the conclusion of the present session of the National Assembly. In the mean while the present rules shall continue.

§. 110.
This Constitution, when sanctioned by the National Assembly, becomes the fundamental law of the Kingdom.

If experience should prove, that any part of it ought to be altered, a proposal concerning that affair shall be made in an ordinary session of the National Assembly and be published in print. But it is the business of the next National Assembly to decide, whether the alteration proposed shall take place or not. Yet such an alteration must never be inconsistent with the principles of this fundamentel law, but only concern modifications in particular cases, which do not alter the spirit of this Constitution, to which alteration the consent of two thirds of the National Assembly is required.

We the signed, Deputies of the Kingdom of Norway, hereby declare this Constitution, sanctioned by the National Assembly, to be the fundamental law

of the Kingdom of Norway, which all and every one shall obey. In witness whereof we have signed these Presents and thereto put our seals.
Eidswold the 17th of May 1814

Peder Anker. [L. S.][2]	C. M. Falsen. [L. S.]	Christensen. [L. S.]	C. Sibbern. [L. S.]
F. Stabell. [L. S.]	Z. Mellebye. [L. S.]	Alexand. Chr. Möller [L. S.]	Motzfeldt. [L. S.]
H. Haslum. [L. S.]	Christie. [L. S.]	F. Meltzer. [L. S.] J. Rolfsen. [L. S.]	J. Rein. [L. S.]
A. v. W. Koren. [L. S.]	G. B. Jersin. [L. S.]	R. Gierager. [L. S.] Irgens. [L. S.]	Nielsen. [L. S.]
P. Hiermand. [L. S.]	C. Holck. [L. S.]	N. Loftesnæs. [L. S.] F. Schmidt. [L. S.]	J. Collett. [L. S.]
C. Hoen. [L. S.]	Lövenskiold. [L. S.]	P. Cloumann. [L. S.]	T. O. Huvestad. [L. S.]
Sverdrup. [L. S.]	Omsen. [L. S.]	Wergeland. [L. S.] O. C. Mörch. [L. S.]	Weidemann. [L. S.]
Stabel. [L. S.]	Lysgaard. [L. S.]	J. Moses. [L. S.] N. Scheitlie. [L. S.]	Dahl. [L. S.]
A.M. Heiberg. [L. S.]	Bendeke. [L. S.]	A. König. [L. S.] Evenstad. [L. S.]	H. H. Nysom. [L. S.]
H. Wedel-Jarls-berg. [L. S.]	Blom. [L. S.]	O. R. Apeness. [L. S.]	A. Sibbern. [L. S.]
P. Steenstrup. [L. S.]	C. H. Hornemann. [L. S.]	Diriks. [L. S.]	J. Hesselberg. [L. S.]

A.
Grönneberg.
[L. S.]

O. Amundsröd.
[L. S.]

G. Lund, jun.
[L. S.]

Erichstrup.
[L. S.]

T. J. T.
Lundegaard.
[L. S.]

O. Lömsland.
[L. S.]

E. Jaabech.
[L. S.]

S. Eeg.
[L. S.]

F. Motzfeldt.
[L. S.]

G. Wulfsberg.
[L. S.]

J. Aall, jun.
[L. S.]

Grögaard.
[L. S.]

T. R.
Lilleholt.
[L. S.]

Prydz.
[L. S.]

H. Waagaard.
[L. S.]

Fleischer.
[L. S.]

N. Dyhren.
[L. S.]

D. Hegermann.
[L. S.]

Haraldstad.
[L. S.]

J. Aall.
[L. S.]

T. Bryn.
[L. S.]

E. T. Lande.
[L. S.]

O. K.
Tvedten.
[L. S.]

Krohg.
[L. S.]

J. Stub.
[L. S.]

E. Walböe.
[L. S.]

R. Floer.
[L. S.]

Hount.
[L. S.]

J. Hansen.
[L. S.]

D. Cappelen.
[L. S.]

P. V.
Rosenkilde.
[L. S.]

Oftedahl.
[L. S.]

C. Mölbach.
[L. S.]

A.
Regelstad.
[L. S.]

F. Fabricius.
[L. S.]

F. Konow.
[L. S.]

P. Johnson.
[L. S.]

E. Thorsen
[L. S.]

Petersen.
[L. S.]

O. Svendsen.
[L. S.]

P. Ramm.
[L. S.]

Balke.
[L. S.]

E. Höyum.
[L. S.]

G. Röed.
[L. S.]

A. Rogert.
[L. S.]

P. Schmidt, jun.
[L. S.]

J. H. Darre.
[L. S.]

H.
Rambech.
[L. S.]

L. Forsæth.
[L. S.]

C. Midelfart.
[L. S.]

H. Heyerdahl.
[L. S.]

S. Bratberg.
[L. S.]

Wasmuth.
[L. S.]

D. Schevig.
[L. S.]

J. Lange.
[L. S.]

H.
Giedeboe.
[L. S.]

F.   P. Ertzgaard.   C. Stoltenberg.   J. Ely.
Heidmann.   [L. S.]   [L. S.]   [L. S.]
[L. S.]

  O. B. Bercheland.   H. Carstensen.[3]
        [L. S.]   [L. S.]

Address from the Deputies of the people of Norway about the conferring the Norwegian crown upon the Regent of Norway, His Royal Highness, Prince Christian Frederik.

We the signed, Deputies from the Kingdom of Norway, make hereby known, that, according to the desire of the people and to the proclamation of Your Royal Higness, we have joined, pursuant to our full-powers, in order to draw up a fundamental law for the Kingdom of Norway, so as to the best of our judgment we should think it most beneficial to the Kingdom. To that effect, we have endeavoured to distribute the sovereign power, in such a manner, that legislation is deposited into the hands of the people, and the executive power into the hands of the King.

Having finished this fundamental law, it became a dear and sacred duty to us to elect a King, who, by the wisdom and energy of his government, was able to ensure and support the safety, welfare and glory of the Kingdom.

The Deputies of the Norwegian people could not hesitate a moment whom they should select to this elevated and important post. Confidence, gratitude and love equally forced us to fix our regards on Your Royal Highness. You arrived among us in the time of danger and misery. With the most constant zeal You always directed your actions and thoughts to the benefit of the country; You inseparately tied Your fate to ours, and, as Regent of the country, You have expressed no less a regard to the rights of the people than zeal for the promoting of its prosperity and glory.

We are convinced, that we have compleated the desire and will of the Norwegian people, by electing You this day King of Norway, and, on presenting to Your Royal Highness this fundamental law of the country, we rejoice in the hope, that it may be found worthy of Your approbation, and that You will accept of a crown, voluntarily offered You by a free people. At the Diet at Eidswold, the 17th of May 1814.

According to the resolution of the National Assembly signed in behalf af all the Deputies, by

G. Sverdrup   Motzfeldt   Christie
President.   Vice-President.   Secretary.

His Royal Highness' the Prince Regents Answer in the National Assembly to the Adress above.

Norwegians! The high calling, to which you are elected by the trust of your fellow-citizens, is finished. The Constitution of Norway is founded; the Norwegian people has maintained its rights through you, its selected Deputies; it has maintained them for futurity, and, by a sage distribution of the power, secured civil Liberty and that public order which the executive power is obliged and able to preserve.

The experience for which other states must suffer has taught the Deputies of the Norwegian people to guard the Constitution equally against the marks of despotism as against the abuses of a popular government.

This old Kingdom calls for a King, but he should no more be a despot in the form than in the government;—no he should be the first friend and father to his people. This the people expects to find in me, and its confidence is to me a sacred calling, notwithstanding the dangers and pains that attend me, entirely to devote myself to the welfare and glory of Norway.

With these honest views, and strengthened by a confidence on the assistance of God Almighty, I hope to answer the expectations of this nation.

I accept the crown of Norway as the gift of a constant and sincere people, as a pledge of its attachment to me and my royal family.

1 promise and swear to reign the Kingdom of Norway according to its Constitution and Laws; so help me God and his holy word.

Eidswold, the 19th of May 1814

Christian Frederik.

We the Signed, chosen by the Deputies of the Norwegian people to publish in print the transactions of the National Assembly do hereby attest, that this fundamental law of the Kingdom of Norway and the documents annexed to it, are, word for word, conformable to the chief records of the National Assembly.

Christiania, the 31st of May 1814.

  G. Sverdrup   L. Stoud Platou   Omsen

NOTES

1. As discussed in "Note on Interdisciplinarity and Stylistic Conventions" in this volume, the English-language version reprinted in Appendix B is not a precise translation of the Norwegian version reprinted in Appendix A. Differences between the versions include differences in format, punctuation, diction, and spelling of signatures. In addition, the English-language version contains several spelling mistakes and inconsistencies. Please note that following the deputies' signatures, Appendix A comprises Christian Frederik's signature whereas Appendix B comprises an address from the deputies to Christian Frederik, his answer, and an attestation.

2. The Latin phrase *logus sigilli*, abbreviated *L.S.*, means "place of the seal."
3. The Constitutional Assembly protocols did not include electoral districts in the list of framers. Electoral districts are included in some later printed versions.

▶• •◀

Bibliography

Primary Sources

Adler, Johan Gunder and Christian Magnus Falsen. (1814) "Udkast til en Constitution for Kongeriget Norge." Unpublished manuscript. Norwegian University of Science and Technology University Library website. n.d. Accessed 11 April 2014. http://www.ntnu. no/ub/spesialsamlingene/digital/pdf/05a099214.pdf

Andersen, Hans Christian. (1868) 1967. "Laserne." In *H.C. Andersens Eventyr*, ed. Erik Dal, 5:113–114. Copenhagen: Hans Reitzel.

Anker, Carsten J. 1904. *Christian Frederik og Carsten Ankers Brevveksling 1814, samt Uddrag af deres Breve fra 1801–13 og fra 1815–17.* Christiania: Aschehoug.

Anordning, angaaende Sommer- og Høste-Tingenes Holdelse udi Bergens Stift, Fredensborg Slot, den 23de Maji Ao. 1755. 1755. Copenhagen: Directeuren over hans Kong. Majests. og Univ. Bogtrykkeri Johan Jørgen Høpffner.

"Åpen høring i Stortingets kontroll- og konstitusjonskomité torsdag 1. mars 2012 kl. 12:00" [Open hearing in the Constitutional Committee, video record, 1 March]. 2012. Stortinget website. http://www.stortinget.no/no/Hva-skjer-pa-Stortinget/Videoarkiv/Arkiv-TV-sendinger/?mbid=/2012/H264-full/Hoeringssal1/03/01/hoeringssal1-20120301-115520.mp4&msid=280&dateid=10003442.

[Bie, Jacob Christian]. 1771. *Samtale mellem Einar Jermonsøn og Reiar Randulvsøn paa Opland i Aggerhuus-Stift i Norge.* Copenhagen: J.R. Thiele.

Bjerregaard, Henrik Anker, and Christian Blom. n.d. *Den kronede norske Nationalsang.* Christiania: Winther.

Bjørnson, Bjørnstjerne. 1880. "Vor Grundlov en Kontrakt, du? Det har jeg aldrig vidst." *Fedraheimen*, 5 June.

Blackstone, William. 1765–1769. *Commentaries on the Laws of England.* 4 vols. Oxford: Claredon Press.

Blair, Hugh. 1783. *Lectures on Rhetoric and Belles Lettres.* Dublin: printed for Messrs. Whitestone, Colles, Burnet, Moncrieffe, Gilbert, [and 8 others in Dublin].

Blaustein, Albert P., and Jay A. Sigler. 1988. *Constitutions That Made History.* New York: Paragon House.

Bolingbroke, Henry St. John, 1st Viscount. (1733–1734) 1809. *A Dissertation Upon Parties: In The Works of the Late Honourable Henry St. John, Lord Viscount Bolingbroke.* London: J. Johnson et al.

Burke, Edmund. (1791) 1999. *Selected Works of Edmund Burke.* Vol. 2, *Reflections on the Revolution in France.* Indianapolis: Liberty Fund.

Burlamaqui, Jean-Jacques. 1760. *Grundsætninger til Stats-Retten.* Translated by A.S. Dellgast. Copenhagen: Lars Nielsen Svare.

Calamandrei, Piero. (1955) 2008. "Discorso sulla Costituzione" di Piero Calamandrei". *19 Luglio 1992* website. Accessed 11 April 2014. http://www.19luglio1992.com/index.php?option=com_content&view=article&id=781:qdiscorso-sulla-costituzioneq-di-pietro-calamandrei&catid=20:altri-documenti&Itemid=43.

Campbell, David F.J., Paul Pölzlbauer, Thorsten D. Barth, and Georg Pölzlbauer. 2013. *Democracy Ranking 2013 (Scores).* Vienna: Democracy Ranking. Accessed 7 April 2014. http://democracyranking.org/wordpress/ranking/2013/data/Scores_of_the_Democracy_Ranking_2013_a4.pdf.

Catechism of the Catholic Church. 2006. The Vatican website. Accessed 3 April 2014. http://www.vatican.va/archive/ENG0015/_INDEX.HTM.

Codice Penale italiano [Italian criminal code]. n.d. Testo Legge website. Accessed 3 April 2014. http://www.testolegge.com/italia/codice-penale.

The Constitution—Complete Text: The Constitution, as Laid Down on 17 May 1814 by the Constituent Assembly at Eidsvoll and Subsequently Amended. 2013. Stortinget website. Accessed 3 April 2014. http://www.stortinget.no/en/In-English/About-the-Storting/The-Constitution/The-Constitution/.

Constitution de la République Batave. 1805. La Haye: Imprimerie d'Etat.

Constitution du canton de VAUD. 1803. Website of the research project "The Rise of Modern Constitutionalism, 1776–1849." Accessed 11 April 2014. http://www.modern-constitutions.de/nbu.php?page_id=02a1b5a86ff139471c0b1c57f23ac196&show_doc=CH-VD-1803-02-19-fr.

Constitution of the Italian Republic. n.d. The Italian Senate website. Accessed 3 April 2014. www.senato.it/documenti/repository/istituzione/costituzione_inglese.pdf.

The Constitution of the Kingdom of Norway: Given by the Constituent Assembly at Eidsvold on May 17th, 1814, and Now, on the Occasion of the Union Between the Realms of Norway and Sweden Decreed by the Storthing in Extra Session at Christiania, Revised and Affirmed on November 4th, 1814; with amendments. 1895. Translated by US Senator Knute Nelson. Chicago: John Anderson.

The Constitution of the Kingdom of Norway: Translated Pursuant to Order of Government. 1814. Christiania: Jacob Lehmann.

"Constitutions of the World from the late 18th Century to the Middle of the 19th Century Online." n.d. Website of the research project "The Rise of Modern Constitutionalism, 1776–1849." Accessed 3 April 2014. http://www.modern-constitutions.de/.

Costituzione della Repubblica italiana. n.d. Website of the Italian government. Accessed 3 April 2014. http://www.governo.it/governo/costituzione/costituzionerepubblicaitaliana.pdf.

Democracy Index 2012: Democracy at a standstill. 2012. The Economist Intelligence Unit website. Accessed 7 April 2014. http://pages.eiu.com/rs/eiu2/images/Democracy-Index-2012.pdf.

Dokument 3 (1961–1962): Utredninger m.v. om Det europeiske økonomiske fellesskap i forhold til den norske Grunnlov. Oslo: Stortinget, Den utvidede utenriks-og konstitusjonskomité.

Dokument 12:2 (2003–2004): Grunnlovsforslag fra Jens Stoltenberg, Jørgen Kosmo, Carl I. Hagen, Berit Brørby og Kjell Engebretsen om endringer i Grunnloven §§ 15 (ny), 20, 23, 82 (ny), 86 og 87 med sikte på å innføre en ordning med oppløsningsrett og positiv parlamentarisme (investitur). Oslo: Stortinget, Representanter.

Dokument 12:30 to 12:36 (2011–2012). In *Grunnlovsforslag fremsatt på det 156. storting samt Norges grunnlov.* Oslo: Stortinget.

Dokument 16 (2011–2012): Rapport til Stortingets presidentskap fra Menneskerettighetsutvalget om menneskerettigheter i Grunnloven. Oslo: Stortinget, Presidentskapet.

Dokument 19 (2011–2012): Rapport fra Grunnlovsspråkutvalget om utarbeidelse av språklig oppdaterte tekstversjoner av Grunnloven på bokmål og nynorsk. Oslo: Stortingets administrasjon.

Dokumentet Grunnlova av 17. mai 1814. 1814. Unpublished manuscript. Stortinget website. Accessed 11 April 2014. https://www.stortinget.no/Global/pdf/Stortingsarkivet/17.%20mai-grunnloven.pdf.

Entwurf der Constitutions-Urkunde. 1849. Kaiserlich-königliche Hof- und Staatsdruckerei: Kremsier.

Falsen, Enevold. (1802) 1821. "Hvad er Frihet, og hvor skulle vi søge den?" In *Envold Falsens Skrifter,* 1:131–166. Christiania: Jacob Lehmann.

Fure, Eli, ed. 1989. *Eidsvoll 1814: Hvordan grunnloven ble til.* Oslo: Dreyer.

Grunnloven fra 1814. 1814. Unpublished manuscript. Stortinget website. Accessed 3 April 2014. http://www.stortinget.no/no/Stortinget-og-demokratiet/Lover-og-instrukser/Grunnloven-fra-1814/.

Grunnlovsforslag nr. 8 (2003–2004): Grunnlovsforslag fra Aanund Hylland og Finn-Erik Vinje, vedtatt til fremsettelse av Jørgen Kosmo og Kjell Engebretsen, om endringer i Grunnloven §§ 3, 6, 12, 14, 26, 41, 50, 60, 63, 68, 75, 87, 93, 110 og 110 a (retting av språklige feil). Accessed 3 April 2014. Stortinget website. http://www.stortinget.no/Global/pdf/Dokumentserien/2003-2004/dok12-200304.pdf.

Grunnlovsforslag nr. 15 (2007–2008): Grunnlovsforslag fra Aanund Hylland og Finn-Erik Vinje, vedtatt til fremsettelse av Carl I. Hagen, Inge Lønning, Berit Brørby, Ola T. Lånke og Olav Gunnar Ballo, om endringer i Grunnloven §§ 30, 61, 100 og 106 (retting av språklige feil). Stortinget website. Accessed 3 April 2014. http://www.stortinget.no/Global/pdf/Dokumentserien/2007-2008/dok12-200708-15.pdf.

Grunnlovsforslag nr. 16 (2007–2008): Grunnlovsforslag fra Carl I. Hagen og Finn-Erik Vinje, vedtatt til fremsettelse av Carl I. Hagen om språklig fornyelse av Grunnloven. Stortinget website. Accessed 3 April 2014. http://www.stortinget.no/Global/pdf/Dokumentserien/2007-2008/dok12-16-2008.pdf.

Grunnlovsforslag nr. 21 (2003–2004): Grunnlovsforslag fra Ågot Valle, Martin Engeset, Kjell Engebretsen, Carl I. Hagen og Modulf Aukan om endring av Grunnloven § 100 (ytringsfrihet). Stortinget website. Accessed 3 April 2014. http://www.stortinget.no/Global/pdf/Dokumentserien/2003-2004/dok12-200304-021.pdf.

Grunnlovsforslag nr. 21 (2011–2012): Grunnlovsforslag fra Anders Anundsen, Per-Kristian Foss, Carl I. Hagen, Michael Tetzschner og Finn-Erik Vinje, vedtatt til fremsettelse av Anders Anundsen, Per-Kristian Foss og Michael Tetzschner om språklig fornyelse av Grunn-

loven. Stortinget website. Accessed 3 April 2014. http://www.stortinget.no/Global/pdf/ Grunnlovsforslag/2011-2012/dok12-201112-021.pdf.

Grunnlovsforslag nr. 22 (2011–2012): Grunnlovsforslag fra Anders Anundsen og Per-Kristian Foss om en nynorsk versjon av Grunnloven. Stortinget website. Accessed 3 April 2014. http://www.stortinget.no/no/Saker-og-publikasjoner/Publikasjoner/ Grunnlovsforslag/2011-2012/dok12-201112-022/.

Grunnlovsforslag nr. 25 (2011–2012): Grunnlovsforslag fra Marit Nybakk, Martin Kolberg, Jette F. Christensen, Hallgeir H. Langeland og Per Olaf Lundteigen om vedtak av Grunnloven på tidsmessig bokmål og nynorsk. Stortinget website. Accessed 3 April 2014. http:// www.stortinget.no/Global/pdf/Grunnlovsforslag/2011-2012/dok12-201112-025.pdf.

Grunnlovsforslag nr. 27 (2011–2012): Grunnlovsforslag frå Per Olaf Lundteigen, Lars Peder Brekk, Jenny Klinge, Hallgeir H. Langeland og Jette F. Christensen om ny § 38 (grunnlovfesting av kroner og øre som norsk pengeeining). Stortinget website. Accessed 3 April 2014. https://www.stortinget.no/Global/pdf/Grunnlovsforslag/2011-2012/dok12-201112-027.pdf

Höjer, Andreas. (1737–1738) 1783. *Jus Publicum det er Stats-Ret eller Statsforfatning og Rettigheder for Danmark, Noreg og Fyrstedommene forklaret ved private Forelæsninger eller Kollegio.* Christiania: Jens Ørbek Berg.

Holberg, Ludvig. 1716. *Introduction til Naturens- og Folke-Rettens Kundskab.* 2 vols. Copenhagen: Johan Kruse.

Innst. S. nr. 270 (2003–2004) Innstilling fra kontroll- og konstitusjonskomiteen om endring av Grunnloven § 100. Oslo: Stortinget, Kontroll- og konstitusjonskomiteen.

Innstilling 254 S (2009–2010) til Grunnlovsforslag nr. 15 (2007–2008). Stortinget website. Accessed 3 April 2014. http://www.stortinget.no/no/Saker-og-publikasjoner/ Publikasjoner/Innstillinger/Stortinget/2009-2010/inns-200910-254/.

Jæger, Herman, Didrik Arup Seip, Halvdan Koht, and Einar Høigaard. 1932. *Henrik Wergeland Samlede skrifter: Artikler og småstykker.* Vol. 3, bk 1. Kristiania: Steenske forlag.

Journal encyclopédique ou universel. 1780. Number 5.

Jungmann, Josef. [1838] 1989–1990. *Slownjk česko-německý.* Prague: Academica. 5 vols.

"Kongelig Reskript af 14. September 1770." 1786. In *Kongelige Rescripter, Resolutioner og Collegialbreve for Danmark og Norge udtogsviis udgivne i chronologisk Orden,* ed. Laurids Fogtmann. 6th section, vol.1 (1776–1786), 252–253. Copenhagen: Gyldendal.

Kongeriget Norges fjerde ordentlige Storthings Forhandlinger i Aaret 1824. 1825. Vol. 2. Christiania: Chr. Grøndahl.

Kongeriget Norges Grundlov, given i Rigsforsamlingen paa Eidsvold den 17de Mai 1814. 2012. Lovdata, the website of the Ministry of Justice and the Faculty of Law in Oslo. Accessed 3 April 2014. http://lovdata.no/dokument/NL/lov/1814-05-17.

Kongeriget Norges Grundlov, given i Rigsforsamlingen paa Eidsvold den 17de Mai 1814 og nu, i Anledning af Norges og Sveriges Rigers Forening, nærmere bestemt i Norges overordentlige Storthing i Christiania den 4de November 1814. 1814. Christiania: Jacob Lehmann.

Kongeriket Norges Grunnlov gitt i riksforsamlingen på Eidsvoll den 17. mai 1814, slik den lyder etter senere endringer, senest stortingsvedtak av 27. mai 2014. [Current Norwegian Constitution]. 2014. Lovdata, the website of the Ministry of Justice and the Faculty of Law in Oslo. Accessed 27 June 2014. http://lovdata.no/dokument/NL/lov/1814-05-17.

Kongeriget Norges Grunnlov og øvrige Forfatningsdokumenter. 1903. Oslo: Stortinget.

Kongsspegelen. Unpublished manuscript about 1230. 1976. Oslo: Det norske samlaget.

Lov om målbruk i offentleg teneste. 1980. Lovdata, the website of the Ministry of Justice and the Faculty of Law in Oslo. Accessed 3 April 2014. http://lovdata.no/dokument/NL/lov/1980-04-11-5.

Montesquieu, Charles de. (1748) 1961. *De l'Esprit des lois.* 2 vols. Paris: Garnier Frères.

Mounier, Jean-Joseph. 1789. *Nouvelles observations sur les états-généraux de France.* Paris: Publisher unknown.

Národní nowiny, 8 March 1849, 10 March 1849, 13 March 1849, and 14 March 1849.

Nordahl Brun, Johan. 1772. *Einer Tambeskielver: Et Sørgespil i fem Optog til Brug for den kongelige danske Skueplads.* Copenhagen: Godiches Efterleverske.

Nørregaard, Lauritz. 1784. *Natur- og Folke-Rettens første Grunde.* 2nd ed. Copenhagen: Gyldendal.

NOU. 1999. *"Ytringsfrihed bør finde Sted": Forslag til ny Grunnlov § 100.* Oslo: Justis- og politidepartementet.

———. 2005. *"There Shall Be Freedom of Expression": Proposed New Article 100 of the Norwegian Constitution: Report: Excerpts.* Oslo: Justis- og politidepartmentet.

———. 2007. *Formål for framtida: Formål for barnehagen og opplæringen.* Oslo: Departementenes servicesenter.

———. 2011. *Bedre integrering: Mål, strategier, tiltak.* Oslo: Departementenes servicesenter.

Offizielle stenographische Berichte über die Verhandlungen des österr. Reichstages. n.d. Website of the Joint Czech and Slovak Digital Parliamentary Library. Accessed 3 April 2014. http://www.psp.cz/eknih/1848urrs/stenprot/index.htm.

Olafsen, Arnet. 1914. *Riksforsamlingens forhandlinger 1ste del. Protokoller med bilag og tillæg.* Kristiania: Grøndahl & Søns Boktrykkeri.

Øverland, Arnulf. 1946. "Vår frihetsdag: Djurgården, Stockholm, 17. mai 1945." In *Det har ringt for annen gang: Taler og artikler,* 56–62. Oslo: Aschehoug.

Paine, Thomas. (1776) 2004. *Common Sense.* Edited by Edward Larkin. Peterborough, Ontario: Broadview Press.

Paine, Thomas. (1791) 1894. "Rights of Man." In *The Writings of Thomas Paine,* ed. Moncure Daniel Conway, 258–389. New York: G.P. Putnam's Sons.

Peaslee, Amos J. 1956. *Constitutions of Nations.* 3 vols. The Hague: Martinus Nijhoff.

Peterson, Mathias Conrad. 1798. "Min Troes Bekjendelse." *Qvartbladet,* vol. 1, no. 1: 1–4.

Platou, Carl Stoud. 1871. *Ludvig Stoud Platous Optegnelser for Aaret 1814.* Kristiania: Mallings Bogtrykker.

Pražské nowiny, 27 April 1848, 9 March 1849, and 11 March 1849.

Qvartbladet. 1798–1799, 2 vols.

Raabe, Jens. 1914. *Kong Christian Frederiks dagbok: Fra hans opphold i Norge i 1814.* Kristiania: Grøndahl & Søns Boktrykkeri.

Referat Stortinget. 2006a. 2 February. Stortinget website. Accessed 11 April 2014. https://www.stortinget.no/no/Saker-og-publikasjoner/Publikasjoner/Referater/Stortinget/2005–2006/060202/2/.

_____. 2006b. 2 February. Stortinget website. Accessed 11 April 2014. https://www.stortinget.no/no/Saker-og-publikasjoner/Publikasjoner/Referater/Stortinget/2005-2006/060202/1/.

_____. 2012. 21 May. Stortinget website. Accessed 11 April 2014. https://www.stortinget.no/no/Saker-og-publikasjoner/Publikasjoner/Referater/Stortinget/2011-2012/120521/2/.

Representantforslag 87 S (2010–2011): Representantforslag fra stortingsrepresentantene Trine Skei Grande og Borghild Tenden om å revidere Grunnloven. Stortinget website. Accessed 3 April 2014. http://www.stortinget.no/no/Saker-og-publikasjoner/Publikasjoner/Representantforslag/.

Riis, Claus Pavels. 1864. *Claus Pavels' Biografi og Dagbøger.* Bergen: C. Floors Forlag.

Riksforsamlingens forhandlinger. 1914–1918. 5 vols. Kristiania: Grøndahl & Søns Boktrykkeri.

Rosted, Jakob. 1810. *Forsøg til en rhetorik i ett udtog af Hugo Blairs forelæsninger over rhetoriken, med hensyn til underviisningen i de lærde skoler.* Christiania: Lehmann.

Rothe, Tyge. 1781–1782. *Nordens Staetsforfatning før Lehnstiden, og da Odelskab med Folkefriehed: I Lehnstiden og da Birkerettighed, Hoverie, Livegenskab med Aristokratie.* 2 vols. Copenhagen: Gyldendal.

Rousseau, Jean-Jacques. (1762) 1978. *On the Social Contract, with Geneva Manuscript.* Edited by Roger D. Masters. Translated by Judith R. Masters. New York: St. Martin's Press.

Salamin, Michel, ed. 1969. *Documents d'histoire suisse, 1798–1847.* Sierre: Avenue Général Guisan, 29, chez l'auteur.

Schlegel, Johan Frederik Vilhelm. 1797. "Erindringer imod Hr. Birckners Skrift." *Astræa* 1: 345–488.

_____. 1798. *Naturrettens eller den almindelige Retslæres Grundsætninger.* 1st ed. 2 vols. Copenhagen: J.F. Schultz

_____. 1805. *Naturrettens eller den almindelige Retslæres Grundsætninger.* 2nd ed. 2 vols. Copenhagen: J.F. Schultz.

Schytte, Andreas. 1773–1776. *Staternes indvortes Regiering.* 5 vols. Copenhagen: Gyldendal.

_____. 1777. *Danmarks og Norges naturlige og politiske Forfatning.* Copenhagen: Gyldendal.

Sneedorff, Frederik. 1795. *Frederik Sneedorffs samlede Skrifter.* Vol. 2, *Indledning til Statistiken og om Europa i Almindelighed.* Copenhagen: Gyldendal.

Sneedorff, Jens Schielderup. (1757) 1776. *Sneedorffs samtlige Skrifter.* Vol. 7, *Om den borgerlige Regiering.* Copenhagen: Gyldendal.

Stampe, Henrik. 1793–1807. *Erklæringer, Breve og Forestillinger, General-Prokureur-Embedet vedkommende.* 6 vols. Copenhagen: Gyldendal.

Stang, Frederik. 1833. *Systematisk Fremstilling af Kongeriget Norges constitutionelle eller grundlovbestemte Ret.* Christiania: P.J. Hoppes forlag.

Statuto Albertino 1848: Lo Statuto di Carlo Alberto secondo i processi verbali del Consiglio di Conferenza dal 3 febbraio al 4 marzo 1848. 1898. Edited by Domenico Zanichelli. Rome: Dante Alighieri.

Storthings-Efterretninger 1814–1833. 1874. Vol. 1. Christiania: Dybwad.

Stortingets presidentskap til professor Finn-Erik Vinje. 2004. "Grunnlovens språk." Letter, 9 January.

Stortingets presidentskap ved Thorbjørn Jagland til stortingsrepresentantene og partigruppene. 2008. "Språklig kvalitetssikring av grunnlovsforslag." Letter, 28 April.

Throndhjemske Tidende, no. 44, 1799, no. 45, 1799, no. 46, 1799, and no. 47, 1799.

Trykkefrihetsforordningen av 27. september 1799. 1800. In *Chronologisk register over de kongelige forordninger og åbne breve, del 12: 1797–1799,* ed. Jacob Henrich Schou, 674–688. Copenhagen: Gyldendalske Boghandels Forlag.

Vattel, Emmerich de. 1758. *Le droit des gens ou principes de la loi naturelle.* London: Publisher unknown.

Voltaire. 1771. *Hr. F.A. de Voltaires Brev til Hans Majestet Kongen af Danmark angaaende den udi hans Stater forundte Tryk-Frihed.* Copenhagen: L.N. Svare.

Wergeland, Henrik. 1841–1843. *Norges Konstitutions Historie.* Kristiania: Guldberg and Dzwonkowski.

Wergeland, Nicolai. 1830. *Fortrolige Breve til en Ven, Skrevet fra Eidsvold i aaret 1814 af Et Medlem af Rigsforsamlingen.* Christiania: Malling, and 25 April 1848, and 8 March 1849.

Wolff, Jens. 1814. "The New Constitution of Norway." In *Sketches on a Tour to Copenhagen, Through Norway and Sweden, Interspersed with Historical and Other Anecdotes of Public and Private Characters, to Which is Added an Appendix, Relative to the Present Political State of Norway,* cxi–cxxvi. London: Longman, Hurst, Rees, Orme, and Brown.

Secondary Sources

Andenæs, Johs, and Arne Fliflet. 2006. *Statsforfatningen i Norge.* Oslo: Universitetsforlaget.

An-Na'im, Abdullahi Ahmed. 2008. *Islam and the Secular State: Negotiating the Future of Shari'a.* Cambridge, MA: Harvard University Press.

Arendt, Hannah. 1963. *On Revolution.* London: Penguin.

———. 2000. *The Portable Hannah Arendt.* Edited by Peter Baehr. New York: Penguin.

Aristotle. 1996. *The Politics and the Constitution of Athens.* Edited by Stephen Everson. Cambridge: Cambridge University Press.

Armitage, David. 2007. *The Declaration of Independence: A Global History.* Cambridge, MA: Harvard University Press.

Aschehoug, Torkel Halvorsen. 1891–1893. *Norges nuværende statsforfatning.* 3 vols. Christiania: P.T. Mallings boghandels forlag.

Austin, John L. 1962. *How to Do Things with Words: The William James Lectures Delivered at Harvard University in 1955.* Cambridge, MA: Harvard University Press.

Baker, Keith Michael. 1990. *Inventing the French Revolution.* Cambridge: Cambridge University Press.

Balibar, Francoise, Philippe Büttgen, and Barbara Cassin. 2004. "Moment, Instant, Occasion." In *Vocabulaire européen des philosophies: Dictionnaire des intraduisibles,* ed. Barbara Cassin, 813–818. Paris: Le Robert/Seuil.

Bambi, Federigo. 2011. "Constitutio, Constitution, Costituzione." *La Crusca per Voi: Foglio dell' Accademia della Crusca* 43: 7–8.

Barendt, Eric. 2005. *Freedom of Speech*. Oxford: Oxford University Press.

Bastid, Paul. 1985. *L'idée de constitution*. Paris: Economica.

Baxter, Hugh. 2011. *Habermas: The Discourse Theory of Law and Democracy*. Palo Alto, CA: Stanford University Press.

Beaud, Olivier. 2009. "L'histoire du concept de constitution en France: De la constitution politique à la constitution comme statut juridique de l'Etat." *Jus Politicum* 3: 1–29.

Beevor, Antony. 2012. *The Second World War*. New York: Little, Brown.

Bellah, Robert N. 1976. "The Revolution and the Civil Religion." In *Religion and the American Revolution*, ed. Jerald C. Brauer, 55–73. Philadelphia: Fortress Press.

Bentham, Jeremy. 1995. *The Panopticon Writings*. Edited by Miran Bozovic. London: Verso.

Berge, Kjell Lars. 1991. "Samtalen mellom Einar og Reiar: et symptom på tekstnormendringer i 1700-tallets skriftkultur?" *Arkiv för nordisk filologi* 106: 137–163.

———. 1998. "Den offentlige meningens genrer." In *Norsk litteraturhistorie: Sakprosa fra 1750 til 1995*, ed. Trond Berg-Eriksen and Egil B. Johnsen, 136–156. Oslo: Universitetsforlaget.

———. 2010. "Trondhjem: Selskapenes offentlighet." In *Norsk presses historie: 1-4 (1660–2010), bind 1: En samfunnsmakt blir til 1660–1880*, ed. Martin Eide and Hans Fredrik Dahl, 129–146. Oslo: Universitetsforlaget.

Berge, Kjell Lars, and Trygve Riiser Gundersen. 2010. "'Det pressemessige' før pressen: Et marked tar form." In *Norsk presses historie: 1-4 (1660–2010), bind 1: En samfunnsmakt blir til 1660–1880*, ed. Martin Eide and Hans Fredrik Dahl, 15–41. Oslo: Universitetsforlaget.

Bergsgård, Arne. 1943. *Året 1814*. Oslo: Aschehoug.

———. 1945. *Unionen*. Oslo: Aschehoug.

Berlant, Lauren. 1991. *The Anatomy of National Fantasy: Hawthorne, Utopia, and Everyday Life*. Chicago: Chicago University Press.

Berlin, Isaiah. 1969. *Four Essays on Liberty*. Oxford: Oxford University Press.

Blehr, Barbro. 2000. *En norsk besvärjelse: 17. maj-firande vid 1900-talets slut*. Nora, Sweden: Nya Doxa.

Böckenförde, Ernst-Wolfgang. 1991. "Die Entstehung des Staates als Vorgang der Säkularisation." In *Recht, Staat, Freiheit: Studien zur Rechtsphilosophie, Staatstheorie und Verfassungsgeschichte*, 92–114. Frankfurt am Main: Suhrkamp.

Brauneder, Wilhelm. 2000. "Die Verfassungsentwicklung in Österreich 1848 bis 1918." In *Die Habsburgermonarchie 1848–1918*, vol. 7, bk. 1, ed. Helmut Rumpler and Peter Urbanitsch, 69–237. Vienna: Österreichische Akademie der Wissenschaften.

Bregnsbo, Michael. 1997. *Folk skriver til kongen: Supplikkerne og deres funktion i den dansk-norske enevælde i 1700-tallet*. Copenhagen: Selskapet for Udgivelse af Kilder til Dansk Historie.

Byberg, Lis. 2008. "Leseferdighet og skolevesen 1740–1830." *Heimen* 45: 1–12.

Caenegem, R.C. van. 1995. *A Historical Introduction to Western Constitutional Law*. Cambridge: Cambridge University Press.

———. 2009. "Constitutional History: Chance or Grand Design." *European Constitutional Law Review* 5: 447–463.

Cao, Deborah. 2009. *Translating Law*. Clevedon, UK: Multilingual Matters.

Carcaterra, Gaetano. 1994. "Norme costitutive." In *Il linguaggio del diritto*, ed. Uberto Scarpelli and Paolo Di Lucia, 219–231. Milan: LED.

Casper, Gerhard. 1997. *Separating Power: Essays on the Founding Period*. Cambridge, MA: Harvard University Press.

Castberg, Frede. 1964. *Norges statsforfatning*. 2 vols. Oslo: Universitetsforlaget.

Čermák, František. 2010. *Lexikon a sémantika*. Prague: Lidové noviny.

Charnock, Ross. 2009. "When May Means Must: Deontic Modality in English Statutes Construction." In *Modality in English: Theory and Description*, ed. Raphael Salkie, Pierre Busuttil, and Johan van der Auwera, 177–198. Berlin: Mouton de Gruyter.

Chilton, Paul. 2004. *Analysing Political Discourse: Theory and Practice*. London: Routledge.

Cignetti, Luca. 2005. "Sfondi e rilievi testuali nella Costituzione della Repubblica italiana." In *Rilievi: Le gerarchie semantico-pragmatiche di alcuni tipi di testo*, ed. Angela Ferrari, 85–134. Florence: Cesati.

Conte, Amedeo. 2002. "Atto performativo." In *Atto giuridico*, ed. Giuseppe Lorini, 29–108. Bari: Adriatica.

Dahl, Robert A. 1989. *Democracy and its Critics*. New Haven, CT: Yale University Press.

———. 1994. "A Democratic Dilemma: System Effectiveness Versus Citizen Participation." *Political Science Quarterly* 109: 23–34.

———. 2003. *How Democratic is the American Constitution?* 2nd ed. New Haven: Yale University Press.

Dahl, Robert A., and Bruce Stinebrickner. 2003. *Modern Political Analysis*. Upper Saddle River, NJ: Prentice Hall.

De Mauro, Tullio. 2006. "Introduction." In *Costituzione della Repubblica Italiana (1947)*, vii–xxxii. Turin: UTET.

———. 2011. "1947. Costituzione." In *Itabolario*, ed. Massimo Arcangeli, 184–186. Rome: Carocci.

Derrida, Jacques. 1967. *De la grammatologie*. Paris: Minuit.

———. 1986. "Declarations of Independence." *New Political Science* 7: 7–15.

De Wolfe Howe, Mark. 1965. *The Garden and the Wilderness: Religion and Government in American Constitutional History*. Chicago: University of Chicago Press.

Dickinson, Harry T., ed. 2005. *Constitutional Documents of the United Kingdom 1782–1835*. Munich: K.G. Saur Verlag.

Diderot, Denis. 1766. *Article Jésuite tiré de l'Encyclopédie*. London: Compagnie 1766.

Di Lucia, Paolo. 1997. *L'universale della promessa*. Milan: Giuffrè.

Dippel, Horst. 2005. "Modern Constitutionalism: An Introduction to a History in Need of Writing." *The Legal History Review* 73: 154–156.

Dölemeyer, Barbara. 2005. "Thing Site, Tie, Ting Place: Venues for the Administration of Law." In *Making Things Public: Atmospheres of Democracy*, ed. Bruno Latour and Peter Weibel, 260–267. Cambridge, MA: MIT Press and ZKM Publications.

Dryzek, John S., and Simon Niemeyer. 2010. *Foundations and Frontiers of Deliberative Governance*. Oxford: Oxford University Press.

Dyrvik, Ståle. 2005. *Året 1814*. Oslo: Samlaget.

Efmertová, Marcela, and Nikolaj Savický. 2009. *České země 1848–1918: Díl I. Od březnové revoluce do požáru Národního divadla*. Prague: Libri.

Elias, Arthur. 2001. "La néerlandicité de la constitution de 1798." *Annales historiques de la Révolution française* 326: 43–52.

Elster, Jon. 1995. "Forces and Mechanisms in the Constitution-Making Process." *Duke Law Journal* 45: 364–396.

———. 1998. "Deliberation and Constitution Making." In *Deliberate Democracy,* ed. Jon Elster, 97–122. Cambridge: Cambridge University Press.

Falsen, Christian Magnus. 1817. *Norges Grundlov, gjennemgaaet i Spørgsmaal og Svar.* Bergen: R. Dahls Enke og Søn.

Faye, Andreas. 1863. *Norge i 1814.* Christiania: Mallings Bogtrykkeri.

Feldbæk, Ole. 1982. *Tiden 1730–1814.* Copenhagen: Gyldendal.

Fet, Jostein. 1995. *Lesande bønder: Litterær kultur i norske allmugesamfunn før 1840.* Oslo: Universitetsforlaget.

———. 2003. *Skrivande bønder: Skriftkultur på Nord-Vestlandet 1600–1850.* Oslo: Samlaget.

Fischel, Alfred. 1912. *Die Protokolle des Verfassungsausschusses über die Grundrechte: Ein Beitrag zur Geschichte des österreichischen Reichstags vom Jahre 1848.* Vienna: Gerlach & Wiedling.

Fure, Eli, ed. 1989. *Eidsvoll 1814: Hvordan grunnloven ble til.* Oslo: Dreyer.

Gammelgaard, Karen. 2003. *Tekstens mening: En introduktion til Pragerskolen.* Copenhagen: Roskilde universitetsforlag.

Garzone, Giuliana. 2001. "Deontic modality and performativity." In *Modality in Specialized Texts,* ed. Maurizio Gotti and Marina Dossena, 153–173. Bern: Peter Lang.

Giddens, Anthony. 1976. *New Rules of Sociological Method: A Positive Critique of Interpretative Sociologies.* New York: Basic Books.

Giesey, Ralph E. 1987. *Le roi ne meurt jamais: Les obsèques royales dans la France de la Renaissance.* Translated by Dominique Ebnöther. Paris: Flammarion.

Glenthøj, Rasmus. 2012. *Skilsmissen: Dansk og norsk identitet før og efter 1814.* Odense: Syddansk Universitetsforlag.

Grimm, Dieter. 1990. "Verfassung (II)." In *Geschichtliche Grundbegriffe: Historisches Lexikon zur politisch-sozialen Sprache in Deutschland,* vol. 6, ed. Otto Brunner, Werner Conze, and Reinhart Koselleck, 863–899. Stuttgart: Klett.

Grimm, Dieter, and Heinz Mohnhaupt. 1995. *Verfassung: Zur Geschichte des Begriff von der Antike bis zur Gegenwart.* Berlin: Duncker & Humblot.

Habermas, Jürgen. 1962. *Strukturwandel der Öffentlichkeit: Untersuchungen zu einer Kategorie der bürgerlichen Gesellschaft.* Neuwied: Luchterhand.

———. (1967) 1988. *On the Logic of the Social Sciences.* Cambridge: Polity Press.

———. 1981. *Theorie des kommunikativen Handelns.* 2 vols. Frankfurt am Main: Suhrkamp.

———. 1984–1987. *The Theory of Communicative Action.* 2 vols. Cambridge, MA: MIT Press. Originally published as *Theorie des kommunikativen Handelns* (Frankfurt am Main: Suhrkamp, 1981).

———. 1989. *The Transformation of the Public Sphere.* Cambridge, MA: MIT Press. Originally published as *Strukturwandel der Öffentlichkeit: Untersuchungen zu einer Kategorie der bürgerlichen Gesellschaft* (Neuwied: Luchterhand, 1962).

———. 1992a. *Autonomy and Solidarity: Interviews with Jürgen Habermas.* Edited by Peter Dews. London: Verso.

_____. 1992b. "Further Reflections on the Public Sphere." In *Habermas and the Public Sphere*, ed. Craig Calhoun, 421–461. Cambridge: MIT Press.

_____. 1994. "Struggles for Recognition in the Democratic Constitutional State." In *Multiculturalism: Examining the Politics of Recognition*, ed. Amy Gutmann, 107–148. Princeton, NJ: Princeton University Press.

_____. 1996. *Between Facts and Norms: Contributions to a Discourse Theory of Law and Democracy*. Cambridge, MA: MIT Press.

_____. 1998. "Civil Society and the Constitutional State." In *Habermas and the Korean Debate*, ed. Sang-Jin Han, 273–288. Seoul: Seoul National University Press.

_____. 2006. *Between Naturalism and Religion*. Cambridge: Polity Press.

_____. 2009. *Europe: The Faltering Project*. Cambridge: Polity Press.

_____. 2012. *The Crisis of the European Union*. Cambridge: Polity Press.

Hamilton, Alexander, James Madison, and John Jay. 2009. *The Federalist Papers*. Chicago: American Bar Association.

Han, Sang-Jin. 1998. *Habermas and the Korean Debate*. Seoul: Seoul National University Press.

Hase, Thomas. 2001. *Zivilreligion: Religionswissenschaftliche Überlegungen zu einem theoretischen Konzept am Beispiel der USA*. Würzburg: Ergon.

Hawgood, John A. 1939. *Modern Constitutions Since 1787*. London: MacMillan.

Hegel, Georg Wilhelm Friedrich. 1935. *Die Verfassung des Deutschen Reichs: Eine politische Flugschrift*. Stuttgart: Fromanns.

_____. 1952. *The Philosophy of Right: The Philosophy of History*. Chicago, London, and Toronto: Encyclopaedia Britannica.

_____. 1975. *Aesthetics: Lectures on Fine Arts*. Translated by T.M. Knox. 2 vols. Oxford: Clarendon.

Heggtveit, Hallvard G. 1888. *Eidsvoldsmænd: Biografiske Skisser samt Mindekvad*. Kristiania: H. Aschehoug.

Helset, Per, and Bjørn Stordrange. 1998. *Norsk statsforfatningsrett*. Oslo: Gyldendal.

Hemstad, Ruth. 2012. "Grunnloven i glass og ramme." *Nasjonens hukommelse*. Website of the National Library of Norway. Accessed 3 April 2014. http://www.nb.no/nasjonenshukommelse/category/reklame/?nr=338.

_____. 2013. "'[…] oversvømmet Norge med oprørske Proclamationer': Svensk propaganda i Norge 1812–1813." In *Veivalg for Norden: 1809–1813*, ed. Bård Frydenlund and Odd Arvid Storsveen, 87–109. Oslo: Akademika.

Herlitz, Nils. 1967. *Grunddragen av det svenska statsskickets historia*. Stockholm: Norstedts.

Hlavačka, Milan. 2005. "Užívání jazyka v byrokratizované komunikaci a samospráva v Čechách 1792–1914." *Český časopis historický* 103: 800–827.

Höbelt, Lothar. 2006. "Die deutsche Presselandschaft." In *Die Habsburgermonarchie 1848–1918*, vol. 8, bk. 2, ed. Helmut Rumpler and Peter Urbanitsch, 1819–1894. Vienna: Österreichische Akademie der Wissenschaften.

Höjer, Niels. 1882. *Norska Grundlagen och dess källor*. Stockholm: Aktieb. Hiertas bokförlag.

Holmøyvik, Eirik. 2008. "Mellom to konstitusjonelle epokar. Nicolai Wergeland sitt grunnlovsutkast i 1814." In *Forfatningsteori møter 1814*, ed. Dag Michalsen, 182–214. Oslo: Akademisk publisering.

———. 2010. "Nikolaus Gjelsvik og rettsmålet." In *Juristmållaget 75 år,* ed. Gunnar O. Hæreid, Kåre Lilleholt, Ingvild Risnes Skeie, and Merete Tollefsen, 79–89. Oslo: Privatrettsfondet.

———. 2012. *Maktfordeling og 1814.* Bergen: Fagbokforlaget.

———, ed. 2013. *Tolkingar av Grunnlova: Om forfatningsutviklinga 1814–2014.* Oslo: Pax forlag.

Huff, Toby E. 1993. *The Rise of Early Modern Science: Islam, China and the West.* New York: Cambridge University Press.

Hunt, Lynn. 2007. *Inventing Human Rights: A History.* New York: W.W. Norton.

Hylland, Aanund. 1989. "Om språket i grunnloven." *Norsk statsvitenskapelig tidsskrift* 4: 345–364.

Hyvik, Jens Johan. 2010. *Språk og nasjon 1739–1868.* Oslo: Samlaget.

Jæger, Tycho C. 1916. "Valgene til Riksforsamlingen." *Historisk tidsskrift* 3: 365–389, 472–494.

Jarausch, Konrad H. 2006. *After Hitler. Recivilizing Germans, 1945–1995.* Oxford: Oxford University Press.

Jenkins, Iredell. 1980. *Social Order and the Limits of Law: A Theoretical Essay.* Princeton, NJ: Princeton University Press.

Jordheim, Helge. 2007. "Conceptual History between *Chronos* and *Kairos*: The Case of 'Empire.'" *Redescriptions: Yearbook of Political Thought and Conceptual History* 11: 115–145.

———. 2012. "Against Periodization: On Koselleck's Theory of Multiple Temporalities." *History and Theory* 51: 151–171.

Kagan, Robert. 2006. *Dangerous Nation: America and the World 1600–1898.* London: Atlantic Books.

Kalleberg, Ragnvald. 2005a. "Samfunnsfagene i samfunnet." In *Introduksjon til samfunnsfag: Vitenskapsteori, argumentasjon og faghistorie,* ed. Fredrik Engelstad, Carl Erik Grenness, Ragnvald Kalleberg, and Raino Malnes, 276–324. Oslo: Gyldendal.

———. 2005b. "Samfunnsvitenskapenes oppgaver, arbeidsmåter og grunnlagsproblemer." In *Introduksjon til samfunnsfag: Vitenskapsteori, argumentasjon og faghistorie,* ed. Fredrik Engelstad, Carl Erik Grenness, Ragnvald Kalleberg, and Raino Malnes, 92–193. Oslo: Gyldendal.

———. 2007. "A Reconstruction of the Ethos of Science." *Journal of Classical Sociology* 7: 137–160.

———. 2008. "Sociologists as Public Intellectuals During Three Centuries of the Norwegian Project of Enlightenment." In *Academics as Public Intellectuals,* ed. Sven Eliaeson and Ragnvald Kalleberg, 17–48. Newcastle, UK: Cambridge Scholars Publishing.

———. 2009. "Can normative disputes be settled rationally? On Sociology as a normative discipline." In *Raymond Boudon: A Life in Sociology,* ed. Mohamed Cherkaoui and Peter Hamilton, vol. 2, 251–269. Oxford: Bardwell Press.

———. 2010. "The Ethos of Science and the Ethos of Democracy." In *Robert K. Merton: Sociology of Science and Sociology as Science,* ed. Craig Calhoun, 182–213. New York: Columbia University Press.

_____. 2011. "The Cultural and Democratic Obligations of Universities." In *Academic Identities—Academic Challenges? American and European Experience of the Transformation of Higher Education and Research*, ed. Tor Halvorsen and Atle Nyhagen, 88–125. Newcastle, UK: Cambridge Scholars Publishing.

Kann, Robert A. 1974. *A History of the Habsburg Empire 1526–1918*. Berkeley: University of California Press.

Kant, Immanuel. 1797. *Die Metaphysik der Sitten*. Hamburg: Felix Meiner.

Kantorowicz, Ernst H. 1997. *The King's Two Bodies: A Study in Mediaeval Political Theology*. Princeton, NJ: Princeton University Press.

Keel, Aldo. 1999. *Bjørnstjerne Bjørnson: En biografi 1880–1910*. Oslo: Gyldendal.

Kierulf, Anine. 2012. "Hvilken rolle spiller Grunnloven § 100 i Høyesteretts ytringsfrihetspraksis?" *Lov og rett* 51, no. 3: 131–150.

Kinneavy, James L., and Catherine R. Eskin. 1998. "Kairos." In *Historisches Wörterbuch der Rhetorik*, vol. 4, ed. Gerd Ueding, 836–844. Tübingen: Max Niemeyer Verlag.

Kopp, Peter F. 1992. *Peter Ochs*. Basel: Basler Zeitung.

Korzen, Iorn. 2010. "Lingua, cognizione e due Costituzioni." In *Lingua e diritto*, ed. Jacqueline Visconti, 163–202. Milan: LED.

Koselleck, Reinhart. (1972) 2000. "Über die Theoriebedürftigkeit der Geschichtswissenschaft." In *Zeitschichten: Studien zur Historik*, 298–316. Frankfurt am Main: Suhrkamp.

_____. 1979. "Einleitung." In *Geschichtliche Grundbegriffe*, ed. Otto Bruner, Werner Conze, and Reinhart Koselleck, i–xv. Stuttgart: Klett-Cotta.

_____. 1983. "Begriffsgeschichtliche Probleme der Verfassungsgeschichtsschreibung." *Der Staat Beiheft* 6: 7–46.

_____. 2004. *Futures Past: On the Semantics of Historical Time*. Translated by Keith Tribe. New York: Columbia University Press.

Koskenniemi, Martti. 2011. *The Politics of International Law*. Oxford: Hart Publishing.

Kuhnle, Stein. 1972. "Stemmeretten i 1814." *Historisk tidsskrift* 51: 373–389.

Kydland, Anne Jorunn. 1995. *Sangen har lysning: Studentersang i Norge på 1800-tallet*. Oslo: Solum.

Lafferty, William M. 2012. "Governance for sustainable development: The impasse of dysfunctional democracy." In *Governance, Democracy and Sustainable Development: Moving Beyond the Impasse?*, ed. James Meadowcroft, Oluf Langhelle, and Audun Ruud, 297–337. London: Edward Elgar.

Lagerroth, Frederik. 1973. *Sverige och Eidsvollsförfattningen*. Lund: Gleerup.

Langeland, Nils Rune. 2005. *Siste ord: Høgsterett i norsk historie 1814–1905*. Oslo: Cappelen.

Lauten, Maren Dahle. 2010. *"Borgeraand udvikler sig kun almindelig der, hvor hver Enkelt har Leilighed til Politisk Virksomhed": Framveksten av eit moderne demokratiomgrep under debatten om formannsskapslova av 1837*. Master's thesis, University of Oslo.

Lefort, Claude. 1988. *Democracy and Political Theory*. Translated by David Macey. Minneapolis: University of Minnesota Press.

Leso, Erasmo. 2012. "27 dicembre 1947: Lingua della Costituzione e lingua di tutti." In *Un secolo per la Costituzione (1848–1948): Concetti e parole nello svolgersi del lessico costituzionale italiano*, ed. Frederigo Bambi, 277–290. Florence: Accademia della Crusca.

Lucas, Stephen E. 1989. "Justifying America: The Declaration of Independence as a Rhetorical Document." In *American Rhetoric: Context and Criticism Carbondale*, ed. Thomas W. Benson, 67–130. Carbondale: Southern Illinois Press.

———. 1990. "The Stylistic Artistry of the Declaration of Independence." *Prologue: Quarterly of the National Archives* 22: 25–43.

Luhmann, Niklas. 1995. *Social Systems*. Palo Alto, CA: Stanford University Press.

———. 2005. *Law as a Social System*. Oxford: Oxford University Press.

Lüsebrink, Hans Jürgen, and Rolf Reichardt. 1997. *The Bastille: A History of a Symbol of Despotism and Freedom*. Durham, NC: Duke University Press.

Lyon, Ann. 2003. *Constitutional History of the United Kingdom*. London: Routledge-Cavendish.

Madzharova Bruteig, Yordanka. 2010. "Czech Parliamentary Discourse: Parliamentary Interactions and the Construction of the Addressee." In *European Parliaments under Scrutiny*, ed. Cornelia Ilie, 265–302. Amsterdam: John Benjamins.

Mauss, Marcel. 1954. *The Gift: Forms and Functions of Exchange in Archaic Societies*. London: Cohen & West.

McIlwain, Charles Howard. 1940. *Constitutionalism: Ancient and Modern*. Ithaca, NY: Cornell University Press.

Mestad, Ola. 2005. "Unionsoppløysinga i 1905: Parlamentarisme, strategi og statsrett." In *Rett, nasjon, union: Den svensk-norske unionens rettslige historie 1814–1905*, ed. Ola Mestad and Dag Michalsen, 334–419. Oslo: Universitetsforlaget.

Michalsen, Dag. 2005. "Rett, metafor og bilde." *Kritisk Juss* 31: 222–228.

———, ed. 2008. *Forfatningsteori møter 1814*. Oslo: Akademisk publisering.

———. 2011. *Rett: En international historie*. Oslo: Pax forlag.

Miller, Carolyn. 1984. "Genre as Social Action." *Quarterly Journal of Speech* 70: 151–167.

Modeer, Kjell Åke, and Martin Sunnqvist, eds. 2012. *Legal Stagings: The Visualization, Medialization and Ritualization of Law in Language, Literature, Media, Art and Architecture*. Copenhagen: Museum Tusculanum Press.

Mohnhaupt, Heinz. 2006. "Das Verhältnis der drei Gewalten in der Constitution der Cortes vom 19. März 1812." In *Konstitutionalismus und Verfassungskonflikt*, ed. Ulrike Müssig, 79–99. Tübingen: Morh Siebeck.

Morgenstierne, Bredo. 1926–1927. *Lærebok i den norske statsforfatningsret*. 2 vols. Oslo: O. Christiansens boktrykkeri.

Mortara Garavelli, Bice. 2001. *Le parole e la giustizia: Divagazioni grammaticali e retoriche su testi giuridici italiani*. Turin: Einaudi.

———. 2011a. "L'italiano della Repubblica: Caratteri linguistici della Costituzione." In *L'italiano dalla nazione allo Stato*, ed. Vittorio Coletti, 211–218. Florence: Le Lettere.

———. 2011b. "La lingua delle Costituzioni italiane 1848–2011." *La Crusca per Voi: Foglio dell' Accademia della Crusca* 43: 4–7.

Moyn, Samuel. 2010. *The Last Utopia: Human Rights in History*. Cambridge, MA: Belknap Press of Harvard University Press.

Müller, Jan-Werner. 2007. *Constitutional Patriotism*. Princeton, NJ: Princeton University Press.

Nilsen, Ragnar Anker. 1997. *Hva fikk nordmennene å lese i 1814? En bibliografi med beskriv-else av skrifter og trykk utgitt i Norge i grunnlovsåret*. Oslo: Universitetsbiblioteket i Oslo.

Oleschowski, Thomas. 2006. "Das Preßrecht in der Habsburgermonarchie: Politische Öffentlichkeit und Zivilgesellschaft." In *Die Habsburgermonarchie 1848–1918*, vol. 8, bk. 2, ed. Helmut Rumpler and Peter Urbanitsch, 1493–1533. Vienna: Österreichische Akademie der Wissenschaften.

Olivecrona, Karl. 1971. *Law as Fact*. London: Stevens.

Olsen, Johan P. 2010. *Governing Through Institution Building: Institutional Theory and Recent European Experiments in Democratic Organization*. Oxford: Oxford University Press.

Palonen, Kari. 1999. "Rhetorical and Temporal Perspectives on Conceptual Change." *Finnish Yearbook of Political Thought* 3: 41–59.

———. 2008. *The Politics of Limited Times: The Rhetoric of Temporal Judgment in Parliamentary Democracies*. Baden-Baden: Nomos.

Parent, Joseph M. 2011. *Uniting States: Voluntary Union in World Politics*. Oxford: Oxford University Press.

Pettit, Phillip. 1996. "Freedom as Antipower." *Ethics* 106: 576–604.

Pflanze, Otto. 1998. *Bismarck: Der Reichskanzler*. Munich: C.H. Beck.

Pocock, J.G.A. 1975. *The Machiavellian Moment: Florentine Political Thought and the Atlantic Republican Tradition*. Princeton, NJ: Princeton University Press.

Popper, Karl. 1945. *The Open Society and Its Enemies*. London: Routledge.

Rasch, Bjørn-Erik. 2000. "Grunnloven er moden for forandringer." *Aftenposten*, 11 May.

———. 2011. "Veto Points, Qualified Majorities, and Agenda-Setting Rules in Constitutional Amendment Procedures." Paper presented at the 2nd International Conference on Democracy as Idea and Practice, Oslo, Norway, 13–14 January.

Ringvej, Mona. 2011. "Communicative Power and the Absolutist State: Denmark-Norway c. 1750–1800." In *Scandinavia in the Age of Revolution: Nordic Political Cultures, 1740–1820*, ed. Pasi Ihalainen, Michael Bregnsbo, Karin Sennefelt, and Patrik Winton, 301–315. Farnham, UK: Ashgate.

Ritter, Joachim. 1965. *Hegel und die französische Revolution*. Frankfurt am Main: Suhrkamp.

Rotteck, Carl von, and Karl Theodor Welcker. 1834–1843. *Staats-Lexikon, oder Encyklopädie der Staatswissenschaften*. 15 vols. Altona: Johann Friedrich Hammerich.

Rumpler, Helmut. 1997. *Eine Chance für Mitteleuropa: Bürgerliche Emanzipation und Staatsverfall in der Habsburgermonarchie*. Vienna: Ueberreuter.

Sand, Inger-Johanne. 2010. "Constitutionalism and the Multi-Coded Treaties of the EU." In *The Many Constitutions of Europe*, ed. Kaarlo Tuori and Suvi Sankari, 49–67. Farnham, UK: Ashgate.

Sandel, Michael J. 2012. *What Money Can't Buy: The Moral Limits of Markets*. London: Alan Lane.

Sandvik, Hilde, ed. 2010. *Demokratisk teori og historisk praksis*. Oslo: SAP.

Sassen, Saskia. 2006. *Territory, Authority, Rights*. Princeton, NJ: Princeton University Press.

Schmidgen, Wolfram. 2012. *Exquisite Mixture: The Virtues of Impurity in Early Modern England*. Philadelphia: University of Pennsylvania Press.

Seip, Jens Arup. 2002. *Utsikt over Norges historie*. Vol. 1, *Tidsrommet 1814 - ca. 1860*. Oslo: Gyldendal.

Sejersted, Francis. 1978. *Den vanskelige frihet 1814–1851*. Oslo: Cappelen Forlag.

———. 1997. "Den gamle og den nye kommunikasjonsstat." *Nytt Norsk Tidsskrift* 3: 216–227.

———. 2011. *The Age of Social Democracy: Norway and Sweden in the Twentieth Century*. Princeton, NJ: Princeton University Press.

Sieyès, Emmanuel-Joseph. (1789) 1994. *Ecrits politiques*. Edited by Robberto Zapperi. Paris: Editions des Archives Contemporaines.

Siskin, Clifford. 2010. "Mediated Enlightenment: The System of the World." In *This Is Enlightenment*, ed. Clifford Siskin and William Warner, 164–172. Chicago: University of Chicago Press.

Skinner, Quentin. 2001. "A Third Concept of Liberty." *Proceedings of the British Academy* 117: 237–268.

———. 2002. *Visions of Politics*. Vol. 1, *Regarding Method*. Cambridge: Cambridge University Press.

———. 2009. "A Genealogy of the Modern State." *Proceedings of the British Academy* 162: 325–370.

Skirbekk, Gunnar. 1998. "'Din tanke er fri ...': Om å grunngi det rettslege vern av ytringsfridom." In *Vit og vitskap*, 88–106. Bergen: Fagbokforlaget.

Smith, Eivind. 2012. *Konstitusjonelt demokrati*. Bergen: Fagbokforlaget.

Specter, Matthew G. 2010. *Habermas: An Intellectual Biography*. Cambridge: Cambridge University Press.

Spiegelberg, Herbert. 1935. *Gesetz und Sittengesetz: Strukturanalytische und Historische Vorstudien zu einer Gesetzfreien Ethik*. Zurich: Max Niehans.

Steen, Sverre. 1954. *Det frie Norge*. Vol. 3, *Krise og avspenning*. Oslo: J.W. Cappelens forlag.

Steinberg, Michael. 2004. *Listening to Reason: Culture, Subjectivity, and Nineteenth-Century Music*. Princeton, NJ: Princeton University Press.

Stolleis, Michael. 1988. *Geschichte des öffentlichen Rects in Deutschland*. Munich: C.H. Beck.

———. 2009. *The Eye of the Law: Two Essays on Legal History*. Abingdon, UK: Birkbeck Law Press.

Storsveen, Odd Arvid. 1997. *Henrik Wergelands norske historie: Et bidrag til nasjonalhistoriens mythos*. Oslo: Norges forskningsråd.

Stourzh, Gerald. 1975. "Vom aristotelischen zum liberalen Verfassungsbegriff." In *Fürst, Bürger, Mensch: Untersuchungen zu politischen und soziokulturellen Wandlungsprozessen im vorrevolutionären Europa*, ed. Friedrich Engel-Janosi, Grete Klingestein, and Heinrich Lutz, 97–122. Munich: Oldenbourg.

———. 1988. "Constitution: Changing Meanings of the Term from the Early Seventeenth to the Late Eighteenth Century." In *Conceptual Change and the Constitution*, ed. Terence Ball and J.G.A. Pocock, 35–54. Lawrence: University Press of Kansas.

Supphellen, Steinar. 1978. "Supplikken som institusjon i norsk historie." *Historisk tidsskrift* 57: 152–186.

Tamm, Ditlev. 1997. "Den danske 'Constitution' og den franske revolution." In *Med lov skal land bygges II*, ed. Henrik Stevnsborg and Ditlev Tamm, 172–183. Copenhagen: Jurist- og Økonomforbundets Forlag.

Teubert, Wolfgang. 2010. *Meaning, Discourse and Society*. Cambridge: Cambridge University Press.

Tønnesson, Kåre. 1990. "Menneskerettighetserklæringene i det attende århundre og den norske grunnloven." In *Menneskerettighetene i den nasjonale rett i Frankrike og Norge*, ed. Eivind Smith, 30–38. Oslo: Universitetsforlaget.

Tretvik, Aud Mikkelsen. 2000. *Tretter, ting og tillitsmenn: En undersøkelse av konflikthåndtering i det norske bygdesamfunnet på 1700-tallet*. Trondheim: Skriftserie fra Historisk institutt, NTNU.

Troper, Michel. 1980. *La séparation des pouvoirs et l'historie constitutionnelle française*. Paris: Librairie générale de droit et de jurisprudence.

Tuori, Kaarlo, and Suvi Sankari, eds. 2010. *The Many Constitutions of Europe*. Farnham, UK: Ashgate.

van Dijk, Teun A. 2008. *Discourse and Context: A Sociocognitive Approach*. Cambridge: Cambridge University Press.

Vikør, Lars S., and Arne Torp. 2000. *Hovuddrag i norsk språkhistorie*. Oslo: Gyldendal akademisk.

Vile, John R. 1997. *A Companion to the United States Constitution and Its Amendments*. Westport, CT: Praeger.

Vinje, Finn-Erik. 2002. *Frihetens palladium—i språklig belysning: Om språket i Grunnloven*. Oslo: Stortinget.

Visconti, Jacqueline. 2009a. "A Modular Approach to Legal Drafting and Translation." In *Formal Linguistics and Law*, ed. Günther Grewendorf and Monika Rathert, 401–426. Berlin: Walter de Gruyter.

_____. 2009b. "Speech Acts in Legal Language: Introduction." *Journal of Pragmatics* 41: 393–400.

Warner, Michael. 1990. *The Letters of the Republic: Publication and the Public Sphere in Eighteenth-Century America*. Cambridge, MA: Harvard University Press.

Warner, William. 2013. *Protocols of Liberty: Communication Innovation and the American Revolution*. Chicago: Chicago University Press.

Williams, Christopher. 2006. "Fuzziness in Legal English: What Shall We Do About Shall?" In *Legal Language and the Search for Clarity*, ed. Anne Wagner and Sophie Cacciaguidi-Fahy, 237–264. Bern: Peter Lang.

_____. 2007. *Tradition and Change in Legal English: Verbal Constructions in Prescriptive Texts*. Bern: Peter Lang.

_____. 2009. "Legal English and the Modal Revolution." In *Modality in English: Theory and Description*, ed. Raphael Salkie, Pierre Busuttil, and Johan van der Auwera, 199–210. Berlin: Mouton de Gruyter.

Yunis, Harvey. 1996. *Taming Democracy: Models of Political Rhetoric in Classical Athens*. Ithaca, NY: Cornell University Press.

Contributors

Kjell Lars Berge
Professor of Nordic Languages and Literature at the Department of Linguistics and Scandinavian Studies at the University of Oslo.

Karen Gammelgaard
Professor of Czech Language and Literature at the Department of Literature, Area Studies, and European Languages at the University of Oslo.

Eirik Holmøyvik
Professor at the Faculty of Law at the University of Bergen (Norway).

Helge Jordheim
Professor of Cultural History at the Department of Culture Studies and Oriental Languages at the University of Oslo.

Ragnvald Kalleberg
Professor Emeritus of Sociology at the Department of Sociology and Human Geography at the University of Oslo.

Yordanka Madzharova Bruteig
PhD, researcher affiliated with the University of Oslo.

Dag Michalsen
Professor of Legal History at the Department of Public and International Law at the University of Oslo.

Mona Ringvej
Researcher and Project Manager at the Department of Archaeology, Conservation, and History at the University of Oslo.

Inger-Johanne Sand
Professor of Public Law at the Department of Public and International Law at the University of Oslo.

Ulrich Schmid
Professor of Russian Culture and Society at the School of Humanities and Social Sciences at University of St. Gallen (Switzerland).

Jacqueline Visconti
Associate Professor at the Faculty of Foreign Languages and Literatures at the University of Genoa (Italy) and Honorary Research Fellow at the Department of Italian Studies at the University of Birmingham (England).

William B. Warner
Professor of English at the Department of English at the University of California, Santa Barbara.

Index

Constitutions